HANDBOOK OF
HISPANIC SOURCE MATERIALS
AND RESEARCH ORGANIZATIONS
IN THE UNITED STATES

Handbook of

HISPANIC

SOURCE MATERIALS AND
RESEARCH ORGANIZATIONS

in the United States

SECOND EDITION

EDITED BY RONALD HILTON
Director of Hispanic American Studies
Stanford University

STANFORD UNIVERSITY PRESS • STANFORD, CALIFORNIA

1956

STANFORD UNIVERSITY PRESS, STANFORD, CALIFORNIA

Published in Great Britain and India by Geoffrey Cumberlege,
Oxford University Press, London and Bombay

SECOND EDITION
May 1956

The first edition of this work was published in 1942 by the
University of Toronto Press, Toronto, Canada, under the title
Handbook of Hispanic Source Materials in the United States,
and was edited by Ronald Hilton.

Printed and bound in the United States of America
Library of Congress Catalog Card Number: 56-6178

PREFACE

The first edition of this <u>Handbook</u> was published by the University of Toronto Press in 1942. It was reviewed not unkindly, and received some unexpected compliments; it quickly went out of print, several libraries complained that their copies had been stolen, and the book sold on the secondhand market for three times the original price. But recalling the tedious research which had gone into its preparation, the editor had no intention of succumbing again to the enthusiasm which led him to the initial project. However, it became clear that the <u>Handbook</u> served a real scholarly need, and he agreed to undertake the work necessary for a second edition. Indeed, he now hopes that this <u>Handbook</u> may be revised and reissued every ten years or so.

The term "Hispanic" is used in the title to embrace Spain, Portugal, and Latin America of the pre- and post-Columbian periods; Florida, Texas, the Southwest, and California are included until their annexation by the United States. The material surveyed belongs to the humanities, the fine arts, and the social sciences; the natural sciences have been included in the case of some exceptional collections. The <u>Handbook</u> seeks to perform the important service of calling the attention of both American and foreign scholars to the vast wealth of Hispanic material deposited and in some cases one might say lost in the collections of the country.

It would have been possible to arrange this <u>Handbook</u> in a variety of ways, but it was finally decided that the most practical would be to describe the various collections by state and locality, and to refer to the index those who would seek precise items.

It would perhaps have been possible to enforce an artificial consistency in the descriptions contained in the book, but it was clear that such uniformity would have dessicated the whole project; each statement is phrased in the form which seems best fitted to the collection described. The alternative of giving the information in a tabulated form was rejected. The original statements have been left, so far as possible, in the terms in which they were drawn up, since they represent a formal statement by the institution concerned. It is appropriate here to express our gratitude to all the institutions described, since they had frequently to engage in veritable research projects to bring to light their Hispanic resources. Anyone familiar with this kind of work will immediately realize the time which had to be expended on the preparation of many of these statements.

The statements in the <u>Handbook</u> have, however, been subjected to scrutiny. In almost every case, the collection was examined by the editor or one of his colleagues, its importance for the scholar

v

was assessed, and an approximate length was set for the statement describing it. Arrangements were then made for some scholar to prepare the description—nearly always the person best acquainted with the collection. The description, once received, was reviewed carefully, and was frequently the subject of correspondence and telephone calls. In some instances the editor cut out items which were in his judgment not as rare as the institution claimed, while in others he requested additions about items which seemed to him unusual. He was sometimes under pressure to include items which seemed important to the contributor, while to the editor they reflected a preoccupation with one discipline or institution. In difficult cases, the question was referred to other experts, and the editor accepted their judgment.

Obviously, in a survey of this kind there can be no absolute criterion of rarity or value. The selection made simply represents the honest opinion of the editor and his colleagues. While recognizing that such decisions are not infallible, and that every reader will expect detailed coverage of his particular field and his own institution, the editor is obliged to point out that this is impossible. The Hand-book seeks not to give a complete description of general collections, but rather of those collections or items which are sufficiently unusual to be of interest to the Hispanic researcher. While the editor will of course stand by the decisions made, he will be grateful if readers send him comments and suggestions for any future editions. In particular, he will welcome information about new acquisitions. It is believed that in general the information in this edition is up to date as of January 1, 1956.

While it would scarcely be feasible to list the hundreds of persons who have been helpful in one way or another, we must at least list the distinguished Latin Americanists who formed a kind of ad hoc committee for the revision of the Handbook. They are Dr. Howard F. Cline, Director of the Hispanic Foundation, Library of Congress, Washington, D. C.; Professor George P. Hammond, Director of the Bancroft Library, University of California; Professor Lewis Hanke, Professor of Latin American History and Director of the Latin American Institute of the University of Texas; Professor Francis M. Rogers, Dean of the Graduate School of Harvard University; and Professor Arthur P. Whitaker of the History Department of the University of Pennsylvania. These colleagues undertook a final check of the collections in their respective areas, and the editor is deeply appreciative of the substantial assistance they have afforded

Ronald Hilton
Editor

TABLE OF CONTENTS

xiv   [Table of Contents]

Museum of Northern Arizona
Flagstaff, Arizona

The Museum of Northern Arizona has for over thirty years conducted an archeological survey of the region around Flagstaff. The sites number over 3,500 and date from about 700 A.D. to the present time. Excavation of over a hundred sites dating from about 800 to 1200 A.D. has been undertaken. From this it was found that until 900 A.D. the prehistoric population was small. About 876 A.D. the eruption of Sunset Crater (twenty miles northeast of Flagstaff) occurred, and spread a layer of fine volcanic ash over an area of a thousand square miles. This ash made agriculture possible where it had been impossible before, by forming a mulch on the land. A vast population swarmed in from all directions and remained until the late 1100's when the mulch of ash was blown away. The population which had lived in scattered earth lodges and, later, small masonry houses, began to concentrate in larger and larger houses until, in 1276, when the great drought (1276-96) began, only a few large pueblos existed, Thereafter, various large pueblos were abandoned, and the people concentrated in the already populous Hopi villages which were occupied through Spanish times (1540-1680). After the Pueblo Rebellion of 1680, many of the villages moved to the mesa tops, which were easily fortified, and have remained there to the present day.

The few Spanish and Mexican objects in the collections of the museum are from the Spanish missions of the period 1620-80. They consist of a few random articles from surface collections, such as potsherds of Spanish and Mexican majolicas, fragments of bronze church bells, and an exact replica of the only beam now in existence from the mission church of San Francisco at Oraibi (a Hopi pueblo), and sketches and measurements of another, formerly at Shipolovi, which belonged to the mission of San Bartolomé de Shongopovi.

In its monthly leaflet Plateau, formerly Museum Notes, the museum has published numerous papers which bear on the Spanish period. The following longer studies have appeared in the Museum of Northern Arizona Bulletin:

Nequatewa, Edmund. "The Truth of a Hopi and Other Clan Stories of Shungopovi" (VIII, 1936), describes the Hopi view of the establishment of the missions and their final destruction in 1680.
Whiting, Alfred F. "The Ethnobotany of the Hopi Indians" (XV, 1938), is a detailed study of the plants introduced by the Spanish and still extensively cultivated.

1

Arizona Department of Library and Archives
Phoenix

The Arizona Department of Library and Archives (formerly the State Library) includes its Hispanic materials under the general classification of "Arizoniana." This collection is housed in adequate quarters in a new wing of the state capitol at Phoenix, designed and constructed chiefly for the department. It embraces some 6,000 volumes, the accumulation of which began almost as early as the authorization of the first territorial library in 1864, but did not become an orderly process until 1917 (when the State Library was created by law as a separate entity), and was not emphasized until 1932. The contents of the collection were acquired almost entirely by purchase.

The bulk of this collection of Arizoniana relates to the post-Spanish era, and more particularly to the early territorial and American pioneer period. It is in this respect, if any, that it is particularly strong. The aim of its builders, however, has been to add all available material in both English and Spanish text concerning those portions of Mexico out of which Arizona was formed, or to which the area was directly related. This material has to do with the early activities of the Catholic church and its padres and missions, war, boundary survey, and collateral subjects. A few fairly rare items are worthy of note, including manuscripts and documents attributed to Fathers Junípero Serra and Garcés. The collection of maps of the Southwest, Mexico, and Central America is fairly complete.

Arizona Pioneers Historical Society
949 East Second Street
Tucson

The library of the Arizona Pioneers Historical Society has over 20,000 volumes and is said to have the most complete collection on all aspects of Arizona, as well as extensive coverage of the entire Southwest. Among the rare items is an excellent set of Kingsborough Antiquities of Mexico. The library has fairly good files of Arizona newspapers, extending back about a hundred years and completely cross-filed. The collection includes the diaries of a number of Spanish priests who came to Arizona and over 18,000 pictures of Arizona people, places, and missions.

University of Arizona
Arizona State Museum
Tucson

The Arizona State Museum was founded in 1893 as a territorial museum and later, upon Arizona's admission to statehood in 1913, it became the official depository in the state. It has extensive archeological collections of pottery, basketry, textiles, and stone and bone tools from Basketmaker II through Pueblo IV of the Anasazi Culture. Pueblo III and IV in the Kayenta, Little Colorado, and White Mountain areas are particularly well illustrated. Excellent collections of study materials are also available from sites of the Mogollon and Hohokam Cultures of east central and south central Arizona, respectively. In recent years, studies in problems related to early man have resulted in extensive collections of specimens dating from the time of Christ to approximately ten thousand years ago. The archeological collections total nearly 25,000 specimens.

In ethnology, the Apache, Navajo, Hopi, Zuni, Pima, Papago, Maricopa, Yaqui, and Seri tribes are represented in a collection aggregating roughly 10,000 specimens.

Because other institutions in Arizona have specialized in Spanish and Mexican objects of the Conquest period, the Arizona State Museum has not emphasized these. Certain objects from missions have been returned to their place of origin if local museums have been established.

University of Arizona
Library
Tucson

The University of Arizona Library has a moderately good collection of Hispanic materials, strongest in Mexican literature. Since 1920, when the library published a bibliographical description of its holdings in Mexican Writers, the collection has grown considerably, and additions are made currently. The library has a strong Arizona collection with some materials of interest for the history of Mexico, especially the Sonora-Arizona region. Held on deposit for an indefinite period is the W. J. Holliday collection of early Sonora and Sinaloa imprints, a typewritten check list of which is available for loan. See Mexican Writers; a Catalogue of Books in the University of Arizona Library, with a Synopsis and Bibliographical Notes. Prepared by Estelle Lutrell, librarian (Tucson, 1920. 83 pp.).

CALIFORNIA

Spanish Missions

Select bibliography:*

Anza's California Expeditions, edited by Herbert Eugene Bolton, 5
   vols. (Berkeley, 1930).
Bancroft, Hubert Howe. California Pastoral (San Francisco, 1888).
____. History of California, 7 vols. (San Francisco, 1884-90).
Bolton, Herbert Eugene. The Colonization of North America (New
   York, 1920).
____. Fray Juan Crespi, Missionary Explorer (Berkeley, 1927).
____. Guide to Materials for the History of the United States in the
   Principal Archives of Mexico (Washington, D.C., 1913).
____. Spanish Exploration in the Southwest, 1542-1706 (New York,
   1916).
Bourne, E. G. Spain in America (New York, 1906).
Carter, Charles Franklin. The Missions of Nueva California (San
   Francisco, 1900).
Caughey, John Walton. California (New York, 1940).
Chapman, Charles Edward. Catalogue of Materials in the Archivo
   General de Indias for the History of the Pacific Coast and the
   American Southwest (Berkeley, 1919).
____. The Founding of Spanish California (New York, 1916).
____. A History of California: The Spanish Period (New York, 1916,
   1930).
Clinch, Bryan James. California and Its Missions; Their History to
   the Treaty of Guadalupe Hidalgo, 2 vols. (San Francisco, 1904).
Costanso, Miguel. The Narrative of the Portolá Expedition of 1769-
   1770, edited by Frederick J. Teggart (Berkeley, 1910).
Coues, Elliott. On the Trail of a Spanish Pioneer: The Diary and
   Itinerary of Francisco Garcés...1775-1776, 2 vols. (New York,
   1900).
Coulter, Thomas. Notes on Upper California (Los Angeles, 1835).
Cowan, Robert E. A Bibliography of the History of California, 1510-
   1930, 3 vols. (San Francisco, 1933).
Da Silva, Owen Francis. Mission Music of California, a Collection
   of Old California Mission Hymns and Masses (Los Angeles, 1941).
Dana, Richard Henry. Two Years before the Mast (1st ed., New York,
   1840; New York, 1936, introduction by James D. Hart).
Davis, William Heath. Sixty Years in California (San Francisco, 1889).
Denis, Alberta Johnson. Spanish Alta California (New York, 1927).

_____

   *The Bancroft Library at the University of California (q.v.)
has the best collection on the California missions.

Doyle, John T. Some Account of the Pious Fund of California and
the Litigation to Recover It (San Francisco, 1880).

Dunne, Peter Masten. Black Robes in Lower California (Berkeley,
1952).

___. Pioneer Black Robes on the West Coast (Berkeley, 1940).

Engelhardt, Padre Zephyrin (Charles Anthony). The Missions and
Missionaries of California, 4 vols. (San Francisco, 1908-16).

Fitch, Abigail H. Junípero Serra (Chicago, 1914).

Forbes, Alexander. California: A History of Upper and Lower
California (London, 1839).

Garcés, Francisco T. H. On the Trail of a Spanish Pioneer, translated and edited by Elliott Coues (New York, 1900).

Geary, Gerald J. The Secularization of the California Missions
(Washington, D. C., 1934).

Geiger, Maynard J. Calendar of Documents in the Santa Barbara
Mission Archives (Washington, D. C., 1947).

Hallenbeck, Cleve. Spanish Missions of the Old Southwest (Garden
City, N. Y., 1926).

Hawthorne, Hildegarde. California's Missions, Their Romance and
Beauty (New York, 1942).

Hittell, Theodore H. History of California, 4 vols. (San Francisco,
1885-97).

James, George W. In and Out of the Old Missions of California
(Boston, 1916).

Keys, James M. Las Misiones españoles de California (Madrid,
1950).

Kino, Eusebio Francisco. Kino Reports to Headquarters; Correspondence of Eusebio F. Kino from New Spain with Rome (Rome,
1954).

Landaeta, Martín de. Noticias acerca del puerto de San Francisco
(Alta California). Anotaciones de José C. Valadés (Mexico,
1949).

Lummis, Charles Fletcher. The Spanish Pioneers and the California
Missions (Chicago, 1929).

McGroarty, John S. California: Its History and Romance (Los
Angeles, 1911).

___. Mission Memories (Los Angeles, 1929).

Miller, Henry. Account of a Tour of the California Missions, 1856,
edited by Edith M. Coulter and Eleanor A. Bancroft (San Francisco,
1952).

Newcomb, Rexford. The Old Mission Churches and Historic Houses
of California, Their History, Architecture, Art and Lore
(Philadelphia, 1925).

Palou, Francisco. Junípero Serra (Mexico, 1787; translated and
annotated by Maynard J. Geiger, Washington, D. C., 1955).

——. Noticias de la Nueva California (completed in 1783, published in Spanish in 1857 and 1874; translated and edited by Herbert E. Bolton as Historical Memoirs of New California, 4 vols., Berkele 1926).

Pattie, James Ohio. The Personal Narrative of James O. Pattie (Cincinnati, 1831).

Picolo, Francesco María. Informe del estado de la nueva cristianidad de California (Mexico, 1702).

Powers, Laura Bride. The Missions of California: Their Establishment, Progress, and Decay (San Francisco, 1893).

Priestley, Herbert Ingram. Franciscan Explorations in California, edited by Lillian Estelle Fisher (Glendale, Calif., 1946).

——. A Historical, Political and Natural Description of California by Pedro Fages (Berkeley, 1937).

——. José de Gálvez, Visitor-General of New Spain, 1765-1771 (Berkeley, 1916).

Richman, Irving B. California under Spain and Mexico, 1535-1847 (Boston, 1911).

Robinson, Alfred. Life in California (New York, 1846; Oakland, 1947, foreword by Joseph A. Sullivan).

San Martín, José. Memoria y proposiciones del señor don José San Martín sobre las Californias con ocasión de no haber jurado su intendente la independencia por la preponderancia de aquellos religiosos misioneros, Mexico, 1822 (Mexico, 1943; translated into English, with an introduction, by Henry R. Wagner, San Francisco, 1945).

Sánchez, Nellie Van de Grift. Spanish Arcadia (Los Angeles, 1929).

Saunders, Charles Francis. The California Padres and Their Missions (Boston, 1915).

Simpson, Sir George. California: Its History, Population, Climate, Soil, Productions, and Harbors (Cincinnati, 1848).

Sullivan, Ella C. The Story of the Old Spanish Missions of the Southwest (Chicago, 1927).

Van Nostrand, Jeanne, and Coulter, Edith M. California Pictorial (Berkeley and Los Angeles, 1948).

Venegas, Miguel. Juan María de Salvatierra of the Company of Jesus, translated into English, edited and annotated by Marguerite Eyer Wilbur (Cleveland, 1929).

——. Noticia de la California y de su conquista temporal y espiritual hasta el tiempo presente [1739] (Madrid, 1757, 3 vols.; Mexico, 1943-44, 3 vols.; English translation, London, 1759, 2 vols.).

Vischer, Edward. Missions of Upper California, a supplement to Pictorial of California (San Francisco, 1872).

——. Pictorial of California (San Francisco, 1872).

Walsh, Marie T.   The Mission Bells of California (San Francisco,
   1834).
Waters, Willard Otis.   Franciscan Missions of Upper California as
   Seen by Foreign Visitors and Residents (Los Angeles, 1954).
Watson, Douglas E.   The Spanish Occupation of California (San
   Francisco, 1934).
Webb, Edith Buckland.   Indian Life at the Old Missions (Los Angeles,
   1952).

University of California
General Library
Berkeley

A pioneer center of Hispanic studies and one of the first universities to offer a course on Hispanic American history, the University of California at Berkeley contains a notable collection for
research.   The University Library began early to provide necessary
research materials, and over the past fifty years the collections
have been strengthened not only by the active interest of members
of the faculty but by friends of the library and of California.   The
University Library's full resources in Hispanic material consist of
collections in the General Library, the Bancroft Library, and the
Law Library.   For detailed information regarding the Bancroft
Library's holdings, consult the separate statement which follows.

Early in the first decade of this century, Dr. Rudolph Schevill
laid the foundation for the library's Hispanic collection of Spanish
language and literature.   The library has complete runs of scholarly
journals such as Zeitschrift für romanische philologie, 1877 to date.
In addition, Dr. Schevill's personal library was donated posthumously
by his son, Karl Schevill.   As an authority on Cervantes and an editor
of a definitive edition of his works, Dr. Schevill had accumulated a
notable working collection, which contains a number of sets of complete works of Cervantes; the most important editions of Don Quixote,
including facsimiles of the first edition; Spanish, French, German,
and other translations; and much valuable material on the Spanish
author.   Among the items is the scarce title Pedanius Dioscorides,
Pedacio Dioscorides... acerca de la materia medicinal, y los venenos
mortiferos (Antwerp, 1555).

Another contributing factor toward the enlargement of the
library's Hispanic collection was the interest of the Catalan engineer,
Juan C. Cebrián, of San Francisco, who wished to have in the West
a center for the dissemination of Spain's cultural heritage.   Due to
his generosity and his scholarly interests, the library had received
by 1925 nearly 9,000 volumes and pamphlets.   In the 1928 publication

of Spain and Spanish America in the Libraries of the University of California, a Catalogue of Books... V. 1: The General and Departmental Libraries, a third of the titles were Cebrián gifts. The subject index shows thirty pages of titles on history and description and seventeen on Spanish language and literature. One of the most valuable gifts is the famous Salva edition of the Comedias of Lope de Vega, published in 1609-47.

Early in the 1930's, the working library of Elijah C. Hills, th philologist, was added to these holdings. The collection contained 1,600 bound volumes and "seventeen shelves of unbound periodicals, reprints and miscellaneous pamphlets." It included a number of rare dictionaries and glossaries dealing primarily with Spanish and other Romance languages.

These early acquisitions resulted in the library's possessing an outstanding collection of material on Cervantes, Lope de Vega, the drama and novel of the nineteenth century, and early nineteenth-century periodicals.

In the field of language, the library's holdings were greatly enlarged in 1942 by the purchase of the Santamaría Library of American Linguistics. The 2,000 volumes had been used by Francisco J. Santamaría, the Mexican scholar, in the compilation of the Diccionario general de americanismos. One part, the Colección Bibliográfica Tabasco, is housed in the Bancroft Library. The othe the Colección Lingüística, retained in the General Library, includes the valuable item Esteban Pichardo y Tapia, Diccionario provincial casi razonado de voces cubanas, 3d ed. (Havana: Impr. la Antilla, 1862).

In the field of Hispanic American literature, the collection shows the painstaking effort of a faculty committee, active for eight or ten years, to build up systematically materials for research. To aid in these objectives, the library's Humanities Reference Service, in collaboration with faculty members, began in 1951 a project for the acquisition of all published works of selected authors. Today the list includes 28 authors for Spanish America and 10 for Brazil. Consequently, the library's collection is of excellent quality, strong in the modern phases of Hispanic American literature, and unique in its coverage of certain literary types and authors, such as the Chilean novel, Peruvian poetry, the Mexican corrido, and the Uruguayan writer, José Enrique Rodó.

The library's Hispanic material in the social sciences is outstanding for its extensive coverage. In 1951, the library's Catalog Department estimated 23,000 volumes in this field, and a random sampling in history revealed that 63 per cent of the titles had a Latin American imprint. The initial nucleus was the Bernard Moses collection of 1,541 bound volumes, including 291 of the donor's own writings and 309 unbound periodicals, most of which deal principally with the Philippines and Spanish America. Also included are 52 volumes of the Registro Nacional de la República Argentina.

In the last few years several factors have been responsible for the extensive additions to the collection. One is the gradual accumulation of periodicals through gifts and exchange. Since the university had so many series to offer, it was able to establish very satisfactory exchange relations with societies and institutions from which the library received material available only from these sources. In the early 1940's a comprehensive check of Latin American serials bibliographies was begun. As a result, the library now receives 1,437 titles, including 89 exchanges in Buenos Aires, 42 in Rio de Janeiro, and 26 in Bogotá. The collection, strong on the areas of Argentina, Brazil, Chile, Colombia, and Venezuela, reflects the results of travels in Latin America by vaious members of the faculty: Charles E. Chapman in Chile, Engel Sluiter and James F. King in the River Plate area, and John H. Rowe in Peru. Another factor in the growth is the survey made in 1950 by interested faculty members to determine the strength of the collection in certain areas and fields. Their findings brought about the establishment of an area fund and of special procedures for filling gaps. Lastly, much has been done by a unified purchase plan by a faculty committee representing interdepartmental interests, especially those in the social sciences.

In 1947, the university purchased the Feuille collection of legal source materials on Costa Rica, Guatemala, Ecuador, Cuba, Panama, and Venezuela for the Law Library, which now has a good working collection of Latin American codes, laws, and gazettes. In this acquisition are many legal periodicals, complete runs from 1821 for Colombia, 1830 for Ecuador, and 1832 for Costa Rica. These supplement the holdings in the library's Documents Department of informes of the executive governments, legislative proceedings, and official gazettes.

Although the Biology Library does not consider Latin America as one of its areas of prime interest, its botany holdings are noteworthy. In 1947-49, the library initiated a project of photographing the early and rare items of the Gray Herbarium at Harvard University. Research formerly done only at Harvard can now be undertaken at the University of California. A special effort is made to keep up to date with current serials and documents, especially in public health, entomology, and zoology for Argentina, Brazil, Chile, and Mexico.

Since the university began as a land-grant institution, the Agriculture Reference Service has acquired a comprehensive coverage of serial publications and has maintained an extensive exchange with foreign governments, experiment stations, important agricultural societies, and countries which have the same interests and products as California. With the exception of the library in the United States Department of Agriculture, the university library has the largest foreign-exchange program in the country. One of the newer exchanges, stemming from technical-assistance programs of the United Nations and the United States, is the output of the co-operative United States—Peruvian program in agriculture. The major strength of the Agriculture Reference Service's Hispanic collection is in serials publications, such as the Review of the River Plate.

University of California
Bancroft Library
Berkeley

In the latter 1850's Hubert Howe Bancroft, San Francisco bookseller and stationer, casually began to fill a shelf with reference books on California as a part of his firm's work in publishing a Pacific Coast handbook. By 1859 he had about seventy-five volumes, a nucleus which inspired him to set about collecting in earnest. As Bancroft gathered materials on local history, he became more and more interested in the background of California-- his scope widened to include Latin America and even Spain. As he traveled and collected, he acquired everything he could which applied to the history of California, the Pacific West, and Spanish North America. When Bancroft, after twenty-five years, had amassed a library of over 50,000 items, he determined to write a general history of California and the West, and he left no corner unexplored in his attempt to make his library as complete as possible.

Bancroft's efforts were by no means confined to printed works, for the manuscripts he accumulated, which are of inestimable value, relate the history of three centuries, and more than half a continent. Realizing that there were also vast resources in the private papers of some of the early California families, he tried to secure as many of these as possible before they were lost or destroyed. It is fortunate that a man of such foresight should have begun his activities at a time when many of these early settlers or their immediate descendants were still alive, and before their valuable records were scattered. Besides private papers, Bancroft spent great sums of money on the copying of such documents as mission records and California provincial and departmental archives, a wise investment, for the originals of some of these have since been destroyed.

As Bancroft assembled this great mass of sources of every conceivable nature, he set a corps of helpers to work, under Henry L. Oak, extracting the material from which were written the famous histories of California, the Pacific Coast states, Mexico, Central America, and others.

In 1905, Bancroft's entire collection was purchased by the University of California, a move led by Henry Morse Stephens, head of the history department, and Benjamin Ide Wheeler, president of the university. Since that time, the library has continued to grow steadily, its books, manuscripts, maps, and newspapers increased by both gifts and purchases. Its geographical scope has remained essentially the same as that defined by Bancroft's original interests, although microfilm and other modern techniques have enabled the library to include pertinent material from such previously inaccessible sources as the archives of England, France, Spain, Portugal, Mexico, and other countries.

Bancroft's works contained volumes and sets on the early history of the West Indies, Central America, Peru, Mexico, Texas, California, Arizona, New Mexico, Utah, Oregon, Washington, Idaho, Montana, Colorado, Wyoming, British Columbia, and Alaska. The present library undertakes collection of historical materials in those areas, although in recent years rather special emphasis has been given to California, the Southwest, Mexico, and Central America.

The materials in the library may be classified as manuscripts, rare books and other printed materials, photographs, pamphlets, maps, and newspapers. Printed sources in the fields of Spanish and Spanish American history and literature have been listed in the second volume of Spain and Spanish America in the Libraries of the University of California, compiled by Eleanor Ashby Bancroft and published in 1930. Many items, of course, have been added since that time.

Among the rarer manuscripts are many relating to Mexico from the sixteenth century and even earlier. A pre-Cortesian Zapotecan codex, a number of illuminated manuscripts including several Aztec sermonarios, a fourteenth-century parchment copy of Pope Gregory's Moralia, Indian calendars, and Artes of various languages compose part of the linguistics collection.

Other interesting manuscripts include: a pastoral of Bishop Zumárraga, 1534, on the founding of the cathedral; another on the College of Guadalupe de Zacatecas; sundry prayers and sermons; the proceedings of the four provincial councils of the church. Alonso Zurita's Relación, a libro de cabildo (Mexico), and Durán's Historia repose with manuscripts by Las Casas, a portion of Muñoz' gatherings, diaries, and crónicas; instrucciones of several viceroys, records of trials, and so forth, represent accessions not easily obtainable in the days before government archives were available to students. Not the least in importance are several diaries of voyages and geographical descriptions, such as a copy of Bishop Tamarón's Visita of the Mexican northwest (1754). Eleven sixteenth-century originals, gramáticas, and letters are of interest. There are numerous later linguistic items, originals from Mexico. There is also a unique collection of originals and facsimiles of manuscripts for the history of the Jesuits on the Pacific slope of Mexico in the sixteenth, seventeenth, and eighteenth centuries.

Californiana is, of course, the Bancroft Library's greatest field of specialization. With such nuggets as the Larkin and Vallejo* papers, Hubert Howe Bancroft created a magnificent manuscript collection dealing with the Spanish and Mexican periods, as well as the early American period, in California. To this the library has constantly added diaries, journals, logbooks, and innumerable collections of private papers, local archives, and business records. As examples of the materials the library is now collecting, such items might be cited as the minutes of the San Francisco Board of Aldermen for 1852-55, the papers of such prominent California figures as Chester H. Rowell, James D. Phelan, and Governors Olson and Pardee, or a recently acquired collection of more than 100 John Muir letters. The library has fallen heir to the voluminous records of the Panama Pacific International Exposition, as well as large files of records of various California business enterprises.

In terms of bulk alone, the greatest addition to the manuscript collection in the past few years has been the vast accumulation of reproductions of manuscripts from foreign archives. For a number of years these were limited to transcripts, and thousands of pages of these were made from documents primarily in the archives of Spain and Mexico. More recently photoreproduction has facilitated the copying of these treasures, and the library's foreign microfilm project has brought in material from the principal archives of Mexico, Spain, Portugal, France, England, and the Netherlands. The library now has well over 2,000,000 exposures of microfilm, as well as many enlargement prints. These photographs come from the Archivo General de la Nación in Mexico, the Archivo General de Indias in Seville, the Arquivo Histórico Colonial in Lisbon, the Algemeen Rijksarchief at the Hague, the Public Record Office of the British Museum, and other archives.

*See Doris Marion Wright, A Guide to the Mariano Guadalupe Vallejo Documentos para la Historia de California, 1780-1875 (Berkeley: University of California Press, 1953).

In "Bancroft Library Microfilm: Portugal and Her Empire,"
The Hispanic American Historical Review (Feb. 1954, XXXIV,
114-25), Gwendolin B. Cobb describes the historical documentation
microfilmed by her between 1949 and 1951 in Portuguese archives
for the Bancroft Library. The documents relate mainly to Brazil
and date from between the late sixteenth and the early eighteenth
centuries. Descriptions of several Portuguese libraries are included, especially of the Arquivo Histórico Colonial and the Tôrre
do Tombo in Lisbon.

The library's collection of books and pamphlets is largest
for California, followed by Mexico, Cuba, Venezuela, and Colombia.
The Mexican group includes rare sixteenth- and seventeenth-century
geographical titles, imprints, and historical writings. Recently
it has been brought up to date with the purchase in Mexico of over
1,000 volumes, which help substantially to fill in the gaps of the war
and postwar years in Mexican publications.

"Papeles Varios" is a fine collection of Mexican pamphlets
(and imprints), comprising 230 thick volumes of miscellaneous
records. It contains more than 3,000 different publications—
mostly pamphlets—written by church leaders, government and
military officials, doctors, lawyers, and men of letters. Only a
small part of these "Papeles" dates from the seventeenth and eighteenth centuries and consists of sermons and ecclesiastical edicts.
The major part, which relates to the nineteenth century, is chiefly
political and historical in character and touches all phases of Mexican
history in that period.

The Franz Blom papers consist of diaries, notebooks, reports
of expeditions and travels, and transcripts and photocopies of documents, as well as articles from periodicals and newspapers. These
archeological papers, 1919-40, relate chiefly to Yucatán, Tabasco,
and Chiapas, in Mexico, and to Guatemala and Honduras.

The holdings on Cuba, increased in 1936 by the gift of Professor Francis S. Philbrock of the University of Pennsylvania Law
School, consist of over 2,000 items. The library acquired, in 1943,
the Theo H. Crook collection, consisting of several thousand volumes,
chiefly relating to Colombia and Venezuela. The collection is amaz-
ingly complete and deals with both the colonial and national periods.

Archeological writings for the Americas include nearly all
the classic titles; to these have been added many on Mexico, such
as copies of codices, and a representative, although not inclusive,
collection of modern studies from institutions engaged in field work.

Codes, laws, and briefs formed, from the library's inception, a large division of materials, especially for California, Mexico, and Central America. To these have been added various editions of the Recopilaciones, the records of the Cortes of Leon, Castile, and Aragon, with numerous treatises and concordances, and English translations of laws of interest to Americans. The Diario Oficial of Mexico is present in a long run; several similar diarios have been added, as have the Actas of the Cabildo of Mexico, of Buenos Aires, and of other cities, and several Spanish treatises by Escriche, Dánvila y Collado, Pérez y López, and others.

Newspapers in the Bancroft Library are chiefly important in the field of California and Southwest history, as files of the rare Californian, California Star, and San Francisco Alta California testify. There are, however, important files of papers for Mexico, Cuba, and a few other Latin American countries. The library no longer collects newspapers published after 1905, this function having been assumed by the Newspaper Division of the General Library. The library does continue to receive certain other periodicals from various parts of Latin America. From Mexico these include publications and documents from both national and state governments.

The library's collection of maps, exclusive of those in atlases and books, numbers several thousand. To these are added sets of sheet maps, such as of the Geologic Survey of the United States, and sets of Mexican topographical maps, numbering several hundred items. The library has a number of very valuable manuscript maps, some of them dating from the sixteenth century. There are many maps of the early railroads—United States transcontinental and local—beginning with the 1850's; also those of Canada, Mexico, and Central America; maps of the pre-railroad explorations; maps of the public surveys in California and the West (U.S. General Land Office); mining maps; coast and geodetic surveys of Pacific Coast harbors. There are many scarce real-estate maps of California cities and colonies in their early stages; several series of commercial county and city maps; a number of original diseños of individual grants; and numerous maps of ranchos. Both manuscript and printed maps are constantly being added to the collection. Photographic copies include such items as a full collection of Kino's maps.

Early in 1950 the Bancroft Library moved from its cramped location on the fourth floor of the General Library to larger quarters in the new Library Annex. The move not only provided much-needed space for books and scholars, but allowed a certain amount of re-organization. A division of manuscripts was created, where special facilities for the care, use, and supervision of rare materials have been provided. A room was created for storage and reading of the library's growing collection of microfilm. Materials in the library are noncirculating, although the library is open to the public. Manuscripts and rare items may be used by accredited researchers.

The library is supported in its aims and activities by the Friends of the Bancroft Library. Since its organization several years ago, this group has annually published some book in the Bancroft field. It also sponsors an occasional publication, Bancroftiana, which carries news of the library's activities, recent acquisitions, and other events.

Guides to several of the important early California manuscript collections have been completed, and at least one such collection, the Thomas Oliver Larkin papers, is being published in full.

A part of the publication program of the Bancroft Library is its sponsorship of the Cortés Society, whose purpose is to publish, in English translation, documents and more general works relating to the Spanish conquest of Mexico.

University of California
Bancroft Library
Cortés Society
Berkeley

The Cortés Society, organized in 1917 by Marshall H. Saville and others in the Museum of the American Indian, New York, planned the publication of documents relating to the discovery and conquest of Latin America. In the succeeding years, it issued the following volumes, published in New York:

I.   Narrative of Some Things of New Spain by the Anonymous Conqueror, a Companion of Cortés, edited by Marshall H. Saville (1917).

II. An Account of the Conquest of Peru by Pedro Sancho, Secretary to Pizarro, edited by Philip Ainsworth Means (1917).

III. An Account of the Conquest of Guatemala in 1524 by Pedro de Alvarado, edited by Sedley J. Mackie (1924).

IV. Relation of the Discovery and Conquest of Peru by Pedro Pizarro, 2 vols., edited by Philip Ainsworth Means (1921).

V.   The Histories of Brazil by Pero de Magalhães, 2 vols., edited by John B. Stetson, Jr. (1922).

After the death of Mr. Saville, Herbert I. Priestley (of the Bancroft Library), Henry R. Wagner (of San Marino, California),

Thomas W. Streeter (of Morristown, New Jersey), and others re-
vived and reorganized the society. A new series, with the following
titles, was begun, published in Berkeley, California:

I. The Discovery of New Spain in 1518 by
Juan de Grijalva, edited by Henry R.
Wagner (1942).

II. The Discovery of Yucatan by Francisco
Hernández de Córdoba, edited by Henry
R. Wagner (1942).

III. The Rise of Fernando Cortés, by Henry
R. Wagner (1944).

IV. Motolinía's History of the Indians of
New Spain, edited by Elizabeth Andros
Foster (1950).

University of California
Bancroft Library
Quivira Society
Berkeley

The Quivira Society was organized in 1929 by a group of investigators engaged in research pertaining to the early history of
northern Mexico and the southwestern part of the United States.
Its purpose is to make accessible to the English-speaking public
the most important original Spanish documents relating to this vast
and interesting field. The society has published the following
volumes:

I. The Espejo Expedition into New Mexico, Luxán, translated
and edited by George P. Hammond and Agapito Rey (1929).

II. Indian Uprising in Lower California, 1734-1737, Taraval,
translated and edited by Marguerite Eyer Wilbur (1931).

III. The Mercurio Volante of Don Carlos de Sigüenza y
Góngora, translated, with introduction and notes, by
Irving A. Leonard (1932).

IV. History of New Mexico by Gaspar Pérez de Villagrá
Alcalá, 1610, translated by Gilberto Espinosa,
introduction and notes by F. W. Hodge (1933).

V. Diary of the Alarcón Expedition into Texas,
1718-1719, by Fray Francisco Céliz, translated
and edited by Fritz Leo Hoffmann (1935).

VI. History of Texas, 1673-1779, by Fray Juan Agustín
Morfi, in two parts, translated, with biographical
introduction and annotations, by Carlos Eduardo
Castañeda (1935).

VII. The Spanish Southwest, 1542-1794, in two parts,
with an annotated bibliography by Henry R. Wagner (1937).

VIII. New Mexico in 1602; or, Juan de Montoya's Relation
of the Discovery of New Mexico, translated and edited
by George P. Hammond and Agapito Rey (1938).

IX. The Reconnaissance of Pensacola Bay, 1689-1693,
translated and edited by Irving A. Leonard (1939).

X. A Scientist on the Trail; Travel Letters of A. F.
Bandelier, 1880-1881, edited by George P. Hammond
and Edgar F. Goad (1949).

XI. Three New Mexico Chronicles: the Exposición of Don
Pedro Bautista Pino, 1812; the Ojeada of Lic. Antonio
Barreiro, 1832; and the additions by Don José Agustín
de Escudero, 1849, edited by H. Bailey Carroll and J.
Villasana Haggard (1942).

XII. Instructions for Governing the Interior Provinces of
New Spain, 1786, by Bernardo de Galvez, translated
and edited by Donald E. Worcester (1951).

University of California
"Ibero-Americana"
Berkeley

In 1931 Herbert E. Bolton, A. L. Kroeber, and C. O. Sauer
established "Ibero-Americana" as one of the series published by
he University of California Press. The original statement of its
purpose was given in the following words: "The series Ibero-
Americana is to form a collection of studies in Latin American
cultures, native and transplanted, pre-European, colonial, and
modern. Physical and racial backgrounds have a place in the col-
ection, but it is anticipated that the studies will be in the main
contributions to culture history. The studies will be issued occasionally as individually paged numbers, and will be of variable
size and cost." Volume one of this series was published on April
9, 1932.

Among the volumes published are:

Barlow, R. H. The Extent of the Empire of the Culhúa Mexico
(1949).

Beals, Ralph L. The Aboriginal Culture of the Cáhita Indians (1943).

——. The Acaxee, a Mountain Tribe of Durango and Sinaloa (1933).

——. The Comparative Ethnology of Northern Mexico Before 1750
(1932).

Borah, Woodrow. New Spain's Century of Depression (1951).

—. Silk Raising in Colonial Mexico (1943).
Cook, S. F. The Conflict Between the California Indian and White
   Civilization, 4 parts (1943).
—. The Extent and Significance of Disease Among the Indians of
   Baja California, 1697-1773 (1937)
—. The Historical Demography and Ecology of the Teotlalpán (1949).
—. Soil Erosion and Population in Central Mexico (1949).
Cook, S. F., and Simpson, Lesley B. The Population of Central
   Mexico in the Sixteenth Century (1948).
Kelly, Isabel. The Archeology of the Autlán-Tuxcacuesco Area of
   Jalisco, 2 vols. (1945 and 1949).
—. Excavations at Chametla, Sinaloa (1938).
—. Excavations at Culiacán, Sinaloa (1945).
Kroeber, A. L. Uto-Aztecan Languages of Mexico (1934).
Radin, Paul. An Historical Legend of the Zapotecs (1935).
Sauer, Carl. Aboriginal Population of Northwestern Mexico (1935).
—. Colima of New Spain in the Sixteenth Century (1948).
—. The Distribution of Aboriginal Tribes and Languages in North-
   western Mexico (1934).
—. The Road to Cíbola (1932).
Sauer, Carl, and Brand, Donald. Aztatlán, Prehistoric Mexican
   Frontier on the Pacific Coast (1932).
Simpson, Lesley Byrd. Studies in the Administration of the Indians
   in New Spain (1934, 1938, 1940).
Taylor, Paul S. A Spanish-Mexican Peasant Community: Arandas
   in Jalisco, Mexico (1933).
West, Robert C. The Mining Community in Northern New Spain:
   The Parral Mining District (1949).

University of California
Museum of Anthropology
Berkeley

     The University of California Museum of Anthropology is a
part of the department of anthropology but has its own staff. The
principal collections and workrooms occupy the whole of a four-
story building on the campus, plus collections in five other buildings.

     Its most important Latin American collection is the pre-
Hispanic archeological material assembled by Max Uhle between
1899 and 1905, through the support of Mrs. Phoebe A. Hearst.
Uhle's main collection (9,413 specimens) is described in Catalogue
IV of the museum, with the same permanent specimen numbers as
were in his field notes, the endeavor being to treat his material as

a type collection with as little "translation" as possible. The bulk
of this collection represents Uhle's own excavations. It is the first
major Peruvian collection accompanied by scientific data and still
remains the largest one thus assembled. The excavations were conducted in a series of coastal valleys from the north to the south of
Peru and at a couple of interior points. Much of the now currently
accepted distinction of Peruvian types and periods rests upon this
work of Uhle. In the course of it, he first distinguished early from
late Chimu, the proto-Lima culture, the Ica from the Nazca phases
of the southern coastal culture, and so forth. Uhle's intended monographic publications shriveled to a number of short but important
papers in journals and in the proceedings of the International Congress of Americanists. The deficiency has been partly made good
by a series of papers—chiefly by Kroeber, Strong, Uhle, O'Neale,
Gayton, and Kelly—published in volumes of the University series
in American Archaeology and Ethnology, and in Anthropological
Records. These papers analyze chiefly Uhle's pottery and textile
finds. A paper by L. M. O'Neale and A. L. Kroeber on "Textile
Periods in Ancient Peru" lays the foundation for the history of the
textile art in Peru.

The skeletal material and the photographic negatives from
Peru are not catalogued separately but with skeletons and negatives
from other parts of the world.

From the remainder of South America, the museum's collections are much more scattered. They include some ethnological
lots from the Amazonian region, some archeological ones from
Venezuela, a gift of archeological material from Ancón, Peru, by
Mrs. Uhle, and so forth. The 7, 942 specimens are described in
Catalogue XVI. Included in the same catalogue are also some extras
and some unidentified pieces of the Uhle collection.

Catalogue III describes the 32, 548 specimens from Mexico
and Central America. From the higher or classical native civilization of Mexico, the museum has relatively little. It does possess,
however, the following from the west coast of Mexico (Sonora,
Sinaloa, Jalisco, and Nayarit): an excellent collection of pottery
from Ixtlán; various sherd collections formed as a by-product of
Sauer and Brand's reconnaissances in Sinaloa and Sonora; the bulk
of the collection made by Isabel T. Kelly at sites in Sinaloa and
Jalisco, under contract with the Mexican government, the latter
retaining the majority of complete objects, but authorizing the
museum to keep most of the broken ones, which are the great majority. A collection of kitchen midden material has been excavated
in the coastal Maya area of British Honduras.

Since the series of "Ibero-Americana" (q. v.) was instituted in 1932, some work by members of the department or the museum having reference to Latin America has appeared in that series rather than in the two departmental series previously mentioned.

The California catalogue contains something over 170, 000 entries. While many of the specimens are archeological fragments, nevertheless this is the largest and strongest unit in the museum. As regards intrinsic value, it is about equally divided between ethnology and archeology. For purposes of catalogue grouping, California is defined in terms of the present political boundaries.

The Southwestern material, both archeological and ethnological, is included in a class which covers North America except for California and Mexico. Catalogue II describes the 29, 500 specimens.

In addition to the above-mentioned material, Catalogue XII (Physical Anthropology) lists more than 600 specimens from Hispanic America.

University of California
Museum of Vertebrate Zoology
Berkeley

The Museum of Vertebrate Zoology was founded and endowed by Miss Annie M. Alexander in 1908 as a repository for specimens and information relative to the higher vertebrate animals of western North America. The particular groups with which it is most concerned are mammals, birds, reptiles, and amphibians. The collection is large and constantly growing.

Most of the specimens are from western North America, including the Mexican states of Sonora, Lower California, Guerrero, Chihuahua, Coahuila, Sinaloa, Jalisco, and Chiapas.

The materials from Lower California were collected in the period 1925 to 1931. They include approximately 11, 000 specimens, more than half of which are birds, a third mammals, and the remainder reptiles and amphibians. The collecting was done under the direction of the late Joseph Grinnell, who participated in the first field work in the Sierra San Pedro Mártir section. In the course of the work, the entire length of the peninsula was traversed several times, and various adjacent islands (Cedros, Magdalena, Espíritu Santo, San José, and San Francisco) were visited. Study of the birds by Dr. Grinnell resulted in the descriptions of many new forms and culminated in his A Distributional Summation of the Ornithology of Lower California, published by the University of

California Press in 1928.   This work includes a study of all the
scientific literature concerning the birds of Lower California; it is
the most important and authoritative work on the birds of that region.
The reptiles and amphibians collected were reported on by J. M.
Linsdale.   Papers based on the mammal collection have been written
by Seth B. Benson, Joseph Grinnell, and E. R. Hall.

In 1936, the museum initiated a program of field work in northern Mexico under the direction of Seth B. Benson and with the co-
operation of the Departamento Forestal y de Caza y Pesca.   Later
this was extended through intensive work in all parts of the country
by A. Starker Leopold, from 1944 on, in preparation of a book on
the game mammals and birds of Mexico.   Alden H. Miller began
extensive work on Mexican birds in 1948, both in the field and at
the museum, in editing and writing a distributional check list of the
birds of Mexico; Part I was issued in 1950.   Frank A. Pitelka has
made a special study of the jays of Mexico, particularly in Chiapas.
In 1947, the museum received a gift of 6, 000 specimens of birds
from Guerrero, from the estate of Milton S. Ray.

Apart from the materials mentioned above, there are considerable collections in the museum from El Salvador and Colombia.

Pomona College
Claremont

In 1930, José Clemente Orozco was brought to Pomona College
to decorate a dining room in one of the halls.   He chose the Prometheus
theme.   The fresco covers over a hundred square yards of plaster
laid on acousticon.

The items in the Pomona College Library relating particularly
to Hispanic studies are contained largely in the Mason Library of
California and Western American History, and the Henry R. Wagner
Collection of History and Cartography of the North Pacific.   Both
collections are housed in the rare book room.

The Mason Library was the gift of Mr. William Smith Mason
to Pomona College and has been maintained and enlarged through
an annual stipend from the donor.   At the time of the acquisition of
the library by Pomona College in 1914, it consisted of some 1, 800
volumes, which have since been increased through gifts of books and
by purchase to over 4, 800 volumes.   Due to the wide scope of the
collection, there has been little or no attempt to purchase manuscripts,
and it consists principally of printed books relating to New Spain
and the trans-Mississippi West, with particular emphasis on the
Pacific Coast from precolonial times to the present.   Among the few

manuscripts in the collection, the page entitled "Estado de las missiones de la nueva California, " dated 1785, and containing a summary of the possessions of each mission as of that year, is of interest. There is no published catalogue or bibliography of the Mason Library.

The Wagner collection, gift to Pomona College of Mr. Henry Raup Wagner in 1936, consists of approximately 500 printed volumes, 44 bound volumes of photostats and transcripts, 50 packages of photostats and transcripts, and 629 maps, of which some are originals and the majority photostats. A few maps, formerly contained in the Mason Library, have been catalogued with these. This material relates almost entirely to the Spanish exploration of the North Pacific Coast prior to 1800, with some accounts of land expeditions into the southwestern quarter of the present United States, as well as including books, manuscripts, and maps regarding Spanish and Portuguese exploration and trade in the East Indies and Asia. There is a considerable section of books dealing with navigation in the sixteenth and seventeenth centuries. This collection is probably unsurpassed as to size and completeness in its field, and constitutes a prime source for research. There is no printed guide or catalogue to the books or copies of manuscripts, but the list of maps in Volume II of Henry Raup Wagner, The Cartography of the Northwest Coast of America to the Year 1800 (Berkeley: University of California Press, 1937), notes the maps which are in this collection and forms an excellent check list.

In 1949, the library acquired a number of books from Mr. Henry R. Wagner's Cortés collection.

Los Angeles County Museum
Exposition Park
Los Angeles 7

The collection of paintings in the Los Angeles County Museum has been formed in very recent years. In 1946 a reorganization of the art division was undertaken. During the years 1946 and 1947, the late William Randolph Hearst provided the museum with a special fund in order to fill gaps in the collection. In addition, Mr. Hearst presented to the museum numerous paintings and sculptures from his vast collections. Other donors, both in this country and in Europe, have contributed to the museum's collections during the past few years.

Included among the Spanish paintings are the following:

Cano, Alonso. "The Virgin Appearing to St. Anthony of Padua, "
seventeenth century, oil on canvas.
—. "Christ in Limbo, " oil on canvas.
Greco, El. "St. Andrew, " oil on canvas. Formerly in the church
of Almadrones, Guadalajara, Spain, where it formed a part of
an incomplete series of eight Apostle figures, four of which were
acquired by the Prado Museum of Madrid in 1946. Of the remain-
ing four, one was retained by the bishop of the church and three
came to the United States.
—. Some rare drawings in red chalk—preliminary sketches for the
"St. Andrew" and for another work, the head of a spectator in
"The Despoiling of Christ. "
Leonardo, José. "St. John the Baptist in the Desert, " ca. 1635,
oil on canvas.
Mazo, Juan Bautista del. "Young Princess Praying, " seventeenth
century, oil on canvas.
Ribera. "St. Joseph, " seventeenth century, oil on canvas.
Valencia, School of. "St. Michael Fighting the Dragon, " fifteenth
century, tempera on wood.
Zurbarán. "The Young Christ Wounded by a Thorn, " seventeenth
century, oil on canvas.

Also represented in the museum are several Mexican painters,
including Diego Rivera and Juan de Correa.

Spanish sculpture in the museum includes:

Processional Crucifix, engraved on both sides, late fourteenth
or early fifteenth century.
St. Ildefonso as the Archbishop of Toledo, wood, gilded and poly-
chromed, ca. 1500; center figure of reredos, church of San
Ildefonso in Husillos (Palencia).
Two alabaster reliefs of angels from tomb of Don García Osorio
(d. 1502?) and his wife, formerly in San Pedro at Ocaña.
Alabaster tombstone of a knight of Santiago, School of Castile,
early sixteenth century.
Alabaster tomb of a knight, School of Castile, ca. 1550.

There are also a silver almsplate with gilt-silver figures
(Cordoba, late sixteenth century), a silver ciborium (Catalan, fourteenth century), and from the sixteenth century a silver taza, cross,
and chalice.

Hispanic American materials in the anthropology division of
the Los Angeles County Museum include the following.

Mexico and early California:

In the Native Sons of the Golden West collection, 273 items con-
sisting of arms, costume, and implements.
In the Coronel collection, 1,276 items of Mexican California days,
consisting of furniture, costume, and tools.
Examples of pottery and textiles from Mexico in a collection of the
Museum Associates.
In the Del Valle collection, 1,938 items from Spanish, Mexican, and
aboriginal California.
In the Mrs. Walter J. Barlow collection, 457 items of American
Indian, Mexican, and other origins.
In the Hearst collection, 221 Navajo and Mexican woolen blankets.
Also a collection of over 2,000 California Indian archeological items.

Central America:

In the Gump collection, 34 pre-Spanish pottery items from Ometepec
Island, Nicaragua.
Central American pottery (531 pieces) in plainware and polychrome
exteriors.

Panama:

In the E.A. Salisbury collection, 57 items of modern Panamanian
Indian objects such as textiles, beads, and wood carvings.

Ecuador:

In the E. Bergen collection, 19 pieces of Jívaro Indian featherwork;
37 anthropological items from the Amazon area; and 22 items of
San Blas Indian material of ethnographic interest.

Peru:

In the Ida P. Osborn collection, 80 historical and archeological
objects.

In the history division of the Los Angeles County Museum, the
early history of California is well represented by over 8,500 items.
A number are of Spanish origin, some are Mexican, others a combination
of these plus variations of a purely local character. In the California
History Hall, there are dioramas representing various episodes of
California history during the Spanish and Mexican periods.

The library of the museum is permeated with material on Latin
America. Items of special interest are: a collection of seventeenth-
century maps of the New World; manuscript collections of the Del
Valle family, of Antonio Franco Coronel, and of the Historical Society
of Southern California; a set of the nineteenth-century Spanish-
language newspaper La Crónica. There are important collections of
scientific works concerning northern Mexico and Lower California.

Los Angeles Public Library
630 West Fifth Street
Los Angeles 13

The Los Angeles Public Library is departmentalized, so that books are shelved according to subjects, geographical considerations being secondary. Mexico and the Spanish period of the Southwest are represented primarily in the department of Hispanic Americana. The value of the collection to students is in its scope and catholicity. It extends from books printed by Spanish and Mexican presses in the early seventeenth century to current books, pamphlets, and serials. The basic collection was acquired during the years 1898-1909, at the suggestion of Miss Anna Beckley, reference librarian, and Mr. Charles F. Lummis, distinguished Southwestern author. They were purchased from Mr. Francis S. Barton, a Protestant missionary and book collector of Mexico City, the library of the Rev. Juan Cavallería of the Iglesia de Nuestra Señora of Los Angeles, and trade agencies.

Ancient Mexico is represented in the great codices (Vaticanus, Magliabecchi, Mendocino, Ramírez, Troano), the Anales of the Museo Nacional, and the works of Lord Kingsborough, Maudslay, and recent archeologists and philologists such as Earl H. Morris and Ralph L. Roys.

The early chroniclers of the general history of the Indies— Juan de Torquemada (ed. 1723) and Antonio de Herrera (ed. 1726-27), together with the long list of such sources as Bernal Díaz del Castillo, Fernando Alva Ixtlilxochitl, and Diego de Landa—tell the story of Indian civilization and Spanish conquest. The collection is especially rich for the viceregal period, including vidas, such as those of Antonio Margil de Jesús of Guatemala and Junípero Serra of California, confesionarios, sermons, early parochial histories, and the narratives of outstanding ecclesiastics such as Jerónimo Mendieta, Isidro Féliz Espinosa, Francisco Javier Alegre, and Francisco Javier Clavijero. In this division there is a unique collection of Guadalupana including the Maravilla americana (1756) of the famous Miguel Cabrera. Art, mining, medicine, and cookery are also represented. There is a small collection of linguistics, distinguished by several interesting titles: Martín de León, Camino del cielo en lengua mexicana (1611), Ignacio de Paredes, Catecismo mexicano (1758), Horacio Carochi, Compendio del arte de la lengua mexicana (1759), and the well-known Fr. Andrés de Olmos, Arte para aprender la lengua mexicana. Legislation of the period is found in the colonial code, Recopilación de leyes de los reinos de las Indias (1681). In the general division of legislation are available a short list of significant works, among them Manuel Dublán, Legislación mexicana (42 volumes covering the years 1687-1910), and the Diario de los Debates for 1862-63 and 1869-1913.

Contributions of the eminent Mexican scholars of the nineteenth and present centuries are fully represented (García Icazbalceta, Riva Palacio, Bustamante, Peñafiel, Castillo Negrete, Genaro García, Zamacois, the Colección de documentos inéditos of Pacheco and Cárdenas, and the Colección de documentos relativos al Departamento de Californias), as well as the works of American and British writers.

The collection of travel and description is notable. It includes Mapas españoles de América, siglos XV-XVII, the Boletín of the Sociedad de Geografía y Estadística, the works of Humboldt, Henry George Ward, John Lloyd Stephens, Mrs. Calderón de la Barca, Joel R. Poinsett, and Waddy Thompson, as well as innumerable sketches and impressions of other past and contemporary writers.

Many of the works mentioned include materials on the Hispanic frontier area now within the confines of the United States. For California, there is an extensive specialized collection including manuscripts of the Mercury case (an official record of 1,137 pages of the seizure of the contraband ship Mercury); copies of de la Guerra letters; certified typewritten copies of the Pedro Font Diario and Junípero Serra Diario, and photostats of pertinent materials; early editions of the Serra (1787) by Palou, the Salvatierra (1754) by Venegas, the Noticia de la California (1757), now attributed to Burriel, Francesco María Picolo, Informe (1702), the Diario histórico (1770) of Miguel Costansó.

The collection of genealogy and heraldry is noted for containing such works as those of García Carraffa, the Academia Mexicana de Genealogía y Heráldica, Ortega y Pérez Gallardo's Historia genealógica de las familias más antiguas de México, Lohmann Villena's Los Americanos en las órdenes nobiliarias, 1529-1900, Martínez Cosío's Caballeros de las órdenes militares en México, books of Villar Villamil, and source material and mission records on Spanish California families.

The collection is completed by the works of recent writers, files of the Academy of Pacific Coast History, publications of the Southwest Museum, state historical society papers, and all current publications available.

Southwest Museum
Highland Park
Los Angeles

The Southwest Museum of Los Angeles offers to the student two kinds of Hispanic material: books, and objects illustrating the history and culture of Spanish America, especially of the former Spanish possessions of California, New Mexico, and Arizona. The books are housed in the museum library. The other material is in the "Casa de Adobe, " a full-size reconstruction of a Spanish-Californian ranch house, situated near the museum, to which it was presented by the Hispanic Society of California in 1925.

While no count of the Spanish American material in the library of the museum has been made, it may be said that published material pertaining especially to the archeology, ethnology, history, and linguistics of Mexico, southwestern United States, and California, is fairly rich, since the major portion of one collection, that of the late Dr. Charles F. Lummis, the founder and first secretary of the Southwest Museum, belongs to this field. There is considerably less relating to Central and South America. The Munk collection is classified as Arizoniana, but is really of the Southwest and contains materials on the Spanish and Mexican periods of Southwestern history. The Munk library provided the basis for Hector Alliot's Bibliography of Arizona (Los Angeles: Southwest Museum, 1914). The library of the Southwest Museum has received the Maya collection of Theodore T. Willard, and the library of Professor Kenneth Macgowan, used by him in writing his Early Man in the New World (New York: The Macmillan Co., 1950).

The Casa de Adobe comprises twenty rooms surrounding a patio. Four of the rooms form the private quarters of the resident hostess; three are storage rooms; and two are devoted to museum case displays. The rest of the house, including a sala or parlor, a music room, a dining room, a kitchen, an oven room, a bathroom, a priest's room, a chapel, and three bedrooms, are furnished appropriately as exhibits.

The furniture displayed in these ten rooms is such as a Californian ranch house would have accumulated in fifty years of occupancy, beginning about 1800; in fact, many of the pieces originally stood in such houses and have been lent or given to the museum by members of the old families.

The early period is represented by chairs, tables, and the like, originating in Mexico and Spain in the seventeenth and eighteenth centuries; there is also furniture of the Empire style, some from Spain, some from the eastern United States, and early Victorian furniture from the latter source.

In one museum room of the Casa are exhibits illustrating the ranchos of California, the costumes of the Spanish period, and the characteristic weapons of the time, all labeled and enlivened with illustrations and miniature models. In the other museum room are exhibits similarly illustrating the Franciscan missions and their industries.

On the walls of the mission museum room and elsewhere in the Casa may be seen old paintings from the Caballeria collection, most of which once hung in the Franciscan missions of California. Dispersed after the missions were secularized, they were located and purchased many years later by an energetic priest, Father Juan Caballeria, and finally found their way to the Southwest Museum.

Noteworthy among the personal relics displayed at the Casa are a small wooden shrine of San Antonio and a small religious picture, both said to have belonged to Fray Junípero Serra, and a photostat copy of his original journal describing his first trip to Alta California. There are also various articles from the Sepúlveda, de la Guerra, Ortega, and Pico families of California, and the Delgado family of New Mexcio.

The Southwest Museum proper is devoted to the American Indian, ancient and modern, especially the Indians of the Southwest and California, but there are excellent objects from almost the entire Western Hemisphere. It is especially rich in baskets from many tribes, and in blankets and other textiles from the Navajo and from the Pueblo villages. Case exhibits are changed from time to time, and there is always study material in reserve. Besides such case displays, there are a number of small groups or dioramas, and miniature figures, illustrating the lives and dress of various tribes. The Prehistoric Room is devoted to the archeology of the Southwest, with the exhibits arranged in sequence from the earliest known times to the coming of the whites. The Fred K. Hinchman hall on the floor beneath is devoted to the arts and customs of the modern tribes of the Southwest. In the lobby are shown archeological and ethnological collections from Spanish America, and synoptic exhibits of Indian projectile points, shellwork, and of the useful plants and plant products for which the world is indebted to the American Indian.

The library, outside of its Hispanic collections, is devoted largely to the American Indian. The publications of the museum deal mainly with Indian subjects and include the following:

Amsden, Charles Avery. Navaho Weaving, Its Technic and History,
2d ed., 1949. (Published by the University of New Mexico Press
in co-operation with the Southwest Museum.)

——. Prehistoric Southwesterners, from Basketmaker to Pueblo
(1949).

Cordry, Donald B. and Dorothy M. Costumes and Textiles of the
Aztec Indians of the Cuetzalán Region, Puebla, Mexico (1940).

——. Costumes and Weaving of the Zoque Indians of Chiapas, Mexico
(1941).

Hodge, F. W. The History of Hawikuh, New Mexico, One of the
So-Called Cities of Cíbola (1937).

Lothrop, S. K. Inca Treasure as Depicted by Spanish Historians
(1938).

Van de Velde, Paul and Henrietta R. The Black Pottery of Coyotepec,
Oaxaca, Mexico (1939).

University of California *
The Library
Los Angeles

The library's general collection is strong in the Hispanic
field. Periodicals and standard works relating to Spain and Latin
America are in the main stacks. Rare books, manuscripts, newspapers, maps, and other fragile or non-book materials are kept
in the Department of Special Collections.

The Robert Ernest Cowan collection of over 3,000 volumes,
pamphlets, maps, manuscripts, and newspapers pertaining to
California and the American West contains many of the key items
relating to the activities of Spain and Mexico in these regions.

The following materials of Hispanic interest are in the Department of Special Collections:

Amesti, José. "Cuaderno de cuentos de la casa del J[os]e Amesti
del año de 1840 [i.e., 1839] a 1850"; account book of José Amesti,
merchant and prominent citizen of the district of Monterey,
California, during the Mexican and early American periods;
128 numbered pages (some blank). Robert Ernest Cowan collection.

Bernaldes, Andres. "Historia de los Reyes Catolicos D. Fernando
y Da. Ysabel, escrita por el Bachiller Andres Bernaldes, "
Seville, 1682; 398 leaves, with index. Bound manuscripts collection.

Castro, Manuel. Correspondence and papers, 1837-70; consist
chiefly of the correspondence and business papers of Manuel Castro,

* See Supplement, p. 388, for additional data.

but containing a few papers of Juan Bautista, José, Jesús
María, Víctor, and Simón Castro; 2 folders. Robert Ernest
Cowan collection.

Commonplace book containing sermons and notes in Spanish (18th
century?); 576 pp. (pages 1 and 2 are missing). Bound manuscripts collection.

Crespi, Juan. Letters—Nov. 24, 1769 to Francisco Palou, and
June 11, 1770 to Juan Andres; copied from British Museum MS
13974 for George Davidson, 1890; 49 leaves. Robert Ernest
Cowan collection.

"Documentos historicos mexicanos" [binder's title]; copies of
documents of the late seventeenth and early eighteenth centuries
relating to various land grants in the viceroyalty of New Spain
(many pages are missing). Bound manuscripts collection.

Enriquez de Ribera, Payo, abp., viceroy of Mexico, 1612-84.
"Explicatio apologetica nonnullarum propositionum a theologo
quodam non dextere notatarum sive: Quaestiones variae, quarum
explicationi occasionem dedit theologi cuiusdam non satis accurata
notatio. Goatemalae: Apud Iosephum de Pineda y Ybarra, 1663."
The only copy in the United States of the first book printed in
Guatemala.

Font, Pedro. Journal prepared by Padre Fray Pedro Font, apostolic
preacher of the College of Santa Cruz de Querétaro from the
minutes written on the road during a journey to Monterey and
the Port of San Francisco in company with Don Juan Bautista de
Anza..., Sept. 29, 1775 to June 23, 1776; translated from the Spanish
by Marie Doyle; 119 pp. Tipped in at end of manuscript: a.l. s.
from Robert E. Cowan to Lawrence Clark Powell, Los Angeles,
May 2, 1938, explaining that the translation of the Font diary
was purchased by Cowan at the sale of the John Doyle library
in 1912; 1 p. Robert Ernest Cowan collection.

Gaffey collection. A collection of letters and documents from
the family archives of Margaret (Gaffey) Kilroy, daughter of John
T. Gaffey:

Bandini, Juan (1800-59). Correspondence and papers, 1837-89;
includes correspondence, accounts, and legal documents; a
few papers of his son Juan B. Bandini; accounts relating to his
partnership with Abel Stearns; original expediente for his Rancho
Tecate in Lower California; and an account book for Rancho San
Rafael, Lower California; 74 items.

Bandini, Juan B. Diary, Santa Monica, Calif., April 1, 1883 to
August 6, 1905 (Nov. 2, 1896 to Nov. 19, 1900 not included).

Gaffey, John T. Letters and documents, 1885-1910; letters to

Gaffey from Mariano Ruiz, and including a memorandum and description of his mines in the territory of Tepic, Mexico; 12 items in folder.

Ruiz, Mariano. "Leyenda historica de los estados de Michoacan, Jalisco y Nayarit, escrita por el General de Division, Mariano Ruiz, dedicada a la honorada dama, Mrs. Arcadia Bandini de Gaffey, de San Pedro, Calif., E.U.A., 1927"; many photographs, portraits, and reproduction of drawings by Ana Maria B. Ruiz tipped in; 187 numbered leaves, typescript.

—. "Leyenda historica del territoria de Tepic, escrita por el Señor General Mariano Ruiz, dedicada a los niños de las escuelas nacionales del referido territorio, México, enero 30 de 1914"; portraits of the author and Manuel Lozada tipped in; 3 vols. in two, typescripts.

—. "Reminiscencias historicas, escrita por el Señor de División, Mariano Ruiz, veteran de 1862. Dedicadas a su honorado amigo, Mr. John T. Gaffey, de San Pedro, Calif., E.U.A., Mexico, 16 de Septiembre de 1926"; portraits and photographs tipped in; 3 vols. in one.

Galvez, José de. Instructions for Don Vicente Villa—copy for the Commandant of the Troops, Don Pedro Fages, La Paz, Jan. 5, 1768; translated from the Spanish [by Robert Ernest Cowan?]; 14 leaves. Robert Ernest Cowan collection.

Gillespie, Archibald Hamilton, Private and public papers of Archibald H. Gillespie, special messenger from the President of the United States to Colonel John C. Fremont, Captain and Brevet Major of the California Battalion of Mounted Riflemen and Commandant of the Southern Department of the Territory of California during the conquest, 1846-47; many of the papers are in Spanish and written by prominent members of the Mexican population of California during this period; 464 numbered letters and documents.

Ixtlilxochitl, Fernando de Alva. History of the Chichimeca nation, its settlement and establishment in the land of Anahuac, known today as the Kingdom of New Spain; beginning and progress of the powerful Tetzcucano empire and successions of its monarchs until its destruction by the invasion of the Spaniards who conquered it; translated from the Mexican edition by Frank de Thoma; 235 MS leaves (incomplete). Robert Ernest Cowan collection.

Joven Guipuzcuana (bark). Cuaderno del cargam la Barca Joven Guipuzcuana y devitos a Don Jose Antonio Aguirre, Fort Vancouver, Jan. 27, 1849; 5 MS pages. Robert Ernest Cowan collection.

Linares, Fernando de Alencastre, duke, viceroy of Mexico. "Instruccion de govierno..."; Andrade's copy of the Duke of Linares' instructions to his successor; 66 leaves, 65 pp.

Pardo y Urbina, Manuel. "Ligeros estudios hechos sobre la historia, siembra y cultivo del tabaco"; thesis presented to the Escuela Nacional de Agricultura, Mexico, June 1, 1888; 250 holograph pp., signed.

Posesion que tomo el Doctor Geronimo de la Villa de Robladillo, Aug. 2, 1551; 8 pp., 4 MS leaves.

Sarria, Vincente de. "Panegirico de la gloriossa Sta. Anna madre de la madre de Dios. Predicado en Echabarri en su festividad ano de 1796"; 5 holograph pp., signed. Robert Ernest Cowan collection.

—— "Panegirico de la gloriossa Sta. Anna madre de la madre de Dios. En Echabarri, 1797"; 7 holograph pp., signed. Robert Ernest Cowan collection.

Sociedad de Colonizacion al Estado de Sonora, San Francisco. Correspondence and papers, Feb. 14 to May 4, 1855; most of the documents are written and signed by Francisco Casanueva, secretary of the society; 11 letters and documents.

Valde, Lucas. "Carta critica sobre los libros i memoriales del pe Francisco de Soto i Marne, 1752"; 162 holograph pp., signed.

Villa, Simeon A. Flight and wanderings of Emilio Aguinaldo from his abandonment of Bayamborg until his capture in Palanan: a diary by Simeon A. Villa, a member of his staff, Nov. 13, 1899 to March 22, 1901; typescript copy of an English translation; 129 numbered leaves.

University of California
William Andrews Clark Memorial Library
Los Angeles

Manuscripts of Hispanic interest:

Alegre y Capetillo, José Ignazio María. "Derrotiero que hize Fr. José Ignazio María Alegre y Capetillo con particular Razon de todos los acaecim [ien] tos y cosas dignas de mem. ria del viaje, que hize con Don Hugo de Oconor"; voyage begun from Mexico in 1771; 86 leaves, 172 pp.

"El Ap[ostoli]co Colegio de Sōr Fernando de Meq. co. Da cuenta à V. R. M. [unknown] de los nuevos descubrimtos hechos con felicida (sobre lo antiquam. te conquistado de la California) desde el ano de 1769, hasta el presente de 1776... Copia"; 14 leaves, 28 pp.

Azanza, Miguel José de, Virrey de Nueva España. A.l. s. to Diego de Agreda; Mexico, April 13, 1799; commissioning de Agreda to contract for a voyage to Alta California; 2 pp.; with copies of the conditions and estimates for the voyage; 2 pp.

Bolívar, Simón, Libertador y Presidente de la República de Colombia.
"Al Presidente de los Estadoz Unidoz Mejicanoz"; signed August
14, 1828; 1 leaf, 1 p.

Calzada, Juan (Rev. Padre Guardian Fray). "Respuesta del R. P.
Guardian F. Juan Calzada al Exĩno Señor Virey dando las razones
por que no se han entregado a la Jurisdicion ordinaria Ecleciastica
las Misiones de la Alta California"; dated 1818; with one folding
plate of statistics sewn in, and one page of statistics laid in; 25
leaves, 48 pp.

Candelaria, Juan. "Noticias que da Juan Candelaria Vecino de esta
villa de San Francisco Xavier de Albuquerque de edad de 84 años
nacio el año del 1692"; dated 1776; 8 leaves, 15 pp.

Cassio, Pedro Antonio de. "Nuevo Reglamento para el antiguo y
nuevos establecimientos de Californias—Año 1781"; signed MS;
48 leaves, 95 pp.

Collection of six related pieces: (a) "Extracto—sobre establecimiento
de Missiones y dos Presidios en los Rios Colorado y Gila y sobre
abrir comunicaz.n con el Nuevo Mexico desde Sonora y a Monterrey
desde el Nuevo Mexico"; ca. 1775; 18 leaves, 52 pp. (b) "Indice
de los documentos que tratan de ereccion de Missiones en los Rios
Colorado y Gila...Establecimiento de dos Presidios y apertura de
comunicaz.n desde Sonora al Nuevo Mexico, y desde esta Prov.a
a Monterrey"; ca. 1776; 2 leaves, 4 pp. (c) "Papel util sobre
comunicaz.n con los nuevos establecim.tos—Descripcion del Moqui
y otras tierras—papel que presente al Virrey"; ca. 1776; 15 leaves,
28 pp. (d) "Sublevacion de los Yumas..."; December 26, 1781;
1 p. (e) "Sublevacion de Pecos"; August 15, 17—; folio, 2 pp.
(f) Index of the above papers; fragment; folio, 1 p.

Conch, Fernando de la, Gov.or de Nuevo Mexico. "Explicacion de
la Cruz, y Caracteres pressedene.s que en una Gamussa...la
Nacion Juta me entrego..."; signed MS; November 7, 1787; with
one page of diagram; 3 leaves, 5 pp.

"Convite evangelico..."; account of Indian uprisings, 1751-66, against
the Jesuit Missions of Mexico, Arizona, and California; 38 leaves,
75 pp.

Corrêa da Serra, José Francisco. A.l.s. from Philadelphia, October 28, 1820, to Francis Walker Gilmer; gives lexicographical
information as requested; 1 leaf, 1 p.

"Descripcion...del Palacio llamado vulgarm.te de Moctezuma...";
with one page of diagram; folio, 3 pp.

"Diario de lo acacido y practicado en la entrada que se hizo a la Ysla
del Tiburon este ano 1750"; bound with MS. poem, "Sur, " 16 pp.,
at end; with poem, 53 leaves, 104 pp.

Dominguez, Francisco Atancio (Fray) and Velez de Escalante,

Silvestre (Fray). A.l.s. to Don Pedro Fermin de Mendinueta,
the Mission of Guadalupe Zuñi, November 25, 1776; contemporary
copy; 4 pp.

Echeandía, José María de. "Territorio de la Alta California";
document in the hand of Augustin Zamarano, signed by Echeandía,
September 22, 1829; concerning political divisions and officers of
Alta and Baja California; 4 leaves, 7 pp.

Ferrer, Vicente (Padre Fray). A.l.s. to Padre Fray Junípero Serra,
November 28, 1775; 10 leaves, 20 pp.

[Galvez y Gallardo, Bernardo, Conde de—signature found in several
places.] "Instruccion formada, en virtud de Real Orden, para
govierno del Senor Comandante General de Provincias Internas
[Jacobo Ugante y Loyola] en el ano de 1786"; 18 various signatures at end; 56 leaves, 110 pp.

"Instruccion hecha por el Governador y tropa de los nuevos establecimientos de California"; MS in two hands; ca. 1776; 6 leaves, 12
pp.

[Jefferson, Thomas] A.l.s. "Extracts from a letter to Mr. Char-
michael dated August 2, 1790"; instruction for negotiations with
Spain; 1 leaf, 2 pp.

Jefferson, Thomas. Manuscript memorandum signed, August 2,
1790; a plan for forcing Spain to accede to the Louisiana Purchase;
2 leaves, 2 pp.

———. A.l.s., New York, August 10, 1790, to William Short [chargé
d'affaires at Paris]; instructions for negotiations with France;
allusions to Louisiana country; folio, 4 pp.

———. A.l.s. to James Monroe, in hand of a secretary, London,
February 2, 1804; regarding the relations of the United States
with Spain and Spanish America after the Louisiana Purchase;
2 folios, 7 pp.

Maurelle, Francisco Antonio. Narration of the voyage made in 1779
to the coasts of California by Bruno Heceta; 62 leaves, 124 pp.

Narvaez, José María. Manuscript diary of navigation, 1788; 31 pp.

"Noticias, y reflexiones sobre la Guerra que se tiene con los Yndios
Apaches en las Provincias de la Nueva españa. Caracter de los
Yndios"; ca. 1790; 8 leaves, 16 pp.

Oñate, Juan de. "Asiento que Don Jhoan de Oñate Vez[ino] de
Cacatecas haze con el Rey ñro señor, sobre el descubrimiento
y poblacion del nuevo Mexico, echas por el s.r Don Luis de
Velasco, Virrey desta nueva espana. 1595"; with title; 5 leaves,
9 pp.

O'Reilly, Alexander, Governor of Louisiana. Document, in French,
signed, August 21, 1763; proclamation issued in the name of the
King of Spain, appealing to the people of Louisiana to acquiesce
to the rule of Spain; broadside.

Paredes,———, Conde de, Virrey de Nueva España. Document
signed, May 7, 1681, regarding the first permanent settlement
in California; 1 leaf, 2 pp.

—, Document signed, regarding the outfitting of ships for California; May 9, 1681; folio, 2 pp.

Prudean [?], Carlos, Agrimensor Real y Particular de la Provincia
de la Luisiana. Survey, signed, with diagram of the district of
La Feliciana in Louisiana; 1 leaf, 2 pp.

"[Reconocomiento de las costas de la California--Expediccion de
1774]... La expediccion que por Mar se hizo el año pasado de
1774 con destino de reconocer las Costas de la California
septentrional hasta la altura de 60 grados de Latitude al Norte
..."; an extract of the voyage which includes: "Estado de la
Misiones de Monterrey hasta 31. de Diziembre de 74"; folio,
4 pp.

"Relacion de el attaque, que las tropas de S. M. dieron a los
enemigos Indios Pimais, Ceris, y Yaquis en... Cerro prietto
el 25. de Novriembre de 1768"; 4 leaves, 8 pp.

Tamiriz, Francisco de Paula. "Ynforme sobre fomento y reforma
de abusos en la California Alta ó Nueva Alvion"; continuation:
Rivas, Juan (Fray). "Ynforme ó memoría en respuesta del
informe anterior de Tamariz. 1814"; 36 leaves, 71 pp.

Maps of Hispanic interest:

[Bodega y Cuadra, Juan Francisco de.] "Puerto del Capitan Bodega
descubierto con la Goleta Sonora..."; October 3, [1775]; pen
and ink; double page.

"Desde el puerto, o boca de s.m fran.co asta el Puerto de la bodega
en derechura ay ocho leguas, y por la costa 12 leguas"; pen and
ink; double page.

Vial, Pedro. "Mapa et tierra que yos. Pedro Vial taingo tran-
zitare en S. t Tafee este dia 18 de Osictubre de 1787"; pen
and ink, with color; double page; with: "Alturas de los Sitios
abaso omencionado de la Sonora á la nueva California segun el
ultimo viaje"; folio MS; 1 p; "Noticias de Viale en extracto de
su viaje"; folio MS; 3 pp.

The following are printed maps:

Greuter, Mattheus. "Terrestrial globe." Rome: Dominici de
Rubeis [Dominico Rossi], 1695.

"Hispaniae novae sivae magnae, recens et vera descriptio.
1579"; double page; on verso: "Espaigne nevve"; 1 printed page.

First Theater in California
Monterey

The theater is an adobe structure built in 1844. It was presented in 1906 to the State of California by William Randolph Hearst, individually and as a trustee of the Landmarks Fund. Its exhibits consist of early Californiana, including a wooden drop curtain, baptismal font, and weights and measures.

Monterey Custom House Museum
Monterey

This old Mexican stone and adobe structure with balconies and arcade is the property of the United States Government, which leases it to the State of California for museum purposes. Like the First Theater in California, it is controlled by the State Department of Natural Resources. Its exhibits consist of early Californiana (pictures, manuscripts, flags) loaned by citizens of Monterey and of California.

Mills College
Art Gallery
Oakland 13

The collection of Guatemalan textiles in the Art Gallery was presented to Mills College by one of its trustees, Prentiss N. Gray, of New York City. This collection, assembled by Mrs. E. A. Osborne, of the Historical Society of Guatemala, represents the hand-loom work of different tribes and provinces. Unusual and varied weaves, dyes, and symbols are shown, which should prove of interest to the layman as well as to the professional student. Many of the pieces are notable for their beauty of pattern and for their inventive and abstract representation of birds and animals. It is believed that the flower designs, which appear occasionally, are the result of the influence of German settlers. Most of the designs are worked out as the weaving proceeds, only a few tribes embroidering the pattern after the article is taken from the loom.

Many of the garments are of a shirt-like character called huipil, which is a word of the Cakchiquel language meaning "my covering." The more remote and primitive the tribe, the more plain and simple is the huipil. The parts of the garment are put together with a randa, a stitch common to nearly all the tribes. The corte or skirt is usually made on a large foot loom, and varies in color according to the tribe. The cincho (belt) is usually closely woven and is worn tightly wrapped around the body. The perraje (shawl), of

silk or wool, comes from the mountain regions. The flat pieces,
called sutes or servilletas, are used as kerchiefs in which to carry
food, money, or small articles, to cover baskets of produce, or
even as head or neck coverings. An example of the telar (loom)
is included in the collection.

On indefinite loan from the Food Technology Foundation is a
collection of pre-Columbian Peruvian textiles which has been collected by the architect Leonard Priess in Seattle. It consists of
approximately 60 pieces, 5 of which are more than six feet high.
The areas and cultures represented are Tihuanaco, Chimu, and
Inca. All techniques from featherwork to tapestry weaving and
veils are included. Every item is under glass and framed. The
collection may easily be one of the finest on the Pacific Coast.

The Art Gallery has several hundred photographs from Mexico,
Guatemala, Colombia, Ecuador, Peru, and Brazil, collected by
the director of the gallery, Dr. Alfred Neumeyer. Special emphasis
has been placed on architecture and architectural decoration.

There is also a collection of books on Spanish and Portuguese
colonial art, comprising the basic literature in this field. Together
with the library of contemporary Latin American literature, a well-
rounded library can be found at Mills College, sufficient for graduate studies in Latin American culture.

Mission Inn
Riverside

Riverside, on the site of the Jurupa rancho of the Mexican
period, was started in 1869 as an American community by a colony
from the eastern states. The town itself was not settled by the
Spanish, and there never was a mission here. C. C. Miller, of
Tomah, Wisconsin, who was engaged in 1873 as the colony's
engineer, built an adobe home in 1875, the first solid-walled house
in town. This homestead was the small beginning of the present
Mission Inn. It is still existing on its original site in the outer
patio.

The salary of a small colony engineer was very meager, so
in 1876 Mrs. Miller began taking boarders. The name "Glenwood
Cottage" was first chosen for the budding hotel but later that of
"Mission Inn" was adopted.

In the early nineties, Mr. Miller, Charles F. Lummis, and
a few other active Californians formed "The Landmarks Club" to
call attention to the historic interest of the old Spanish Franciscan

Missions and to seek ways and means to preserve and restore them. Soon a further idea began to take form in Mr. Miller's mind: to build a hotel of brick and concrete based on the architecture of the missions. Thus arose in 1902-3 "New Glenwood," the first California Mission Hotel. This is the building surrounding the entrance court, having the one-story original adobe in the center, and called today the "Mission Wings."

A journey to Spain was made in 1911 to see the source of Californian and Spanish colonial art. Bells and crosses, grilles, tiles, carvings, and vestments were collected to start furnishing the cloister, and as a basis for an antique department at the inn.

More of the frame buildings were removed in 1914 to make way for the "Spanish Wings," containing the Spanish art gallery, dining room, kitchen, and open dining patio. The art gallery contains the paintings, tapestries, and furniture brought from Spain, while the dining room is tiled like Hispano-Moresque rooms. Mexico was visited soon after this. In 1920, an especially important art acquisition was made—the Rayas gold-leaf altar from Mexico.

The Mission Inn has in its art collection "The Immaculate Conception with the Mirror" by Murillo. It was painted for the Convent of the Barefoot Carmelite Nuns at Madrid, and was there from 1678 to 1807.

Fine Arts Gallery
San Diego

I. Classical period

Paintings:

Berruguete, Pedro (attributed to). "St. Peter," a panel from a polyptych in an altarpiece in the Church of Santa María del Campo, south of Burgos. Gift of the Ehrich Galleries, New York.

Coello, Alonso Sánchez. "Isabel de Francia," ca. 1560. Collections: Count Avogli; Trotti and Co., Paris; R. Heilbuth, Copenhagen.

__. "Philip II of Spain as a Boy." Gift of the Misses Anne and Amy Putnam.

Giner, Tomás (attributed to). "Crucifixion"; a replica of this work exists in the Milá collection at Barcelona, Spain. Gift of Mr. Samuel H. Kress, New York.

Goya. "Marquis de Sofraga," painted about 1795. The picture has remained in the possession of the sitter's family, from whom

it now comes. There is a copy in the Academy of History in
Madrid, which is reproduced by Vicente Castañeda y Alcover,
La Real Academia de la Historia 1735-1930 (Madrid, 1930). Pl.
VI. This picture is reproduced in Art News, outside cover,
January 14, 1939.

Greco, El. "St. Francis of Assisi, " ca. 1580. Collections:
    private collection, Madrid; Hahle; Axel Beskow, Stockholm.
    Gift of Mr. and Mrs. Appelton S. Bridges, San Diego.

Martínez del Mazo, Juan Bautista. "Philip IV of Spain. " Gift
    of Felix Wildenstein, New York.

Master of Budapest (school of). "Deposition. " Purchased from
    the Van Deimen Galleries, New York. Described and illustrated
    by Chandler R. Post, History of Spanish Painting, IV, pp. 326-28.

Master of St. Nicholas. "St. John the Evangelist, " fifteenth
    century. Gift of Mr. Bertram M. Newhouse, New York.

Murillo. "Penitent Magdalen. " Collections: King Louis Philippe
    of France; Marquis de Llano, Paris and Madrid. Gift of Mr.
    and Mrs. H. H. Timken, Canton, Ohio.

Ribera. "Sibyl. " Gift of Mr. and Mrs. H. H. Timken.

Unknown, fifteenth century. West Aragonese retablo, ca. 1430-40.
    "St. John the Baptist, " and four scenes from his life: "Birth, "
    "Preaching, " "Denunciation of Herod, " and "Decapitation. "
    Gift of Mr. Samuel H. Kress. Described and illustrated by
    Chandler R. Post, op. cit., IV, pp. 663-65.

Unknown, sixteenth century. "Dormition of the Virgin, " detail
    from. Collections: John Singer Sargent.

Velázquez (school of). "Portrait of a Young Soldier. " Purchased
    from Dr. Arthur Edwin Bye, Philadelphia.

Zurbarán. "St. Jerome, " ca. 1638. Collections: King Louis
    Philippe of France; Lord Heytesbury, London.

__. "The Virgin and Child with St. John, " 1653. Collections:
    The Marquis of Stafford; the Duke of Sutherland; Dr. Gottler,
    Munich; the Altamira Collection.

    Illuminated manuscript:

Patent of Nobility, in favor of Eugenio Alfonso de Rioja, with seal
    of Philip II of Spain, Valladolid, 1583. Gift of Post 6 of the
    American Legion, through Dr. B. L. Riese.

    Sculpture:

Ortiz, Pablo, fifteenth century. Saint in niche; carved marble.
Other pieces: Madonna, early sixteenth century, of polychromed
    carved wood, formerly in collection of Count Domínguez, Spain;

polychromed carved wood figure of a bishop, seventeenth century; St. Anne, seventeenth century, carved wood, gift of the
late Mrs. William C. Poland; balustrade columns of carved
wood, seventeenth century, showing eastern influence.

Furniture:

Bridal chest, Spanish Plateresque sixteenth century; refectory
table, Spanish eighteenth century, showing French influence;
brazier, early seventeenth century; chair, medieval Spanish,
Moorish influence; 2 candlestands, turned wood, gold-leaf
finish, late Spanish; old brass charger, with repoussé figure of
a bishop; old carved ebony coffer, Portuguese; and tooled leather
chair, old Portuguese.

Textiles:

Cope, sixteenth century, silk and metallic embroidery; altar frontal,
linen with embroidered floral design, eighteenth century; 2 chasubles,
used by the Franciscan monks of Quito, Ecuador, eighteenth century; Spanish silk lace fichu, pillow lace, nineteenth century; and
Spanish shawl, embroidered on net, made for the Seville Exposition,
and purchased there by the donor.

Ceramics:

Two architectural revetment tiles from Valencia, Spain, dated 1413
and representing "The Dragon and the Bull"; 2 tiles, sixteenth
century, from Teruel, from the house of the Marquesa Esquivel
in Seville, Spain; 2 Hispano-Moresque lustre dishes, sixteenth
century; small Hispano-Moresque bowl, seventeenth century;
small bowl, Puente del Arzobispo, seventeenth century; Hispano-
Moresque plate, seventeenth century; blue and white Talavera
fruit dish, seventeenth century; blue and white Talavera bowl,
eighteenth century; inkstand, Alcora, eighteenth century; pitcher,
Alcora, eighteenth century; Moorish oil bottle; old Spanish glass
tumbler; vase, Talavera type, seventeenth or eighteenth century;
and Spanish plate, "The Risen Christ, " by Daniel Zuloaga, late
of Segovia, Spain.

II. Contemporary period

Oil painting:

Caviedes, Hipólito Hidalgo de. "Elvira and Tiberio, " South American
Negro couple seated stiffly on Empire sofa in their "Sunday best. "
Purchased out of the 1935 Carnegie International Exhibition, where
it received the first prize. Reproduced Art Digest, October 15,
1935.

Frau, José. "The Almond Tree and the White Street." Gift of Mr.
   and Mrs. J. Erskine Campbell.
Junyer, Joan. "Composition Head" and "Les Plongeurs."
Pruna, Pedro. "Blanche." Purchased out of the 1928 Carnegie
   International Exhibition at which Pruna received the first award.
Sorolla. "Boating," oil sketch. Gift of Mr. R. C. Jackson.
—. "Maria in the Gardens of La Granja." Portrait of Sorolla's
   daughter. Gift of Mr. Archer M. Huntington.
—. "Self Portrait." Gift of Mr. Paul R. Mabury.
Viladrich, Miguel. "Hamlet." Gift of Mr. Archer M. Huntington.
Zubiaurre, Ramón de. "Sailors of Ondorroa." Gift of Mr. and Mrs.
   Appleton S. Bridges.
Zubiaurre, Valentín de. "Abuelos."
—. "Golden Wedding." Gift of Mrs. Henry A. Everett.
Zuloaga. "Antonio la Gallega." Gift of Mr. and Mrs. Appleton S.
   Bridges.

Sculpture:

Manolo (Manuel Martínez Hugue). "La Danseuse à l'Eventail," terra-
   cotta sculpture.

Graphic art (Spanish):

Orovida. "The Scarf Game," etching.
Picasso. "The Three Graces," etching.
Pruna, Pedro. "Love Thoughts," pen sketch with water-color wash.
Quintanilla, Luis. "Emigrants," etching.

Graphic art (Mexican):

Charlot, Jean. Eighty-two colored lithographs with titles by the
   French poet Paul Claudel.
Méndez, Leopoldo. "The Producer," woodcut.
Orozco, José Clemente. "Three Generations," lithograph.
Ramos Martínez, Alfredo. "Friars and Nuns," pastel drawing.

San Diego Museum of Man
Balboa Park

The San Diego Museum of Man's ethnological collections pertaining to the aborigines of the districts which collectively later became known as Latin America are broad in their geographical scope
but discontinuous in the field concerned. In South America, Peru
is represented with ceramic, metal, stone, textile, and skeletal
items. There is considerable pathological material from Peru in
the physical anthropological collection. From the Pacific coast of
Colombia and Panama, there is a large collection of Chocó Indian
materials.

The museum's greatest resources in Middle American ethnology have to do with Mexico. In this field, all the major cultures, such as the Mayan, Toltec, etc., are comprehensively represented by originals and replicas.

Collections in the Southwestern field are large and fairly representative, with the emphasis on ceramics. Although the materials are in the main prehistoric, most post-Spanish items are also included.

Results of research are published occasionally by the institution in a format known as San Diego Museum Papers and in El Museo.

California Academy of Sciences
Golden Gate Park
San Francisco 18

The California Academy of Sciences has a most extensive collection of natural history specimens from the Galapagos Islands. Its investigations began with an expedition on the schooner Academy in 1905 and have continued systematically to the present time. The field notebooks of the personnel of these trips are on file, and some two thousand pages of scientific reports have been published by the academy.

The academy's Galapagos plant and insect collections are the largest to be found in any museum in the world. The reptile collection is considered complete, with every known species of tortoise represented. The bird collection is the largest, next to Lord Rothschild's. The mammal fauna of the Galapagos is small, nor is the fish collection complete. A good representation of marine and non-marine mollusks from the islands is included among the collections of the department of geology. Its marine Pliocene and Pleistocene invertebrate fossils collection is the best ever assembled.

The academy's library contains the scientific literature on the Galapagos as represented in the proceedings and transactions of learned societies; also special books and monographs, and many of the original sources in the George Davidson library of Pacific voyages. Mr. Joseph Slevin of the academy's staff has recently completed in manuscript a history of the Galapagos Islands from their discovery to the present time. He has acquired a photostat collection of pertinent material from the archives of the Public Records Office, the British Admiralty, the British Museum Library, and other bureaus in London.

California Palace of the Legion of Honor
San Francisco 21

The California Palace of the Legion of Honor has in its permanent collections the following Hispanic paintings and prints:

Carreño de Miranda, Juan. "Portrait of King Charles II of Spain, "
    oil on canvas, seventeenth century; in the Williams collection.
Dali, Salvador. "St. George and the Dragon, " etching, dated 1944.
Goya. "Disasters of War, " 80 aquatints.
—. "The Proverbs, " 16 aquatints.
Hispano-Italian School. "Portrait of a Man, " oil on canvas, seventeenth century; in the Williams collection.
Murillo. "Portrait of a Nun, " oil on canvas, seventeenth century;
    in the Williams collection.
Sorolla. "Children Running on the Beach, " oil on canvas; gift of
    Sir Joseph Duveen.
—. "On the Beach, " oil on canvas; gift of Mr. Archer M. Huntington.

California State Library
Sutro Branch
San Francisco

In 1913, the heirs of Mr. Adolph Sutro, San Francisco mining engineer and civic leader, presented the Sutro library to the State of California with the understanding that it be maintained in San Francisco as a part of the California State Library. The Sutro library originally contained around 250, 000 volumes, but the fire of 1906 destroyed more than half of these, leaving an estimated total of 90, 000 volumes. Mr. Sutro had, during the eighties, bought widely in the book markets of Europe and in Mexico, with the idea of building up a large reference library on the Pacific Coast.

In Mexico he bought many thousands of books, Spanish and Mexican; about 50, 000 pamphlets, nearly all of Mexican imprint of the eighteenth and nineteenth centuries; and several hundred manuscripts. The Spanish books cover a miscellaneous field; religion, medicine, literature, history, and science are all represented with works from the sixteenth century on. The collection of law books is particularly complete; the earliest edition of the collected Spanish laws is that of 1598. The Mexican laws begin with the compilation of Mendoza, printed in Mexico in 1548. There are several hundred books on medicine in Spanish and in Latin. Many of the early books of travel and collections of voyages are also in the library.

The Mexican pamphlet collection is of great importance. Many political pamphlets, government publications, newspapers, and other periodicals thoroughly cover the period of Mexico's changes of government during the first half of the nineteenth century. The library is particularly rich in the writings of Fernández de Lizardi, "El Pensador Mejicano." Nearly all known writings of his are represented, and many of the books and pamphlets were his property at one time.

Texas, too, is represented by several pamphlets, one of them being an autographed copy of Stephen Austin, Translation of the Laws, Orders and Contracts on Colonization (1829), his presentation copy to Dr. Lucas Alamán, one of the outstanding leaders of Mexican independence.

The several hundred Mexican manuscripts in the collection include letters; financial accounts of the Convent of Santiago Tlatilolco; some records of the book dealer, Abadiano; military, technical, and religious treatises; some dramatic works; and Mexican manuscript copies of printed books. The manuscripts have not been completely studied and evaluated.

The most valuable manuscript from the point of view of a California library is a volume called Memorias de viajes. It contains a manuscript copy of Costansó's Diario as well as Vila's logbook of the San Carlos on its outward voyage, January 9 to May 12, 1769, and of the return, August 1 to 24, 1770. These were printed, with translation, in the Publications of the Academy of Pacific Coast History, Vol. 2, 1911.

Another interesting manuscript is the Diario de lo acaecido en Manila durante el tiempo que se mantuvieron en estas Yslas los Yngleses el año de 1763. The library has a few leaves of an early Mexican codex on maguey paper.

Many of the papers and correspondence of Sir Joseph Banks, long president of the Royal Society, are in the library. Among them are some letters that have to do with Vancouver, Mackenzie, Dixon, and others, and the west coast of North America. Several of these were reprinted in a small edition by a local private press. Others have appeared in the Pacific Northwest Quarterly, British Columbia Historical Quarterly, and Pacific Historical Review. The Creassy manuscript concerning his plan to seize Panama is among the Banks papers, which are currently being catalogued.

A mimeographed catalogue of Mexican pamphlets chronologically arranged was issued by the library with WPA help in 1939-41. At the same time bibliographies of poems and pamphlets of Lizardi, Dávila, and other writers of the period of the first revolution

in Mexico were issued. Reprints of certain rare items by Lizardi
and others were included in the bibliographies. A catalogue of works
by Spanish and Portuguese writers in the Sutro collection relating to
the Catholic Church was also begun. Only 128 pages of the catalogue
were published.

The library has complete chronological files of its Mexican
pamphlets as well as an author index in its card catalogue. All books
in the Spanish language are segregated in the card catalogue. They
appear also under author in the mail file and in the subject files.
Mexican official publications have been checked with the Library of
Congress' Mexican government publications, compiled by Annita
Melville Kerr and issued in 1940.

An addition of several hundred Mexican legal pamphlets, all
dating before 1900, was made to the collection several years ago.
These, and gifts made by friends in Mexico, have enlarged the number of Mexican provincial imprints in the library. Several Sutro
rarities in this field have been described by Joaquín Fernández de
Córdoba in his scholarly bibliographies.

The files of Mexican periodicals and almanacs are good. The
library lacks only Vol. 9 of the second series of the Diario de México,
1805-17. The Gazeta de México is complete, including the first series
No. 1-6 for January to June, 1722, and the second series No. 1-157
for 1728 to 1742. Other periodicals and newspapers to about 1850
are equally interesting.

A fortunate arrangement with the San Francisco Public Library
has made it possible to house the Sutro collection in the public library building. The reference and general works in the public library can thus be used in connection with the older books and the
rarities of the Sutro library.

M. H. de Young Memorial Museum
San Francisco 18

In the M. H. de Young Memorial Museum, the pre-white era
of the Americas is represented by ethnological material from California, the Southwest, Mexico, Central America, and Peru. This
material—whether purchased, presented to the museum, or lent for
either a definite or an indefinite time—has been acquired over a
period of some fifty years, and the sources are consequently many
and varied.

The most significant single collection with regard to California
ethnology is the group of Yokut Indian baskets given to the museum

by Mr. H. H. Welsh. Together with a number of Pomo, Washo, Maidu,
Pit River, Yurok, and Piute baskets, this collection forms the nucleus for a fairly comprehensive representation of the art of basketry
in California.

The typical pottery vessels and coiled baskets of the American
Southwest constitute a small exhibit from that region, one which has
frequently been augmented by temporary exhibitions from local collectors.

Among the Mexican and Central American material, the most
outstanding collection is the one presented to the museum by Dr.
Ernest Forbes. The collection includes a large number of exquisitely
worked gold articles of personal adornment, such as earplugs, la-
brets, and pendants from Ecuador, Colombia, and Panama. There
are Zapotecan funeral urns and Aztecan and Mayan vessels and masks.
The pieces are largely of pottery, with a few exceptions in carved
stone. In addition to the Forbes group, the museum has numerous
variously acquired objects in the same general category, supplemented by articles which carry the chronology through the Archaic,
Totonac, Zapotec, Toltec, and Aztec horizons in the Valley of Mexico
with less complete representations of the Mayan and Colombian regions. Three metates, tentatively identified as Chorotegan, are
noteworthy in the Central American division.

In the Peruvian section, especially worthy of mention are the
pottery vessels owned by the museum from the valleys of Chancay
and Chillón. Pottery, textiles, and metal objects from the more
advanced civilizations of Nazca and Chimu are of particular importance. There are magnificent tapestry-weave textiles from the coast
al region, on loan from Dr. Hans Gaffron. Included from his collection is a large fragment of a most exceptional feather cloak. Shown
in contrast to this cloak is the museum's fine silver breastplate from
Trujillo, Peru, of about 1300-1600 A.D. The museum also owns
various other Peruvian textiles representative of other techniques.

Since the M. H. de Young Memorial Museum is an art museum
the ethnological exhibits are selected more from the point of artistic than of cultural interest. Color, form, design elements, and
general esthetic value, therefore, are the principal considerations
in selecting such material for exhibition in the primitive arts and
crafts galleries.

The museum also possesses the following objects of Spanish
origin:

Covarrubias, Marcos. Embroidered velvet altar frontal, made at the order of Charles V for the Church of San Juan de los Reyes, Toledo.

Flandes, Juan de. "Christ Carrying the Cross." Although Flemish born, the artist was active in Spain from 1496 until his death in 1519.

Greco, El. "St. Francis." This painting was included in the Kress Memorial Collection inaugurated in the museum February 18, 1955. It was purchased by the Kress Foundation, upon the personal recommendation of Mr. Rush H. Kress, to honor the city of San Francisco.

——. "St. Jerome," terra cotta; possibly one of the rare sculptural works by the painter.

——. "St. John the Baptist," painted about 1597-1602; signed in Greek script at lower right on rock. Formerly in the convent of the Carmelitas Descalzas, San José, Malagón.

Unknown, second half of thirteenth century. "Madonna and Child," polychrome wood, north Spanish.

There is also a magnificent fifteenth-century Spanish ceiling, donated to the museum by Mr. and Mrs. Chauncey McCormick, of Chicago, and installed in a room specially designed to receive it in 1952. This mudéjar ceiling came from the palace of Altamira in Torrijos, Madrid, and is in an exceptionally good state of preservation (carved wood). There is an interesting legend attached to this particular piece: it is known that the family who built the palace were affiliated with Ferdinand and Isabella; and although there is no proof, it is said that under this ceiling they conferred with Columbus and authorized his trip to America.

San Francisco Museum of Art
War Memorial, Civic Center
San Francisco

Because of California's Mexican tradition as well as because of the great influence, notable in the case of Diego Rivera, Mexican art has had upon contemporary California painting, a representative collection of Mexican paintings, water colors, drawings, and prints is being assembled by the museum. These paintings are contemporary, for contemporary art is the field to which the museum is devoted. The paintings represent about ten different artists. Notable items are Diego Rivera, "Flower Vendor," "Little Girl with Coral Necklace," "Symbolic Landscape," "Mother and Child"; Ramos Martínez, "Hats," "Flower Carrier," "Aboriginal Americans"; Carlos Mérida, "Composition," "Pisces and Cancer"; Roberto Montenegro, "Still Life"; Rufino Tamayo, "Window," "The Lovers";

José Orozco, "Sleeping." In the other categories, the museum owns an important group of drawings by Diego Rivera; some water colors by the same artist; a not quite complete series of Orozco's prints; and drawings, water colors, and prints by Ramos Martínez and other Mexicans.

As an extension of this interest in the art of Mexico, the museum collects painting, sculpture, water colors, drawings, and prints of all the Latin American countries, notably major works by Emilio Pettoruti and Onofrio Pacenza (Argentina), José Perotti (Chile), Luis Alberto Acuña (Colombia), Eduardo Kingman (Ecuador), Julio Codesido (Peru), Joaquín Torres-García (Uruguay), Héctor Poleo (Venezuela).

The museum has as well a representative collection of international contemporary art, including that of Picasso. It has a large collection of the art of the region and a representative group of Americana. In its library, study room, and activities, it includes art and culture of all the American countries in its general collections and program.

University of San Francisco
Library
San Francisco 17

The library of the University of San Francisco contains the following Hispanic material:

Manuscripts—Libro de casamientos y difuntos (of Mission Santa Rosalía Mulegé, Baja California); Informe de la Misión de Santa Rosalía Mulegé, 1730 (by P. Juan Luyando).

Microfilm—Archivo histórico de hacienda, Mexico City (hundreds of pages pertaining to Jesuit economic matters); Archivo general de Indias (letters and reports concerning Baja California); Ignacio Lizasoain's official report on the condition of the Jesuit missions of northern Mexico, 1761-63 (original in University of Texas library); report on Lorentio Ricci, Jesuit General, 1758-73; mission records of San José de Comondú, ca. 1769-1826; El Atlante de las Californias (sketch of Ugarte's life), n.d.; 9 letters of Juan Nentvig, 1764-67.

Photostats—Letters of Lambert Hostell from Stöcklein's Neue Welt-Bott, numbers 760-63 (not available in the United States); Annua mexicana (Jesuit yearly reports), 1757-63 (original in Bolton collection, University of California); 10 letters of Antonius Maria Benz, German Jesuit missionary to northern Mexico, 1750 (typescripts in Bancroft Library).

Henry E. Huntington Library
San Marino

The value of the Henry E. Huntington Library's collections for
Hispanic study lies chiefly in its materials dealing with the exploration and early colonization of the Western hemisphere. Outside of
this field, only its Spanish and Portuguese incunabula deserve special
mention. Any American library possessing 134 Spanish and 6 Portuguese incunabula cannot but receive attention from students of late
medieval and early modern history. H. R. Mead, Incunabula in the
Huntington Library (San Marino, 1937), completely covers this point
(pp. 231-38, 244).

In the American historical field, it is difficult to give a brief
description of the Hispanic collections, as they comprise both printed books and archival materials, and the library has issued no check
lists or summary catalogues involving any of this material. In fact,
as regards the archival materials, none of these has been listed in
any way whatever, due to the fact that they have not been considered
as important for the research work of the institution as those dealing with English history and literature, and the development of what
is now the United States.

Printed source materials covering the discovery of the Americas
are quite abundant. Perhaps no better general guide to this part of
the collections can be mentioned than George Watson Cole, Catalogue
of Books Relating to the Discovery and Early History of North and
South America Forming a Part of the Library of E. D. Church, 5
vols. (New York: Dodd Mead, 1907). Mr. Huntington acquired this
entire collection, and while not all the Church copies are still in
this institution, duplicates of the titles listed by Dr. Cole are to be
found here. In general, however, printed and manuscript source
materials for Central and South American history were not gathered
by Mr. Huntington beyond the year 1600. Of "Mexican incunabula,"
books printed from the beginning of printing in Mexico up to and including the year 1600, the library has 49, mainly religious in subject matter but well representing the output of the press in that
country and period.

After the year 1600, the Huntington Library's only interest in
Hispanic matters is in connection with the North American possessions of Spain which are now part of the United States: the states
of California, Arizona, New Mexico, and Texas. Apart from de Bry's,
Hulsius', and Hakluyt's Voyages and some ecclesiastical histories,
there is little in the library bearing directly on the general history
of Mexico. The history of the Spanish Southwest is, however, well

covered in printed materials, and the library's collection on what
is now the State of California is one of the finest for historical research. An excellent description of this portion of the library is
given by the late John C. Parish in the Huntington Library Bulletin, No. 7, April 1935.

Manuscript materials of value for Hispanic research begin
with one of the copies of Christopher Columbus, Book of Privileges,
and continue with the Pazarro—La Gasca papers. The latter are
the official correspondence of Pedro de la Gasca, sent as pacifica-
tor to Peru by the Emperor Charles V of Spain, plus the official
papers which La Gasca captured when he finally subdued the rebellion headed by Gonzalo Pizarro. Among these papers, some 3,000
folios in number, are letters and documents bearing the rubrics or
actual signatures of such royalty, conquistadores, and government
officials as Charles V and Philip II of Spain; Francisco, Hernando,
Gonzalo, and Pedro Pizarro; Diego de Almagro; Pedro de Valdivia;
Oviedo y Valdés; Pedro de la Gasca; and Francisco de Carvajal.
Two other interesting sixteenth-century manuscripts fitting in well
with the Pizarro papers are Pedro Pizarro, Relacion del descubrimiento y conquista del Piru, and Books IV, VI, VII, IX, XI, XXXII,
and XXXVII of Oviedo y Valdés, Historia de las Indias.

Passing from the sixteenth century to manuscripts of a later
date, a link is provided by approximately 50 original documents recording the proceedings of cases brought against various individuals
by the Spanish Inquisition in Mexico from about 1583 to the year
1824. Of the late seventeenth century are the library's Father Kino
correspondence, some 30 letters relating to the establishment of
missions in what is now known as Lower California, and to such
material should be added the manuscripts compiled by Andrés
Burriel, now known as Venegas, Noticia de la California. The
Gálvez collection includes about 1,500 pieces, mainly letters from
José de Gálvez to the viceroys of Mexico, with drafts of their replies, roughly dating from 1763 to 1772, and including much of value
regarding the first settlement of Alta California. In addition to this
material, there are several miscellaneous volumes of manuscript
material relating to Mexico in the eighteenth century, largely material of an ecclesiastical nature, as it came originally from the
library of Father Fischer, the confesor to Maximilian.

The Spanish manuscripts relating to the Pacific coast of what
is now the United States and British Columbia, while few in number,
have much of interest for the student; and there are also some 200
manuscript pages relating to Florida in the late eighteenth and early
nineteenth centuries. For the history of southern California in the

Mexican period, there are some documents in the Stearns, Gaffey, and Wilson papers.

Frances and MacKinley Helm Collection
of Contemporary Mexican Art
435 East Pedregosa Street
Santa Barbara

Dr. and Mrs. MacKinley Helm began to form their collection of contemporary Mexican art in 1938, shortly after their first view of the paintings of David Siqueiros and Jesús Guerrero Galván in William Spratling's collection in Taxco. The first item in the new collection was "The Letter, " a transitional painting of Guerrero Galván. This picture, like the greater part of the collection that followed, was purchased from Miss Inés Amor at the Galería de Arte Mexicano in Mexico City. Designed at first to be broadly illustrative of the whole school of Mexico City, as defined in Dr. Helm's Modern Mexican Painters, the collection has been narrowed down through gifts to museums, notably to the Philadelphia Museum of Art, and now includes examples of drawings and paintings—early, middle, and late—of the following artists: José Clemente Orozco; David Alfaro Siqueiros, who is represented by figure pieces, abstractions, and fantastic landscapes, as well as an unusual working cartoon from Chile; Rufino Tamayo, with several examples of the earlier work; Carlos Mérida, from 1924; Carlos Orozco Romero, in several media, including the widely reproduced "Luz Misteriosa"; Federico Cantú, with scores of paintings, drawings, and engravings; Jesús Guerrero Galván, with many paintings and drawings from 1937, including "La Concepción" from his first urban manner, and several examples of the later mystical palette; Raúl Anguiano, with oil paintings and sepia washes; Francisco Gutiérrez, with the Manhattan series of twelve water colors; Ricardo Martínez de Hoyos, in oil color and gouache; Alfredo Zalce, in the largely neglected landscape and still-life métier; and the new young genius Guillermo Meza, with twenty-four examples from the fifteen-year corpus of his astonishing work. The housing of this collection is divided between Brookline, Massachusetts, and Santa Barbara, California.

Old Mission
Santa Barbara

At Old Mission Santa Barbara (founded by the Franciscans in 1786 and still maintained by them) there are three distinct collections of material of interest to historians.

The first is the archives, which are within the monastic enclosure and may not be entered by the laity. However, the archivist in charge will bring out designated documents to serious research workers. In no case may the documents be taken off the mission premises. There is a printed catalogue of the mission documents: Calendar of Documents in the Santa Barbara Mission Archives, by Maynard J. Geiger (Washington, D.C.: Academy of American Franciscan History, 1947).

The original documents, about 3,000 in number, cover the period of missionary activity in California from 1769 to 1853. They include the annual and biennial reports of nearly all the twenty-one missions, a number of inventarios of several missions, and the official church registers of Mission Santa Barbara. Besides these, there are letters and reports of the presidentes and missionaries of the California missions, letters and reports of the California governors and officials, orders and instructions from the viceroys of New Spain, the college of San Fernando in Mexico, and the Bishop of Sonora, in whose jurisdiction California lay. Most of these documents are in a good state of preservation and are easily decipherable. The documents are shelved in chronological order.

Besides the above, there are about 700 printed pamphlets in Spanish, covering the nineteenth century, most of them emanating from Mexico. They deal with topics of Church and State. Many of them are pastoral letters of Mexican bishops, essays, sermons, and calendars.

Furthermore, there is a large collection known as the Engelhardt transcripts, copied from the Bancroft Library at Berkeley, the Archbishop's Archives in San Francisco, church registers of California missions other than Santa Barbara, as well as notes and transcripts concerning Spanish Florida, Texas, New Mexico, and Arizona. They vary greatly in size. As yet these have not been organized, and cannot be put at the disposition of research workers until they are organized and classified.

The Hispanic American library is an integral part of the archives. It contains about 700 books in the Hispanic American field, practically all being histories. Most of them were printed within the last two hundred years, but some go back to the seventeenth century. The majority are in Spanish and English; a number are in Latin; the rest are in Portuguese, French, and German. Among these books are such standard works as Recopilación de las leyes de Indias (ed. of 1681), Mendieta, Torquemada, Sahagún, Izaguirre, Icazbalceta, Pimentel, Solórzano Pereira, Alcedo. There is also a practically complete set of the Catholic Directory from 1836 to date, the Archivo Ibero-Americano (Madrid, 1914-36), the Pan American Bulletin from 1890 to date, and incomplete collections of other historical magazines.   There are a number of chronicles of the Franciscan missionary colleges, as well as books on California relating to the nineteenth century.

The second section is the Old Mission Library.   This contains about 18, 000 books and is for the private use of the friars of the mission in their professional work.   This library is also within the monastic enclosure and is not accessible to the laity; nor may these books be loaned out.   The library emphasizes theology, general history, and literature.   About 1, 000 of these books date back to old Mission days (1769-1853) and are some of the books the Franciscan padres used in their missionary work.   Practically all of these refer to dogmatic and moral theology, canon law, liturgy, and homiletics.   They are of little interest except to those engaged in theology or in the historical study of books or printing.   Most of the books are in Spanish or Latin.   A card index has been made.

The third section is the curio department, which is open to the public every day in the year.   It contains quite a range of relics of old mission days, including mission furniture, church goods, the personal belongings of the friars, and odds and ends such as books, coins, Indian utensils, and drawings.   In the mission church proper, there are some paintings and statues which were brought to California from Mexico and Spain during the mission period.

Santa Barbara Museum of Art
1130 State Street

In addition to a collection of some 12 santos (both bultos and retablos), the Santa Barbara Museum of Art owns the following Hispanic works:

Martínez, Alfredo (Mexican, 1872-1946).   "Madonna, " ink, crayon, and water color.

Unknown, seventeenth-eighteenth century.   Painting of St. Francis Xavier.

Unknown, seventeenth-eighteenth century.   Painting of St. Ignatius of Loyola (companion piece to above).

Unknown, fifteenth-sixteenth century.   Tabernacle of carved and painted wood.

Vargueño of walnut with ivory inlay, sixteenth century.

General Vallejo's Home Museum
Third Street, West
Sonoma

The home of the outstanding figure of Mexican California was transformed into a museum in 1923 and put under the supervision of one of the general's children—Mrs. Louisa Vallejo Emparán. Although it houses a small and varied collection, the interest of this building lies chiefly in its memories of Vallejo.

Stanford University
Art Gallery and Museum

The Art Gallery of Stanford University has only one piece of Hispanic material: a silver ciborium of the late sixteenth century, the gift of Mortimer C. Leventritt.

The Stanford Museum owns the following Spanish works:
A pair of reliquary busts, wood gilt and polychrome, early seventeenth century.
San Joaquín, wood polychrome, seventeenth century.
Madonna and Child, wood polychrome, Catalan, seventeenth century.
St. Barbara, wood polychrome, seventeenth century.
Group of Apostles and Christ, wood gilt and polychrome, sixteenth century.
An antiphonary, dated 1782.
Part of an altar screen, wood gilt and polychrome, seventeenth century.
Tabernacle finial, gilt, set with lapis, eighteenth century.

In addition, there is the Paul P. Page collection of prehistoric ceramics from Ixtlán del Río, Mexico, comprising several hundred figurines, pots, spindle whorls, etc., primarily from the early period of the region.

Stanford University
Hispanic American Report

The Hispanic American Report, which was established in 1948 by Professor Ronald Hilton, director of Hispanic American Studies at Stanford University, is issued monthly. It is prepared by the Hispanic World Affairs Seminar; Professor Hilton is the editor, and Professor Martin B. Travis, Jr., of the Political Science Department, the associate editor. The seminar works in close collaboration with the Stanford Advisory Board, the members of which are at present as follows: Weldon B. Gibson, Paul F. Griffin, Ralph

F. Harris, Charles F. Park, Jr., Juan B. Rael, A. Kenneth
Schellinger, Bernard J. Siegel, Carl B. Spaeth, Eugene Staley,
William C. Steere, Graham Stuart, Hans E. Thalmann, James S.
Triolo, James T. Watkins IV, Ira L. Wiggins, Joseph E. Williams.
The Hispanic American Report seeks to give an accurate account of
political and social developments in Spain, Portugal, and Latin
America.

The Report is based on a wide variety of sources, some printed, such as newspapers, and some unprinted. Informants who have
recently returned from Spain, Portugal, or Latin America provide
valuable facts and interpretations. The Report receives a steady
flow of data from correspondents in the countries studied. All the
information received is carefully assessed in terms of its source.
A cumulative index of Volumes I to VII is now available. These
volumes may be obtained on microfilm from University Microfilms, 313 N. First Street, Ann Arbor, Michigan.

In connection with the accumulation of source materials each
month, a system of vertical files was established in January 1954.
It is hoped that these files will in due course become an important
source for the study of contemporary Latin America.

In addition to the Stanford Advisory Board, there is an Inter-
national Advisory Board consisting of the following members:
Charles Aubrun (University of Paris), Russell H. Fitzgibbon (Uni-
versity of California at Los Angeles), John Gange (University of
Virginia), John Gillin (University of North Carolina), Preston E.
James (Syracuse University), Irving A. Leonard (University of
Michigan), J. Lloyd Mecham (University of Texas), Arturo Torres-
Rioseco (University of California at Berkeley), and Arthur P. Whit-
aker (University of Pennsylvania).

Stanford University
Hoover Library on War, Revolution, and Peace

The resources of the Hoover Library on War, Revolution, and
Peace for Hispanic countries are centered chiefly in government documents, newspapers, books, and pamphlets.

Its documents include official gazettes, parliamentary debates,
laws and decrees, and publications of ministries in the fields of the
social sciences. The holdings cover chiefly the period from the
outbreak of World War I (1914) through the mid-twenties (1925).
For certain countries, namely, Portugal and Spain, the documentary collections include publications for the period 1925 to date. The

majority of the library's documentary holdings, however, lie within the period of the first quarter of the twentieth century.

The library's newspaper files are limited chiefly to Spain and Portugal. Typical holdings are: from Lisbon, Portugal, Diario da Manha, 1947 to date, and Diario de Noticias, 1947 to date; from Madrid, Spain, ABC, 1913-19, 1936-39, Arriba, 1939 to date, and Ya, 1939 to date.

Special collections include the following:

The Portuguese and Spanish sections of the Library of the British Ministry of Information, 1914-18, consisting of some 250 books and propaganda pamphlets distributed during World War I by the Allies and by the Central Powers.

Delegation propaganda of the Paris Peace Conference, 1919, comprised of documents presented and distributed by the delegations of Argentina, Bolivia, Chile, Costa Rica, Panama, Peru, and Portugal.

Minutes, reports and memoranda of the Special Neutrality Commission of the Pan American Union, which met from December 16, 1914 to December 16, 1915.

The Burnett and Gladys Bolloten collection on the Spanish Civil War, 1936-39. This unit, the outstanding collection in America on the Spanish Civil War, consists of over 500 books and pamphlets, a splendidly organized clipping collection, and bound volumes of some 30 newspaper titles, issued chiefly in northern Spain during the years 1936-39. The newspaper section of the collection includes the following titles:

1. Diario de Burgos, published at Burgos, seat of the Franco government.
2. Heraldo de Aragón, the principal paper of Aragón.
3. El Norte de Castilla, the most important paper of Valladolid.
4. La Gaceta Regional, the principal paper of Salamanca, General Franco's military headquarters.
5. F. E., the well-known Falange paper of Seville.
6. Libertad, the Falangist journal of Valladolid.
7. Domingo, the leading weekly of San Sebastián.

The collection is likewise rich in typewritten copies of important letters and reports by political and military leaders, reports by partisans operating in Franco territory, and similar manuscript materials.

The Bolloten collection is supplemented by additional newspapers, periodicals, and book and pamphlet material published by both Spanish factions.   Special attention has been given to Basque, Catalan, and Galician groups during the civil war period.   After the defeat of the Loyalists and the rise of important Spanish emigré centers outside of Spain, the library acquired Spanish emigré publications from over a hundred organizations all over the world.

The Hoover Library's current acquisition program includes the procurement of materials from both Spain and Portugal which are essential to the study of current political, economic, and social developments within the two countries.   By an agreement of February 23, 1954, the Hoover Library has transferred substantially all of its Latin American collections to the Stanford University General Library.

Also in the Hoover Library are an ancient embroidered mantle of alpaca wool dyed with vegetable dyes, from the pre-Incan culture of Paracas, and a golden mask of the early Inca period.   These were presented to President-elect Herbert Hoover in December 1928 by Augusto B. Leguía, President of Peru.

Stanford University
Lane Medical Library

The historical collection in the Lane Medical Library contains a considerable body of materials for the study of the history of the biological sciences in Latin America, especially Mexico and Central America.   Included in these holdings are most of the major histories of medicine dealing with Latin America, as well as the significant monographs concerned with individual persons or nations.   Efforts have been made to obtain so far as possible texts of great historical significance either in the original editions or at least in later reprints, as well as those works by European writers which represent the first or early significant descriptions of Latin America, e.g., Monardes, Piso, etc.   The largest portion of the collection is that dealing with Mexico, represented by many important medical texts from the sixteenth century onward; included is the manuscript of Gregorio López, Tesoro de medicina.   Guatemala is represented by, among other things, the first medical book to be printed in that country, José Flores' Especifico nuevamente descubierto en el reyno de Guatemala, 1782.   Cuba is well represented, especially in regard to the question of yellow fever.

Stanford University
Natural History Museum

The Natural History Museum of Stanford University is at

present the foremost center of research on the fresh-water fishes
of South America. Under the direction of Professor George S.
Myers, extensive work is being done on the fishes of many parts
of Hispanic America, especially Brazil, eastern Peru, Venezuela,
and the coasts of Peru and Ecuador. This is the only North American institution offering students the opportunity of pursuing advanced
work on South American fresh-water fishes. Training is given not
only in fish classification, but also in practical fisheries, biology,
conservation, and administration. The museum possesses large
and growing collections of the fishes of the interior of Chile, Argentina, Brazil, Peru, Ecuador, Guiana, Venezuela, Panama, and
Mexico, as well as extensive series of the oceanic fishes of Mexico,
the West Indies, Panama, Colombia, Peru, Ecuador, and the Galápagos Islands. The museum has also what is probably the most
complete existing collection of the shore and fresh-water fishes of
the Philippines, largely collected by Dr. A. W. C. T. Herre, and
important representations of the fishes of Mozambique and Madeira.
Studies on the fishes of many parts of the world are continually in
progress at the museum, most of them involving some Hispanic
area, directly or indirectly. Results of research are being published in various journals, among them Stanford Ichthyological
Bulletin and Copeia.

The Hispanic American entomological collections of the Natural History Museum of Stanford University are important in regard to but one field. They contain probably the largest amount
of material of the Homopterous superfamily Coccoidea from Mexico
and Central America that is in existence. This material is being
reported upon by Professor G. F. Ferris as part of an extensive
work entitled Atlas of the Scale Insects of North America. The
material has been accumulated from various sources, but primarily
during two expeditions by Professor Ferris, one to Mexico in 1925-
26 as a fellow of the Guggenheim Foundation, and another to western Panama made during the summer of 1938.

The Dudley Herbarium contains herbarium material from
Hispanic America, especially from Baja California and Sonora in
Mexico, Ecuador, and the Galápagos Islands. Notable among the
Galápagos collections is a full set of the Snodgrass and Heller col-
lections made on the Stanford-Hopkins Expedition. From Mexico
and Central America are collections by Pringle, Purpus, Orcutt,
Anthony, Ortega, Gentry, Hinton, and others. Of the herbarium
staff, Mrs. Roxana Ferris has collected in Baja California, Sonora,
Sinaloa, Colima and Nayarit, Mexico. Dr. Ira L. Wiggins has
made several extended expeditions to Baja California and Sonora

and is preparing a systematic flora of these desert regions. The
Contributions from the Dudley Herbarium, a bulletin published by
the herbarium, contains several papers on these Mexican collections by Dr. Wiggins and Mrs. Ferris. The extensive herbarium
of Gaston Gautier of the plants of the Mediterranean basin, acquired
by the bequest of Herman L. Knoche, is very rich in collections
from Spain and Portugal. A collection of Ecuadorean specimens
was made by Dr. Wiggins in 1944 and is also housed in the herbarium.

Stanford University
Library

The Branner Brazilian collection:

The section of the Stanford University General Library devoted to Hispanic American history and institutions is unique in
only one particular, namely, a rather unusual collection of Brazil-
iana. The personal collection of Dr. John Casper Branner, second president of the university and a great friend and admirer of
Brazil and its people, forms the basis of the library's section on
this country. The original collection numbered over 6,000 items
and has since been supplemented with many valuable additions.
Special attention has been paid to the acquisition of Brazilian government documents, several hundred volumes of parliamentary
and ministerial debates and reports of the Empire and early republican period having been added to the holdings in recent years.

In the field of history proper, practically all the standard works
were to be found in Dr. Branner's collection. In additon to such
well-known books as Rocha Pitta's and Southey's histories of colonial Brazil, the library contains the most important works dealing with the period of the Dutch occupation of Brazil. The authoritative work in Latin by the Dutch writer Barlaeus, Brasilia (Amsterdam, 1647), Joannes de Laet's history of the activities of the
West India Company in the original Dutch and in a French translation,
and Nieuhof's account of Brazil and of the work of the West India
Company may be found. A twenty-six volume work, Les Lettres
édifiantes et curieuses écrites des missions étrangères par quelques
missionaires de la Compagnie de Jésus (Paris, 1736), is one of the
most important sources for the activities of the Jesuits in Brazil.

Perhaps the most valuable serial is the quarterly review published by the Brazilian Historical and Geographical Society, with
holdings beginning with the founding of the society in 1839 and extending up to the present. The library also has another important

serial, the Laws of Brazil, a complete set of the legislation under the monarchy (1808-89) and a set for most of the years of the republic. A long series of scholarly books of travel dealing with economic, political, and social conditions, flora and fauna, anthropology, and ethnology may be found.

Portuguese history and literature also found a relatively large place in Dr. Branner's collection. There are several fine editions of Camões' great epic poem Os Lusiadas, describing the exploits of the Portuguese in the days of Vasco da Gama, and a complete set of the historical works of Portugal's greatest historian, Alexander Herculano, in twenty-six volumes.

The collection also contains the standard dictionaries, bibliographies, and works of reference in fields of Portuguese and Brazilian studies. The Bibliotheca brasiliense of J. C. Rodrigues is the most important bibliographical guide to Brazilian history and institutions.

Folklore collection:

The Stanford University Library may be considered as one of the best equipped centers for research in folklore, especially in the Hispanic field, in the United States. The some two thousand titles listed in the bibliography and notes of Dr. Aurelio M. Espinosa's Cuentos populares españoles, 3 vols. (Madrid: Consejo Superior de Investigaciones Científicas, 1946-47), give an idea of the importance of the Stanford collection, since almost all of these titles are included in the Stanford library.

The library possesses not only the standard reference works, bibliographies, and similar aids to research in folklore, but also contains numerous special studies and monographs. With respect to the Hispanic materials, all the important regions and all branches of folklore are represented, although the library is perhaps strongest in the fields of the folk tale, balladry, and folk poetry. A few examples will give a general idea of the scope of the collection: A. M. Alcover, Aplech de rondaies mallorquines, 9 vols. (Barcelona, 1913-26); T. Braga, Contos tradicionaes do povo portuguez, 2 vols. (Oporto, n. d.); Fernán Caballero, Cuentos, oraciones, adivinas y refranes populares e infantiles (Leipzig, 1878); F. Carreras Candí, Folklore y costumbres de España, 3 vols. (Barcelona, 1931-33); J. A. Carrizo, Cancinero popular de Tucumán,

2 vols. (Buenos Aires, 1937); and Vicente T. Mendoza, El Romance español y el corrido mejicano (Mexico, 1939).

Of interest to folklorists is the large number of periodicals devoted to, or containing, folklore materials. Among the more important are the following: Anales de la Universidad de Chile (Santiago, since 1843); Archivos del folklore cubano, 5 vols. (Havana, 1924-30); Biblioteca de las tradiciones populares españolas, 11 vols. (Seville-Madrid, 1883-86; Journal of American Folklore (Boston-New York, since 1888); Revista de dialectología y tradiciones populares (Madrid, since 1944); and Revista lusitana, 37 vols. (Oporto-Lisbon, 1887-1939).

Memorial Library of Music:

The Memorial Library of Music, under the direction of Dr. Nathan van Patten, has acquired a number of manuscripts and first editions of scores by Hispanic American composers. Among these are the following items: the original manuscript with signature and the first edition inscribed by the composer, of the Sinfonía de Antigona, by Carlos Chávez; a signed manuscript fragment of El Amor brujo, by Manuel de Falla; the original manuscripts of Polka de concierto, by Carlos Härtling, and Marcha General Francisco Morazán, by Lupe de Härtling; first editions of three works by Joaquín Turina; and the first edition, inscribed by the composer, of Heitor Villa-Lobos' Historietas—canto e piano.

Newspapers and government documents of Latin America:

These collections have been consolidated in the General Library by agreement with the Hoover Library, which recently transferred to it its Latin American newspaper files, including Noticias Gráficas (Buenos Aires, 1941-50), La Prensa (Buenos Aires, 1946 to date), La Nación (Santiago de Chile, 1941 to date), and El Nacional (Mexico City, 1942-47).

The Rafael Heliodoro Valle Collection of Latin American Materials:

This collection presents a cross-section of political activity within this geographic area; it consists of ephemeral materials, pamphlets, periodicals, and newspapers originating chiefly in Mexico. The collection includes materials illustrative of various radical and Communist movements in Latin America during and since the era of World War I. Until recently this collection was housed in the Hoover Library, which still retains the section consisting of publications of European emigré groups and political factions in exile.

Stanford University
Who's Who in Latin America

Who's Who in Latin America, a biographical dictionary, was
originally directed by the late Professor Percy Alvin Martin, who
published two editions, each appearing in single volumes. The
first, containing about 1,000 biographies, was published in 1935;
the second, with approximately 1,500 biographies, in 1940. The
third edition, consisting of seven volumes, was completed in 1951
under the direction of Professor Ronald Hilton. It makes available
a total of about 10,000 biographies. Each volume is devoted to
one or more countries, grouped according to geographic position,
as follows:

I. Mexico.
II. Central America and Panama.
III. Colombia, Ecuador, and Venezuela.
IV. Bolivia, Chile, and Peru.
V. Argentina, Paraguay, and Uruguay.
VI.Brazil.
VII.Cuba, Dominican Republic, and Haiti.

Colorado Springs Fine Arts Center
Taylor Museum
Colorado Springs

The Taylor Museum of the Colorado Springs Fine Arts Center was founded, and the original collections made, by Alice Bemis
Taylor of Colorado Springs. The museum's field of activity was
originally defined as the Spanish colonial period in the Southwestern
states, but in recent times more attention has been given to Mexico,
both colonial and contemporary.

The Spanish American religious art of New Mexico (ca. 1700-
1900) is represented by approximately 800 specimens of wood
carving and painting, bultos, and retablos. In this number are
many pieces from the collection of the late Frank Applegate of
Santa Fe, New Mexico, as well as an outstanding group of specimens attributed to the lay order Los Hermanos Penitentes. Many
specimens, while belonging to the Penitente moradas, were formerly
in the local churches. Others, however, have been successfully
traced to their origin in the Penitente order.

Native religious art in New Mexico is a rapidly disappearing
craft. For this reason the museum has made additions to its collections whenever possible. A photographic record is maintained

of all specimens examined, whether later acquired by the museum
or not. In this way a check list has been prepared covering all
private and public collections examined by the staff members. This
is by no means a complete index to all extant specimens but serves
as a guide to the student. The great majority of santos are privately
owned and difficult of access. Photographs of all specimens may be
consulted at the museum, although the furnishing of reprints is subject to the will of the owner. Photographs of all specimens belonging to the museum are available at a nominal charge. No descriptions or catalogues are in print.

Items of especial interest are: retablo of San José, originally
in the Church of Santa Cruz, Santa Cruz, New Mexico, and one of the
few dated specimens in existence; "The Angel of Death" ("El Muerto").
from Cordova, New Mexico, long used by the Cordova morada.
The latter is attributed to a member of the López family of wood
carvers. José López is important in New Mexican religious art
as he was, before his death in 1937, probably the last of the san-
teros. In 1949, the museum acquired a notable group from the
Durán chapel of Talpa, New Mexico. Included are the reredos from
the chapel together with all the altar furnishings and figures, probably the work of one man. The group is outstanding because of the
excellent condition of the santos, the result of careful handling by
the Durán family; the chapel was never open to the public.

The collection is a comprehensive one, the endeavor being to
represent the many techniques and phases of the crafts. Additions
are being made constantly.

The textile collection includes:

Spanish American—Rio Grande (Chimayo) blankets; and embroidered
    colchas (approximately 100 specimens in all).
Mexican—a growing collection of textiles, both ecclesiastical and
    utilitarian. The museum is making an effort to build a com-
    prehensive collection of these materials with a view to study
    and publication.

Specimens from many representative crafts are gradually
being accumulated from all points in Latin America—ironwork,
ceramics, leather, glass. At present these are not extensive
enough to warrant separate listing.

Denver Art Museum
Fourteenth Avenue and Acoma Street
Denver 4

The Latin American collections of the Denver Art Museum
are comprised of Peruvian, Guatemalan, Mexican colonial, and
contemporary folk art, including textiles, tin and silver, leatherwork, and ceramics. The chief holdings in this field are knitted-
wool face masks, cocoa bags, caps, fine eighteenth- and nineteenth-
century Saltillos, tooled leather leggings, tin and wooden masks,
and a variety of jars, flasks, and bowls.

Collections of Latin American religious folk art from the southwestern United States contain approximately 40 works. Included
are an eight-paneled painted altarpiece ascribed to the Taos painter,
a near-life-sized crucifix, and a standing Christ from the morada
at Mora; a very early flat-style bulto of "Nuestra Señora del Rosario";
an early retablo, "Los Tres Archangelos," bearing the date 1620;
an eighteenth-century straw inlaid cross from Las Cruces; a life-
sized Death Cart made in Colorado about 1875; a modern bulto,
"Adam and Eve in the Garden of Eden," by López; a retablo of "St.
Veronica's Veil with the Trinity"; and many other excellent examples
of the folk art of the Rio Grande Valley.

The Spanish collections of the museum include a Spanish
seventeenth-century room with embossed and polychromed cordova
leather walls and walnut dados and doors. This room has a blue
and gilt wooden ceiling with a relief medallion of "St. George and
the Dragon." Furniture, paintings, sculpture, and crafts of the
period complete the room.

Among the other Spanish material in the museum is the Charles
Bayly bullfight collection composed of many hundred items including prints, drawings, paintings, sculpture, costumes, swords, and
other paraphernalia. There is also a complete library of books,
magazine articles, and photographs on bullfighting. This collection
is one of the largest and most complete of its kind.

Freyer Collection of Hispano-Peruvian Art
933 Pennsylvania Street
Denver

The Hispano-Peruvian collection of Mrs. Frank Barrows
Freyer consists of late sixteenth-, seventeenth-, and eighteenth-
century paintings and furniture, silver, leather boxes, and other
art objects. These were acquired in Cuzco, Peru, during the years

1920-23. Following is a list of the paintings included in the collection; all are unsigned and the artists unknown:

"Our Lady of Victory of Malaga, " late sixteenth century.
"Defense of the Host, " late sixteenth century.
"Virgin of the Distaff, " late sixteenth century.
"St. Ursula, " early seventeenth century.
"Rest on the Flight to Egypt, " early seventeenth century.
"Our Lord of Earthquakes, " early seventeenth century.
"Sleeping Christ Child, " early seventeenth century.
"Spiritual Marriage of St. Catherine, " seventeenth century.
"St. Joseph and Christ Child, " seventeenth century.
"Gloria in Excelsis Deo, " seventeenth century.
"St. John the Evangelist, " seventeenth century.
"Adoration of the Magi, " seventeenth century.
"Queen of Angels, " seventeenth century.
"San Bruno, " seventeenth century.
"Assumption of the Virgin, " seventeenth century.
"St. Rose of Lima, " small canvas.
"Madonna and Child, " small canvas.
"Holy Family, " small canvas.
"St. Francis, " small canvas.
"The Christ, " 14 by 12 inches, on metal.
"St. Dominic, " small wood panel.
"St. Catherine, " small wood panel.

Photographs of some of the paintings and furniture have been reproduced by Philip Means in his Fall of the Inca Empire. The Hispanic Society of America has published photographs of some of the paintings; and Pál Kelemen shows five of the paintings in his Baroque and Rococo in Latin America.

The collection is open to the public on certain days of the week when Mrs. Freyer is in Denver. Otherwise it is exhibited by the Colorado Springs Fine Arts Center.

Wadsworth Atheneum
25 Atheneum Square, North
Hartford 3

Following is a list of the Spanish paintings in the Wadsworth Atheneum:

Dali, Salvador. "Apparition of Face and Fruit-dish on a Beach, " oil.
—. "La Solitude, " oil.
—. "Paranoiac-astral image, " oil on panel.

Dosal, Francisco. "Portrait of King Alphonso XIII as a Boy, " oil.
Fernández, Luis. "Still Life, " oil on panel.
Fortuny, Mariano, "Sketch of a Head, " oil.
García, José. "Death of St. Francis Xavier, " oil.
Goya. "Gossiping Women, " oil.
Greco, El. "Virgin and Child with St. Anne, " oil.
Lucas, the Younger, Eugenio. "The Chastisement of Luxury, "
    oil on cradled panel.
—. "Walpurgisnacht, " oil on cradled panel.
Meléndez, Luis. "Still Life with Bread, Birds, " oil.
Miró, Joan. "Composition, " 1924, oil on wood.
—. "Composition, " 1933, oil.
Murillo. "St. Francis Xavier, " oil.
Picasso. "Study of a Woman, " oil on panel.
Ribera. "Crown of Thorns, " oil.
Valdés Leal, Juan de. "Vanitas, " oil.
Zurbarán. "St. Serapión, " oil.

The Mexican paintings are:

Guerrero Galván, Jesús. "La Vigornia, " 1937, oil on masonite.
Páez, José de (1715-90). "Cardinal D. Alonzo Núñez, Archbishop
    of Mexico, " oil.
Rivera, Diego. "Girl with Mask, " 1938, oil.
Tinoco, Juan (ca. 1650-1700). "St. Jerome in his Study, " oil.
Unknown, eighteenth century. "Virgin of the Rosary, " oil.
—. "Baby with Silver Rattle, " oil.
—. "Trinity, " oil.
—. "Madonna and Child Enthroned (Virgin of Carmen), " oil.
—. "Queen María Isabel Francisca of Spain, " oil.
Unknown, late eighteenth-nineteenth century. "Portrait of Manuel
    Marcos de Ybarra García Figueroa Uera, " oil.
Unknown, nineteenth century. "Portrait of Doña María de la Luz
    Rosano, " oil.
—. "Still Life, Vase of Flowers, " oil.
—. "Still Life, Pot with Saucer and Eggs, " oil.
—. "Still Life, Wine Bottles, " oil.
Villalpando, Cristóbal de. "Archangel Michael, " oil.

The museum also owns an oil painting, "Prescience, " by the
Chilean artist Matta; and a "Portrait of J. Pierpont Morgan, " done
in 1910 by the Peruvian artist Carlos Baca-Flor.

In addition, the museum has 42 water colors of Peruvian
costume by Margot Schmidt y Pizarro; drawings by Dali, Goya,
Matta, Picasso, Raúl Anguiano; and a water color by Amador Lugo.

There are prints by the following Mexicans—Raúl Anguiano, Roberto Guardia Berdecio, Jesús Escobedo, Leopoldo Méndez, José Chávez Morado, Fernando Castro Pacheco, José Guadalupe Posada, and Rufino Tamayo; the Spaniards Goya and Picasso; the Uruguayan Antonio Frasconi; and the Argentine Demetrio Urruchua.

The Serge Lifar collection of designs for the Russian Ballet include 3 water colors done in 1923 by Juan Gris, plus a pencil sketch of a costume for Pierrot; 2 canvases (one a curtain) done in 1927 by Joan Miró; 5 pencil or pen-and-ink drawings by Picasso; 10 water colors—program cover, curtain, decor, various costumes—done in 1925 and 1927 by Pedro Pruna; and a water color by José-María Sert.

As to Spanish sculpture, the museum has 2 pairs of seventeenth-century wood candlesticks; a sixteenth-century wood group— "Flight into Egypt"; a seventeenth-century sculptor's model of the "Virgin of the Immaculate Conception, " made of gilt plaster and metal on a brass globe representing the earth; a twelfth-century polychrome limestone corner capital.

There are some pre-Columbian pieces from Mexico and Costa Rica, and a bronze, "Ma Chanson, " by the Brazilian sculptress Maria Martins.

The Atheneum owns a number of Peruvian textiles, some dating from the second century. These come from the Chicama, Nazca, and Ica valleys and from the Paracas peninsula. There are also pieces of tapestry and embroidery.

The silver and silver-gilt pieces include a mug by the Mexican Cañas (ca. 1810), a Spanish processional cross (Gothic, early fourteenth century), a chalice from Barcelona (fifteenth century), and various Peruvian pins, rings, bells, and tweezers.

The Mexican ceramics in the Atheneum are mainly nineteenth or twentieth century; but there is a large covered jar from Puebla (ca. 1700), a head from the Papaloapam basin (eleventh-thirteenth century), agricultural god (Zapotec culture, 500-1000 A.D.). The collection of Peruvian ceramics is larger and includes jugs, goblets, silvadors, and figure vessels. An interesting piece is a portrait vase of a priestly personage, from Chimbote, north coast of Peru (proto-Chimu, third-seventh century). The Spanish collection consists of eighteenth- and nineteenth-century vases, teapots, and pitchers.

Other Hispanic pieces include a portable Spanish writing

desk of rosewood inlaid with brass, a painted Spanish bed, and a copy of Don Quixote, published by Juan de la Cuesta, Madrid, 1605. This book of 316 sheets and tabla is bound in parchment.

Yale University
Library
New Haven

The Yale University Library's collection of Latin American literature is largely due to the interest and efforts of four men who have given collections of books to Yale in order to strengthen the understanding and the relations between the Americas.

The first of these gifts of books came from Professor Hiram Bingham, a graduate of Yale in the class of 1898, who was for years professor of Latin American history at Yale, and later curator of the American Historical Collection in the Yale Library. Professor Bingham's chief interest was in Peru, as was natural from the fact that he was the explorer who rediscovered Cuzco and published books about that Peruvian city, and who was the head of the Yale Peruvian Expeditions of 1911, 1912, 1914, and 1915. His Machu Picchu, a Citadel of the Incas, describing his discovery, is a classic in its field.

In June 1907, Dr. Bingham gave to the Yale University Library his collection of about 2,000 volumes and pamphlets relating to the history and geography of South America. This collection was supplemented at later dates and in 1916 exceeded 4,500 volumes. Among the printed material are found many volumes of South American newspapers and periodicals, literary, scientific, and political, besides a large number of official publications, especially of Colombia and Venezuela. Writing in 1908 of the Latin American collections in the Yale Library, of which his gift is a part, Dr. Bingham said in an article published in the Monthly Bulletin of the International Bureau of the American Republics (February 1908):

"It is probably true that the Yale Library has the best single collection of South American material in the country. This collection includes over seven thousand volumes of printed sources, official documents, laws, codes and decrees, periodicals and newspapers, political pamphlets, and secondary works. Among these are three hundred volumes of Spanish American newspapers and journals—official, ecclesiastical, political and literary. Some of the official newspapers, notably the Diario Oficial of Colombia (eighty volumes), offer an unusual opportunity for monographs in political science. Of interest in this connection are some five hundred volumes of the official publications of Colombia and Venezuela. The laws, codes and commentaries of those countries are represented by some 350 volumes and an interesting collection of manuscript volumes, illustrative of the process of codifying the laws of Colombia. The number of minor printed sources and secondary works is unusually large. This is due chiefly to the collection of South Americana made by Don Jorge Pombo of Bogotá, an indefatigable collector for over twenty years, two thousand of whose books have recently been acquired by the Library. "

In 1920, Dr. Bingham gave to the library the noteworthy Peruvian collection purchased in 1911 from Señor Pérez de Velasco. Many books in this latter collection were formerly the property of the Peruvian historian, Manuel de Odriozola.

The Bingham collection also includes manuscripts which relate to the colonial period in Peru. Some are account books of government offices or church institutions, and several volumes contain decrees and other documents issued by the viceroys. A few relate to Indian affairs, and there are also some poems and historical treatises. The earliest manuscript, dated in 1548, is a deed to property belonging to the Convento de la Merced in Lima.

Another great collection was made by Henry R. Wagner of the Yale class of 1884, who lived for many years in Chile and Mexico, and built up collections of books on those countries which Yale has since acquired. In 1906, he gave to the Yale Library some 600 books and pamphlets which he collected during his travels in South America. Many of these items are rare Spanish literature of the revolutionary period. Of the later general historians, the collection includes numerous writings by Vicuña Mackenna. It also includes more or less extensive parts of such South American periodicals as Almanaque Peruano Ilustrado, Anales de la Universidad de Chile, Calendario y Guía de Foresteros de Lima, El Mercurio Chileno, El Museo de Ambas Américas, El Repositorio Peruano, Revista de Ciencias y Letras, Revista Chilena, Revista de Archivos y Bibliotecas Nacionales, Revista de Lima, Revista de Santiago, Revista de Valparaíso, Revista del Pacífico, Revista Peruana, Sud-América, and a complete file of the first volume of Aurora, the first newspaper published in Chile. In this gift is also Odriozola, Colección de documentos literarios del Perú and Documentos históricos del Perú. The literature of geography and travels is extensively represented by a variety of publications on exploration of the Andes and other parts of the continent. The literature covering the political differences between the various South American republics is also well represented. Mr. Wagner supplemented this initial gift, so that by 1916 the Henry Raup Wagner collection on South America amounted to 7,000 volumes.

In July 1915, the collection of Mexican books made by Mr. Wagner became a part of the Yale University Library. The collection consists of 531 manuscripts, 9,653 printed volumes, 2,600 broadsides and folios, and a large number of newspapers. In addition to books on Mexico, this collection includes printed and manuscript material relating to Central America, South America, the Philippines, Cuba, the West Indies, and Spain. Outside of a number of standard, high-class early chronicles and voyages, of considerable commercial value and of the greatest significance to scholars, the great bulk of the collection consists of manuscript material and pamphlets which Mr. Wagner spent eight years in collecting, with infinite pains and with as thorough a knowledge of the subject as a foreigner can obtain.

The library also possesses Mr. Wagner's collection on mining and metallurgy. It consists of 600 technical and statistical books and pamphlets on mining with a large proportion relating to South America. It contains several early works in Italian, and the original Spanish edition (1640) of Barba's Arte de los metales, as well as all the French, English, and German editions.

Yale University acquired Mr. Wagner's collection on Texas and the Midwest in 1920. It contains about 2,000 books and pamphlets and 1,000 manuscripts and newspapers. There are numerous Spanish works on Texas and the Mexican War, some of which are quite rare. There are also 124 broadsides of which, in most instances, the Yale Library and the University of Texas possess the only known copies.

One of the most important and useful parts of the Yale Latin American collection is the group of 500 volumes given by Mr. Carlos A. Tornquist, of Buenos Aires, which came in April 1921, through Mr. Tomás A. LeBreton, the Ambassador from Argentina, and which was formally presented to the university by Mr. Enrique Gil, appointed by Ambassador LeBreton to represent Mr. Tornquist, in November of that year. In a letter to President Angell of Yale University, Mr. Tornquist says:

"In forming this little library I endeavored to have represent-

ed the principal authors in all branches of science and letters
with the exception of mathematics, engineering, and special technical subjects, having given particular preference to letters, oratory, history, law, and sociological subjects."

All the principal authors of Argentina are represented in
this collection, which Mr. Tornquist spent years assembling.

Still another collection was that given in 1929 by Ernesto
Stelling, of Valencia, Venezuela, a graduate of the Sheffield Scientific School of Yale University in 1924. It consists of over 300 of
the best books written in Venezuela since 1900. The volumes represent 174 authors and are mostly in belles-lettres, although some
are in history and science. This gift constitutes a splendid supplement to the library's collection of older Venezuelan literature.
Mr. Stelling adds to this collection periodically.

In addition to these four collections, the library is exceptionally strong in Spanish drama of the nineteenth century and in
Spanish American drama of all periods.

Professor Bingham was succeeded as curator of Latin Americana
in the library by Professor Frederick B. Luquiens, who in 1939
published the valuable bibliography Spanish American Literature
in the Yale University Library, a description of some 5,600 titles
in literature in the collection. The present curator is Professor
José Juan Arrom.

The recent accession of the William Robertson Coe collection of Western Americana has brought additional books and manuscripts of Hispanic interest to the library. The manuscript items
are fully described in Mary C. Withington's Catalogue of Manuscripts in the Western Americana Collection (New Haven, Conn.:
Yale University Press, 1952).

The library's Hispanic collection as a whole is one of the
best in the field, and in some branches is unrivaled. It is well
rounded in its coverage both by subject and by region, especially
emphasizing the history and literature of the areas. Materials
relating to Mexico and Peru are so extensive as to constitute a
unique resource for study of these countries, and Venezuela,
Argentina, and Chile are well represented. The collections in
history, geography, literature, and the social and political sciences
number more than 58,000 volumes, and there are extensive further
holdings dealing with the fine arts, natural sciences, law, and
bibliography.

Yale University
Peabody Museum of Natural History
New Haven

The Peabody Museum of Natural History at Yale University contains four groups of collections which may be of interest to Hispanists.

The first group is headed by the Avery Judd Skilton collection of Mexican antiquities. This collection was received in the museum in 1879 from Dr. Julius A. Skilton, United States Consul in Mexico City, who assembled it. About three-fifths of the collection had originally been made for Emperor Maximilian, between the years 1864 and 1878. The collection contains 384 items, all archeological specimens from Indian sites in central Mexico. Most of these seem to be Aztec or pre-Aztec. Among the more important specimens are a stone collar and a number of fine carved stone figures. Part of the collection is on exhibit in the museum; the rest is stored in easily accessible drawers. None of the collection, to our knowledge, has been published.

In addition to the Skilton collection, there are several smaller collections in the Peabody Museum which contain archeological and ethnological specimens from Mexico. The latter include both Indian and Spanish specimens. The two outstanding specimens in these collections are an obsidian mask and an Aztec calendar stone. The mask is supposedly the finest in existence. The calendar stone is one of three in the world. This stone has been described by George Grant MacCurdy, "An Aztec 'Calendar Stone' in Yale University Museum, " American Anthropologist, N.S. XII (1910), 481-96.

The second group consists of the Bingham Peruvian collections. These were obtained by joint expeditions of Yale University and the National Geographic Society to Peru in 1911-12 and 1914-15. These expeditions, which were headed by Hiram Bingham, worked mainly in the ruins of Machu Picchu, supposedly the last stronghold of the Incas. The material obtained from this site is considered the best collection of pure Inca specimens in the world. It includes pottery, textiles, stone and metal tools, and skeletal material. The Bingham collections also contain representative examples of pottery from coastal sites in Peru, and a few ethnological specimens. Many of these were purchased by Dr. Bingham. They include the Alvistur collection from Cuzco and the Cheney collection. About one-third of the specimens in the Bingham collections are on exhibit or in easily accessible storage in the mu-

seum.   The rest of the specimens are packed away in another
building.   A number of books and papers have been written on the
Inca specimens from Machu Picchu.   They include:

Bingham, Hiram.   Inca Land.   Boston: Houghton Mifflin, 1922.
—. Machu Picchu, a Citadel of the Incas.   New Haven, 1930.
Eaton, George F.   "The Collection of Osteological Material from
    Machu Picchu, " Memoirs of the Connecticut Academy of Arts
    and Sciences, V, May 1916.
Mathewson, C. H.   "A Metallographic Description of Some Ancient
    Peruvian Bronzes from Machu Picchu, " American Journal of
    Science, Fourth Series, XL (1915), 525-616.

The Bingham collections have been enlarged by recent re-
searches in Colombia, Ecuador, and Peru.   Wendell Bennett and
James Ford excavated material in Colombia in 1941; Bennett and
Cornelius Osgood collected in Ecuador in 1944; and Bennett also
worked in Peru in 1946 and 1950.   Principal reports on these re-
searches are as follows:

Bennett, Wendell.   Archeological Regions of Colombia, a Ceramic
    Survey.   Yale University Publications in Anthropology, No. 30
    (1944).
—. Excavations in the Cuenca Region, Ecuador.   Ibid., No. 35
    (1946).
—. The Gallinazo Group, Viru Valley, Peru.   Ibid., No. 43 (1950).
Ford, James A.   Excavations in the Vicinity of Cali, Colombia.
    Ibid., No. 31 (1944).

The third group of specimens comes from Central America.
The Peabody Museum contains some of the largest collections in
existence of artifacts from Indian graves in the province of Chiriquí,
Panama.   The choicest of these was collected from 1859 to 1866
by M. A. de Zeltner, French Consul in Panama.   Others were made
by J. A. McNeil several years later.   The collections include gold
objects, stone implements, metates and stools of stone, and large
amounts of pottery.   Some of the specimens are on exhibit in the
museum.   The rest are in easily accessible storage.   Among
reports on this collection are:

MacCurdy, George Grant.   "A Study of Chiriquian Antiquities, "
    Memoirs of the Connecticut Academy of Arts and Sciences,
    III, 1911.
Zeltner, M. A. de.   Note sur les sépultures indiennes du départe-
    ment de Chiriqui (Etat de Panama).   Panama, 1866.
In addition to the specimens from Chiriquí, the museum also

possesses a representative collection from Costa Rica, acquired by exchange from the Carnegie Museum in Pittsburgh. Like the Chiriq collections, this collection is partially on exhibit, partially in accessible storage.

The final group of collections in the Peabody Museum centers in the West Indies. Expeditions from the museum have been working in the Greater Antilles yearly since 1934. In addition, work has been done in Venezuela, Panama, Florida, and British Guiana. Most of the specimens obtained are potsherds, but there are some stone, bone, and shell artifacts. The main objective of this work is to reconstruct the prehistory of the aboriginal inhabitants of the West Indies. Some attention, however, is being paid to the period of contact with the Spaniards. The following archeological collections were obtained in connection with the museum's Caribbean anthropological program: (1) Cuban material obtained by Cornelius Osgood and Irving Rouse in 1941; (2) Venezuelan collections made by Osgood and George D. Howard in 1941; (3) Florida material collected by Rouse, Vera Masius Ferguson, John M. Goggin, and Fran. H. Sommer from 1944 to 1950; (4) a British Guiana collection made in 1944 by Osgood; (5) Trinidad material excavated by Rouse in 1946 and (6) Venezuelan material excavated by Rouse and J. M. Cruxent in 1950. A bibliography of these collections follows:

Ferguson, Vera Masius. Chronology at South Indian Field, Florida. Yale University Publications in Anthropology, No. 45 (1951).
Goggin, John M., and Sommer, Frank H. Excavations on Upper Matecumbe Key, Florida. Ibid., No. 41 (1949).
Howard, George D. Excavations at Ronquín, Venezuela. Ibid., No. 28 (1943).
——. Prehistoric Ceramic Styles of Lowland South America, Their Distribution and History. Ibid., No. 37 (1947).
Osgood, Cornelius. British Guiana Archeology to 1945. Ibid., No. 36 (1946).
——. The Ciboney Culture of Cayo Redondo, Cuba. Ibid., No. 25 (1942).
——. Excavations at Tocorón, Venezuela. Ibid., No. 29 (1943).
Osgood, Cornelius, and Howard, George D. An Archeological Survey of Venezuela. Ibid., No. 27 (1943).
Rainey, Froelich G. Excavations in the Ft. Liberté Region, Haiti. Ibid., No. 23 (1941).
——. Porto Rican Archeology. New York Academy of Sciences, Scientific Survey of Porto Rico and the Virgin Islands, XVIII, Pt. 1 (1940).
Rouse, Irving. Archeology of the Maniabón Hills, Cuba. Yale

University Publications in Anthropology, No. 26 (1942).
___. Culture of the Ft. Liberté Region, Haiti. Ibid., No. 24 (1941).
___. Porto Rican Prehistory. New York Academy of Sciences,
Scientific Survey of Porto Rico and the Virgin Islands, XVIII,
Pts. 3 and 4 (1951).
___. Prehistory in Haiti, a Study in Method. Yale University Pub-
lications in Anthropology, No. 21 (1939).
___. A Survey of Indian River Archeology, Florida. Ibid., No. 44
(1951).

The Americas
Academy of American Franciscan History
5401 West Cedar Lane

The Americas is a quarterly review devoted to inter-American
cultural history. It is published in July, October, January, and
April. At present the editorial staff consists of Antonine Tibesar,
editor-in-chief; Mathias C. Kiemen, managing editor; Bede A.
Dauphinee, assistant managing editor; and Francis B. Steck (Quincy
College), Maynard Geiger (Santa Barbara Mission), Lazaro Lama-
drid (Washington, D. C.), Fidel Chauvet (Mexico City), Lino G.
Canedo (Washington, D. C.), and Michael B. McCloskey (Siena
College). The advisory editors are George P. Hammond (University of
California), Robert S. Chamberlain (Carnegie Institution of Wash-
ington), Carlos E. Castañeda (University of Texas), John Tate
Lanning (Duke University), J. Manuel Espinosa (Department of
State, Washington, D. C.), France V. Scholes (University of New
Mexico), David Rubio (Madrid, Spain), Manoel Cardozo (Catholic
University of America), Richard F. Pattee (National Catholic Wel-
fare Conference), Lewis Hanke (University of Texas), Irene A.
Wright (Department of State, Washington, D. C.), Ruth Lapham
Butler (Newberry Library, Chicago), Marie R. Madden (Teachers
Institute, Brooklyn), Roscoe R. Hill (National Archives, retired),
Joseph F. Thorning (Carrollton Manor, Md.), William F. Montavon
(National Catholic Welfare Conference), Henry Grattan Doyle (George
Washington University), W. Eugene Shiels (Xavier University, Cincin-
nati, Ohio).

Pre-Columbian Collection of Robert Woods Bliss
2750 Que Street, N. W.

The distinguished American diplomat, Mr. Robert Woods
Bliss, once ambassador to Argentina, devoted his leisure to collecting pre-Columbian art objects from the Latin American republics. Although many of the items are now on display in the Peabody

Museum of Harvard University, the collection still housed in Mr.
Bliss' Washington home is very remarkable; the objects have been
selected with great skill and consummate artistic sense.

The collection was put on exhibition as a loan in the National
Gallery of Art, Washington, D.C., in 1947. The following description, taken from a handbook prepared at that time, will give an
indication of the extent and significance of the collection:

Between 30 and 40 small carved heads or pendants of jadeite, about
    half Zapotec or Mixtec from the Oaxaca area, the others Maya,
    Toltec, Aztec, or Olmec.

Four Aztec crystal and gold objects: a crystal earspool; a pair of
    crystal earspools backed with gold; labret of crystal with gold
    and silver tips (early accounts of Mexico mention bimetallic
    objects such as this piece but only a few are known today); gold
    labret in the form of an eagle's head.

Two Mixtec pieces: a gold necklace of cast filigree beads, the
    beads being flat with three tiny bells attached to each; a pair
    of gold filigree disks surmounted by hummingbirds, the heads
    shown in great detail, with each bird holding in its beak a metal
    plaque from which three tiny bells are suspended (these disks
    were probably ear ornaments).

Four Mexican stone carvings: a human head of diorite; a human
    head of onyx; a circular human head of porphyry; a serpentine
    head of a man with a large nose.

Three alabaster jars: one, representing a monkey encircled by
    his tail, which is held over his head; a flaring jar with short
    tripod legs, one of the largest specimens known; a globular
    jar with tripod legs.

Ten stone carvings in "Totonac" style, dating from approximately
    the ninth and tenth centuries; these consist of ceremonial objects—
    5 axes, 2 palmas, 3 heads.

Eleven Aztec-style sculptures include: a coiled rattlesnake of
    rhyolite-porphyry, elaborately carved on the base; a feathered
    serpent of quartz-diorite, an outstanding example of Aztec
    sculpture and one of the few dated Aztec pieces in the United
    States (1507 A.D.); a basalt figure representing the Aztec
    water goddess (the back is elaborately carved, and there are
    traces of red paint); a clay head representing the Aztec rain
    god, painted after firing in black, white, red, and blue; an
    obsidian head or skull; a shell necklace representing skulls
    with inlaid eyes of unidentified material.

Three "Toltec"-style masks and a figurine of clay.

A "Toltec" fresco found at Tetitla near Teotihuacán, Mexico,
    probable date between 600 and 900 A.D. The fresco, 83 5/8

by 28 5/8 inches, is on plaster. It portrays a road leading to
the doorway of a temple, at the left. To the right is a richly
dressed individual with one knee bent to the ground. He wears
a huge feather headdress and carries a scepter with plumes.
A large tail issues from his back; his sandals are crossed-
laced to his thighs. A huge scroll in front of the face represents his speech.

Four frescoed cylindrical bowls. The outer walls were plastered
and coated after firing and then painted—three with a serpent
as the subject.

Three Olmec carvings: a highly polished statuette of diopside-
jadeite; a head of rock of quartz and chalcedony representing
a jaguar; a head of porphyry representing a jaguar.

Four small clay figurines in Maya style.

An effigy jar in Tarascan style representing a hunter carrying
home a deer.

A polychrome Maya jar, formerly in the collection of Enrique
Cámara of Mérida, Yucatán. Two interrelated scenes are
depicted, both involving a ceremonial connected with deer.

An Aztec-style stone statue of the goddess Tlazolteotl in the act
of childbirth. Holes drilled in the hair, ears, and lower jaw
indicate that it was once embellished with jewels or feathers.
The stone has been identified as wernerite and, more recently,
as aplite speckled with garnets. It is generally regarded as
one of the finest examples of Aztec sculpture. It was taken to
France, probably during the Maximilian regime, where it became part of a geological collection. It later passed into the
hands of a French gynecologist and was ultimately acquired by
the late Joseph Brummer, who brought it to this country.

Nineteen diopside-jadeite pendants from the Nicoya peninsula,
Costa Rica, some in the form of celts, others carved—a woman,
a turtle, axe gods.

Fifteen gold ornaments in the style of Veraguas province, Panama—
crocodile gods, birds, jaguars, varying in length from roughly
1 to 5 inches.

Three gold pendants in the style of Coclé province, Panama.

Nine ornaments of the Quimbaya culture. The Quimbaya tribe,
which occupied approximately the departments of Antioquia
and Caldas in Colombia, produced some of the finest gold
ornaments and utensils in the New World. Most of the metal
is an alloy of copper and gold containing a large amount of
silver as an impurity. The ornaments in the collection consist
of a gold nose pendant in the form of a tapered bar with birds
on the tips; a gold necklace of cast openwork beads; a gold pend-

ant of twin animals; a miniature pendant of cast gold, representing a parrot; a gold-cast insect (probably a grasshopper); a gold anthropomorphic figure, probably representing a crocodile god with bifurcated tail; a gold pin, the head formed by two superimposed crocodiles standing on a coiled serpent; a gold pin, the head formed by two superimposed animals standing on a coiled serpent, the body of the larger animal and the serpent engraved to represent scales; a pendant of cast gold representing a flute player.

Six gold ornaments of the Chibcha culture. The Chibcha tribes lived in the vicinity of Bogotá, Colombia. Included in the collection are: a gold pin with a pair of birds on the head; a cast-gold bird which has no loop for suspension and probably was a toy rather than a pendant; a cast-gold jaguar with arched back, probably also a toy; a gold pendant representing a man with a large headdress; a gold necklace of small birds (beads on the necklace are Peruvian); a gold breastplate with human head in high relief.

From the north coast of Peru and representing the late Chimu culture are: 2 necklaces of gold and turquoise; 14 jaguar heads of beaten gold, pierced on the edges for sewing to a shirt or poncho; 2 ornamented gold cups; a silver cup; 2 bronze or copper knives; a bronze or copper ear spoon; a miniature cast-silver bowl; a wooden crocodile with eyes and nose of shell inlay, attacking a man; balance scales with nets of cotton and beam of bone; 7 wooden spindles.

A hollow silver male figure and solid silver female figure, both Inca.

A fluted pottery jar of late Chancay style from the central coast.

There are 2 interesting pieces from the southern highlands of Peru: an adze of bronze in the form of a bird, with the tail serving as a cutting edge, inlaid with copper and silver; a chopping knife with a handle terminating in a llama head. The shaft of the handle (bronze inlaid with copper and silver) is inlaid with delicate designs consisting of lozenge shapes, wavy lines probably representing snakes, and conventionalized representations of llamas.

From the south coast of Peru come: a shell gorget inlaid with turquoise beads, the top sheathed with gold; a gold pin with relief representing a face; a clay polychrome jar representing a skull; a false head from a mummy bundle. This latter is made of cloth stuffed with cotton; the features are of various colored feathers; now-blackened silver strips below the eyes denote tears.

There are also half of a tapestry tunic of Tiahuanaco style with
warp of cotton and weft of wool (probably vicuña); a tapestry
poncho of the Inca period; a hat of velvet with a running figure
on each side; a hat of velvet with birds shown on each of four
sides; a hat of velvet with geometrical designs on each panel;
an embroidered cotton shawl; various woven headbands; and
fragments of cotton and wool.

A later acquisition is a Chavín-style gold spoon from northern Peru.
The handle consists of a seated man blowing a silver shell. There
are two holes for suspension in the back, which is adorned by
an eagle head pointing upward. This specimen was constructed
by beating out various sections which were joined by welding
or autogenous soldering. It is the oldest bimetallic object now
known in the New World.

Mr. Bliss also has a collection of Latin American colonial
silver, consisting of about 50 or 60 pieces. These are mainly
silver plates, altar fronts, church picture frames, maté cups, and
bombillas. This collection was for some years on loan to the Pan
American Union, but it is now boxed and stored.

Catholic University of America
Oliveira Lima Collection

Dr. Manoel de Oliveira Lima, for years a member of the
Brazilian diplomatic staff, presented his library—the accumulation of a lifetime—to the Catholic University of America. The
collection (about 40, 000 pieces) consists largely of Portuguese
and Brazilian manuscripts and books, although there are not a
few English, French, Dutch, German, and other titles. In the
main, it is historical in character but contains much on literature
and some on other matters. There are a number of unique items
among the books. The only collections of Portuguese materials
in the United States that approach it in any way are those in the
Library of Congress and at Harvard University; so far as works
of an historical character are concerned, it is easily first.

Dr. Oliveira Lima gave this magnificent collection during
his lifetime. He became its curator and a member of the faculty
of the university in the department of constitutional and international law, and in this capacity served until his death in 1928.
It was his fixed hope to found an institute devoted to the study of
Portuguese literature and language.

Part of the collection is noted in Bibliographical and Historical Description of the Rarest Books in the Oliveira Lima Collection in the Catholic University of America, compiled by Miss Ruth Holmes under the direction of Dr. Oliveira Lima.

Library of Congress
Division of Manuscripts

Hispanic material is found in many of the library's manuscript collections, for practically all the presidential papers contain items on Latin America, as do the collections of many statesmen. The papers of such figures as Josephus Daniels naturally have large amounts of manuscripts on Mexico. In addition, there are a number of individual items, particularly on Mexico, such as "Journal of Edward T. Tayloe, " kept while he was secretary to Minister Joel R. Poinsett in Mexico, 1825-28, the notes by Albert Gallatin relating to the Indian tribes of Mexico and adjacent regions, and the letter-book and other papers of Captain Andrew Talcott relating to the building of the Imperial Mexican Railway in 1865-66. A collection of letters written to Mrs. Horace Mann includes 23 from Domingo Faustino Sarmiento and 27 from Manuel R. García, Argentine Minister to the United States, mostly concerned with Sarmiento's educational projects in Argentina. There is much valuable Cuban material in the collection of manuscripts from the private library of Domingo and Leonardo del Monte, as well as in the large collection of the papers of José Ignacio Rodríguez, first librarian of the Columbus Memorial Library of the Pan American Union. The papers of Richard Clough Anderson, Jr., first Minister of the United States to Colombia, contain a number of letters from Pedro Gual and other Colombian officials during the period 1823-25. Yankee contacts with Indians and European settlers in South America between 1838 and 1860 are described in 2 diaries, one by the Reverend Jared Leigh Elliott, a chaplain who accompanied Commodore Charles Wilkes on his exploring expedition of 1838-42, and another by Charles T. Fahs, a surgeon on the U. S. S. Water Witch, when that vessel was sent by President Buchanan on a diplomatic mission to Paraguay in 1858. For Brazil there are 2 interesting manuscripts, the "Record of Facts and Observations of Brazil Under the Monarchy, " by R. Cleary, and "Crónicas lagoanas, " the diary of an American missionary in Rio Grande do Sul in the 1840's. A more substantial body of Brazilian material is found in the 4 volumes containing the minutes of the board of directors of the Recife-São Francisco-Pernambuco Railway Company of London, for 1854-61. Much peripheral material may also be garnered from the papers of the

Riggs Bank (Washington, D. C.), which relate to trade with Central and South America since 1816, and from the family letters
of James O. Harrison (1803-88), which contain accounts of pio-
neering in Texas, Honduras, and Brazil. The library recently
acquired a large group of the papers of Samuel Guy Inman, who
has been active for most of his lifetime in inter-American affairs.

The Hispanic material in the division of manuscripts falls
into two classes: (1) original manuscripts; and (2) copies of
manuscripts in Spanish and Mexican archives relating to the history of the United States. It is, therefore, described under these
two headings in the report given below.

Original Manuscripts

Harkness collection:

Outstanding is the Harkness collection of Spanish manuscripts
concerning Peru and Mexico (4, 344 ff., nearly all sixteenth century: Mexico, 2, 939 ff., concerning the house of Cortés and the
Inquisition in Mexico; Peru, 1, 405 ff., notarial registers, viceregal
decrees, royal cédulas, and two libros de cabildo of frontier
towns). These two extensive and valuable collections relating to
the Spanish occupation of Peru and Mexico were the gift of Mr.
Edward S. Harkness, of New York, who acquired them from Dr.
A. S. W. Rosenbach. The documents from Peru were assembled
by the late Bertram T. Lee, an American businessman and bibliophile, long resident in Peru. The collections are fully described in three publications edited by Miss Stella R. Clemence
and issued by the Library of Congress under the direction of Dr.
J. F. Jameson, late chief of the division of manuscripts: The
Harkness Collection in the Library of Congress: (1) Calendar of
Spanish Manuscripts concerning Peru, 1531-1651, 1932; (2) Documents from Early Peru, 1936; (3) Calendar of Spanish Manuscripts concerning Mexico.

A general idea of the nature of the material may be obtained
from the following extract from Dr. Jameson's account in the
first publication:

"The Mexican papers, the earliest of which is dated in 1525,
only five years after Mexico was won for Spain on the plain of
Otumba, have a certain degree of unity in that most of them are
connected to some extent with the house of Cortés, many of the
documents having arisen from the state trial of Martín Cortés,
son of the conquistador, for conspiracy in 1566, or from later
legal proceedings of the family. The Peruvian documents are

more miscellaneous; in fact, extraordinarily varied in character.
There are few aspects of the early history and life of Spanish
Peru which are not illuminated in one or another of these thousand and odd documents, extending in date from 1531 to 1651
(with one additional document of 1740). Aside from a certain number of cédulas of Charles V and Philip II, they originated in Peru.
Most of them are originals, preserved by notaries, while notarial
copies were sent to Spain. They come from persons of all sorts,
from the Pizarros and Almagros, the viceroys and bishops, down
to secretaries and merchants, pilots and sailors, schoolmasters
and widows. They include decrees and proclamations of viceroys,
orders and instructions of officers to subordinates, contracts and
agreements, commercial accounts and letters, minutes of munici-
palities, manumissions, and many other varieties of document.
There are also two very interesting maps."

Portuguese collection:

The Portuguese collection consists of some 250 bound volumes and a somewhat larger amount of unbound material. These
manuscripts formed part of two large Portuguese collections purchased by the Library of Congress from Maggs Brothers of London, in 1927 and 1929, nearly all of them coming from the private
libraries of two Portuguese collectors. The material is varied
in character and especially strong in Portuguese literature and
history. The largest and most important collections are those
on (1) Sebastianism and mysticism; (2) the Military Orders (over
15,000 ff. covering the years 1248-1837, the greater part of which
are copies apparently made for official reasons or possibly with
the idea of publication); (3) literature, particularly poetry—a few
originals and many copies and composite volumes of both major
and minor authors and from early to modern times, including a
good deal of material on Camões, much of it contributed for the
tricentennial of 1880.

Iturbide papers:

The papers of Agustín de Iturbide, who ruled briefly after
independence as Emperor of Mexico, are housed in the library.
The collection has documents dating from 1799 to 1876 and contains Iturbide's military diary, official and personal correspondence,
and other materials of a historical nature gathered after the
emperor's death. Papers of Vicente Guerrero, Nicolás Bravo,
and Anastasio Bustamante among others are included in the collection.

East and West Florida papers:

The Spanish archives of East Florida, with materials dating from 1777 to 1821, comprise over 1,000 portfolios and include all of the original archives except land documents.

The archives of West Florida, in 7 volumes, are a portion
of the official records of the colony while under British control.
They date from 1764 to 1781.

Miscellaneous:

Miscellaneous small collections and individual manuscripts,
acquired at different times and from various sources, and adding
up to fair-sized collections on the Hispanic American countries,
are listed in the following publications:

Garrison, Curtis Wiswell. "List of Manuscript Collections in
   the Library of Congress to July 1931," American Historical
   Association Report for 1930, I, 123-249.
Handbook of Manuscripts in the Library of Congress, 1918.
Powell, C. Percy. "Manuscript Collections Received in the
   Library of Congress July 1931 to July 1938," American His-
   torical Association Report for 1937. (Reprinted by U.S. Gov-
   ernment Printing Office, 1939, v+35 pp.) Acquisitions since
   1938 are reported in each Annual Report of the Librarian of
   Congress and in the Library's Quarterly Journal of Current
   Acquisitions.

Documents prior to the year 1600 are described in De Ricci
and Wilson, Census of Medieval and Renaissance Manuscripts in
the United States and Canada (New York: H. W. Wilson, 1935).

Among the rare items might be mentioned:

The Columbus Codex, or book of privileges granted to him:
   Written at Seville (1502) and containing an authentic and
   contemporary transcript sent to Ferdinand and Isabel of the
   celebrated bull Dudum quidem of Alexander VI (September 26,
   1493). (Cf. De Ricci and Wilson, op. cit., pp. 183-84.)
Copia de littere mandate per Anzola Trevisan, on the discoveries
   of Columbus, and Portuguese navigation to India (1502).
Hernando Cortés, a.l.s. to Charles V. concerning the treatment
   of Indians (ca. 1541-42). The John Boyd Thacher collection
   of autographs of European notables—a letter or document,
   written or subscribed, from each of the following rulers:
   Catherine of Aragon (Queen of Henry VIII), Charles V, Isabel
   (wife of Charles V), Henry III of Castile, John II of Castile,

Henry IV of Castile, Henry Duke of Segovia, John II of Aragon, Ferdinand V of Aragon, Isabel the Catholic, Germaine de Foix (Queen of Aragon), Juana the Mad, Anne of Austria, Philip II, Philip III, Philip IV, Charles II, Philip V, Charles III, Ferdinand VII, Joseph Bonaparte, Isabel II, and Maria II of Portugal. (For a bibliography, see The Collection of John Boyd Thacher in the Library of Congress [1931], and De Ricci and Wilson, op. cit., pp. 250-66.)

Copies of Manuscripts

The Library of Congress in 1914 initiated a program of copying manuscripts in Spanish archives and libraries relating to the history of the United States. Similar work was undertaken in Mexico in 1919. A small collection (1,260 typewritten pages) of documents in the Archivo Nacional de Cuba, at Havana, was received. All of this material was acquired in transcript form, and during a period of twenty-three years (1905-27) many thousands of transcripts were received.

In 1927, under a grant from Mr. John D. Rockefeller, Jr., a more comprehensive project of copying such material, in practically all the countries of Europe and in Mexico, was undertaken. During the years from 1927 to 1938, under the Rockefeller grant from 1927 to 1934, and subsequently supported from the Wilbur Fund and the Library of Congress appropriations, 330,836 pages have been received from Spain, and 66,671 pages from Mexico.

At the commencement of the Rockefeller project (familiarly known as "Project A"), a change in the form of copying was made, transcripts were discontinued, and photostats or photofilm enlargements were substituted. Thus the larger part of the collection is in photographic form.

The history of the library's acquisitions of reproductions is related in Roscoe Hill's American Missions in European Archives (Mexico, 1951), pp. 65-83. The transcripts received prior to 1918 are described in detail in the Handbook of Manuscripts in the Library of Congress (Washington, D.C., 1918). For the later acquisitions, including the great collection received under the Rockefeller grant, there are adequate manuscript inventories, lists, and card indexes in this division. The printed guides issued by the Carnegie Institution of Washington form the basis upon which the selection of material in the archives in Spain and in Mexico was made. These are: William R. Shepherd, Guide to the Materials for the History of the United States in Spanish Archives (Simancas,

the Archivo Histórico Nacional, and Seville) (Washington, D. C.,
1907); Roscoe R. Hill, Descriptive Catalogue of the Documents
Relating to the History of the United States in the Papeles Proce-
dentes de Cuba, Deposited in the Archivo General de Indias, at
Seville (Washington, D. C., 1916); and for Mexico, Herbert E.
Bolton, Guide to Materials for the History of the United States in
the Principal Archives of Mexico (Washington, D. C., 1913). This
library does not, of course, have all the material noted in the guides;
therefore comparison must be made with inventory lists to determine what particular items have been copied.

The reproductions of manuscripts in foreign archives, with
the exception of a few restricted collections, are available on interlibrary loan.

Owing to the wide range of the collection and the diversity of
subjects included, it is not possible in brief compass to give an
adequate summary of the contents. However, here are listed the
archives, and series therein, from which the major part of the collection has been derived.

Spain:

The material from Spain is found in the following principal
depositories:

The Archivo General de Indias, at Seville; the Archivo General de
Simancas; the Archivo Histórico Nacional, the Biblioteca Nacional,
and the Ministerio de Estado, at Madrid.

From the Archivo General de Indias, there are the following
series:

Audiencia de Santo Domingo. A very large collection of Florida
and Louisiana material (mainly the latter) during the Spanish
period.
Papeles de Cuba. Correspondence of Spanish governors of Florida
and Louisiana (mainly the latter) with the captain general of
Cuba, the supervising authorities in Spain, and other officials.
A large part of the material marked "listed" in Hill, Descriptive
Catalogue (see above) has been copied; the specific volumes are
enumerated in Samuel F. Bemis and Grace G. Griffin, Guide to
the Diplomatic History of the United States, 1775-1921 (Washington, D. C., 1935), p. 905, footnote 57.
Papeles de Estado. From the América en General subdivision,
fifteen legajos (over 10, 000 pages) of papers dealing with the
general relations of the United States to Spain and the Spanish

possessions in the New World, and diplomatic relations of Spain
with European countries arising out of the revolutions in Spanish
America in the early nineteenth century. The Patronato, Conta-
duría, Contratación, Indiferente General, Justicia, Audiencias
de Filipinas, the Guadalajara, Mexico and Santa Fé series,
and the Papeles de Ultramar are also represented.

From the Archivo General de Simancas, there are the following series:

Guerra Moderna. A selection of material regarding military
    affairs and border warfare in Spanish Florida and Louisiana.
Marina. A selection of material regarding Spain's activities in
    the American Revolution.
Papeles de Estado. A number of volumes from each of three sub-
    series: Negociación de Francia, containing American material
    from the correspondence of Spain with its embassy in France,
    1761-83; Negociación de Holanda, American material from the
    correspondence of Spain with its legation in Holland, 1776-82;
    and Negociación de Inglaterra, American material from the
    correspondence of Spain with its embassy in England, 1761-82.

From the Archivo Histórico Nacional: of the Estado series,
practically all the material dealing with the diplomatic relations
of the United States and Spain, 1784-1861.

From the Ministerio de Estado: the Estado series, consisting of legation papers containing original instructions to Spanish
diplomatists in the United States, 1796-1838, drafts of dispatches
from the legation to the Minister of State in Spain, 1835, and correspondence of the Spanish minister in the United States with the
Intendant at Havana, 1835.

The library has had microfilmed the entire residencia of
Hernán Cortés, to supplement the Harkness collection, and the
pleitos of Columbus, which consist of the extensive legal records
of the trials by which the Columbus family attempted to recover
certain rights and privileges from the Spanish crown. Microfilm
copies were secured from the Biblioteca Nacional in Madrid of two
of the foundation documents of American history. The first is the
original manuscript of the Historia de las Indias by Bishop Bartolomé
de las Casas (1474-1566), the well-known apostle to the Indians.
His history covers the period 1492-1520 and has been described
by Samuel Eliot Morison as "the book on the discovery of America
that I should wish to preserve if all others were destroyed. " This
lengthy chronicle of the voyages of Columbus and the early attempts

at colonization by the Spaniards is written in the crabbed and difficult hand of Las Casas himself. Inasmuch as the several printed editions (1875, 1877, 1927) were based on one of the many manuscript copies of the history, the reproduction of the original holograph becomes a significant addition to the Hispanic and Americana collections of the library. The second microfilm, acquired from the same library, is the abstract made by Las Casas of the journal kept by Columbus on his first voyage to America. No other copy is known to exist, and the original has long since disappeared. The document Las Casas saved for posterity has been widely printed and will always be one of the primary sources for the history of the discovery of America.

Mexico:

The material from Mexico is derived from the principal archives of Mexico City and from several local archives.

The library possesses copies of the indexes to the vast collection in the Archivo General y Público de la Nación in Mexico City, as well as material drawn mainly from the following five series:

Californias. Vols. VIII, XXII, XXV, XXIX, XXXV, XXXVII, XXXIX, XLI, XLVII, and LXII (see Bolton's Guide, above, for description of the contents of these volumes).

Historia. A voluminous collection covering a wide range of subjects that relate largely to colonization from Mexico in the Southwest, and exploring expeditions from Mexico to California and the Southwest.

Historia: Operaciones de Guerra. From the Guerra de Independencia—Notas Diplomáticas series, a selection of correspondence of the viceroys and other officials of New Spain with Spanish agents (ministers and consuls) in the United States during the Mexican war of independence, 1810-21.

Marina. A large collection, mainly records of trade, legitimate and contraband, with Mexico in the eighteenth and nineteenth centuries.

Provincias Internas. Papers relating to California, New Mexico, and Texas affairs in the eighteenth and nineteenth centuries. Bandos, Reales Cédulas y Ordenes, Correspondencia de los Virreyes, Guerra, Correspondencia, and Inquisición series are also represented in the collection.

From the Archivo General de la Secretaría de Relaciones Exteriores:

a voluminous collection dealing with the diplomatic relations of
Mexico with the United States, 1821-90.

There are also manuscripts from the following archives:
from the Secretaría de Fomento, Colonización, y Industria, a
selection from the Colonización series, consisting of items regarding Texas in the 1820's and 1830's; from the Secretaría de
Gobernación, a few selections from the Comercio, Indiferente,
and Tranquilidad Pública series; from the Secretaría de Guerra
y Marina, a small collection from the Sección de Varios Asuntos,
comprising miscellaneous items of the eighteenth century.

From the Biblioteca Nacional, Mexico City: a collection of
documents for the history of New Mexico and the Southwest, seventeenth and eighteenth centuries.

Many series of manuscripts, chiefly of the colonial period,
from local archives in several parts of Mexico have been microfilmed. Archives in Guadalajara, Guanajuato, Michoacán, Oaxaca,
Puebla, and Tlaxcala are represented.

In addition to the Spanish and Mexican archival collections
just described, there are three special collections of note:

Connor collection of transcripts and photostats of manuscripts in
    Spanish archives relating to the colonial history of Florida
    which were accumulated by Mrs. Washington E. Connor (Jeanette
    Thurber Connor) and after her death given by Mr. Connor to
    the Library of Congress in 1929. This collection comprises
    several thousand pages. Included are three earlier collections.
    The Mary Brooks and Buckingham Smith collections of tran-
    scripts and translation of documents from Spanish archives,
    relating to Florida. The Brooks group is exclusively from the
    Biblioteca Colombiana, Seville. The collection of transcripts
    assembled by Henry Adams contains many copies of documents
    in Spanish archives. They relate to United States—Spanish
    diplomatic relations in the late eighteenth and early nineteenth
    centuries.
Conway collection of typewritten transcripts and translations of
    manuscripts relating to "Englishmen and the Mexican Inquisi-
    tion," 1559-77, contained in the Mexican National Archives and
    the Archivo General de Indias, at Seville (45 volumes). It was
    donated by Mr. George R. G. Conway, of Mexico City, in 1930,
    and is described in a check list compiled by Dr. Schafer Williams
    and published in the Hispanic American Historical Review, XXV
    (August, 1955), 386-97.

Lowery collection of transcripts of manuscripts relating to Spanish
settlements in the United States, 1522-1803, from originals in
the Spanish archives (19 volumes), received in 1907 under terms
of the will of Woodbury Lowery.

Thus far no projects have been undertaken in Portuguese
archives, and no large projects in South America.   Through
the assistance of Professor Samuel F. Bemis, of Yale University,
a collection of correspondence in the Archivo General de la Nación
in Buenos Aires was copied, comprising some 4,000 pages and
concerning relations between Argentina and the United States during the period 1810-52.

Many copies of manuscripts on Indian languages of the New
World have been added to the library's collections through the
Rudolph Schuller collection and by purchase from William R. Gates.
These manuscripts, written mainly in the sixteenth and seventeenth centuries in different Indian languages of Spanish America,
include dictionaries, vocabularies, grammars, sermons, religious
discourses, and miscellaneous writings, which afford a wealth of
source material for the study of native American languages.   The
library has also a few original vocabularies.

Library of Congress
Government Publications

Every effort is made to have a comprehensive representation
of current official publications from the national governments of
the various Latin American countries.   To this end, executive
agreements to provide for the exchange of all official publications
have been concluded by the Department of State with all except two
of the countries (Uruguay and Venezuela).   The record of the current official publications in the various volumes of the Handbook
of Latin American Studies, edited by Lewis Hanke and more recently by Francisco Aguilera, is based on the material received
by the Library of Congress.

Official gazettes; parliamentary debates, proceedings, and
documents; statistical reports; memorias; and other department
publications are not only well represented currently, but there are
long series of each of these groups.   Constant effort is being made
to augment and to perfect the files of the older materials, particularly of the official gazettes.

As the principal organ of publication for the governments,
special attention is paid to the official gazettes.   In a few countries

these have been confined entirely to laws and regulations having
the force of law, but often they contain other materials such as
news, literary articles, proceedings of legislative bodies, presidential messages, budgets, annual reports, treasury statements,
current statistics, court decisions, legal notices, etc. While
there are many unusual items such as the Gaceta del Gobierno of
Venezuela (September 15, 1827 to February 27, 1830), a few of
the long files may be mentioned as follows:

Chile: El Araucano (1830-76) and Diario Oficial (1877 to date).
Costa Rica: La Gaceta (1877 to date).
Cuba: Gaceta de la Habana (earlier Diario) (1832-1902).
Dominican Republic: El Monitor (1866), Boletín Oficial (1868-73),
    and Gaceta (1874 to date).
Ecuador: Registro Oficial (throughout nearly the whole period
    from 1830 to date).
Haiti: Moniteur (1870 to date).

From all the states of Mexico as well as from the territories,
there is a substantial representation of the official gazettes (usually
designated Periódico Oficial). Between November 1948 and June
1951, microfilming of Mexican state gazettes was carried on in
Mexico City, and more than 700 reels were produced (cf. library's
Microfilm Clearing House Bulletin, Supplement, No. 1).

From the provinces of Argentina, from the states of Brazil,
from the departments of Colombia, and from the states of Venezuela, the representation of official gazettes is mostly limited to
the more recent material.

The proceedings and documents of parliaments constitute
another very important group of official source material. With
the exception of Costa Rica, Haiti, Nicaragua, and El Salvador,
where such materials are ordinarily printed in the gazettes, there
are very considerable files for almost every Latin American country.

In the constitutions of the various Latin American republics
there is usually a provision requiring the principal departments to
present regularly either to the chief executive and thence to congress
or directly to congress, a detailed account of the affairs of the
department during the previous fiscal period. A good sample of
the extent of the representation of these Memorias is a publication
of the Library of Congress given in James B. Childs, The Memorias of the Republics of Central America and of the Antilles
(Washington, D.C., 1931). A later publication, entitled Bibliography

of Official Publications and the Administrative Systems in Latin American Countries (Washington, D.C., 1938), gives a brief statement about each of the principal government departments in the various countries, and should thus render the approach to the material rather easier. In 1940, the library published a guide by Annita Melville Kerr, entitled Mexican Government Publications. In 1943, the Census Library Project produced an annotated bibliography prepared under the supervision of Irene B. Taeuber, entitled General Censuses and Vital Statistics in the Americas.

A more recent indication of the extensive representation of Latin American official publications can be found for each country in A Guide to the Official Publications of the Other American Republics, published in the library's Latin American Series during 1945-49. A part for Mexico was not prepared in view of the guide issued in 1940. Among the many unusual publications represented in the Guide, attention may be particularly called to the detailed first census of Brazil, 1872, printed in 22 parts, 1873 76, of which no other copy has been located in the United States.

Government publications constitute one of the most important groups of materials for research and a very refractory group. The strength of the collections at the library points to the desirability of further work on guides to overcome the refractoriness of the material.

Library of Congress
Hispanic American Material

Books published during the colonial period, including both European and American imprints:

The library possesses rare and valuable works of the sixteenth and seventeenth centuries, the contemporary accounts of the discovery, exploration, and settlement, including the letters and reports of the early navigators and conquistadores, the histories and descriptions of the New World by the royal cronistas de las Indias, and other works of special character.

Of this material, largely European imprints, there is a representative working collection, but of course many rarer items are wanting; e.g., the Columbus apparatus is extensive both in his writings and in critical works, but the 1493 and other practically unobtainable editions of the letters are missing. Of Vespucci and Cortés, the same situation is noted. Of the works of Peter Martyr, the library possesses De Orbe Novo decades (Alcalá, 1516), the

Basle edition of 1533, Eden's translation (London, 1555), and other works and editions; Acosta, Historia natural y moral de las Indias (Seville, 1590), and the Latin edition, De natura Novi Orbis (Cologne, 1596); Oviedo, Historia general de las Indias (Seville, 1535); López de Gómara, Hispania victrix (Medina del Campo, 1553); Martín Cortés, Breve compendio de la sphera (Seville, 1551); Herrera, Historia general (Madrid, 1601-15); the first editions of Garcilaso de la Vega, Primera parte de los Commentarios reales (Lisbon, 1609) and Historia general del Perú (Córdoba, 1617). These titles are cited to indicate the scope of the collection with respect to the rare and valuable source material.

The collections of early works on cosmography and cartography (Ptolemy, Waldseemüller, etc.) and of early voyages (De Bry, Hulsius, Purchas, Hakluyt, and others) are full, and the early works on colonial legislation and administration, commerce, etc. are well represented. Of special interest and value to students of the colonial period are the various chronicles of the religious orders, especially the Jesuits, Franciscans, Augustinians, and Dominicans, that played so distinguished a part not only in the transmission of culture but also in the political and administrative organization of the country. To the acquirement of these, the library has devoted special attention.

Of different character, but of great rarity and importance, are the earlier products of the American presses. The first printing press in the New World was introduced into Mexico by Viceroy Mendoza about 1539. Its activity is attested by the fact that by 1640, in which year the Bay Psalm Book was published in Cambridge, Massachusetts, some 515 publications are listed by Medina as having been produced in the city of Mexico.

The colonial legislation, however, established severe restrictions on the operation of the press. The double censorship, civil and ecclesiastical, was strictly applied. Moreover, Americans and Spaniards domiciled in America were not permitted to publish the results of the studies and observations of colonial affairs without the sanction of the Council of the Indies. As a result, the early books published in the colonies were for the most part educational and devotional. Among the rarer volumes of the period are the various works relating to the native languages—Aztec, Quechua, and others. These include the various artes, vocabularios, confesionarios, and are well represented in the library, which possesses among its many earlier and later works on Indian linguistics, Reinoso, Arte y vocabulario en lengua Mame (1644); the artes of

Carochi (1645), of Molina (1571), of Tapia Zenteno (1753), of
Vázquez Gaztelu (1689, 1693, 1716); Bertoni, Vocabulario (1612);
Domingo de Santo Tomás, Grammatica (1560) and Vocabulario en
la lengua general del Perú (1586); and González Holguín, Vocabulario
(1608).

Books published since the overthrow of Spanish domination:

In regard to books published since the achievement of independence, the library is strong in the fundamental works in the
principal fields of study. It is well equipped in the primary and
secondary works in political, constitutional, and administrative
history. In economic and industrial history, it possesses a working collection as well as material on ethnology and antiquities.
Descriptive works, travel books, etc., are well represented, and
there is considerable material on the geology, mineral resources,
botany, and zoology of the southern republics. The literature of
boundary disputes is full.

The library has received, through international exchange and
special donations, a mass of valuable material comprising not only
documents but also the publications of learned societies and institutions and monographic works.

The important collections have been acquired, as for example:
the Colección de libros raros y curiosos que tratan de América;
Colección de documentos inéditos relativos al descubrimiento,
conquista y organización de las antiguas posesiones españolas de
América y Oceanía; Calvo, Recueil complet des traités; Angelis,
Colección de obras y documentos relativos a las Provincias del
Río de la Plata; Medina, Colección de documentos inéditos para
la historia de Chile; Documentos para los anales de Venezuela;
and Odriozola, Colección de documentos literarios del Perú.

The collection of periodicals, while not so notable, contains
sets, complete or partially complete, of the more important re-
views: Revista de Buenos Aires, Revista Argentina, Revista
Chilena, Revista de Cuba, Cuba Contemporánea, Revista Bimestre
Cubana, Mercurio Peruano, Repertorio Colombiano, El Cojo
Ilustrado, Centro América. Some of the representative newspapers
are being received and preserved, such as La Prensa, of Buenos
Aires; Jornal de Commercio, of Rio de Janeiro; Mercurio, of
Santiago de Chile; Diario de la Marina, of Havana; and El Uni-
versal, of Mexico.

Important, indeed, as source material for the study of administrative history, foreign relations, and domestic, financial, and economic policy, is the collection of documents which is probably the most important on the continent.

Of relatively equal importance and comprehensiveness is the material on law, legislation, and jurisprudence. Records of the legislative bodies and court decisions, national and provincial, codes, compilations, and treatises are available and are kept up to date as far as possible.

The ability of the library to purchase desirable items of the increasing publications in the Hispanic American field was at first limited by pressure upon the funds available for acquisitions. This condition has, however, been most favorably modified by the generous gift by Mr. Archer M. Huntington, in 1927, of a hundred thousand dollars, the return from which fund is to be applied to the purchase of books relating to Spanish, Portuguese, and South American arts, crafts, literature, and history.

Library of Congress
Hispanic Foundation

The Hispanic Foundation in the Library of Congress is a division of the Reference Department and has the general responsibility of overseeing the various Hispanic activities of the Library of Congress as a whole. The Hispanic Foundation was created in 1939 to provide a suitable focus for the many traditional Hispanic interests of the Library of Congress. The continuing responsibilities of the Hispanic Foundation are to provide specialized reference service, undertake bibliographical enterprises, and recommend acquisition by purchase, exchange, and gift of suitable materials for the general collections of the library in all fields with an Hispanic interest. The Library of Congress has defined Hispanic areas as those which include not only the Iberian Peninsula—Spain and Portugal—and the independent republics of Latin America, but also the present or past possessions of Spain and Portugal such as their African and Asiatic colonies and the Philippines. In addition to its normal duties as a working division of the Reference Department, the Hispanic Foundation acts as the liaison between the Library of Congress and a wide array of government agencies, cultural institutions, learned societies, and individual investigators, both in the United States and abroad. The Hispanic Foundation also administers a number of endowments and trust funds given the Library of Congress to carry forward its Hispanic activities. The Hispanic Foundation grants no fellowships, as these funds are for specified purposes that do not include making grants to individual investigators. The Hispanic Foundation was constituted as a "center for the pursuit of studies in Spanish, Portuguese and Latin American culture" and therefore is for most purposes a useful first stop for the investigator of Hispanic matters, as part of the Hispanic Foundation's duties include knowledge of the specialized resources found in the numerous other divisions of the Library of Congress.

The physical locale of the Hispanic Foundation consists of the Hispanic Society Room and a series of administrative offices connected with it. The Hispanic Society Room was designed by the architect Paul Philippe Cret to provide an interior which faithfully reproduces in its details the style of the siglo de oro, the sixteenth- and seventeenth-century taste of Spain and Portugal. The walls of its vestibule are decorated with murals by Cândido Portinari, the Brazilian painter; these murals were a gift of the Brazilian government, and the four panels represent common strands in the history of the American areas—Discovery of the Land, Entrance into the Forest, Teaching the Indians, Exploiting Natural Resources. Along the walls of the Hispanic Society Room is a series of lunettes recording the names of celebrated men of letters in the Hispanic world. At the far end of the room from the vestibule a marble tablet commemorates the fact that the Hispanic Society of America presented this room to the Library of Congress. On the upper half of this south wall is a mural painted on stainless steel by Buell Mullen, representing the arms of Columbus. Exhibit cases in the Hispanic Society Room hold monthly exhibits of significant materials in the Library of Congress collections.

The Hispanic Society Room is a study room. In the several alcoves flanking it is a collection of basic specialized reference works, including bibliographical and biographical guides, which is open to the public. Study space in the room is assigned by the Stack and Reader Division of the Library, which also services the general collections of the library, in which are incorporated much of the Hispanic material. The Hispanic Foundation has no special collections of its own for which it has custodial responsibility, and general readers are advised to avail themselves of the services of the public reading rooms.

The Hispanic Foundation annually prepares the manuscript for the Handbook of Latin American Studies. The Handbook is an annual, selective, and annotated guide to the published literature produced each year on the anthropology, art, economics, education, geography, government, history, international relations, law,

language and belles-lettres, music, philosophy, and sociology of
Latin America. Nearly fifty specialists act as its contributing
editors, providing evaluative notes to the some three or four thousand entries in each Handbook; their bibliographical and critical
contributions are co-ordinated by the editorial staff of the Handbook, headed by Francisco Aguilera, editor-in-chief, and Phyllis
Carter, assistant editor. Initiated in 1935, the Handbook has
appeared regularly; the Library of Congress assumed responsibility
for it in 1948. The first thirteen numbers of the Handbook (covering materials from the years 1935-47) were published by the Harvard University Press; numbers 14 and following have been published by the University of Florida Press. Inquiries concerning
the purchase of these volumes should be directed to the publishers.
Although it is selective, the Handbook acts as a faithful reflector
of acquisitions of the Library of Congress from Latin American
areas; by permission of the director of the Hispanic Foundation,
access to the files of Handbooks in progress is made available
to qualified investigators, as the materials therein represent an
important source of up-to-date bibliographical data on Latin
American matters published throughout the world.

The Hispanic collections of the Library of Congress are
among the most distinguished in the world. Various units of the
library have reported in some detail their specialized holdings
for this volume. The Annual Reports of the Librarian of Congress
and the Quarterly Journal of Current Acquisitions contain a wealth
of detail on materials in the specialized and general collections of
the library. Before mentioning briefly some of the major special
collections in Hispanic fields, it is worth noting that the Library of
Congress holdings in general are a distinguished and outstanding
collection which ranks among the first in this country, and even the
world.

Notable among the special collections acquired by gift or
purchase are large holdings in the Manuscript, Rare Books, Music,
Map, and other special divisions of the library. The Law Library
has an almost unrivaled collection which falls within its separate
acquisitions program. In the general collections of the library are
found items from the large Portuguese collections purchased by
the library some thirty years ago; these are particularly rich in
works on Camões, chronicles of the Portuguese kings, religious
orders, and pamphlets on Portuguese overseas expansion, especially in the eighteenth century, as well as items on diplomatic
relations, art and archeology, and local administration. The

Luis Dobles Segreda collection of some 6, 000 volumes covers nearly all aspects of Costa Rican history and culture.   Through a gift
from Alice B. Gould, the library received a vast body of material
on the history of Puerto Rico to 1898.

There are a number of special collections in the Library of
Congress which have not been fully integrated into the general collections through lack of manpower, but which are available to qualified investigators on proper authorization.   Such collections would
include the Roswell W. Hoes collection of approximately 43, 000 items
concerning Cuba, Puerto Rico, and the Philippines, 1898-1906.   The
library also has some 7, 000 Spanish plays, gift of the Hispanic Society of America, and a number of pamphlets covering numerous
aspects of Hispanic history and culture, especially biographies.
Undoubtedly there are many bibliographic and other treasures in
these collections, which will be put in working order when the resources of the library permit.

A special collection is maintained of Hispanic poets who have
recorded their own verse on records or tapes for the Library of
Congress.   Approximately forty such poets are represented in Portuguese, Catalan, Haitian French, and the Spanish of Spain and
Latin America.   Special permission to use this material is necessary.

In past years the Hispanic Foundation has been instrumental
in arranging large-scale co-operative microfilming efforts on behalf of the Library of Congress and participating institutions.   As
a result, there is a rather large body of microfilm material of archives, newspapers, and other research material available in the
library.   While the library is reviewing some of its policies on Hispanic microfilming, a number of these projects are in abeyance.
Their status can be obtained from the various articles in the Quarterly Journal of Current Acquisitions by the Co-ordinator of Micro-
reproduction Projects, Lester K. Born.   Among the projects completed have been the filming of diplomatic correspondence between
the Mexican Ministry of Foreign Relations and its legation in Washington (1853-98), filming of a large body of Mexican legal gazettes
of the nineteenth century, and the microfilming of numerous state
archives in Mexico.

The Hispanic acquistions program of the Library of Congress
is outlined in some detail in the Quarterly Journal of Current Acquisitions for November 1953 (XI, No. 1), 46-59.   That summary
briefly reviews the operations of the widespread exchange network
which brings nearly 125, 000 pieces per year from Hispanic areas,
the purchase machinery and major policies, and various other

relevant matters clarifying the sustained effort being made by the Library of Congress to maintain its already outstanding holdings of Hispanic items.

The Hispanic Foundation has no continuing publications program. Earlier in its history, the foundation administered outside funds supplied to make possible the preparation of numerous guides and publications which appeared in a Latin American series. The titles in this series are as follows:

1. Legal Codes of the Latin American Republics (1942).
2. A Bibliography of Latin American Bibliographies, by
    C. K. Jones (2d ed., 1942).
3. A Guide to the Law and Legal Literature of Cuba, the
    Dominican Republic, and Haiti, by Crawford M.
    Bishop and Anyda Marchant (1944).
4. A Guide to the Law and Legal Literature of Colombia, by
    Richard C. Backus and Phanor J. Eder (1944).
5. A Guide to Latin American Music, by Gilbert Chase (1945).
6. A Guide to the Law and Legal Literature of Mexico, by
    John T. Vance and Helen L. Clagett (1945).
7. Bibliografías cubanas, by Fermín Peraza y Sarausa (1945).
8. Latin American Periodicals Currently Received in the Li-
    brary of Congress and in the Library of the Depart-
    ment of Agriculture (1944).
9. A Guide to the Official Publications of the Other American
    Republics: I. Argentina, general editor, James B.
    Childs (1945).
10. ——. II. Bolivia, general editor, James B. Childs (1945).
11. ——. VII. Cuba, general editor, James B. Childs (1945).
12. A Guide to the Law and Legal Literature of Bolivia, by
    Helen L. Clagett (1947).
13. A Guide to the Law and Legal Literature of the Mexican
    States, by Helen L. Clagett (1947).
14. A Guide to the Law and Legal Literature of Paraguay,
    by Helen L. Clagett (1947).
15. A Guide to the Official Publications of the Other American
    Republics: XVI. Paraguay, general editor, James
    B. Childs (1947).
16. A Guide to the Law and Legal Literature of Venezuela, by
    Helen L. Clagett (1947).
17. A Guide to the Official Publications of the Other American
    Republics: IV. Chile, general editor, Henry V.
    Besso, compiled by Otto Neuburger (1947).

18.   A Guide to the Law and Legal Literature of Ecuador, by
        Helen L. Clagett (1947).
19.   A Guide to the Official Publications of the Other American
        Republics: X. El Salvador, general editor, Henry
        V. Besso, compiled by John De Noia (1947).
20.   A Guide to the Law and Legal Literature of Peru, by
        Helen L. Clagett (1947).
21.   A Guide to the Art of Latin America, edited by Robert C.
        Smith and Elizabeth Wilder (1948).
22.   A Guide to the Official Publications of the Other American
        Republics: XV. Panama, general editor, Henry V.
        Besso, compiled by John De Noia (1947).
23.   ——. XII. Haiti, general editor, Henry V. Besso (1947).
24.   ——. VI. Costa Rica, compiled by Henry V. Besso (1947).
25.   ——. VIII. Dominican Republic, general editor, Henry V.
        Besso, compiled by John De Noia (1947).
26.   A Guide to the Law and Legal Literature of Uruguay, by
        Helen L. Clagett (1947).
27.   A Guide to the Official Publications of the Other American
        Republics: XIV. Nicaragua, general editor, Henry
        V. Besso, compiled by John De Noia (1947).
28.   A Guide to the Law and Legal Literature of Chile, 1917-
        46, by Helen L. Clagett (1947).
29.   A Guide to the Official Publications of the Other American
        Republics: XIII. Honduras, general editor, Henry
        V. Besso (1947).
30.   ——. XI. Guatemala, compiled by Henry V. Besso (1947).
31.   ——. IX. Ecuador, general editor, Henry V. Besso, com-
        piled by John De Noia (1947).
32.   A Guide to the Law and Legal Literature of Argentina,
        1917-46, by Helen L. Clagett (1948).
33.   A Guide to the Official Publications of the Other American
        Republics: V. Colombia, compiled by James B.
        Childs (1948).
34.   ——. XIX. Venezuela, general editor, Henry V. Besso,
        compiled by Otto Neuburger (1948).
35.   ——. III. Brazil, compiled by John De Noia (1948).
36.   ——. XVII. Peru, general editor, Henry V. Besso, com-
        piled by John De Noia (1948).
37.   ——. XVIII. Uruguay, general editor, Henry V. Besso,
        compiled by John De Noia and Glenda Crevenna
        (1948).

100   [District of Columbia]

Library of Congress
Law Library

The Law Library of the Library of Congress has made a special effort to secure a complete collection of outstanding law books
and legal journals of all Hispanic countries. Inasmuch as Hispanic
scholars have devoted themselves earnestly to the law since the time
of St. Isidore in the eighth century, this task is imposing.

The library's collections have been secured mainly through
purchase and governmental exchange, and a great many have been
received as gifts. The greatest impetus to the Hispanic development of the library came from the late John T. Vance, who became
law librarian in 1923. He made an extensive tour of the Mexican
states in 1924 and acquired a large quantity of publications. In 1941
and 1942, he made two long visits to Latin America, which brought
in additional legal material.

An extensive bibliographical plan was developed in 1942, with
support from the Department of State, by which legal guides were
prepared for nearly every country of Latin America; most of them
were the work of Helen L. Clagett, chief of the Latin American
section of the Law Library.

Among outstanding items in the Library is the famous Cedulari
of Vasco de Puga, which appeared in Mexico in 1563, and which
furnishes further evidence of the typographical skill of Pedro Ochart
Another rarity is the first edition of Nuevas Leyes, decreed by
Charles V in 1543 at the instance of the Dominican friar, Bartolomé
de las Casas, and designed to protect the Indians of the New World
from their Spanish overlords. The Bancroft Library of the Universi
of California has presented to the Law Library a microfilm copy
of the first laws printed in the New World, the Ordenãças y cõpilaciõ
de leyes brought together by the first viceroy of New Spain, Antonio
de Mendoza, and printed in 1548 by Juan Pablos in Mexico City.
Many editions of the fundamental Spanish law code, the Siete Partida
are also in the collections. In 1950, the library was fortunate in
acquiring a perfect incunabular edition of the Siete Partidas, which
was the first edition of October 25, 1491, published in Seville.
Another recent acquisition of note is a copy of the thirteenth century
manuscript of the Fuero Juzgo, now the earliest legal manuscript
in the Library of Congress.

In 1948, the library began a project to microfilm the official
gazettes of every Mexican state and territory up to 1920. When this
work is completed the library will have acquired some 400,000 film

exposures comprising a magnificent source for the history of legal development in Mexico in its first century of independence.

Numerically speaking, the Law Library's collections of Latin American materials are the largest in the United States, and perhaps in the world. As a result of the interest expressed by the American Bar Association and other organizations in the establishment of a Center of Latin American Legal Studies, the nucleus of such an organ was established in 1949, and an index-digest on cards of the legislation and periodical literature of the Latin American countries has been initiated.

Library of Congress
Map Division

There is no numerical summary of the maps in the Library of Congress which show Spain, Portugal, Mexico, and the countries and colonies in Central America, the West Indies, and South America, many of them being in atlases.

Among the cartographic treasures in the Map Division are the following: the portolan charts of the coasts of the Mediterranean and of Central America and South America by Jaume Ollives, Mateus Prunes, Jacobus Scottus, Arnaldo Domenech, Miguel Ferra, and others (2 portolan atlases and 12 Spanish or Portuguese charts drawn during the fifteenth, sixteenth, and seventeenth centuries); the Lowery collection (306 maps, 1502-1820, showing the former Spanish possessions within the present limits of the United States of America); the manuscript Teixeira atlas (28 maps made in 1620 by the cosmographer to the king of Portugal); the cartographic manuscripts from the Royal School of Navigation at Cadiz (385 manuscript maps and charts, 1712-1824, depicting various portions of Hispanic America and of the former Spanish possessions in this country); another Spanish manuscript collection (25 detailed maps of the coast from Acapulco, Mexico, northward through California, Oregon, Washington, and western Canada, to Alaska, all made prior to 1799); Vopel's manuscript four-inch globe published in 1688; and one of the so-called buccaneer's atlases, made about 1690, showing the coast of western South America. The collection also includes photostat copies of a great many manuscript maps from Spanish and Portuguese archives.

The Library of Congress has published a number of works concerning representative selections of Hispanic materials in the field of cartography:

The Lowery Collection, a Descriptive List of Maps of the
Spanish Possessions Within the Present Limits of the United States,
1502-1820 was written by Woodbury Lowery, edited by Philip Lee
Phillips, and published in 1912. The volume comprises 567 pages,
describes 750 maps, and contains biographical notes concerning
many of the cartographers.

A List of Maps of America in the Library of Congress, by
Philip Lee Phillips, was printed in 1901 and comprises 1,137 pages.
This work includes maps of both continents up to 1897. Significant
maps in atlases, rare books, and in manuscript form are each
catalogued separately.

A List of Maps, Charts and Views of the Philippine Islands
in the Library of Congress was prepared by Philip Lee Phillips
and published in 1903. The list comprises 130 pages and describes
860 items.

A List of Geographical Atlases in the Library of Congress
was compiled by Philip Lee Philipps and consists of 4 volumes,
aggregating 3,328 pages, published in 1909, 1914, and 1920. Detailed indexes identify the Hispanic items under the headings Spain,
Portugal, South America, Central America, West Indies, and the
names of individual Latin American countries. Most of the maps
are also indexed under the names of their authors, engravers, or
publishers. It will be recognized that the early maps of the world
and of the Western Hemisphere include many important Hispanic
items. A supplementary Volume 5, covering some 2,000 world
atlases received in the Library of Congress since 1920, was compiled for publication in 1955.

The volume entitled Census of Medieval and Renaissance
Manuscripts in the United States and Canada was written by Seymour
de Ricci and William Jerome Wilson, and published in 1935. Pages
240 and 241 contain a list of 11 manuscript portolan charts in the
Library of Congress. They were made in the fifteenth and sixteenth centuries and show the coasts of the Mediterranean, the
British Isles, western Africa, and portions of the Pacific coasts
of North and South America.

The pamphlet entitled Guiana and Venezuela Cartography was
written by Philip Lee Phillips and published in 1898 as pages 681 to
776 of the annual report of the American Historical Association for
1897. Much of the material described was gathered for the use of
the Venezuelan Boundary Commission.

The pamphlet Maps of Cuba, Porto Rico, and the West Indies

in the Library of Congress was written by Philip Lee Phillips and published in 1898 as pages 41 to 57 of Senate Document 161, Fifty-fifth Congress, Second Session.

The pamphlet A List of Books, Magazine Articles, and Maps Relating to Brazil was compiled by Philip Lee Phillips and published in 1901 as a supplement to the handbook of Brazil compiled by the Bureau of the American Republics, the predecessor of the Pan American Union. The maps are listed upon pages 107 to 145.

The pamphlet entitled A List of Books, Magazine Articles, and Maps Relating to Central America Including the Republics of Costa Rica, Guatemala, Honduras, Nicaragua, and Salvador was written by Philip Lee Phillips and published in 1902. The list was compiled for the Bureau of the American Republics. The maps are described on pages 22-30, 46-50, 64-67, 76-79, 94-102, and 108-9.

The pamphlet A List of Books, Magazine Articles, and Maps Relating to Chile was compiled by Philip Lee Phillips and published in 1903. It was prepared for the Bureau of the American Republics. The maps are described on pages 74 to 110.

The publication entitled Check List of Large Scale Maps Published by Foreign Governments (Great Britain Excepted) in the Library of Congress was compiled by Philip Lee Phillips and published in 1904. It indicates on pages 33-34, 38-39, and 51-56 the modern detailed sheet maps of Portugal, Spain, Mexico, Nicaragua, Salvador, Argentina, Bolivia, Brazil, Chile, Colombia, Ecuador, Paraguay, Peru, and Uruguay which were available in the Library of Congress in 1904. Continuations of these maps have been received in large numbers.

The pamphlet entitled Catalogue of an Exhibition in the Division of Maps [Library of Congress] Comprising some 200 Hispanic American Maps, Atlases, Geographies, Globes, and Portraits of Historical, Diplomatic and Cartographic Interest, Ranging through Four Centuries was prepared by Lawrence Martin, Edith Ritton, and Clarence G. Johnson, published in 1935 and reprinted in 1937.

The pamphlet entitled Disturnell's Map was written by Lawrence Martin and published in 1927. It devotes forty pages to a description of twenty-four editions and twenty facsimiles of the "Mapa de los Estados Unidos de Méjico, Segun lo organizado y definido por las varias actos del Congreso de dicha República: y construido por las mejores autoridades, " 1828-58, and its use in connection with the negotiation and ratification of the Treaty of Guadalupe Hidalgo.

The annual reports of the Librarian of Congress from 1897
to the present briefly describe many Hispanic map accessions which
are not included in the publications referred to above.   Others are
described in the Map Division's Annual Acquisitions Report in the
August issue of the Library of Congress Quarterly Journal of
Current Acquisitions.

A Bibliography of Cartography, consisting of some 45,000
4 x 6 cards is available for consultation in the Map Reading Room.
Positive 16-mm. microfilm copies may be purchased from the
Photoduplication Service, Library of Congress.   The first fifteen
reels cost $105, but supplementary reels of 2,000 to 2,500 entries
are filmed as they accumulate and are sold for $4 per reel.   This
bibliography of cartography contains references to outstanding
Hispanic maps and to many Spanish, Portuguese, and Latin American
cartographers as well as to map makers of other nationalities who
have made maps of Spain, Portugal, and the Americas.

Library of Congress
Music Division

In accordance with its policy of keeping its collections as
complete and as representative as possible, the Music Division
acquires Hispanic musical material of all periods and classes.
Hispanic music and musical literature have come to the library
through various channels, such as copyright, purchase, gift, and
transfer.

Books, musical scores (manuscript and printed), and opera
librettos constitute the various Hispanic holdings of the Music
Division.   Collected sets, intended for the use of scholars and
historians, are represented by the following:

Biblioteca de Catalunya.   "Publicacions del Departament de Musica."
  Barcelona: Institut d'Estudis Catalans, 1921——.
Consejo Superior de Investigaciones Científicias, Instituto Español
  de Musicología.   Monumentos de la música española.   Madrid
  and Barcelona, 1941——.
Eslava, Miguel Hilarión.   Lira sacro-hispana... Madrid: M. Martín
  Salazar, 1869.
Pedrell, Felipe.   Hispaniae schola musica sacra... Barcelona:
  Pujol, 1894-98.
Victoria, Tomás Luis de.   ...Opera omnia... Leipzig: Breitkopf
  and Härtel, 1902-13.

Early sources in this field of music are especially plentiful

in the Library of Congress. A recent count of the early books
(before 1800) on music devoted to that art in the Hispanic countries,
or published in the Hispanic languages, reveals nearly 100 volumes.
Many of these are extremely rare and of great historical importance.
They include works which give a detailed picture of musical practice
and instruction in renaissance Spain and Portugal, the theory of
composition in these countries, and the flowerings of various artistic manifestations. The majority of these books are listed in
the library's published catalogues on early books on music. A few
of the important titles, selected at random, will give a slight indication of the extent of the collection. In the following list, several
outstanding musical imprints have been included:

Bermudo, Ivan. Comiença el libro llamado Declaraciõ de instrumētos
    musicales... Osuna: Juan de León, 1555.
Cabezón, Antonio de. Obras de musica para tecla arpa y vihuela...
    Madrid: Francisco Sanchez, 1578.
Cerone, Domenico Pietro. ...El melopeo y maestro... Naples:
    I. B. Gargano y L. Nucci, 1613.
Corrêa de Araujo, Francisco. Libro de tientos y discursos de
    musica practica, y theorica de organo... Alcalá: Antonio
    Arnao, 1626.
Ferrer, Pedro. Intonario general para todas las yglesias de España...
    Saragossa: Pedro Bernuz, 1548.
Guerau, Francisco. Poema harmonico, compuesto de varios cifras
    por el temple de la guitarra española... Madrid: Manuel Ruiz
    de Murga, 1694.
Tomás de Santa Maria. Libro llamado Arte de tañer fantasia, assi
    para tecla como para vihuela, y todo instrumēto, en que se
    pudiere tañer a tres, y a quatro vozes, y a mas... Valladolid:
    F. Fernandez de Cordova, 1565.
Tovar, Francisco. Libro de musica pratica... Barcelona: Johan
    Rosenbach, 1510.

    The Music Division has co-operated with musicologists of the
United States and Latin America in collecting and preparing for pub-
lic distribution recordings of folk music from Brazil, Mexico, Puerto
Rico, and Venezuela.

    The annual reports of the Librarian of Congress enumerate
the tablatures in the Music Division, including those of interest to
Hispanic students. Opera librettos in Spanish and Portuguese,
printed before 1800, are listed in Sonneck's catalogue. Bibliography:

Chase, Gilbert. A Guide to Latin American Music. Washington
    D.C., 1945.

106   [District of Columbia]

Gregory, Julia. (prepared under the direction of O. G. T. Sonneck).
Catalogue of Early Books on Music [Before 1800]. Washington,
D. C., 1913 [with supplement by Hazel Bartlett, Washington,
D. C., 1944].
Sonneck, Oscar George Theodore. Catalogue of Opera Librettos
Printed before 1800. Washington, D. C., 1914.

Library of Congress
Prints and Photographs Division

The Prints and Photographs Divsion of the Library of Congress
includes in its voluminous files much material of Hispanic interest.
Foremost is the Archive of Hispanic Culture, a collection of some
7,500 photographs and slides of the fine and folk arts of Latin America
including many color transparencies. Special emphasis has been
placed upon the fine arts of Latin America. An annotated bibliography, A Guide to the Art of·Latin America, was prepared by
Robert C. Smith and Elizabeth Wilder, and published by the library
in 1948, with support from the Department of State.

Other collections of the division hold Hispanic material—the
Historic American Buildings Survey and the mass of Farm Security
Administration photographs of almost every aspect of life in the
United States. Both of these collections contain material on the
architecture and life of the Spanish Southwest.

Library of Congress
Rare Books Division

The earliest printed document about the New World which the
Library of Congress possesses is a copy of the second Latin edition
(printed at Rome) of Columbus' letter of April 29, 1493, addressed
to the Royal Treasurer of Spain and detailing his voyage of discovery.
The library also has three copies of the later Latin edition, illustrated with the earliest woodcuts relating to America and appended
to Carolus Verardus' Historia baetica, printed at Basel in 1494.

Henry Harrisse, in Bibliotheca americana vetustissima (1866)
and the Additions (1872), which describe works relating to America
published between the years 1492 and 1551, records 28 genuine titles
that appeared before the beginning of the sixteenth century. Of this
number the library has 11, including the two editions of the Columbus
letter. Of the remaining 9, the most interesting is a broadside which
according to later investigation, was probably printed at Alcalá in

1511. Textually this is regarded as the earliest diplomatic document relating to America, for it records the text of the Bull of Demarcation of Alexander VI, which divided the New World between Spain and Portugal. The library's copy, one of three known to be in existence, is the largest known and contains, interestingly enough, a contemporary manuscript translation of the second part of the codicil of the last will of Queen Isabel of Spain, referring to her very real concern for the welfare of the American Indians. The fifteenth-century references to America other than the Columbus letter are few, and are perhaps chiefly remarkable for the paucity of the information relating to America. Most interesting of these early references in the library's possession are the first editions of Sebastian Brant's Das Narrenschiff in German (Basel, 1494), in Latin (Basel, 1497), and in French (Paris, 1497), the first and last of which are included in the Rosenwald collection. In the oration of Bernardino de Carvajal to Alexander VI in the name of King Ferdinand and Queen Isabel, delivered on June 19, 1493, and presumably printed shortly thereafter, the orator makes an allusion to the recently discovered islands toward the Indies.

The spurious reference to Martin Behaim as the discoverer of America is duly recorded in the Latin and German editions of Schedel's popular Nuremberg Chronicle, both printed in 1493. The remaining fifteenth-century titles of American interest are Zacharias Lilius' De origine et laudibus scientiarum (Florence, 1496), wherein it is reported that the king of Spain is sending ships to explore new shores; and Antonius Nebrissensis' Introductorium in cosmographiam Pomponii Melae (Salamanca, ca. 1498).

The most interesting early piece of Americana in the division's possession is the so-called Trevisan manuscript, the cornerstone of a fine group of titles of American interest in the John Boyd Thacher collection. Transcribed at Venice about 1502, this manuscript contains accounts in Italian of the early American discoveries. These translations appear to have been made from the Latin compilations of Peter Martyr by Angelo Trevisan, a young diplomat attached to the Venetian Embassy in Spain. Trevisan sent them to Venice in four installments to his former employer, Domenico Malipiero, who had them transcribed, together with the covering letters, in the present manuscript volume. Also included in the manuscript are other narratives relating to the early Portuguese navigations to India, and an anonymous account of one of Columbus' voyages in the West Indies. The Trevisan manuscript therefore contains what is probably the earliest account extant of the early voyages to America other than the Columbus letter of 1493.

The portion of this manuscript relating to America was printed at Venice in 1504 in the extremely scarce Libretto, which is
represented in the library's collections by a reproduction. The
text was more widely distributed in the form of the Paesi nouamente
retrouati of 1507. The library's copy of this later printing contains one leaf in facsimile but is otherwise complete. Other editions
of this significant text are represented in the library by the German
translation of 1508 in two copies, one of which is in the Thacher
collection; the Latin translation, also published in 1508; and three
later editions in Italian (Venice, 1517; Milan, 1519; and Venice,
1521), the first two of which are in the Rosenwald collection.

Amerigo Vespucci revealed in a letter to Lorenzo dei Medici
the results of his third voyage to the continent which was later to
bear his name. During this particular voyage Vespucci explored
the east coast of Brazil probably to a point as far south as the Río
de La Plata. Thirteen editions in Latin of Vespucci's letter are
recorded as having been printed between 1503 and 1506. The Library of Congress has 2 editions: "the second issue of the third
edition," entitled Mundus novus, printed at Augsburg by Johann
Otmar in 1504; and the sixth edition (Strassburg, 1505), entitled
De ora Antarctica, which has two interesting woodcuts on the title
page.

There also appeared in 1504 at Venice the second volume of
Marcus Antonius Sabellicus' Enneades ab orbe condito. The earlier
portion, published in 1498, contains no reference to America, but
the later volume, which seems to be most uncommon, contains an
entire page referring to Columbus' first and second voyages. The
library's copy is in the Thacher collection.

The earliest map in a printed book relating to the New World
may well be the edition of Ptolemy's Geographia, printed at Ulm
in 1482, for in an extension in the upper left-hand corner of the
world map appears an island labelled "glacialis" which conceivably
might be identified as Greenland. The library is fortunate to
possess 5 copies of this edition, which the late Alfred Pollard described as one of the finest books printed in Germany during the
century. The library's collection of editions of Ptolemy is especially rich, comprising 92 copies of some thirty-eight editions which
were published before 1700. Apparently the library's collections
(49 copies in the Map Division, 43 in the Rare Books Division) lack
only the edition misdated 1462 (i.e., 1477) and the Paris edition of
1546. Of the early sixteenth-century editions the library has 3
copies of the Rome edition of 1508. This contains the Ruysch world

map in three different states, delineating a large portion of the
coast of South America and a southeastern extension of Asia described as Terra Nova, possibly identified as Florida.

The Strassburg 1513 edition of the Geographia, also available
in 3 copies, contains the two maps of the New World made "per
Admiralem quondam serenissi. Portugalie regis Ferdinandi."
Although not printed until 1513, this remarkable edition of Ptolemy
was commenced about the year 1505 by Martin Waldseemüller, the
geographer of St. Dié.

Waldseemüller's Cosmographiae introductio (St. Dié, 1507),
prepared to accompany a small globe and a world map, is the book
responsible for naming America. Of this most desirable book the
library has 3 editions, all from the Thacher collection, dated April
25, 1507, August 29, 1507, and 1509. The library has 2 copies of
the April 1507 edition.

While the Waldseemüller contains the text of the four voyages
of Vespucci, the culmination of these early accounts of the voyages
of exploration was the 1511 edition of Peter Martyr's Opera, which
appeared at Seville. Peter Martyr, the first historian of America,
obtained at first hand much valuable information regarding the discoveries of the early navigators, whom he knew personally. Unquestionably this is the most important single volume relating to
the voyages of exploration that had appeared up to that time.

In the library's 2 copies of Richard Eden's The Decades of
the Newe Worlde (London, 1555), which is the earliest collection
of voyages in English and the third book in English to relate to
America, there is a description of the voyage which Sebastian Cabot
made to the coast of North America in 1508. This description is
in effect a translation from the Latin text from the third decade of
Peter Martyr's classic work first published in 1516, a copy of which
is available in the Thacher collection. Another early description
is that of Juan de Grijalva's expedition to Yucatán in 1518, written
by Juan de Diaz, the chaplain who accompanied the expedition.
It was first printed as an appendage to the 1520 Venetian edition of
Lodovico de Varthema's Itinerario. One result of this expedition
was the disclosure of the great wealth of Mexico, which ultimately
led to the Spanish conquest.

The first account of Ferdinand Magellan's remarkable voyage
to appear in print is Maximilianus Transylvanus' letter (De Molvccis
insulis) to the Cardinal of Salzburg, dated October 23, 1522, a little
more than six weeks after the return to Spain of one of the five

vessels originally equipped for the voyage. The text of the letter was first printed at Cologne during the month of January 1523, and is in the library's collection, as are also two copies each of the two later Rome editions dated November 1523 and February 1524.

For the period of the conquest of Mexico the library has representative holdings of the standard accounts by Hernando Cortés (2 editions of 1524, and 1 each of 1532 and 1550), Bernal Díaz del Castillo (edition of 1632), Francisco López de Gómara (11 editions, the earliest of which is that of 1553), Antonio de Solís y Rivadeneyra (5 editions), and Agustín Dávila Padilla (2 editions). For the material relating to the conquest of Peru there are 5 early editions, including the first of Pedro de Cieza de León's Cronica, 7 editions of Agustín de Zárate's Historia, 5 editions of Garcilaso de la Vega's Historia, and interesting source material in the writings of Levinus Apollonius and Diego Fernández, not overlooking the 1534 edition of the Summario de la generale historia de l'Indie Occidentali. For the later period, enduring evidence of the Spanish colonization south of the Mexican border is available in the 110 books that were printed on local presses, ranging from the time the press was introduced in Mexico City in 1539 to the year 1700.

Library of Congress
Serials Divison

Competent guides to the library's holdings of Hispanic periodicals are to be found in the annual volumes of the Handbook of Latin American Studies, which list more than 400 periodical titles currently being received in the Library of Congress, and in Latin American Periodicals Currently Received in the Library of Congress and in the Library of the Department of Agriculture, published in 1945. With the outbreak of World War II, increased attention was given to Latin American publications, and every effort has been made to maintain this expanded coverage.

In the field of newspapers, the library's annual List of Newspapers Currently Received continues to reflect our coverage of Latin American newspapers. The Pan American Union has prepared a Union List of Latin American Newspapers, and Library of Congress holdings have been reported.

The Library of Congress has several thousand volumes of Hispanic periodicals of a general character, classified in AP60 to AP68; several thousand volumes of Hispanic historical periodicals in F1201 to F3799; and smaller groups in other classes. All these bound sets are shelved in the general collections and are available in the general reading rooms for the use of students. Current issues, however, are available in the Periodicals Reading Room.

The current Hispanic newspapers, in unbound form, are also served to students in the Periodicals Reading Room, but the older bound sets are served in the Newspapers Reference Room in the · Library Annex. Over 100 volumes are added annually. Although not complete, the collection covers a wide range in time and place, as the following shows:

Argentina: 1815-17, 1821, 1823-46, 1887-88, 1891-92, 1900 to date.
Bolivia: 1846, 1857-58, 1861-62, 1866, 1870-77, 1887-88, 1890, 1892, 1904-5, 1824-25, 1927 to date.
Brazil: 1824, 1826-27, 1831-42, 1856, 1870, 1880, 1883-93, 1895-1919, 1925 to date.
Chile: 1824-33, 1836-40, 1845-46, 1849, 1855, 1879-80, 1908 to date.
Colombia: 1827, 1830-31, 1838-39, 1843, 1845-46, 1859-61, 1863-64, 1869, 1926 to date.
Costa Rica: 1896-1906, 1908-9, 1926 to date.
Cuba: 1800-1805, 1813-14, 1821-22, 1829, 1832-33, 1835-83, 1888-92, 1898 to date.
Dominican Republic: 1936 to date.
Ecuador: 1826-27, 1832-33, 1900, 1903-5, 1918, 1920-23, 1924 to date.
Guatemala: 1820-23, 1836-40, 1890-91, 1926 to date.
Honduras: 1839, 1894-95, 1897-99, 1903-4, 1908-9, 1919, 1925-28, 1932 to date.
Mexico: 1805-12, 1821-51, 1857-60, 1864 to date.
Nicaragua: 1855, 1907-8, 1911-12, 1926 to date.
Panama: 1851-53, 1870, 1876-88, 1900-1902, 1904 to date.
Paraguay: 1887-88, 1901-10, 1924 to date.
Peru: 1826-29, 1830-34, 1836-41, 1855, 1859-60, 1895, 1919 to date.
Philippine Islands: 1898 to date.
Portugal: 1715-58, 1792-94, 1796, 1805, 1809, 1811, 1814, 1824-26, 1828-29, 1900-1903, 1905 to date.
Puerto Rico: 1854-58, 1886, 1899 to date.
Salvador: 1900-1914, 1926-35, 1941 to date.
Spain: 1786-90, 1817-18, 1820-24, 1827, 1836-37, 1840-42, 1845, 1853-55, 1875-76, 1880-81, 1887, 1893, 1898 to date.
Uruguay: 1836-38, 1885, 1899-1909, 1925 to date.
Venezuela: 1820, 1822, 1825-27, 1834, 1836-42, 1845-54, 1859-60, 1882, 1896, 1898-1904, 1925 to date.

National Geographic Society
Sixteenth and M Streets, NW

The library of the National Geographic Society contains a well-chosen assortment of reference and research materials, with particular emphasis on works of travel, exploration, geography, and natural history.

The collection dates from the establishment of the National Geographic Society and the National Geographic Magazine by a group of Washington scientists in 1888 "for the increase and diffusion of geographic knowledge." Thus it includes all books, articles, technical papers, maps, and other valuable publications which have resulted from the society's many expeditions and other world-wide activities for the advancement of knowledge of geography in its broadest sense.

This collection constitutes the private library of the National Geographic Society. In so far as possible, however, the society, of which Dr. Gilbert Grosvenor is board chairman and John Oliver LaGorce is president, makes the facilities of its library available to individuals engaged in serious research.

While the collection does not specialize in Hispanic studies, it contains various materials of interest to the scholar in that field. No general catalogue of the contents of the library is published; the card-index system is used.

For reference to the quantities of material contained in the National Geographic Magazine, the society has printed a Cumulative Index (latest edition, 1946; supplement, 1947-51) listing all the articles and maps which it has published since 1899. This index also includes a list of the society's expeditions and indicates the scientific papers, published separately, which have resulted from those undertakings.

For more detailed reference, the society's library contains a card index, with hundreds of thousands of cards, which serves to locate any name or fact, or any of the photographs which have been published in the profusely illustraded National Geographic Magazine.

Among expeditions of particular interest to Hispanic scholars are those of 1912, 1914, and 1915, directed by Dr. Hiram Bingham and jointly sponsored by the National Geographic Society and friends of Yale University. Machu Picchu, lost city of the Incas on a Peruvian mountain top, was uncovered and excavated, and further explorations were carried on in the land of the Incas. See the Cumulative Index for titles of numerous articles reporting on this work, a reference to which is the article "Peru, Home of the Warlike Inca, " by Kip Ross, in the National Geographic Magazine, October 1950. See also Hiram Bingham, Machu Picchu, a Citadel of the Incas (New Haven: Yale University Press, 1930).

Likewise of interest are eleven archeological expeditions to Middle America in the period 1938 to early 1951, sponsored jointly by the National Geographic Society and the Smithsonian Institution, and led by Dr. Matthew W. Stirling, chief of the Bureau of American Ethnology at the Smithsonian. On the first expedition, 1938-39, Dr. Stirling discovered near Tres Zapotes in the State of Veracruz, Mexico, a stela bearing a date equivalent to November 24, 291 B.C., making it the New World's then oldest known dated work of man. Later expeditions to the same general region uncovered conclusive evidence of a distinct ancient civilization now established as the La Venta culture. They also found ten colossal stone heads, monuments of vanished Americans, the largest weighing thirty tons. (A cast of one of these huge heads has been on exhibition in Explorers Hall at the society's headquarters since 1943. A cast of another of the heads was placed on display in 1950 at the American Museum of Natural History, New York.) The 1948-49 and 1950-51 expeditions delved in ancient burial sites in Panama.

In connection with the several articles resulting from these expeditions and other articles on the Maya, Aztec, and Inca civilizations, color plates have been published in the National Geographic Magazine reproducing paintings depicting the daily life of those ancient peoples, carefully prepared in the light of present archeological knowledge.

Also noteworthy are the society's Pueblo Bonito and Tree Ring expeditions, conducted between 1920 and 1929, which shed new light on the everyday life of the pre-Columbian inhabitants of the Southwestern United States and resulted in the dating of their communal dwellings through a study of the tree rings in their charred and weathered beams. See the Cumulative Index for numerous articles; also, in the National Geographic Society's "Contributed Technical Papers, " A. E. Douglass, Pueblo Bonito Series, No. 1, Dating Pueblo Bonito and Other Ruins of the Southwest (1935).

Other Hispanic materials in the National Geographic Magazine, far too numerous for listing here, will be readily located with the aid of the indexes indicated above.

Columbus Memorial Library
Pan American Union

In an effort to strengthen cultural relations between the peoples of America, the First International Conference of American States, held in Washington in 1889-90, made provisions for the creation of a Pan American library to be established in that city.

Dr. Carlos Martínez Silva, one of the delegates to the conference from Colombia, appreciated, along with other Latin American delegates, the need of a library center and also of constructive action to develop it. In the meeting on April 18, 1890, he proposed the establishment in the city of Washington of a library to which each government should send on its own account the most complete collection possible of works relating to the history and civilization of America, so that the results of intellectual and scientific labor in all America might be collected under a single roof.

The result of this proposal was the adoption by Congress of the following resolution:

"Resolved, That there be established at such location in the city of Washington as the Government of the United States may designate, to commemorate the meeting of the International American Conference, a Latin American Memorial Library, to be formed by contributions from all the Governments represented in this Conference, wherein shall be collected all the historical, geographical, and literary works, maps, manuscripts, and official documents relating to the history and civilization of America, such library to be solemnly dedicated on the day on which the United States celebrates the Fourth Centennial of the Discovery of America."

At the Second International Conference of American States, the scope of the library was extended and the name of "Columbus Memorial Library" was adopted.

Since the library was created by the twenty-one American nations as a general library on those countries, it has been found advisable to retain, as a first fundamental classification, a segregation of material by countries. This results in a library of twenty-one units (one for each republic), in addition to a section for books of a general character or relating to two or more countries. For use under this arrangement by countries, the Library of Congress classification system has been adopted and applied. By construing in the broadest sense the provisions of the resolution of 1890 creating the library, its scope has been extended to include any publication that treats directly or indirectly of Latin America. As a result of this policy, the library now contains over 175, 000 titles, including many of the early books on America, histories, descriptive works, and a collection of over 2, 500 titles of periodical publications; it is especially strong in its collections of laws, government reports, literature, history, and books on economic subjects. In addition, it contains a large collection of directories and telephone guides of all the principal cities; Spanish, Portuguese, and English dictionaries; and general reference books. Many of the more important articles in the periodicals received—particularly in the official newspapers and journals and in scientific, literary, and commercial magazines—are indexed on cards, while the periodicals are bound for permanent reference. This collection of periodicals, with the accompanying index cards, affords an opportunity to consult much valuable material that otherwise would be difficult to find.

Until 1951, the collection contained at least one outstanding newspaper of each nation, in some cases files extending over forty years. However, due to space needs for the maintenance of other material, these files were offered to libraries of various universities and disposed of as follows: the University of North Carolina accepted titles from Argentina, Chile, Brazil, Colombia, Mexico, Peru, Uruguay, and Venezuela; the University of Florida accepted titles from Cuba, the Dominican Republic, Haiti, and Panama; and Tulane University of Louisiana accepted titles from the countries of Central America. Of the titles not wanted by the above universities, the Library of Congress accepted titles from Brazil, Paraguay, Peru, and Uruguay, and several remaining titles stayed at the Pan American Union.

In the bibliographical field, the Columbus Memorial Library has continuously published bibliographical information concerning its recent acquisitions, first through the Bulletin of the Pan American Union; then through the Pan American Bookshelf (El Libro Panamericano); L E A; and currently through its monthly List of Accessions. It began publishing, in January 1951, the Review of Inter-American Bibliography, a quarterly publication devoted to the dissemination of information about bibliographical activities in the field of Latin American studies. From 1928 through 1935, it issued the Library and Bibliography Series and the Serie sobre bibliotecas y bibliografía, now out of print. The Bibliographic Series, begun in 1930 and appearing at irregular intervals, now has reached 43 numbers.

In accordance with the resolution of the Seventh International Conference of American States (1933), a special section known as the "Center of Inter-American Bibliography" was established within the library for the purpose of recording the development of bibliography, and of co-ordinating and co-operating in the constructive work of inter-American bibliography and of mutual aid among the libraries of America. National co-operating committees on bibliography were formed in the countries that are members of the Union, but these committees never became very active and have since ceased to function.

The functions of the Center of Inter-American Bibliography are: to disseminate information on the outstanding books of inter-American interest, issuing annotated lists at regular intervals; to collect all printed bibliographies on Pan American topics; to maintain a file concerning bibliographies in preparation or in manuscript; to undertake the preparation and publication of laws and regulations relating to libraries that are members of the Pan American Union; and to act in an advisory capacity to scientific and other learned societies in arranging for the exchange of publications.

The library has served in an advisory capacity to libraries in Latin America desiring to improve their library methods, has distributed books in the United States for Latin American authors and in Latin America for United States authors, and has aided North American libraries in making arrangements for the exchange of books with libraries in South America. Because of the demand for lists of new books published in Latin America, a campaign was inaugurated in 1937—through correspondence with government officials, book and library journals, and publishers—to have established in each country, where one does not now exist, a quarterly list of all new books published under both government and private auspices.

During the sixty years that have elapsed since the first International Conference of American States, the embryonic International Bureau of American Republics has undergone changes until now as the Pan American Union it has become the Secretariat for the Organization of American States. This organization at the Pan American Union has a staff of 350 specialists and secretariat personnel. The Columbus Memorial Library, as a Division of the Department of Cultural Affairs of the Organization of American States, has co-ordinated its objectives to be consistent with the purposes and functions of the OAS. The Pan American Union is charged with the responsibility for assembling and correlating data and information required by the several councils and departments of the OAS in connection with the studies, reports and recommendations of a cultural, social, economic, and juridical nature under consideration by them.   The primary aim of the library, therefore, is to develop a collection that will be fully responsive to the needs of the Union in the discharge of its responsibilities.   To achieve this aim, it has been essential to stress currency of information and materials as the outstanding characteristic of the collection.

Further implementation of the inter-American relations at the library is achieved by the many Pan American Union periodical, serial, and monographic publications which are used for exchange purposes with libraries and institutions throughout the Americas. Duplicates which come to the library are disposed of by gift or exchange to worthy libraries in the Americas.   Selections in answer to scores of requests for assistance which the library receives from libraries in Latin America are mailed from the duplicate collection.

It is natural that Latin American libraries should turn to the Pan American Union for advice and assistance on professional and technical matters.   Their questions frequently refer to types of classification schemes or cataloging rules to follow, literature on library methods, and the availability of library science manuals and where they may be secured.   From time to time requests refer to personal assistance to reorganize libraries.   The Columbus Memorial Library collects technical information which would be of assistance to the Latin American librarian.   It also collects information concerning libraries, librarians, library schools, associations and governmental agencies, library legislation, and the book trade in Latin America.   From time to time, the library publishes compilations with reference to this information.   Opportunities frequently arise whereby members of its personnel give courses in librarianship in library schools in Latin America, and serve as reference librarians and document officers for inter-American conferences and seminars.   Through the Columbus Memorial Library, the Pan American Union gives support to efforts of other inter-American library agencies, such as the Inter-American Bibliographical and Library Association and the Assembly of Librarians of the Americas.   It has sponsored courses and regional conferences for librarians.

As a lending library, the Columbus Memorial Library makes its rich research collection available to others through its reference services, either directly or through interlibrary loans to scholars, research workers, specialists, university students, and general readers interested in information or engaged in studies concerning Latin America.

Sixty some years after its inception, the Columbus Memorial Library, established as a "Latin American Memorial Library," has brought together a compact and relatively thorough collection of bibliographical resources of current information on Latin America. It is in a strategic position within an inter-American organization to further the development of libraries in Latin America and to promote better inter-American library relations. In recognition of its importance to scholarship and research, a new reference reading room was opened early in 1951 to provide adequate quarters for the consultation of its collection and for the extension of the library's reference services.

Phillips Memorial Gallery
1600 Twenty-first Street

The Hispanic material in the Phillips Memorial Gallery is limited to a small number of paintings and a bronze. The first in point of time is "The Repentant Peter" by El Greco, a fine example of the artist's mystic expressionism, his use of all-over design. Also in the Source Room is a realistic Goya, "The Repentant Peter." All the strength and all the weakness of Peter is shown in this "earthy" peasant fisherman, in contrast to the idealistic mystic of El Greco. Zuloaga is represented by the dark and handsome "Girl of Montmartre."

Picasso is represented in the gallery by 3 paintings and a bronze. The early interior "The Blue Room," shows the artist in his "blue period," in which he used rich Hispano-Moresque colors and the technique of Van Gogh. The bronze is of a young jester and was done in 1905. There is an "Abstraction" (1918), a well-disciplined bit of design and of rich but muted colors; also a water color of the same period (1918-21). "The Bull Fight" (1935) is a dynamic painting depicting the cruelty and fascination of Spain's best-loved sport. There is a small Juan Gris, "Abstraction" (1915), inscribed "A mon ami André Salmon, souvenir affectueux, 1919."

The collection also includes paintings by Sorrolla, Cittadini, La Serna, Tamayo, and Charlot.

Smithsonian Institution
Bureau of American Ethnology

The Bureau of American Ethnology was founded in 1879, thanks
to the efforts of John W. Powell, who became its first director. The
directors who succeeded him were W. H. Holmes, F. W. Hodge,
J. Walter Fewkes, and M. W. Stirling.

At first the bureau studied only those Indians found within the
United States, but its activities were soon extended to include all
the Americas. The bureau's chief publication is its Bulletin. The
first forty-eight Annual Reports also contain extensive scientific
monographs. Among numerous scholarly works appearing in the
Bulletin series should be mentioned the Handbook of South American
Indians (Bulletin No. 143), in 6 volumes, written by various specialists and edited under the direction of Julian H. Steward, 1946-50.

Smithsonian Institution
National Collection of Fine Arts

The Gellatly collection in the National Collection of Fine Arts
contains the following Hispanic material:

Paintings:

Artist undetermined. "St. Anne with Virgin and Child."
Gonzales, Juan. "Nativity."

Sculpture:

St. Anne, wood, about fourteenth century.
St. Barbara, wood, polychromed and gilded, late Renaissance.
Wood figure of a king in armor, carved, sixteenth to seventeenth
    century.

Furniture:

Spanish chair, peacock blue and gold; 3 Spanish leather covered
    chairs; Spanish marquetry chest (Lion d'Or), eighteenth century,
    from Mexico; Spanish writing desk (for child), eighteenth century,
    from Mexico; Spanish table, marquetry, bone inlay; Portuguese
    poudreuse, marquetry; Spanish saddle, mounted as chair; chest,
    inlaid with bone and tortoise shell, probably Spanish; chest,
    inlaid mother-of-pearl, probably Spanish; and Spanish carved and
    gilded columns.

Miscellaneous:

Spanish sixteenth-century pendant; Spanish late sixteenth-century rock-crystal pendant; silver Spanish bénitier, sixteenth century.

Smithsonian Institution

National Gallery of Art

The National Gallery of Art now has several distinguished collections, numbering over 16,000 works of art, including paintings, sculpture, prints and drawings, and items of decorative art.

The paintings and sculpture given by Mr. Andrew W. Mellon, at the establishment of the gallery in 1937, comprise works by many of the greatest masters from the thirteenth to the nineteenth century, and have formed a nucleus of high quality from which the collection has grown. In 1942, Mr. Joseph E. Widener presented the famous collection of paintings, sculpture, and decorative arts formed by him and his father, P. A. B. Widener, and kept until then at his home in Elkins Park, near Philadelphia.

The Spanish paintings in the National Gallery of Art are:

Goya. "The Marquesa de Pontejos, " painted 1785-90. Formerly in collection of the Marqués de Miraflores y de Pontejos, Madrid. Mellon collection, 1937.

—. "Carlos IV of Spain as Huntsman." This portrait appears to be a replica in small scale of the one executed by Goya in 1790 and now at Capodimonte, Naples. A second version is in the Royal Palace, Madrid. The present picture, which differs slightly in design from the other two, was probably painted in 1799 or shortly after, since this year is the earliest date possible for the pendant portrait of María Luisa which it was obviously intended to accompany. Formerly in the collection of the Marquesa de Bermejillo, Madrid. Mellon collection, 1937.

—. "María Luisa, Queen of Spain." Replica of a larger picture in the Royal Palace, Madrid, painted late in 1799 (see above). Another version is in the Prado, Madrid. Mellon collection, 1937.

—. "Señora de Sabasa García." According to a family tradition, Goy first saw the sitter, who was then eighteen, when he was painting her uncle, Don Evaristo Pérez de Castro, later Prime Minister of Spain. Attracted by her charm, he asked to paint her portrait, and presented her with this picture. If this tradition is correct, the painting must date before 1808. In technique, however, the portrait seems later, and corresponds with

Goya's style of about 1814. Formerly in the collection of James Simon, Berlin. Mellon collection, 1937.

——. "Don Bartolomé Sureda." Painted about 1801-4, possibly about the time Sureda was made director of the royal porcelain factory of the Buen Retiro. Collections: the family of the sitter, until recently; Havemeyer, New York. Gift of Mr. and Mrs. P. H. B. Frelinghuysen, 1941.

——. "Doña Teresa Sureda." This is the wife of Don Bartolomé Sureda. The portrait was painted about 1801-4. Gift of Mr. and Mrs. P. H. B. Frelinghuysen, 1942.

Greco, El. "St. Ildefonso," painted 1603-5. This picture is a smaller replica of that in the Hospital de la Caridad at Illescas near Toledo. Once in the possession of Jean François Millet, it was later in the collection of Edgar Degas, Paris. Mellon collection, 1937.

——. "St Martin and the Beggar," painted 1604-14. Generally considered to be the latest of El Greco's several versions of the subject, the earliest of which was given to the National Gallery of Art by Mr. Widener in 1942. Other versions are to be found in the Rumanian Royal Collection (Bucharest), the Art Institute of Chicago, and the collection of Robert Treat Paine (Brookline, Mass.). The present painting was formerly in the collection of Michel Manzi, Paris. Mellon collection, 1937.

——. "Laocoön." Painted about 1610, this is the only classical subject treated by El Greco, as far as is now known. The head of Laocoön follows the model that served for the artist's representations of St. Peter in other paintings. The two figures at the extreme right are interpreted, because of their lofty, impersonal relationship to the tragedy, as deities, possibly Apollo and Artemis. This is probably the large painting of Laocoön listed in 1614 in the inventory of El Greco's estate in Toledo. It has subsequently been in the collections of the Dukes of Montpensier, Seville; Palace of San Telmo, Seville (before 1866); Infante Don Antonio de Orleans, Sanlúcar de Barrameda (1908); E. Fischer, Charlottenburg (1914); Prince Paul of Yugoslavia, Belgrade. Kress collection, 1945.

——. "St. Jerome," painted probably after 1600, though Cossio (1908) dates it 1584-94. Very probably to be identified with the painting of the nude St. Jerome described as unfinished, and with similar dimensions, under item No. 145 in the second inventory of the possessions of El Greco's son, Jorge Manuel. Formerly in the collection of Doña María Montejo, Madrid. Gift of Chester Dale, 1943.

—. "St. Martin and the Beggar," painted 1597-99, for the Chapel of San José, Toledo. Signed in full in Greek characters.

—. "The Virgin with Santa Inés and Santa Tecla," painted 1597-99, for the Chapel of San José, Toledo. Signed with initials in Greek characters. This and the foregoing picture were, with two others, painted on commission by El Greco for the Chapel of San José, Toledo; the contract was dated November 9, 1597. The full story of the chapel and its pictures is told by M. Paul Lafond in the Gazette des Beaux-Arts of November 1906, pp. 382-92. The pictures remained in the Chapel of San José until the latter part of 1906, when they were sold by the authorities of the chapel to a firm of picture dealers in Paris, from whom Mr. Widener purchased these two.

Murillo. "A Girl and Her Duenna" ("Las Gallegas"). Purchased in 1823 by Sir William A'Court (afterward first Baron Heytesbury), British ambassador to Spain, from the Duque de Almodóvar; and from Lord Heytesbury, by Mr. Widener.

—. "The Return of the Prodigal Son." Painted between 1670 and 1674, as one of a series of decorations for the church built by the Brotherhood of La Caridad in Seville in connection with their Hospital of St. George. Murillo painted eight large canvases for the nave walls of the church and three small ones for the altars. The present canvas, together with "Moses Striking the Rock" (still in La Caridad), "Abraham and the Angels" (until recently in Stafford House and now in the National Gallery of Canada), and "San Juan de Dios" (La Caridad), hung on the Gospel side of the nave. On the opposite side its counterpart was "Christ Healing the Paralytic" (George Tomline collection, Suffolk); and the other compositions were the "Miracle of the Loaves and Fishes" (La Caridad), "St. Peter in Prison" (Hermitage, Leningrad), and "St. Elizabeth of Hungary" (Academy of San Fernando, Madrid). Collections: La Caridad, Seville; Marshal Soult, Paris (early nineteenth century); Duke of Sutherland, Stafford House, London (from 1835). Given through the generosity of Ailsa Mellon Bruce, by the Avalon Foundation, 1948.

Velázquez. "Pope Innocent X," painted 1649-50. Formerly in the Hermitage Gallery, Leningrad, to which it came in 1779 from the Walpole collection, of Norfolk, England. Mellon collection, 1937.

—. "The Needlewoman," painted about 1640. Formerly in the collection of Mme. Christiane de Polès, Paris. Mellon collection, 1937.

__. "Portrait of a Young Man." Ascribed to Velázquez by Bredius,
by Justi (who dated it in his middle period), and by Mayer, the
picture has also been called by Gensel and von Loga a school
work. Allende-Salazar has published it as the masterpiece of
the middle period of Juan Bautista del Mazo. Formerly in the
Harrach collection, Vienna. Mellon collection, 1937.

Zurbarán. "St. Lucy," painted about 1625. Probably the earliest
in a series of paintings of female saints by Zurbarán and his
followers. Formerly in the collection of Paul Somazzi, of Smyrna,
Turkey. Gift of Chester Dale, 1943.

__. "Sts. Paula, Eustochia, and Jerome." Probably painted for the
Hieronymite nuns of Seville; from the Samuel H. Kress collection, presented to the National Gallery in 1955.

Smithsonian Institution
United States National Museum

The United States National Museum is an important branch
of the Smithsonian Institution, established by act of Congress in
1846 under the terms of the will of James Smithson. In 1880,
Congress supplemented the act by providing that "all collections
of rocks, minerals, soils, fossils, and objects of natural history,
archeology, and ethnology, made by the Coast and Interior Survey,
the Geological Survey, or by any other parties for the government
of the United States, when no longer needed for investigations in
progress, shall be deposited in the National Museum." The museum's collections are continually increasing, not only as a result
of its own expeditions and explorations, but through private gifts,
until now it possesses over 32,000,000 objects. Its Hispanic material is abundant and is scattered through various sections. Recent
expeditions to Hispanic America have increased the collections,
particularly in the fields of botany, zoology, mineralogy, archeology, and ethnology. Detailed information on the collections may
be found in the Institution's publications.

This report is divided into three parts, dealing respectively
with archeological, ethnological, and natural science collections.
The first two sections are subdivided by regions, the last by subject matter.

Archeological Collections

I. Southwestern United States

There are extensive collections from various ancient Pueblo

ruins in Arizona, New Mexico, Colorado, and Utah, consisting of pottery vessels, stone and bone implements, wooden objects, ornaments, etc.

A. From Sikyatki, Awatobi, and other ruins in Tusayan Province:

Fewkes, J. W.   Annual Report, Smithsonian Institution, 1895 (1896), pp. 557-88.
—. Twenty-second Annual Report, Bureau of American Ethnology, Part I (1903), pp. 3-195.
—. Twenty-eighth Annual Report, Bureau of American Ethnology (1912), pp. 25-179.
Hough, Walter. Annual Report, United States National Museum for 1901 (1903), pp. 279-358.

B. From ruins in Mesa Verde National Park, Colorado, and vicinity:

Fewkes, J. W.   Bureau of American Ethnology, Bulletins 41 (1909), 51 (1911), 70 (1919).
Roberts, F. H. H., Jr. Bureau of American Ethnology, Bulletin 96 (1930).

C. From cave ruins in northern Arizona:

Fewkes, J. W.   Bureau of American Ethnology, Bulletin 50 (1911).
Judd, N. M.   Bureau of American Ethnology, Bulletin 82 (1926).
—. Proceedings United States National Museum No. 2828 (1931).
Mindeleff, Cosmos.   Sixteenth Annual Report, Bureau of American Ethnology (1897).

D. From western New Mexico and east central Arizona:

Judd, N. M. Smithsonian Miscellaneous Collections, CXXIV (1954), pp. iii-398.
Roberts, F. H. H., Jr. Bureau of American Ethnology, Bulletins 92 (1929), 100 (1931), 111 (1932).
E. From Casa Grande and other ruins in southern Arizona and New Mexico:

Fewkes, J. W.   Smithsonian Miscellaneous Collections, L (1907), pp. 289-329.
—. Twenty-eighth Annual Report, Bureau of American Ethnology (1912), pp. 25-179.
Hough, Walter. Annual Report of Smithsonian Institution for 1901 (1903), pp. 279-358.
—. Bureau of American Ethnology, Bulletin 35 (1907).

II. Mexico

A. The Tuxtla Statuette, a jadeite figurine from San Andrés Tuxtla, State of Vera Cruz, acquired in 1903; one of the oldest known dated specimens from the New World, bearing Maya glyphs corresponding to May 16, 98 B.C. This has been described by W. H. Holmes in the American Anthropologist, IX (1907), 691-701; by S. G. Morley in the Bureau of American Ethnology, Bulletin 57 (1915), p. 196; and by H. S. Washington in Proceedings United States National Museum, LX, Part IV (1922), 1-12.

Among archeological materials acquired later by the museum are those from the excavations in Cerro de las Mesas, Vera Cruz, accounts of which appear in the Annual Report of the Smithsonian Institution for 1939 and in the Bureau of American Ethnology Bulletin 141 (1943).

B. Stone implements, textiles, and ornaments from a burial cave in the Gulf of California, collected in 1888 by Edward Palmer and described by him in the Annual Report, United States National Museum, 1888 (1890), pp. 127-29.

Among other ethnological collections should be mentioned that of the Huichol Indians of northern Jalisco, which is described in the Annual Report for 1944.

III. Central America

A. Pottery and stone implements collected by J. F. Bransford in 1876-77, in Ometepec Island, Lake Nicaragua, and described by him in the Smithsonian Contributions to Knowledge, Vol. XXV (1881), and the Annual Report of the Smithsonian Institution for 1882 (1884), pp. 803-26.

B. Pottery, stone and copper ornaments, clay figurines, pottery whistles, and effigies from the Bay Islands and the mainland of Honduras, collected by W. D. Strong in 1933 and 1936, and described by him in Smithsonian Miscellaneous Collections, Vol. XCII, No. 14 (1935), and in Vol. XCVII, No. 1 (1938).

IV. West Indies

A. Greater Antilles: Extensive collections from the Taino and other aboriginal culture horizons of Puerto Rico, Vicques, Santo Domingo, Haiti, Cuba, and Jamaica, consisting of pottery bowls, burial jars, figurines, cylinder and flat disc stamps, carved stone collars and elbow stones, zemis, pestles, axes, celts, implements and utensils, knives and daggers of chipped flint, gorgets, implements of carved shell, bone swallowing sticks, seats and images of carved wood, food products including ears of maize, pins of worked metal, and ornaments of hammered gold. Descriptions of the collections appear in various Smithsonian publications.

Among these are:

Fewkes, J. W. "The Aborigines of Porto Rico and Neighboring Islands, " Twenty-fifth Annual Report, Bureau of American Ethnology (1904).
Krieger, Herbert W. "Aboriginal Indian Pottery of the Dominican Republic, " United States National Museum, Bulletin 156 (1931).
—. "Archeological and Historical Investigations in Samana, Dominican Republic, " United States National Museum, Bulletin 147.

B. Bahama Islands: there are collections from the Lucayan and other culture horizons on Watling (San Salvador), Long Island, Caicos, Great Inagua, Exuma, New Providence, Eleuthera, and Andros, consisting of skeletal remains, polished stone zemis, celts and axes, pottery bowls and potsherds, implements and utensils of worked shell, seats, images and figurines of carved wood, arrows, and swallowing sticks of worked bone.

C. Lesser Antilles: Carib and other aboriginal cultures are represented by specimens from St. Thomas, Anegada, Tortola, and St. Croix of the Virgin Islands; also from Guadeloupe, St. Vincent, Nevis, St. Catherines, St. Bartholomew, Santa Cruz, St. Lucia, St. Kitts, Antigua, Barbados, Navasa, Grenada, and Trinidad. These specimens consist of polished stone axes and celts, pottery bowls, pot rests, spindle whorls and potsherds, zemis in stone, pottery, bone, and shell, polished stone collars and three-pointed stones, knives of chipped flint, beads of drilled stone, and daggers and swallowing sticks of worked bone. Among the bibliography on these collections may be mentioned Otis T. Mason, "The Guesde Collection of Antiquities in Pointe-à-Pitre, Guadeloupe, West Indies, " Smithsonian Annual Report, 1884, pp. 731-837.

The interest of the museum in the Caribbean region has continued in recent years. Mr. H. W. Krieger, chief of the ethnology section since 1945, has taken part in the work to restore Isabella first Spanish establishment in Santo Domingo. Although reconstruction has not been possible because of lack of data, numerous archeological discoveries have been made.

In 1949, the museum acquired the writing desk of Diego Columbus. It was made of hand-carved mahogany in Sango Domingo at the beginning of the sixteenth century.

V. South America
    A. Argentina:

Large pottery vessels, locality not given; received in exchange
from the La Plata Museum, Buenos Aires; 10 specimens; Cat.
Nos. 170789-98.
Pottery, bone, stone, and wooden implements, chiefly from ruins
of Telcara, Province of Jujuy; received in exchange from Museo
Etnográfico, Buenos Aires; 286 specimens; Cat. Nos. 259781-
260000.
Stone implements, from various localities; collected by A. Hrdlicka
and Bailey Willis; 1,066 specimens; Cat. Nos. 263762-962.
Stone implements, from various localities; collected by A. Hrdlicka;
478 specimens; Cat. Nos. 264174-237.
Stone implements, from valleys of the Río Negro and Río Santa
Cruz; collected by C. W. Washburne; 267 specimens; Cat. Nos.
281821-49.

    B. Brazil:

Objects and fragments of pottery from Maranhão Island, Amazon
valley; collected by J. B. Steere; 42 specimens; Cat. Nos.
36526-45.
Large burial vases and pottery vessels from Marajo Island; collected by E. M. Brigham, 1881; 21 specimens; Cat. Nos. 59073-
90.
    C. Chile:

Stone and wooden implements from an island off the coast; received
from the American Museum of Natural History; 14 specimens;
Cat. Nos. 273485-98.
    D. Colombia:

Pottery vases from a grave in Antioquia Province; collected by
Thomas Herran; 2 specimens; Cat. Nos. 147237 8.
Earthenware vessels from Antioquia Province; collected by Thomas
Herran; 23 specimens; Cat. Nos. 35776-98.
Pottery from graves at Cundinamarca and Antioquia; collected by
Thomas Herran; 8 specimens; Cat. Nos. 60751-8.
Gold ornaments from graves at Antioquia; collected by Thomas
Herran (purchased); 26 specimens; Cat. Nos. 148148-74.

    E. Ecuador:

Parts of clay figurines, stone beads, and ornaments from La Plata
Island; collected by G. A. Dorsey; an exchange from Field
Columbian Museum, Chicago; 22 specimens; Cat. Nos. 195585-
606.

Stone chairs and pillar from Province of Manabí; collected by A. Santos; 3 specimens; Cat. Nos. 204904-6.

F. Peru:

Copper objects, earthenware vessels, and stone objects from ancient graves at Cuzco; received from the Field Columbian Museum in exchange; 83 specimens; Cat. Nos. 210352-431.

Pottery vessels, stone objects, and copper ornaments and implements from Cuzco; received from the Field Columbian Museum in exchange; 41 specimens; Cat. Nos. 195526-66.

Woven fabrics from Ancón; collected by G. H. Hurlbut for the Bureau of American Ethnology; 4 specimens; Cat. No. 133385.

Textiles—Inca and pre-Inca; collected by C. A. Pope; 45 specimens; Cat. Nos. 233276-320.

Textiles (mostly), spindle shafts, reeds, bone implements from vicinity of Lima; presented by Mrs. J. P. Compton; 15 specimens; Cat. Nos. 365240-49.

Pottery vessels from Chanchán, Trujillo Valley, Cuzco, and Puno; collected by Dr. B. S. Stephenson; 36 specimens; Cat. Nos. 378101-36.

Textiles, weaving implements, gold and silver ornaments, etc. from Ancón; collected by George Kiefer (1884); 144 specimens; Cat. Nos. 73996-4039.

Textiles and pottery (chiefly) from Ancón; collected by W. E. Curtis (1884); 182 specimens; Cat. Nos. 132473-654.

Textiles, bags, baskets, and gourds containing foodstuffs, from Ancón; collected by W. E. Curtis; 44 specimens; Cat. Nos. 133028-71.

Textiles and pottery from various sites; collected by A. Hrdlicka (1919); 352 specimens; Cat. Nos. 307601-842. See A. Hrdlicka, "Some Results of Recent Anthropological Exploration in Peru, " Smithsonian Miscellaneous Collections, LVI, pp. 1-16.

Woven slings from Nasca and Lomas; collected by A. Hrdlicka (1919); 155 specimens; Cat. Nos. 301001-55. See Philip Ainsworth Means, "Distribution and Use of Slings in Pre-Columbian America, with Descriptive Catalog of Ancient Peruvian Slings in the United States National Museum, " Proceedings United States National Museum, LV (1919), pp. 317-49.

Pottery vessels from Ancón; collected by W. H. Jones and George Kiefer (1884); 127 specimens; Cat. Nos. 107363-489.

Pottery vessels from Marachanga; collected by W. H. Jones; 20 specimens; Cat. Nos. 111224-43.

Pottery, textiles, and stone and metal implements from Chicama Valley; collected by A. Hrdlicka; 80 specimens; Cat. Nos. 264239-319.

Ethnological Collections

Collections are most complete for the Pueblo, Navajo, Apache, and Californian tribes, and for the rain-forest tribes of northeastern South America. Specimens are indexed according to their geographical origin, tribal source, and collector. Descriptive data for each specimen are entered on an individual card identified by the catalogue number of the specimen. The collections have been described in various museum publications. A list of some of the works follows:

Conzemius, Eduard. "Ethnographical Survey of the Miskito and Sumu Indians of Honduras and Nicaragua, " Bureau of American Ethnology, Bulletin 106 (1932).

Densmore, Frances. "Yuman and Yaqui Music, " Bureau of American Ethnology, Bulletin 110 (1932).

Hough, Walter. "Fire-Making Apparatus in the United States National Museum, " Proceedings United States National Museum, LXXIII (1928), 1-72.

Hrdlicka, Ales. "Anthropological Work in Peru in 1913. With Notes on the Pathology of the Ancient Peruvians, " Smithsonian Miscellaneous Collections, LXI (1914).

Krieger, Herbert W. "Material Culture of the People of Southeastern Panama, Based on Specimens in the United States National Museum, " United States National Museum, Bulletin 134, pp. 1-141.

McGee, W. J. "The Seri Indians, " Seventeenth Annual Report of the Bureau of American Ethnology, 1895-96, pp. 1-128.

McGuire, J. D. "A Study of the Primitive Methods of Drilling, " Annual Report, United States National Museum, 1894, pp. 623-756.

__. "Pipes and Smoking Customs of the American Aborigines, Based on Material in the United States National Museum, " Annual Report, United States National Museum, 1897, pp. 351-645.

Mason, Otis T. "Aboriginal American Basketry: Studies in a Textile Art Without Machinery, " Annual Report, United States National Museum, 1902, pp. 171-548.

Roth, Walter E. "An Introductory Study of the Arts, Crafts, and Customs of the Guiana Indians, " Thirty-eighth Annual Report of the Bureau of American Ethnology, 1916-17, pp. 25-720.

__. "Additional Studies of the Arts, Crafts, and Customs of the Guiana Indians, with Special Reference to Those of Southern British Guiana, " Bureau of American Ethnology, Bulletin 91 (1929).

Safford, W. E.   "Narcotic Plants and Stimulants of the Ancient Americans, " Smithsonian Annual Report, 1916, pp. 387-424.

Stevenson, James.   "Illustrated Catalogue of the Collections Obtained from the Indians of New Mexico and Arizona in 1879, " Second Annual Report of the Bureau of American Ethnology, 1880-81, pp. 307-422.

__. "Illustrated Catalogue of the Collections Obtained from Pueblos of Zuni, New Mexico, and Wolpi, Arizona, in 1881, " Third Annual Report of the Bureau of American Ethnology, 1881-82, pp. 511-94.

Stirling, M. W.   "Historical and Ethnographical Material on the Jívaro Indians, " Bureau of American Ethnology, Bulletin 117 (1938).

Natural Sciences

Birds:

There are large collections of birds from Mexico, Costa Rica, the Bahamas and Panama, and from Puerto Rico, Hispaniola, and Cuba; a good deal of material from Argentina, Paraguay, Guatemala, Brazil, and Venezuela; and scattered collections from the other countries.

Fishes:

There are large collections from Panama, Cuba, Hispaniola, Puerto Rico, and the Bahamas; miscellaneous lots from Brazil, Argentina, Mexico, Chile, and other countries.

Insects:

There are large collections of Coleoptera from many localities in the Greater and Lesser Antilles, extensive series of Lepidoptera from Mexico and Central America, many Diptera from Mexico, Central America, Brazil, and Peru, and scattered series in all orders from the whole of Latin America.

Mammals:

There are extensive collections from Mexico and the Canal Zone additional material of some extent from Guatemala, and large collections of bats and other species from Cuba, Jamaica, Hispaniola, Puerto Rico, and elsewhere in the West Indies.   The museum has

considerable material from Colombia and Peru and from scattered
localities in Central and South America. In 1944, the Colombian
collection was increased by the material gathered by Philip
Hershkovitz between 1941 and 1943.

Marine invertebrates:

There are large collections from the Bahamas, Cuba, Puerto
Rico, Panama, and the entire coastal area of South America; also
extensive material from Baja California.

Minerals:

The most complete collections come from Mexico, which has
received special attention. There is considerable material from
northern Chile, particularly of the rarer mineral species. The
museum possesses small collections from Brazil and Bolivia.

Mollusks:

The museum owns large collections of mollusks from the
Bahamas, Jamaica, Cuba, Puerto Rico, and Hispaniola. There is
considerable material from the west coast of Mexico, and scattered
series from elsewhere.

Paleontology:

There are foraminiferal collections of some extent from
Mexico, Cuba, and Venezuela; also miscellaneous invertebrates
from Cuba, Hispaniola, and Puerto Rico, with scattered materials
from elsewhere.

Plants:

The largest collections of plants come from Mexico, Costa
Rica, Panama, Colombia, Venezuela, Brazil, Cuba, Puerto Rico,
Hispaniola, and Jamaica; but there are miscellaneous collections
from elsewhere. In recent years a great deal of material has been
collected in Colombia and Venezuela. In 1942, the Instituto de
Ciencias Naturales de Colombia sent the museum 2,169 specimens
of plants, collected mostly by Dr. José de Cuatrecases.

Reptiles and amphibians:

The museum has large collections from Mexico, Panama,
Cuba, Hispaniola, Puerto Rico, and Brazil; scattered material
from elsewhere.

Textile Museum of the District of Columbia
2330 S Street, NW

The Textile Museum of the District of Columbia has a particularly fine collection of rugs and textiles from Peru. The Peruvian group contains over 500 articles, from the Paracas culture to
the Spanish period. Examples of almost every technique are to be
found: embroidery, tapestry, and works in leather and in gauze.

There are also 15 pieces from Mexico, and 8 from Guatemala.

In addition, the museum owns 21 Spanish rugs from the fifteenth, sixteenth, and seventeenth centuries, and Spanish textiles
from the twelfth, thirteenth, and fourteenth centuries.

United States Department of Commerce
Bureau of the Census

Data for the Hispanic countries are shown in the census reports under country of birth or country of origin, either alone or
in correlation with other subjects. The first federal census of the
population of the United States was taken in 1790, but no inquiry was
made at that census on country of birth of the foreign-born.

Statistics on the country of birth of the foreign-born population of the United States have been included in the census reports,
however, at each census since, and beginning with, 1850, and data
on country of origin of the native white stock of foreign or mixed
parentage since, and beginning with, 1890. The alien population
of the United States, by country of birth, was first presented in
the reports at the census of 1890; statistics on inability to speak
English, in connection with country of origin, at the census of 1900;
year of immigration, by country of origin, at the census of 1930;
and mother tongue, that is language of customary speech in the home
prior to immigration, at the census of 1910. In 1910 and 1920, data
on mother tongue were shown for both the first and second generations of the white population, that is the foreign-born white and the
native white of foreign or mixed parentage; in 1930, these statistics
were presented for the first generation only.

As the census reports have expanded with the growth of population and the increased importance of information on the foreign-
born, data on country of birth have been published in correlation
with many other subjects, and this is particularly true of the 1930
census. In 1930, statistics on country of birth are given under the
following subjects in the general report on population, Fifteenth

Census Reports on Population, Vol. II: Country of Birth of the
Foreign-born; Country of Origin of the Foreign White Stock; Mother
Tongue of the Foreign-born White Population; Citizenship of the
Foreign-born; Year of Immigration of the Foreign-born; Age Dis-
tribution; Marital Condition; Illiteracy; Inability to Speak English.
Data on country of origin alone are presented for states, counties,
and cities of ten thousand inhabitants or more in Fifteenth Census
Reports on Population, Vol. III, Parts I and II.

Two special reports on the foreign-born were also published
in connection with the 1930 census, namely, Age of the Foreign-
born White Population by Country of Birth and Foreign-born White
Families by Country of Birth of Head.

A census of Puerto Rico was taken as of December 1, 1935,
under the auspices of the Puerto Rico Reconstruction Administration,
and under the immediate direction of an official of the Bureau of
the Census in Washington, D.C. The census covered both population and agriculture, and the results were published in bilingual
form in one volume, entitled Census of Puerto Rico: 1935.

The question is often raised as to the national origin of the
entire white population of the United States. The decennial census
distributes the foreign-born white population by country of birth
and the population of immediate foreign parentage by country of
birth of parents but does not give any information regarding the
national origin of those whose European ancestors are more than
two generations removed. The best available data covering the
entire white population are those contained in Table A of the report
Immigration Quotas on the Basis of National Origin, published in
1929 as Senate Document 259. In this report the proportion of the
total white population derived from each country of origin is expressed in terms of the equivalent number of inhabitants. The
totals indicate the national origin of the white population determined
"as nearly as may be" upon the basis of the available data, as required by the provisions of Section 11 (c) of the Immigration Act
of 1924. According to this report, it was estimated that, of the
white population of the United States in 1920, 262,804 persons were
descended from people reporting Portugal as country of birth, and
150,258 from persons reporting Spain as country of birth. Separate
estimates were not presented for other Hispanic countries.

A Census of the Americas in 1950 was undertaken at the
suggestion of Dr. Alberto Arca Parró, former national director
of statistics in Peru. On June 7, 1943 he wrote to the directors
general of statistics in all the American countries suggesting that

a census be taken in every country in 1950. The Inter-American
Congress of Demography, meeting in Mexico City in October of
1943, took up the proposal of Dr. Arca Parró, and asked the Inter-
American Statistical Institute to see about carrying it out. A special committee for this purpose was designated by the Institute in
January of 1946. By this time, the census project had received the
approval of various other organizations. From September 2-16,
1947, about a hundred delegates of twenty-two American nations
met in Washington for the first official session of the Committee
for the Census of the Americas, 1950. This committee was made
up of a technical representative from each nation and observers from
the United Nations, the Pan American Union, and the Food and
Agriculture Organization of the UN.

Following are the figures from each nation—either final or
preliminary:

Argentina. . . . . 15, 893, 827. . . . . May 10, 1947
Bolivia. . . . . .3, 019, 031. . . . . .Sept. 5, 1950
Brazil . . . . .52, 645, 479 . . . . .July 1, 1950
Canada. . . . . 13, 893, 208 . . . . June 1, 1951
Chile. . . . . 5, 930, 809 . . . . April, 1952
Colombia . . . . .11, 537, 000 . . . . May 9, 1951
Costa Rica . . . . 800, 875 . . . . May 22, 1950
Cuba . . . . 5, 823, 187 . . . . .June, 1954
Dominican Republic . . . . . .2, 121, 083. . . . . .Aug. 6, 1950
Ecuador. . . . . 3, 076, 933 . . . . .Nov. 29, 1950
El Salvador . . . . 1, 851, 141 . . . . .June 13, 1950
Guatemala. . . . . 2, 787, 030 . . . . April 18, 1950
Haiti . . . . 3, 111, 973 . . . . .Aug. 7, 1950
Honduras . . . . 1, 368, 605 . . . . .June 18, 1950
Mexico . . . . 25, 581, 250 . . . . June 6, 1950
Nicaragua . . . . 1, 053, 189 . . . . April 15, 1950
Panama . . . . 801, 982 . . . . Dec. 10, 1950
Paraguay . . . . 1, 405, 627 . . . . .Oct. 28, 1950
Peru 8, 509, 846 1952
United States . . . . 150, 697, 361. . . . . .April 1, 1950
Uruguay . . . . 2, 550, 000. . . . . .Dec., 1953
Venezuela. . . . . 4, 985, 716 . . . . .Nov. 7, 1951

Buenos Aires is the largest of the American capitals, with
2, 981, 043 inhabitants. Mexico City is next, with 2, 942, 594; and
Rio de Janeiro third, with 2, 303, 063. Of the remainder, those
over a half million include Washington, D. C. (802, 178) and Bogotá
(643, 187).

A housing census has been undertaken by Canada, Colombia, Costa Rica, El Salvador, Guatemala, Honduras, the United States, and Venezuela; but the total results are known only for Honduras (213,011), El Salvador (133,874, only urban dwellings), and the United States (45,875,000).

Further information on all aspects of the Census of the Americas, 1950, can be had from the Department of Commerce, Bureau of the Census, Washington 29, D.C. See also the article by George C. Compton, "How Many Americans," in the review Americas for July 1949.

United States Department of the Interior

General Land Office:

Of interest to students of Hispanic American affairs are the records pertaining to land titles in existence in Florida, Louisiana Territory, California, and the Southwest at the time of their acquisition by the United States, and the miscellaneous file of "historical maps" dating from the late eighteenth century to the present time.

Among the field notes of surveys of the public domain since 1787 are surveys not only of state boundaries and Indian treaty boundaries but of international boundaries as well.

Division of Territories and Island Possessions:

This division, created in 1934, was entrusted with the records pertaining to Puerto Rico, previously belonging to the Bureau of Insular Affairs of the War Department, and has files relating to its government from 1898 to date. They contain governors' reports, general correspondence, and legislative material. There is also a file of the Gaceta de Puerto Rico for 1874-99. There are papers relating to the Puerto Rico Hurricane Loan Relief Section and the Puerto Rican Relief Commission.

Puerto Rico Reconstruction Administration:

Established in the Department of the Interior in 1935, the administration has as its function the formulation and supervision of a program of work relief and increased employment in Puerto Rico.

United States Department of State
Institute of Social Anthropology
Bureau of Inter-American Affairs

The Institute of Social Anthropology was created as an autonomous section of the Bureau of American Ethnology in the Smithsonian Institution in order to study conditions of social life in Hispanic America and to train Hispanic Americans in the techniques of modern social anthropology. The first director of the institute was Julian H. Steward; he was followed by G. M. Foster. In 1952, the institute was transferred from the Smithsonian Institution to the Bureau of Inter-American Affairs in the Department of State, and its activities ended December 31, 1952. Publications of the institute include the following:

Beals, Ralph L. Houses and House Use of the Sierra Tarascans, 1944.
—. Cheran: A Sierra Tarascan Village, 1946.
Brand, Donald D. Quiroga: A Mexican Municipio, 1951.
Foster, George M. Empire's Children: The People of Tzintzuntzan, 1948.
Foster, Mary L. and George M. Sierra Popoluca Speech, 1948.
Gillin, John. Moche: A Peruvian Coastal Community, 1945.
Holmberg, Allan R. Nomads of the Long Bow: The Siriondo of Eastern Bolivia, 1950.
Oberg, Kalervo. The Terena and the Caduveo of Southern Mato Grosso, Brazil, 1949.
Pierson, Donald. Cruz das Almas: A Brazilian Village, 1951.
Tschopik, Harry, Jr. Highland Communities of Central Peru: A Regional Survey, 1947.
West, Robert C. Cultural Geography of the Modern Tarascan Area, 1948.

United States National Archives

Many records in the National Archives document in detail the relations between the United States and Latin America, Spain, and Portugal, and contain much information on the political, economic, and social development of the Latin American and Iberian peoples during the nineteenth and twentieth centuries. They constitute only a part of the 800,000 cubic feet of permanent valuable records of the United States Government that have been transferred to the National Archives during the last decade and a half from the federal agencies that created them. They consist of photographic, phonographic, and cartographic—as well as documentary—material

The holdings of the National Archives are organized into about 270 record groups, each of which is a major archival unit that usually consists of the records of a single bureau or other major subdivision in an executive department, an independent agency, or several related small agencies.

Most of the records in the National Archives are available for use by the public, but some may be used only by special authorization. Requests for information should be addressed to the General Reference Section, National Archives and Records Service, General Services Administration, Washington 25, D. C. Information about the records and some material from them will be furnished by mail, but the National Archives cannot undertake detailed research in rendering reference service. Regulations for the use of materials in the National Archives were published in the Federal Register on March 28, 1953, and reprints are available upon request.

The best published source of information about the records in the National Archives is the Guide to the Records in the National Archives (Washington, D. C., 1948, 684 pp.), which describes accessions through June 30, 1947. Records received since then are described in the National Archives Accessions, commencing with number 31. Additional information about the records is provided in inventories, special lists, reference information papers, and other finding aids*; some of those that relate to specific record

----

*Some Reference Information Papers, issued by the National Archives, describe material in many record groups relating to certain geographic areas belonging to Spain and Portugal or Latin America. They are entitled Materials in the National Archives Relating to: The Caribbean Region (No. 7, June 1942, 10 pp.); Brazil (No. 8, June 1942, 6 pp.); The West Coast of South America (No. 9, July 1942, 8 pp.); Spanish Possessions in Africa (No. 14, December 1942, 5 pp.); Portuguese Possessions in Africa and the Atlantic (No. 18, April 1943, 4 pp.); Cuba (No. 34, 1948, 13 pp.); The Dominican Republic (No. 35, 1948, 11 pp.); Haiti (No. 40, 1949, 13 pp.); and The Mexican States of Sonora, Sinaloa, and Baja California (No. 42, 1952, 16 pp.). A guide to materials in the National Archives relating to Latin America is being prepared. For a description of some cartographic records in the National Archives relating to Mexico, see Manuel Carrera Stampa, "Mapas y Planos Relativos a México, " Revista Iberoamericana, XII (February 1947), 153-98.

groups are cited elsewhere in this report. * The National Archives
has edited and reproduced on some 4,700 rolls of microfilm many
important bodies of research material in its custody, some of which
relate to Latin American and Iberian affairs. Positive prints of
these microfilms may be purchased. The microfilm publications
available are described in the List of National Archives Microfilm
Publications (Washington, D.C., 1953). Photostat and microfilm
reproduction of records may also be ordered from the National
Archives.

The records in the National Archives are described herein
as parts of the established record groups to which they belong.
As this report is not intended to be an exhaustive study, only those
record groups that have important and valuable materials relating
to Latin America, Spain, and Portugal are discussed. Some documents relating to these areas, of course, may be found in many
other groups. Record groups containing information about many
political, economic, and social matters for half a century or more
are described before those dealing with more limited or special
subjects for shorter periods; those that relate to the two World
Wars are described last.

Because of the major role played by the Department of State
in the conduct of foreign affairs, its records contain a greater
volume of material relating to Latin America, Spain, and Portugal
than exists in the records of any other federal agency. The General Records of the Department of State, Record Group 59, 1774-
1949, consist of diplomatic and consular correspondence, communications to and from representatives of foreign governments, papers
of special agents, general correspondence of the department with
persons in the United States and abroad, territorial papers, and
other materials that were accumulated by the department in Washington. They contain information about nearly all phases of our
relations with Latin America, Spain, and Portugal.

---

* National Archives publications are issued in limited editions for distribution to government agencies, archives and libraries
educational institutions, and scholars. For a list of publications
currently available write to the Exhibits and Publications Section,
National Archives and Records Service, General Services Administration, Washington 25, D. C.

The diplomatic and consular correspondence of the Department of State in the National Archives that relates to Latin American and Iberian affairs consists mainly of (1) communications ("dispatches") to the department from ambassadors, ministers, and consuls of the United States; (2) communications ("instructions") to these foreign-service officials from the department; and (3) communications ("notes") exchanged between the department and Latin American, Spanish, Portuguese, and other diplomatic and consular officials who were in the United States. For the period up to August 1906, there are in the National Archives at least 750 volumes of diplomatic dispatches for the twenty Latin American republics, of which more than 180 volumes relate primarily to Mexican affairs, more than 140 to Spain, and more than 40 volumes to Portugal. There are approximately 1,000 volumes of dispatches from some 180 consular posts in Latin America, Spain, and Portugal, of which more than 130 volumes relate to the consular district of Havana, Cuba, 1799-1906.

These dispatches, instructions, and notes constitute the most important single body of materials in the National Archives for students of Latin American, Spanish, and Portuguese affairs. Considerable information will be found in them relating to such broad subjects as the achievement of independence by the Latin American countries from Spain and Portugal; the economic and social progress of Latin American and Iberian nations in the nineteenth and twentieth centuries; the influence of the Catholic Church in Hispanic countries; the participation of these countries in world affairs; the Pan American and the Pan Hispanic movements; and Anglo-American interest in Latin America. Valuable data about significant leaders of Latin America, Spain, and Portugal are available to students who take the time to search in the records.

For an analysis and description of some of these records, see Claude H. Van Tyne and Waldo G. Leland, Guide to the Archives of the Government of the United States in Washington, 2d ed. (Washington, D.C., 1907), pp. 2-56, and Samuel F. Bemis and Grace G. Griffin, Guide to the Diplomatic History of the United States (Washington, D.C., 1935), part II, chaps. i and ii. Documents in the National Archives relating to the early national history of Argentina have been described in Carlos A. Quesada Zapiola, Catálogo de la Documentación Referente a las Relaciones Diplomáticas entre Estados Unidos de América y la República Argentina, 1810-1830 (Buenos Aires, 1948), 210 pp. See Luis Gonzalo Patrizi, "Documentos Relativos a Venezuela que se conservan en The National Archives de Washington," Boletín de la

Academia Nacional de la Historia (Caracas, 1949), 32: pp. 81-98, for similar summarization, on a much smaller scale, for the period 1835-1906. Gonzalo Patrizi limits himself to a treatment of dispatches from American representatives in Venezuela. Héctor García Chuecos, in his Catálogo de Documentos Referentes a Historia de Venezuela y de América, Existentes en el Archivo Nacional de Washington (Caracas, 1950), 88 pp., briefly abstracted the contents of several hundred diplomatic notes, 1810-34, exchanged between United States Secretaries of State Monroe, John Quincy Adams, Clay, and others, on the one hand, and diplomatic representatives of Gran Colombia in the United States such as Manuel Torres and José María Salazar, on the other. *

The records relating to special agents who were appointed by the President of the United States to carry on negotiations with Latin American countries and with Spain and other European colonial powers concerning their Latin American possessions are bound, as a rule, with the regular diplomatic and consular correspondence. † Much of the correspondence from these agents, however, constitutes a separate series known as "Special Agents." This series contains documents relating to the activities of Poinsett, Worthington, Green, and others, who were sent to various Latin American countries during their wars of independence to make contacts with revolutionary governments.

The general correspondence of the department consists of communications received from individals in the United States and abroad (in the "Miscellaneous Letters" series) and communications addressed by the department to persons in the United States and other countries (in the "Domestic Letters" series). The letters in each series are arranged chronologically, and communications

---

*For names of diplomatic and consular agents of the United States in Latin America, Spain, and Portugal, see the United States Official Register, 1816-59, and the Official Register of the Department of State, 1860___.

† See Henry M. Wriston, Executive Agents in American Foreign Relations (Baltimore, 1929) for references to materials regarding these agents; and National Archives, List of Documents Relating to Special Agents of the Department of State, 1789-1906, compiled by Natalia Summers (Washington, D.C., 1951).

relating to Latin America, Spain, and Portugal are interspersed
throughout both series.*

Material relating to those parts of the United States that
were formerly under the sovereignty of Spain and Mexico constitute
a part of the territorial papers in Record Group 59, General Records of the Department of State. Of particular interest are the
territorial papers of Florida, which include data both on East and
West Florida and on Cuba; Orleans, relating to Louisiana; New
Mexico, referring to the area now included in the present states
of New Mexico and Arizona; and California (although never a
territory of the United States). These papers include some documents dated before the areas became parts of the United States.
Closely related to territorial materials in this record group are
originals and transcripts of documents obtained by Jeremy Robinson
and Nicholas P. Trist in Cuba, 1830-35, ‡ that pertain to the Spanish
territories of Florida and Louisiana.

Records maintained by the diplomatic and consular establishments of the United States in Latin America, Spain, Portugal, and
other countries have been transferred to the National Archives in
accordance with directives of the Department of State. They are in
Record Group 84, Records of the Foreign Service Posts of the Department of State, which contains information about activities at
practically every diplomatic post and about 225 consular posts of
the United States in Latin American countries, Spain, and Portugal.
To a certain extent the materials in the group duplicate those described in Record Group 59, General Records of the Department
of State. The original instructions, with enclosures, sent by the
Department of State to its embassies, legations, and consulates,

---

*For an analysis of some miscellaneous and domestic letters
relating to Latin America, Spain, and Portugal in the National Ar-
chives, see Department of State, Calendar of Miscellaneous Letters
Received by the Department of State from the Organization of the
Government to 1820 (Washington, D.C., 1897) and Miscellaneous
Registers C and D, Being an Index to the Miscellaneous Corres-
pondence to and from the Department of State, from June 1, 1870, to
January 1, 1874 (Washington, D.C., 1874).

‡ See Clarence E. Carter, comp., The Territorial Papers of
the United States (Washington, 1934__). This compilation was begun as a publication of the Department of State; in May 1950 responsibility for the work was transferred to the National Archives.

form a series in Record Group 84 that is of more value to students of Latin American and Iberian affairs than a parallel one in Record Group 59. The following series in Record Group 84 are not duplicated to any appreciable extent elsewhere: communications from diplomatic posts to the consular establishments within their jurisdiction and the replies thereto; general correspondence engaged in by diplomatic and consular representatives with officials and citizens of Latin American states, Spain, and Portugal; and records relating to United States citizens and property in those countries.* The post records have not, as yet, been used extensively by scholars and therefore offer great possibilities for research to students of the relations between the United States and Latin American and Iberian countries.

Treaties, conventions, protocols, and other international agreements that have been concluded between the United States and Spain, Portugal, countries of Latin America, and other states during the nineteenth and twentieth centuries are found primarily in Record Group 11, General Records of the United States Government. These records concern peace and friendship, commerce and navigation, consular privileges, extradition, boundaries, claims, arbitrations, international communications, patents, copyrights, trade-marks, commercial travelers, cessions or leases of territory, and other matters of mutual interest to the United States, to the Latin American states, and to Spain and Portugal. Completed (or "perfected") pacts are available for every one of the twenty Latin American republics and for Spain and Portugal.

Treaties that have been negotiated by the United States but that have not become effective are also of concern to students of Latin American, Spanish, and Portuguese affairs. Some of these uncompleted ("unperfected") treaties relate to the slave trade in Latin America, the proposed construction of an interoceanic canal at one of the points along the Isthmus of Panama from Tehuantepec southward, the proposed cession or lease of strategic areas in Lat-

*See National Archives, List of Foreign Service Post Records in the National Archives, compiled by Mark G. Eckhoff and Alexander P. Mavro (1952, 42 pp.), and John P. Harrison, "The Archives of United States Diplomatic and Consular Posts in Latin America, " in the Hispanic American Historical Review, XXXIII (February 1953), 168-83, reprinted by the National Archives.

in America to the United States, and the proposed settlement of
outstanding claims. *

Records relating to the settlement of boundary and other disputes involving countries and citizens of the Western Hemisphere
contain information of considerable value to students of Latin
American, Spanish, and Portuguese affairs. This material is in
Record Group 76, Records of Boundary and Claims Commissions
and Arbitrations. The definition and description of the southern
boundary of the United States involved both Spain and Mexico,
and records pertaining thereto are in this group. From time to
time the President and other officials of the United States have been
called upon to serve as arbitrators in disputes between other governments, often over boundary questions arising in the Western
Hemisphere. There is material pertaining to the boundary arbitrations between Argentina and Paraguay, Costa Rica and Nicaragua,
Argentina and Brazil, and Chile and Peru; and to United States
mediation in the war between Spain and Peru, Chile, Bolivia, and
Ecuador, 1866-72. Some of the manuscript, annotated, or printed
maps of South America, which date from the seventeenth through
the nineteenth centuries, are highly significant historically as well
as cartographically in that they portray the increase in knowledge
of the geography of the continent. Claims of American citizens
against governments of Latin America, Spain, and Portugal have
usually been settled by claims commissions, by arbitration, or by
outright award. The records resulting from these activities provide considerable information about economic and other conditions
in these countries. †

---

* For treaties that have been published see the Treaty Series
and the Statutes at Large. Also see William M. Malloy, comp.,
Treaties, Conventions, International Acts, Protocols and Agreements Between the United States of America and Other Powers,
1776-1909, 2 vols. (Washington, D. C., 1910); and Hunter Miller,
ed., Treaties and Other International Acts of the United States
(Washington, 1931___). The State Department has published List
of Treaties Submitted to the Senate, 1789-1934 (1935) and List of
Treaties Submitted to the Senate 1789-1931 Which Have Not Gone
into Force (1932).

† See a list in the National Archives Guide, p. 306, of those
countries with which the United States concluded agreements for the
settlement of claims. For information about various claims commissions and arbitrations, see John Bassett Moore, History and
Digest of the International Arbitrations to Which the United States

Record Group 43, Records of United States Participation
in International Conferences, Commissions, and Expositions,
contains materials of especial value to the student of Latin American
and Iberian social, economic, and political matters. Among them
are records relating to the Panama Congress (1826), the First
International Conference of American States at Washington, D.C.
in 1889 and subsequent Pan American conferences, the American
International Monetary Commission at Washington in 1891, the
Washington Conference on Central American Affairs (1922-23),
the Eighth American Scientific Congress at Washington in 1940,
the Inter-American High Commission (1916-34), the American-
Mexican Joint Commission, created in 1916, and the electoral
missions sent from the United States to Nicaragua in 1928-32.
There are also materials relating to the countries under discussion among the records pertaining to the Louisiana Purchase
Exposition at St. Louis in 1904, the Brazilian Exposition in Rio
de Janeiro in 1922-24, and the International Exposition at Seville
in 1929. See National Archives, Preliminary Inventory of Records
of United States Participation in International Conferences, Commissions, and Expositions, compiled by H. Stephen Helton (1955).

The records of the United States Senate, 1789-1948, which
constitute Record Group 46, contain important material relating
to Latin America, Spain, and Portugal, some of which is not
available in print. * The records contain information relating to

_____

has been a Party, 6 vols. (Washington, D.C., 1898), and Digest
of International Law, 8 vols. (Washington, D.C., 1906), as well
as W. R. Manning, Arbitration Treaties Among the American
Nations to the Close of the Year 1910 (New York, 1924). For the
texts of agreement see Miller and Malloy, op. cit. Legislation
relating to the commissions is printed in the Statutes at Large and
publications of many of the commissions are listed in the Superintendent of Documents, Checklist of United States Public Documents,
1789-1909, pp. 909-21, 1508-14, and 1525-30.

*See National Archives, Preliminary Inventory of the Records
of the United States Senate, compiled by Harold E. Hufford and
Watson G. Caudill (1950, 284 pp.), for references to records of
the United States Senate relating to Latin America, Spain and
Portugal.

treaties and conventions negotiated with Latin American states and with European powers pertaining to their Latin American possessions; declarations of war against Mexico and against Spain; the acquisition of the Virgin Islands and territories formerly under the sovereignty of Spain and Mexico; the lease of the Panama Canal Zone; United States intervention in Cuba, Panama, Nicaragua, Haiti, the Dominican Republic, and Mexico; and the protection of American life and property in Latin America. Maps and atlases pertaining to Latin America form separate units in this record group.

Records of many standing committees of the United States Senate, particularly the Committees on Foreign Relations and Naval Affairs, contain material of interest to students of Latin American and Iberian affairs. From time to time the Senate established special committees to deal with particular phases of United States relations with Latin America. Some of these were the Select Committee on the Mexican Boundary Commission, the Select Committee on Mexican Claims, the Select Committee to Inquire into the Claims of American Citizens Against the Government of Nicaragua, the Select Committee on Construction of a Nicaraguan Canal, the Committee on Relations with Cuba, the Committee on Interoceanic Canals, the Committee on Pacific Islands and Porto (sic) Rico, and the Special Committee to Investigate the Administration of the Virgin Islands.

Records of the United States House of Representatives, most of which—from the First through the Eightieth Congresses, 1789-1948—are in the National Archives, constitute Record Group 233. These records, similar to those of the Senate and its committees, contain some materials relating to Latin America, Spain, and Portugal. House records less than fifty years old, except those that have been printed as bills, reports, or documents, may not be examined except upon order of the House.

General records of the Department of Justice, Record Group 60, covering the years 1817-1946, contain information of value relating to Latin America, Spain, and Portugal. The records deal with such subjects as the recognition of Latin American governments, intervention in the affairs of Latin American states, the interpretation of treaty provisions and statutes giving effect to them, boundary questions, the acquisition of new territory formerly under the dominion of Spain and Mexico, the government of these acquired areas, private land claims, blockades, piracy, prizes, the laws of war, and neutrality statutes. Some specific topics about which information is available in these records are the Lat-

in American struggles for independence; the prevention of fili-
bustering from United States ports against the governments of
Latin America; the settlement of land claims in California (at least
25 feet of records), Florida, and the former Louisiana Territory;
the controversy between the Federal Government and the State of
Texas over that state's northern boundary; questions arising out
of the Spanish-American War, particularly those relating to claims
against Spain that originated largely in Cuba (at least 75 feet); and
matters pertaining to the Panama Canal and the Isle of Pines.

Various aspects of the United States—Latin American and
United States—Iberian relations are dealt with in Record Group 80,
General Records of the Department of the Navy, for the period 1804-
1944. Reports received by the Secretary of the Navy contain valuable information about conditions in Latin American countries,
especially during periods of political tension or of United States
intervention in the affairs of those countries. Records relating to
the search for strategic naval bases near possible interoceanic
canal routes will interest students of naval diplomacy. Economic
data relating to critical and strategic raw materials in Latin American countries and to domestic and international communication and
transportation systems and facilities are also available in this record group.

The Naval Records Collection of the Office of Naval Records
and Library, 1775-1942 (Record Group 45), in the National Archives
consists of most of the records of the Office of the Secretary of the
Navy prior to 1886, some records of other Navy offices, bureaus,
shore establishments, and boards and commissions, as well as
materials acquired from other sources. Separate bodies of material
of interest to students of Latin America, Spain, and Portugal include letters copied from various sources relating to Panama, the
Dominican Republic, Haiti, Cuba, Nicaragua, and Honduras, 1903-
11; records of the Rio Grande Station, 1875-79 (1 vol.) and of the
Havana Naval Station, 1899-1903 (8 vols.); and correspondence of
the Naval War Board, 1898 (4 vols.), concerning naval operations
in the Spanish-American War. Other important materials relate
to the activities of naval squadrons and expeditions in Latin American
and Iberian waters, particularly those pertaining to the Brazilian
Squadron, the West Indies Squadron, and the several Atlantic squadrons. For detailed references to records relating to Latin America
in Record Group 45, see National Archives, Preliminary Checklist of the Naval Records Collection of the Office of Naval Records
and Library, 1775-1910, compiled by James R. Masterson (December 1945, 149 pp).

Valuable hydrographic information relating to Latin America, Spain, and Portugal is in Record Group 37, Records of the Hydrographic Office. These records in the National Archives, 1811-1943, relate to surveys in Latin American waters and contain hydrographic and navigational information collected by the Hydrographic Office of the United States. Among the materials relating to Latin America are charts based largely on surveys undertaken by United States naval officers in the Caribbean, along both coasts of Central America, and along portions of the coasts of South America; charts prepared by the office relating to the Caribbean and Central and South America, based chiefly upon data collected from foreign hydrographic bureaus; and aerial photographs of the coastal and navigational areas off Cuba, Central America, Venezuela, and the Galapagos Islands. See National Archives, Preliminary Inventory of the Records of the Hydrographic Office, compiled by Walter W. Weinstein (1952, 17 pp.).

Foreign agriculture is documented primarily in Record Group 166, Records of the Office of Foreign Agricultural Relations, 1901-46. Those records pertaining to Latin America, Spain, and Portugal consist mainly of reports originating with agricultural trade commissioners, agricultural attachés, special agents, and regular consular officials of the United States in those countries. The reports deal with practically every aspect of the agricultural economy and with general economic conditions as well. Reports are available, for example, on agriculture in general, crop conditions, crop-reporting systems, farm management, export policy, land policy, labor, marketing, mechanization, and transportation and shipping, as well as on numerous agricultural crops and products of Latin America, Spain, and Portugal. See National Archives, Preliminary Checklist of Reports Received by the Office of Foreign Agricultural Relations, Department of Agriculture, compiled by Lois Bell Miller (June 1945, 149 pp.).

Records maintained by Spain and Denmark in their former insular possessions of Puerto Rico and the Virgin Islands are now, in accordance with international treaties between the United States and those nations, in the possession of the government of the United States. Some of them are in the National Archives. Record Group 55, Records of the Danish Government of the Virgin Islands, contain records, 1672-1917, chiefly in Danish, which originated for the most part with the Danish administration of St. Thomas, St. John, and St. Croix. They represent a selection (1,200 feet) by the United States Survey of Federal Archives, in co-operation with the government of the Virgin Islands, of material of historical value not needed for official use. They contain legislative, judicial, police, military records, and administrative records such as governors' orders and other official papers, tax lists, and records of commissions

Part of the records of the Spanish government in Puerto Rico were moved between 1899 and 1901 from San Juan, Puerto Rico, to the Library of Congress in Washington. Most of them were returned to Puerto Rico. The remaining records (about 150 feet), dating from 1750 to 1898, were transferred in 1943 from the library to the National Archives, where they constitute Record Group 186, Records of the Spanish Governors of Puerto Rico.

A number of record groups in the National Archives contain substantial information pertaining primarily to political, military, and economic affairs during periods when the United States intervened in Latin America.* Some records of the former Bureau of Insular Affairs of the War Department in the National Archives, which are in Record Group 126, Records of the Division of Territories and Island Possessions, relate to the administration of Cuba by the United States Military Government of Cuba, 1898-1902, and the fiscal control of the Dominican Republic by the United States Dominican Customs Receivership, 1905-35. A detailed analysis of these records is given in several finding aids issued by the National Archives.† Record Group 98, Records of the United States Army Commands, contains the records of the War With Spain Army Corps, 1898, part of which operated in Cuba, and records of the territorial commands in Cuba and Puerto Rico, 1898-1902, together with post records for camps, posts, and stations established on those islands. In addition, there are the records of the Army

---

*See National Archives, Materials in the National Archives Relating to Military Government by the United States in the Caribbean Area, 1898-1934, compiled by Kenneth Munden and Forrest L. Foor (Reference Information Circular, No. 26, February 1944, 14 pp.).

† See National Archives, Records of the Bureau of Insular Affairs Relating to the United States Military Government of Cuba, 1906-1909, a List of Selected Files, compiled by Kenneth Munden (February 1943, 43 pp.); List of Records of the Bureau of Insular Affairs Relating to the Dominican Customs Receivership, 1905-1940, compiled by Kenneth Munden (May 1943, 29 pp.); and Records of the Bureau of Insular Affairs Relating to Puerto Rico, 1898-1934, a List of Selected Files, compiled by Kenneth Munden and Milton Greenbaum (March 1943, 47 pp.).

of Cuban Pacification, 1906-9. Record Group 165, Records of the War Department General Staff, contains materials relating to Cuba that were compiled largely by the Army of Cuban Pacification, 1906-7; reports from military attachés in Latin America; and maps relating to Cuba in the Spanish-American War and to the Mexican Punitive Expedition. See National Archives, Preliminary Checklist of the Records of the War Department General Staff, compiled by Elizabeth Bethel (April 1945, 31 pp.).

Records of the United States Marine Corps, Record Group 127, contain materials relating to Latin America. They include correspondence; intelligence, operational, and other reports; and photographic and cartographic records dealing with Marine Corps operations in Mexico, Guatemala, Honduras, Nicaragua, Costa Rica, Panama, Cuba, Haiti, and the Dominican Republic. Some operational reports deal with air missions in Nicaragua, 1927-32; and maps prepared or used by the Marine Corps relate principally to areas in Central America, Haiti, and the Dominican Republic. Records of the Marine detachments at Guantánamo, Cuba (1911-14), in Haiti (1915-34), and in Nicaragua (1928-30) were brought to the United States and are now in the National Archives (50 feet). See National Archives, Preliminary Checklist of the Records of the United States Marine Corps, 1798-1944, compiled by Fred G. Halley (September 1946, 21 pp.); and Preliminary Inventory of the Cartographic Records of the United States Marine Corps, compiled by Charlotte M. Ashby (1954, 17 pp.).

All the records of the Military Government of Cuba, 1898-1903, except those that were turned over to the government of Cuba, were shipped from Cuba to Washington in 1903. Subsequently these records and those of the late Military Government of Cuba, an agency established in 1903 in Washington, D.C. to settle unfinished business, were transferred to the National Archives, where they form Record Group 140 (341 feet). They include correspondence and other papers of the Military Governor, the Auditor for the Island of Cuba, and the Collector of Customs; and incomplete records of the Director of the Census, the Captain of the Port of Havana, the Chief Engineer of Havana, the Engineer of the Department of Cuba, the Superintendent of Schools, the Inspector General, the Director General of Posts, the Disbursing Quartermaster, and the Judge Advocate General. See National Archives, Preliminary Checklist of the Records of the Military Government of Cuba, 1899-1903, compiled by Margareth Jorgensen (September 1946, 52 pp.).

In 1906, in the face of an insurrection in Cuba, the United

States established the Provisional Government of Cuba, and the small amount (16 feet) of its records, 1906-9, now in the National Archives, constitutes Record Group 199. These records consist primarily of correspondence of the Provisional Governor and reports and other papers of various officials of the Provisional Government relating to its fiscal responsibilities. One series of reports of the Provisional Government's National Board of Health deals with cases of yellow fever and other contagious diseases in Cuba.

Some records of the Dominican Customs Receivership, which was established in 1905 to adjust the foreign and domestic debt of the Dominican Republic and avert threatened intervention by other foreign powers, were shipped to Washington, D. C. at the termination of the receivership and were turned over to the National Archives. They make up Record Group 139 and consist primarily of correspondence of the General Receivers and other officials of the receivership relating to its operations, 1905-41 (33 feet). In 1916, the United States established the Military Government of Santo Domingo in the Dominican Republic under the direction of the Navy Department. After the Military Government was terminated in 1924, about 50 feet of its records were brought to Washington, D. C. and are now in the National Archives as a part of Record Group 38, Records of the Office of the Chief of Naval Operations. Primarily they consist of correspondence, reports, executive orders, regulations, and proclamations, 1917-24, of the Military Governor; files (4 feet) of the Gaceta Oficial, 1904-24, an official publication of the Dominican Republic that was continued by the Military Government; and some letters of Sumner Welles, American High Commissioner, 1922-23. Both the records of the Dominican Customs Receivership and the Military Government of Santo Domingo contain valuable data relating to general economic conditions, improvement of roads, sanitation and medicine, and commerce and transportation in the Dominican Republic during the period of United States intervention. See National Archives, Preliminary Checklist of the Records of the Military Government of Santo Domingo, 1916-1924, compiled by Lyman Hinckley (September 1945, 10 pp.).

Record Group 38, Records of the Office of the Chief of Naval Operations, includes other significant materials, most important of which are the reports of naval attachés and intelligence officers to the Department of the Navy concerning almost every Latin American country, Spain, and Portugal. They contain information about a variety of naval, military, political, economic, and scientific matters.

Shortly after the "Tampico Incident" in April 1914, the United States established the Military Government of Veracruz. Some (47 feet) of its records, 1914, were shipped to the United States and now constitute Record Group 141 in the National Archives. They pertain to the government of the city and port of Veracruz by the United States Army and consist of correspondence and orders of the Military Governor and other officials, and reports, legal opinions, and other material relating to customhouse operations, court proceedings, civil claims, sanitation, the food supply, and the maintenance of order.

Intervention by the United States in Haiti resulted in the appointment of the President's Commission for the Study and Review of Conditions in the Republic of Haiti. Its records, a part of Record Group 220, Records of Presidential Committees, Commissions, and Boards, consist principally of correspondence, reports, petitions, minutes, and materials assembled by the Commission in Haiti relating to the political aspects of United States intervention, the effectiveness of United States administration, and social and economic conditions in Haiti. See the Report of the President's Commission for the Study and Review of Conditions in the Republic of Haiti (Washington, D.C., 1930).

The records of several canal commissions in the National Archives provide background data for students concerned with the establishment of the state of Panama, the lease of the Panama Canal Zone by the United States, the construction of the Panama Canal, and the proposed construction of another interoceanic canal across the Isthmus of Panama. Record Group 185, Records of the Panama Canal, consists chiefly of records of the first Isthmian Canal Commission, 1899-1902, with a small quantity of records of the Nicaragua Canal Commission, 1897-1902, and some maps of two French Panama Canal companies, 1881-1900. In addition to correspondence, fiscal materials, and engineering notes, the records include topographic maps, profiles, geological sections, soundings, drawings of locks, tracings, blueprints, and cross sections.

Most of the permanent, noncurrent records of emergency agencies of World Wars I and II are in the National Archives. Detailed information about records of World War I federal agencies is available in the Handbook of Federal World War Agencies and Their Records, 1917-21 (Washington, D.C., 1943, 666 pp.). Records of the World War II period that are in the National Archives and elsewhere are described in detail in the Federal Records of World War II, 2 vols. (Washington, D.C., 1950-51). Other details about World Wars I and II documentation may be obtained from National Archives, Reference Information Circulars Nos. 11 and 39, entitled respectively Materials Relating to Latin America in Records of Emergency War Agencies, 1917-19, in the National Archives (October 1942, 17 pp.) and Materials in the National Archives Relating to World War II (1949, 31 pp.). Some of the records for these two periods that are concerned with Latin America, Spain, and Portugal are described below.

Records of the Committee on Public Information, Record Group 63, deal with the establishment of journalistic contacts abroad and the distribution of propaganda favorable to the United States and the Allies in newspapers and periodicals in foreign countries during World War I. The activities of the committee in Latin America and in Spain were handled by its New York office and branches in Buenos Aires, Lima, Mexico City, Santiago de Chile, and Madrid.* Material concerning Latin America consists of incomplete files of press releases in Spanish and Portuguese and of mimeographed releases in English and Spanish that were issued by the committee's Latin American offices.

A large quantity and a wide variety of information concerning the internal and external economy of Latin American countries during World War I is available in Records of the United States Food Administration, Record Group 4, in the National Archives. Included are materials relating to the production and supply of essential foods like sugar, meat, and wheat in Latin American countries, the admission of agricultural laborers to the United States from Mexico, the provision of water transportation for bringing essential commodities from Latin America, and the efforts by Latin American governments to check smuggling, profiteering, and hoarding. Of particular interest are the records of the Food Administration's Mexican Relations Division, and Office of the Federal Food Administrator for Puerto Rico. †

---

*For a discussion of these activities, based in part on records of the Committee in the National Archives, see James Mock, "The Creel Committee in Latin America," Hispanic American Historical Review, May 1942, 22: 262-79.

†See National Archives, Preliminary Inventory of the Records of the United States Food Administration, 1917-1920, Part I: The Headquarters Organization (July 1943, 335 pp.) and G. Leighton La Fuze, "The Puerto Rico Food Administration and Its Organization and Papers," Hispanic American Historical Review, August 1941, 21: 499-504.

Since one of the two principal functions of the United States Sugar Equalization Board, Inc., was to buy and distribute the 1918-19 crop of Cuban sugar, a considerable part (137 feet) of its records, 1918-26, relate to this activity. These records, which constitute Record Group 6, contain information relating to economic relations between the United States and Cuba during World War I and the subsequent period of reconstruction. A small amount of material relates to coffee imports, which were controlled by the board for a time.

Material concerning maritime commerce during World War I with Latin America—and to a lesser extent with Spain and Portugal—is in Record Group 32, Records of the United States Shipping Board. These records include those of its subsidiary, the United States Shipping Board Emergency Fleet Corporation. They contain information about the servicing of companies operating in the West Indies and on the east and west coasts of Mexico and Central and South America; the blacklisting of firms trading with the enemy; the disposition and operation of enemy vessels off Brazil, Cuba, Peru, and Uruguay; the treatment accorded German shipping in neutral countries such as Argentina, Colombia, and Mexico; the construction of ships and port facilities in Latin American countries; and British interference with American trade in Argentina. Of particular interest are the informational materials gathered by Ricardo de Villafranca, statistician, translator, and interpreter in the Fleet Corporation's South American Trades Department. Students of shipping relating to Spain and Portugal will be interested in records relating to the Atlantic and the Mediterranean—South Atlantic Conferences in this record group. A preliminary inventory of the records of the United States Shipping Board has been compiled by Forrest R. Holdcamper and will be published by the National Archives.

Interspersed throughout Record Group 61, Records of the War Industries Board, mainly 1918-19, is a significant amount of material relating to Latin America.* Some of it is filed by country, but most is in commodity files. These files contain correspondence, memoranda, statistical tables and graphs, work sheets, mimeographed releases, press clippings, and pamphlets concerning particular products and manufactures. They are invaluable sources of information on the shipment of machinery and other industrial

---

*See National Archives, Preliminary Inventory of the War Industries Board Records (May 1941, 134 pp.).

equipment from the United States to Latin America and on the history of the production, exportation from the country of origin, importation into the United States, and consumption in North America and Europe of many Latin American raw materials of great importance in wartime. Some of the commodities about which there is information are coal, copper, nitrates, tin, and wool.

Valuable sources of information for students of economic, informational, and social relations between the United States and Latin America during World War II are in Record Group 229, Records of the Office of Inter-American Affairs, which contains records (395 feet) of that agency and its predecessor and successor units, 1940-47. The office concerned itself with such matters as basic economy, economic development, transportation, science and education, the press, motion pictures, and radio. Its records include correspondence, memoranda, reports, press releases, drawings, and minutes of meetings, and relate to a variety of transportation projects in Latin America, including transportation facilities, missions, quotas, and priorities; the activities of the United States Railroad Mission in Mexico; the radio, press, motion picture, and other activities of the co-ordination committees that were established in practically every Latin American capital; the preparation of pamphlets and posters for distribution throughout Latin America; and the authorization of all kinds of projects in Latin America that would promote hemispheric solidarity and help win the war. In addition, in this record group are sets of En Guardia (in Spanish, Portuguese, and French) and the American News Letter, both of which were issued by the Office of Inter-American Affairs; and English, Spanish, and Portuguese versions of sound motion pictures and sound recordings produced or released by the office for distribution in Latin American countries for information and propaganda purposes. See National Archives, Preliminary Inventory of the Records of the Office of Inter-American Affairs, compiled by H. Stephen Helton (1952, 138 pp.).

Records of the Foreign Economic Administration, Record Group 169, contain records of that agency and its predecessor and successor agencies, 1939-47. Many materials of value to students of economic warfare, lend-lease, and other economic aspects of the World War II period affecting the Latin American countries, Spain, and Portugal are in these records. Probably the most valuable are the files (118 feet) of the Pan American Branch, 1942-45, which include materials relating to the development and control of economic warfare programs in Latin America, reports from Foreign Economic Administration missions, correspondence with

private individuals and firms and with Latin American embassies
relating to foreign trade with Latin America, and reports of the
United States Purchasing Commission on mica production in Brazil.
Other materials in this record group include studies and memoranda
on contract termination policies for Latin America, reports relating to a survey of Axis connections with Latin American tele-
communication companies, reports on petroleum programs for
Spain and Portugal, "Statements of Cargo Availability" supplied
for certain commercial cargoes destined for Latin American ports
via sea freight (188 feet), and reports by field technicians concerning the procurement of wild rubber in Mexico and Central and South
America, together with maps, sketches, and photographs (8 feet).
See National Archives, Preliminary Inventory of the Records of
the Foreign Economic Administration, compiled by H. Stephen
Helton (1951, 180 pp.).

University of Miami
University Library
Coral Gables

The University of Miami has only recently begun the development of its collection of research materials in Hispanic studies.
Consequently, the amount of source material is relatively small.

The holdings of the University Library have been based largely on two acquisitions, the personal library of Dr. A. Curtis Wilgus
and that of a private scholar in the field of Hispanic bibliography.
These, together with subsequent smaller purchases, have resulted
in a useful working collection of bibliographical materials ranging
from such large works as Medina's Biblioteca Hispano-Americana
and Nicholas Antonio's Bibliothecas to smaller more specialized
works such as Ximeno Gallardo, Escritores del Reyno de Valencia,
2 vols., 1747-49, and Pérez Pastor's La Imprenta en Medina del
Campo. Mention should also be made of the recent acquisition of
Colección de documentos inéditos relativos al discubrimiento,
conquista y organización de las antiguas posesiones españolas de
América y Oceania.

The Hispanic American Institute, which co-ordinates research
in Hispanic fields, publishes the University of Miami Hispanic
American Studies. The most important library material in the
institute is the personal library of Dr. Ralph S. Boggs, which is
housed in stacks adjacent to Dr. Boggs' office. Although this collection covers the entire field of folklore, it is strongest in Hispanic materials. It is open to use by qualified scholars at all times.

The university works closely with the Historical Society of South Florida, and the University Library offers the society's publication Tequesta on current exchange.

The N. B. T. Roney collection of maps of Florida and the Antilles, housed in the library, consists of about 100 maps of the sixteenth through the nineteenth centuries.

Although the Mark F. Boyd library of material on Florida and the West Indies has not yet been transferred to the University Library, it is listed in the official catalogue, and until the books are housed at the university, they are available by mail through the university to any scholar who has a need for them.

University of Florida
Florida Historical Society
Gainesville

The only Hispanic material to be mentioned are the Panton Leslie papers. This collection consists of hundreds of papers and business items belonging to the Indian trading firm of Panton Leslie and Company, Pensacola, Spanish West Florida. During the second Spanish occupation of Florida, this firm carried on an extensive Indian trade, particularly with the Creek Indians.

University of Florida
P. K. Yonge Library of Florida History
Gainesville

The P. K. Yonge Library now includes the photostats from Spanish archives of the former Florida State Historical Society. The society was founded in 1922, chiefly through the interest of Mr. John B. Stetson, Jr., aided by Mrs. Jeanette Thurber Connor. Through the agency of Miss Irene A. Wright, a survey of manuscripts on Spanish Florida in the Archivo General de las Indias was begun. This was followed by the photostating of manuscripts by Miss Wright, and for the next six or seven years she continued to survey manuscripts in the different fondos. There are in the collection well over 100,000 pages of material, all on Spanish Florida. The first document dates from 1519, and the last from about 1819. These papers provide the documentary background for the history of Spanish Florida. The collection is especially rich in government material (including many expedientes), ecclesiastical papers, and social and economic papers. It contains rich material for the study of the Florida missions, of the relations with the

Indians, of British attacks from the north, and of military matters, including expeditions of various kinds. From this material, Mrs. Connor published several volumes of Spanish Colonial Records. It was the policy of the society to publish the old Spanish manuscripts in both the original and the page-for-page translation. Among these may be mentioned a facsimile of the book of the unknown Gentleman of Elvas, together with a new translation of it made by James A. Robertson (Deland, 1932-33). A 2-volume set of Luna Papers was edited, with a translation, by Herbert I. Priestly; and The Reconnaissance of Pensacola Bay, 1689-1693 was printed under the auspices of the Quivira Society in 1939, the documents having been translated and edited by Irving A. Leonard, mainly from the photostats owned by the Florida State Historical Society.

Printed works in the P. K. Yonge Library include:

[Barcia Carballido y Zúñiga]. Ensayo cronológico para la historia
general de la Florida. Madrid, 1723.
Diario de las operaciones...Galvez. [Havana, 1781 (?)]
Herrera, Antonio de. Historia general de los hechos de los
castellanos en las islas Tierra Firma del mar oceano, 9 vols.
in 4. Madrid, 1726.
Historia de la conquista del Nuevo Mundo, 9 vols. Madrid, 1829.
Ogilby, John. America... London, 1671.
Recopilacion de leyes de los reynos de las Indias, 4 vols. Madrid,
1756.
Smith, Buckingham. Coleccion de varios documentos para la
historia de la Florida y tierras adjacentes. London, 1857.
Stevens, John. The Spanish Rule of Trade to the West Indies
(transcript). London, 1702.
Two Friends, the narrative of a voyage to the Spanish Main in the
ship Two Friends. London, 1819.
White, Jos. M. A New Collection of Laws...of Great Britain,
France and Spain Relating to Concessions of Land, 2 vols.
Philadelphia, 1839.

Microfilms in the P. K. Yonge Library include the following, the originals of which are in the Library of Congress: Correspondence of Governors Justis and Montiano of East Florida with the Captain General and Governor of Cuba, 1737-41, 664 pp.; East Florida Papers, 1783-1821, microfilms of 1,355 selected documents; Woodbury Lowery transcripts and notes from Spanish sources relating to Florida, 1551-1680, 10 vols. From the General Records of the Department of State in the National Archives, there are microfilms of Florida Territorial papers, 1811-21, 11 vols. Other microfilms include: Archivo General de Indias, Papeles de Cuba (copies of legajos, complete—1874, 1875, 1876A, 1876B, 1789, 1790, 1791A, 1791B, 1797, 1792, 1856), a total of 5,998 documents; Buckingham Smith transcripts from Spanish archives, 1500-1786, 3,300 sheets (originals in New York Historical Society); Establecimiento de las Indios Panzacolenos, 1764, 134 sheets (from Archivo General de México); Sigüenza y Góngora's Reconocimiento ...Baia de Pansacola, 1693, 52 sheets (from Newberry Library); Documents pertaining to the history of Florida in Mexico City archives, 1,200 sheets including calendar (collected by Rev. Charles W. Spellman); and microfilms of photostats and transcripts of Spanish material relating to the southeastern United States in the archives of the North Carolina Historical Commission, 1650-1783, 16,000 pages from A. G. I., A. H. N., and Simancas (with calendar).

University of Florida
University Library
Gainesville

The reasonably adequate resources for studies in Hispanic fields to be found in the University of Florida Library are primarily a matter of growth during the past decade. Such progress as has been achieved has been without outside funds and with no large donations of books. The first sizable gift, and a very helpful one, was that of a thousand or so volumes from the Latin American library of the late Joseph B. Lockey. They were preponderantly monographs but included also several valuable collections, notably handsomely bound sets of the "Biblioteca Ayacucho" (63 vols.), directed by Blanco Fombona, of Documentos para la historia de la vida pública del Libertador... (14 vols.), edited by José F. Blanco and R. Azpurúa, and of the Memorias del General O'Leary (32 vols.).

Another thousand or more volumes were later acquired by inheritance from the university's Institute of Inter-American Affairs and from the personal library of A. Curtis Wilgus, when the institute was superseded by the School of Inter-American Studies and Dr. Wilgus became its director in 1951. These consisted largely of government documents, periodicals, and learned journals from Latin America, a valuable addition to previous holdings. Other donations have so far consisted mainly of small but greatly appreciated gifts from individuals such as those from former Latin American students or from visitors to the annual Caribbean conferences.

It is obvious that this library can never seek to rival the old
and rich holdings of, for instance, the John Carter Brown Library,
but it has undertaken to make one unique contribution. As the
Farmington Plan representative for the Caribbean area, the University of Florida Library is responsible for the acquisition of all
current publications of Caribbean imprint of presumed research
value. Excluded by the agreement are government documents,
newspapers, periodicals, maps, and sets of books in progress
before the plan went into effect. While the library counts it a
privilege to assume this responsibility, it does find that for its own
immediate needs some of the materials not included by the plan
are extremely important and constitute a large portion of current
acquisitions.

Through the efforts of the serials division, there are now
becoming available to the economics or other interested departments the principal anuarios estadísticos, various of the boletines
estadísticos, and some of the publications of the bancos centrales.
The memorias or corresponding annuals of other governmental
units, especially of foreign affairs, of commerce or interior or
treasury, and of agriculture, are received from a number of countries. Argentina, Colombia, Venezuela, and the Dominican Republic have been particularly generous, so that some files now
extend back a number of years. Full information concerning the
results of the Census of the Americas is being obtained as rapidly
as it becomes available. The library receives the diario oficial
from five countries: Colombia, Mexico, Chile, Peru, and Uruguay.

Of non-book materials a noteworthy acquistion is that of
some 70,000 feet of microfilm copy of the diplomatic correspondence of the United States and Latin America, one of the largest
collections outside the National Archives. Its value is enhanced
by the fact that the library has a complete microfilm copy of the
New York Times from its founding (1851) to date. For earlier
years a supplement useful in some respects is the microfilm of
The Times of London, 1785-1850.

Latin American newspapers currently received are El Día
from Montevideo, Correio do Povo from Pôrto Alegre, Tribuna
Libre from El Salvador, El Mundo from San Juan, Puerto Rico,
La Nación from Ciudad Trujillo, and from Cuba, El Mundo, The
Havana Post, and El Diario de la Marina. For the last named
the library's subscription is being changed to microfilm.

Recognizing that serial publications contain much source
material not otherwise available, the library plans to expand sys-

tematically and extensively its holdings in Latin American periodicals. Of those currently received whose chief fields are the humanities or the social sciences, there are a number of which the library has complete bound sets to date: Boletín bibliográfico de antropología (Mexico, 1937___), Filosofía y letras (Mexico, 1941--), Revista Hispanica Moderna (New York and Buenos Aires, 1934--), Revista de Historia de América (Mexico, 1938--), Revista Nacional (Montevideo, 1938--).

Among those for which the holdings are sizable but as yet incomplete are: Atenea (Chile, 1924--), Boletín de Historia y Antigüedades (Colombia, 1902--), Cuadernos Americanos (Mexico, 1942--), Repertorio Americano (Costa Rica, 1919--), Revista Brasileira de Estatística (Rio de Janeiro, 1940--), Revista de las Indias (Colombia, 1936--), Revista do Serviço Público (Rio de Janeiro, 1937--), Revista Iberoamericana (Mexico, 1939--), Revista Nacional de Cultura (Venezuela, 1938--), Sur (Buenos Aires, 1931--), Tiempo (Hispanoamericano) (Mexico, 1942--), Universidad de la Habana (Cuba, 1934--).

The library possesses more or less complete files of most of the major periodicals relating specifically to Hispanic studies published in the United States, England, and France, and it is attempting to fill the more serious gaps. The current list of Spanish journals in the fields of history, political science, and literature is reasonably good, and there is a complete bound set to date of the Boletín de la Real Academia de la Historia (Madrid, 1877--). Portugal is better represented by periodicals than in other respects.

The library has a creditable bibliographical collection to which additions are constantly being made. Noteworthy Latin American possessions are the Medinas, of which the library has secured most of the major bibliographies except the Biblioteca Hispano-Chileno, and practically all the Imprentas except that of the Antiguo Virreinato del Río de la Plata. Most of the other basic general or national bibliographies have also been obtained or are on order, and current national bibliographical and archival publications, particularly of the Caribbean area, are being acquired as rapidly as possible.

From the Iberian peninsula, Spanish bibliographies, retrospective and current, are rather strong, but there is a general dearth of Portuguese materials. It is hoped that the arrival of the numerous volumes of the Grande Enciclopédia Portuguesa e Brasileira will remedy somewhat the general weakness where

Portugal is concerned. For that country, the single outstanding
item in the collection is the set (4 parts in 18 volumes) of the
Academia das Sciencias de Lisboa's Portugaliae Monumenta Historica a Saeculo Octavo...usque ad Quintumdecimum (Olisipone,
Typis Academicis, 1856-1917).

Resources for the study of Spanish history and literature,
from the medieval period on, are reasonably good but scarcely
extraordinary. Sets of documents include the four major Colección
[es] de documentos inéditos...(DII, 42 vols.; DIU, 25 vols.; DIH,
14 vols.; DIE, 113 vols.) with few missing volumes. There are
at least partial sets of lesser collections and almost all of the
Colección de Libros Raros y Curiosos que Tratan de América
(22 vols.).

For studies involving Spanish legislation, the most valuable
sets include the Actas de las Cortes de Castilla, 1563-1713 (26
vols., of which vol. 24 is lacking), and those of Aragón, Valencia,
and Catuluña, also in 26 volumes.

For nineteenth-century Spain, there are most of the successive
sets of the Diario de Sesiones de las Cortes Constituyentes from
1836 to 1878. For the recent Spanish Republic, there is the 26-
volume set covering 1936-1939, Legislación del Nuevo Estado.

Of comparable materials relating to Spanish America, there
are—besides the Recopilación de Leyes and divers relaciones,
memorias, etc.—several complete or partial sets of actas de cabildo
and of documents and archival records of different areas and periods.
Chile, Cuba, and Mexico are to date the best represented numerically, followed by Argentina and by small sets or scattered volumes for other countries, chiefly of the Caribbean area. Basic
materials on the constitutional history of Argentina in the early
nineteenth century are excellent. For legislation of the national
period, Mexico is the best represented, especially in the pre-
revolution period. Colombia is next, and for several of the other
Caribbean countries there are significant holdings.

In the matter of documents, the Brazilian collection is best.
The library has 60 of the 69 volumes of the Annaes de Biblioteca
Nacional, issued at Rio de Janeiro from 1876 up to 1950, and
practically all of the 93 volumes of the Documentos históricos
published up to 1951, also by the Biblioteca Nacional. The library
was recently given twenty-odd of the earlier 35 volumes of the
rather general set with the series title "Documentos brasileiros."
Medina's Colección de Documentos Inéditos para la Historia de

Chile is complete, and there are scattered volumes of the Colección de Historiadores... Of the Publicaciones del Archivo General de la Nación which Mexico began to publish in 1910, the library has the 36 volumes through 1945.

As for general coverage, the best is that of the sixteenth-century period of conquest and settlement, for which are available the major collections of legislation and works of the chroniclers and the contemporary historians.

Travel literature, mostly in reprint editions, is fairly strong. Holdings include Dampier's A New Voyage Around the World, 3d ed., (London, 1698-1709; Navarrete's Colección de... Viages y Descubrimientos...; several titles by Hakluyt and Works Issued by the Hakluyt Society (1st series, 100 vols.; 2d series, 99 vols.; extra series, 12 vols.). There are 40 or more volumes of Humboldt's works, of which the most important is the somewhat rare Voyage de Humboldt et Bonpland, 23 vols. (Paris, 1805-34).

As for the study of Hispanic literatures, the library provides reasonably good resources for that of Spain, but so far those of Spanish America and of Brazil are at best spotty. Histories of national literatures are fairly adequate, and there are sets of the more or less "complete works" of several authors of varying importance. These include Andrés Bello, Gertrudis Gómez de Avellaneda, José Martí, Eugenio M. de Hostos, Francisco Pimentel, Enrique José Varona, Medardo Rivas, Aluizio de Azevedo, and Machado de Assis. Of the innumerable "bibliotecas" which in so many cases include subject matter of various fields, our most nearly complete sets are of "Grandes escritores argentinos," "Biblioteca de cultura peruana," "Biblioteca de escritores de Chile," and about 200 of the earlier volumes of the wide-ranging "Biblioteca pedagógica brasileira." Next in order would come the "Biblioteca aldeana de Colombia" and "Escritores mexicanos."

Basic geographic coverage and materials, including the 1:1,000,000 map of Hispanic America, are fairly good. They are strongest for the Caribbean area.

For Latin American studies in sociology, economics, political science, geography, and anthropology, the fact that independence upon periodicals and government publications as compared with book materials is relatively heavy is being borne in mind in the acquisition program. The same is more or less true for several fields in which the development of university courses as they relate to Latin America and of relevant library holdings is in its initial stages   agriculture,   art,   music,   medical   sciences,   and public health.

University of Florida
University Library
Inter-American Bibliographical and Library Association
Gainesville

The association, at first called the Inter-American Biblio-graphical Association, was created in Washington, D. C., in May 1930, largely through the efforts of Dr. E. Gil Borges, at that time the assistant director of the Pan American Union, to-gether with the co-operation of Dr. James A. Robertson and other persons interested in bibliographical activity. One of the first steps was the creation of an organizing and co-ordinating commit-tee, which included Dr. H. H. B. Meyer, Dr. Ernest K. Jones, Mr. James B. Childs, Mr. John T. Vance, Dr. A. Curtis Wilgus, Mr. E. Kletsch, and Dr. E. Gil Borges. Meetings of this com-mittee were held every two weeks in the Pan American Union or the Library of Congress, and organization and activities were dis-cussed. As a result, the constitution was drawn up and printed, dues were fixed for individuals at one dollar per year, and the com-mittee proceeded to encourage the preparation of bibliographies by various individuals which the Pan American Union distributed to the association members.

However, it soon became evident that the association's in-terests included libraries, and, in December 1934, the name of the organization was changed to the Inter-American Bibliographical and Library Association, with headquarters in the Library of Con-gress until 1951, when the move to Gainesville took place.

The objects of the association are the promotion of inter-American bibliographical work by means of co-operation with bibliographical organizations, bibliographical experts, libraries, and other related agencies in all countries of the Americas; and the lending of assistance in research work on subjects relating thereto.

At first membership was limited to persons nominated by the committee. Later all persons interested in the aims of the organization, wherever they might reside, were invited to join.

In 1935, the association began to print an annual volume in what is known as Series I. The following volumes have thus far appeared in this series:

Boggs, Ralph S. Bibliography of Latin American Folklore, 1940.
Davis, Harold E. Latin American Leaders, 1949.
—. Makers of Democracy in Latin America, 1945.
—. Social Science Trends in Latin America, 1950.
Gosnell, Charles F. Spanish Personal Names, 1938.
Kantor, Harry. A Bibliography of Unpublished Doctoral Disser-
    tations and Masters Theses Dealing with the Governments,
    Politics, and International Relations of Latin America, 1953.
McLean, Malcolm. El Contenido literario de "El Siglo Diez y
    Nueve, " 1940.
Nichols, Madaline W. The Gaucho: Cattle Hunter, Cavalryman,
    Ideal of Romance, 1942.
Roberts, Sarah E. José Toribio Medina: His Life and Works, 1941.
Rubio, David, and Sullivan, M. C. A Glossary of Technical Li-
    brary and Allied Terms in Spanish and English, 1936.
Topete, José Manuel. A Working Bibliography of Latin American
    Literature, 1952.
Weil, Felix J. Argentine Riddle, 1944.
Wilgus, A. Curtis. Histories and Historians of Hispanic America,
    1936.

    With the inception of the annual convention, it was felt neces-
sary to publish the papers submitted for the convention. Thus in
1938, Series II, called the Proceedings, was begun.

    A third series consists of works which the association wishes
to sponsor. The only volume which has appeared in this series is
Raymond L. Grismer's A Reference Index to Twelve Thousand
Spanish American Authors, which has also been issued in a Spanish
edition.

    A new (1954) bibliographic quarterly, Doors to Latin America,
issued by the Inter-American Bibliographical and Library Association and the University of Florida, is compiled by A. Curtis Wilgus.
It lists a wide variety of works on Latin America along with informative notes.

Monastery of San Bernardo
Miami

    The monastery of San Bernardo in Sacramenia, Old Castile,
was built in 1141 by Alfonso VII. This Cistercian monastery was
sold by the Spanish government in 1835 to a local farmer, who used
it as a barn. It was purchased by William Randolph Hearst in 1920
for $500,000. He had it shipped to the United States, stone by stone,
in 10,751 crates, but the depression of 1929 prevented him from

rebuilding it in California. For almost thirty years, the crates
stood in San Francisco's Golden Gate Park, but after Hearst's
death, when the materials were offered virtually without cost to
anyone who would undertake to reconstruct the convent, it proved
impossible to raise the necessary funds in California. Two Ohio
businessmen, E. Raymond Moss and William S. Edgemon, there-
upon bought the materials and, with great care, re-erected the
convent thirty miles north of Miami, Florida, where it was opened
to the public in 1954.

John and Mable Ringling Museum of Art
Sarasota

There are 28 paintings in the Spanish section of the collection at the John and Mable Ringling Museum of Art. They represent chiefly the great Spanish painters of the seventeenth century.

Among the most important canvases are: 2 portraits by
Velázquez; an "Immaculate Conception" and 3 other canvases by Murillo;
"Christ on the Cross, " by El Greco; "La Madonna de la Leche, "
by Ribera; "The Flight into Egypt, " one of only three known signed
paintings by Pareja; "Saint Joseph and the Infant Christ, " by
Zurbarán; a portrait of the Duchess of Alba by Goya. Other artists represented are Alonso Cano, Antonio Pereda, Juan de Valdés-
Leal, and El Greco's son, Jorge Manuel Theotocopuli. Two portraits
of Mariana of Austria hang side by side: one as a young woman,
by Velázquez; the other as a nun, by Juan Carreño de Miranda.

Among the lesser works of art are a more-than-life-sized
seventeenth-century Spanish polychromed and gilded wood sculptured figure, and several pieces of late fifteenth-century Hispano-
Moresque faience.

Florida State University
Tallahassee

The library of Florida State University has 65 reels of microfilm of East Florida papers (MSS), the originals of which are in
the Library of Congress. It owns Nicolás León's Bibliografía
mexicana del siglo XVIII, 6 vols., 1902-8. It also has the following
works of the Chilean bibliographer José Toribio Medina: Biblioteca
hispanoamericana (1493-1810), 7 vols., 1898-1907; Bibliografía
de la imprenta en Santiago de Chile desde sus orígenes hasta febrero
de 1817, 1939; La Imprenta en Bogotá (1739-1821), 1904; La

166   [Florida]

Imprenta en Guadalajara de México (1793-1821), 1904; La Imprenta
en Guatemala (1660-1821), 1910; La Imprenta en Lima (1584-1824),
1904-7; La Imprenta en México (1539-1821), 8 vols., 1907-12;
La Imprenta en Veracruz (1794-1821), 1904.

The library also owns the following works:

Acosta, José de. Histoire naturelle et moralle des Indes, tant
    orientalles qu'-occidentalles, 1598.
Anghiera, Pietro Martier de. The Historie of the West Indies,
    containing the Actes and Adventures of the Spaniards, 1625.
Casas, Bartolomé de las. Breuissima relacion de la destruycion
    de las Indias, 1552.
___. A Relation of the First Voyages and Discoveries made by the
    Spaniards in America, 1699.
Cortés, Hernando. Historia de Nueva-España, escrita por su
    esclarecido conquistador Hernán Cortés, 1770.
___. Praeclara Ferdinãdi. Cortesii de Noua maris Oceani Hyspania
    Narratio Sacratissimo, 1524.
Díaz del Castillo, Bernal. The True History of the Conquest of
    Mexico, 1800.
Fernández de Oviedo, Gonzalo. L'Histoire naturelle et generalle
    des Indies, isles, et terre ferme de la grand mer oceane, 1556.
Garcilaso de la Vega. Histoire des Incas, 1737.
___. Historia general del Peru trata el descubrimiento del; y como
    lo ganaron los Españoles, 1617.
Herrera y Tordesillas, Antonio de. Description des Indes
    Occidentales, qu'on appelle aujourdhuy le Nouveau monde,
    1622.
___. Historia general de los hechos de los castellanos en las islas
    i tierra firme del mar oceano, 1726-27.
Le Moyne de Morgues, Jacques. Brevis narratio eorum quae
    en Florida Americae provîcia Gallis acciderunt, 1591.
López de Gómara, Francisco. Historia de Mexico, 1554.
Pigafetta, Antonio. Premier voyage autour de monde, 1801.
Ulloa, Antonio de. A Voyage to South America. Describing, at
    large, the Spanish Cities, Towns, Provinces, etc. on that
    Extensive Continent, 1772.

Among the collections owned by the library are:

Biblioteca aldeana de Colombia, vols. 1-100, Bogotá, 1935-36.
Biblioteca de autores españoles, vols. 1-71, Madrid, 1848-1926.
Colección de documentos inéditos para la historia de Hispano-
    América, 14 vols., 1927-32.
Colección de documentos inéditos relativos al descubrimiento,

conquista y organización de las antiguas posesiones españolas de América y Oceania, 42 vols., 1864-84.
Colección de documentos inéditos relativos al descubrimiento, conquista y organización de las antiguas posesiones españolas de ultramar, 2 series, 25 vols., 1885-1932.
Libros de Cabildos de Lima, 16 vols. and 2 index vols., 1534-39, 1544-1611, 1935-47.
Odriozola, Manuel de, comp. Colección de documentos literarios del Perú, 11 vols., 1732-1877.
—. Documentos históricos del Perú, 10 vols., 1863-77.
Peru. Memorias de los virreyes que han gobernado el Perú, 6 vols., 1859.
Ravignani, Emilio. Asambleas constituyentes argentinas, 6 vols., 1813-98.
Sociedad de bibliófilos españoles. Libros publicados, Series 2, 27 vols., 1923-43.
Spain (Ministerio de Fomento). Relaciones geográficas de Indias: Perú, 4 vols., 1881-97.

The library's periodicals include:

Anales de la Universidad de Chile, Series 1-4 (odd vols. in each series), 1872-1946.
Hispanic Review, 1933 to date.
Revista Bimestre Cubana, 1939 to date.
Revista de Archivos, Bibliotecas y Museos, Series 3, vols. 1-51, 1897-1931.
Revista de Filología Española, vols. 1-32, 1914-48.
Revista del Archivo Nacional del Perú, vols. 1-16, 1920-43.
Revue Hispanique, vols. 1-81 (lacks 8 vols.), 1894-1933.

In the map collection of the library may be found:

Twenty world atlases of the seventeenth, eighteenth, and nineteenth centuries, such as the 1612 edition of Ortelius' Theatro del Mondo, Mercator's Atlas (1630), and Atlas Maritimus and Commercialis, published by John Senex in 1728.
Nine regional and national atlases include Thomas Jefferys' West India Atlas (1775) and Antonio García Cubas' Atlas Geográfico, Estadístico e Histórico de la República Mexicana (1858).
Some 75 unbound early maps of Florida and the Caribbean area include representative works from each of the national schools of cartography.
Among current material is the American Geographical Society's Map of Hispanic America, 1:1,000,000, and nautical charts from the U.S. Coast and Geodetic Survey and the Hydrographic Office.

The university museum of Florida State University contains the John and Mary Carter collection of prehistoric Peruvian materials. This collection includes a good selection of Nazca, Chimu, and Mochica wooden, stone, bone, shell, gold, silver, textile, and ceramic pieces. The museum also contains the Bellamy collection of prehistoric Panamanian artifacts. A Panamanian ethnobotanical collection is also available for study. Representative archeological collections of Cuban and Haitian materials are also to be found. Prehistoric Florida materials include those excavated by the department of anthropology of Florida State University, the Florida Geological Survey, and the American Philosophical Society.

Art Institute of Chicago
Chicago 3

Among the Spanish paintings in the Art Institute of Chicago, the following are the most notable:

Bermejo. "A Saint, " ca. 1480.

Goya. "Six Episodes in the Capture of the Bandit Margato by the Monk Pedro de Zaldivia, " ca. 1806; "Hanging of the Monk, " 1810; "Isidoro Máiquez, " ca. 1807.

Greco, El. "Assumption of the Virgin, " dated 1577; "St. Martin and the Beggar, " 1599-1604; "Feast in the House of Simon, " before 1604; "St. Francis and the Skull, " ca. 1594.

Martorell. "St. George and the Dragon, " late 1430's.

Murillo. "Two Monks in a Landscape, " ca. 1645.

Navarre, School of. "The Ayala Altarpiece, with Scenes from the Life of Christ and the Life of the Virgin, " dated 1396.

Picasso. "On the Upper Deck, " 1901; "Woman with Cats, " 1901; "The Old Guitarist, " 1903; "Head of Acrobat's Wife, " 1904; "Woman with Mirror, " 1909; "Henry Kahnweiler, " 1910; "Figure, " 1927; "Still Life, " 1922; "Bathing Woman, " 1927; "Figure" (African period), n.d. ; "Head, " n.d. ; "Musical Instruments, " 1916; "Man with Pipe, " 1916; "Maternity, " 1921; "Mother and Child, " 1921; "Still Life" (drawing with water color), 1907-8.

Velázquez. "The Servant, " ca. 1620; "St. John, " 1620-22; "Job, " 1617.

Zurbarán. "Still Life—Fruit and Flowers, " late 1630's; "San Román, " 1638. In March of 1955, the Art Institue acquired a dramatic "Crucifixion" of Zurbarán in what was hailed as "One of the most remarkable 'recoveries' in art history. " It was originally painted in 1627 for Seville's white-robed Dominicans, was seized by Napoleon's troops in 1807, was presented in 1880 by the Duke of Alba to a Jesuit seminary in Canterbury, and then

disappeared until rediscovered by Daniel Catton Rich, Director
of the Art Institute, who describes it as "one of the greatest
paintings by Zurbarán."

Also represented are Dali, Gris, and Miró.

In the department of decorative arts, Gallery A13 is devoted
to a collection of Spanish Renaissance furniture, silver, vestments,
embroidered altar frontals, statues, and lustered majolica. The
medieval collection includes a large crucifix of polychromed wood,
Catalonian, from the district of Banolas of about 1200. The department also possesses two leather chests of the eighteenth century,
textiles from the twelfth through the nineteenth centuries, and a
large collection of Mexican pottery of the seventeenth through the
nineteenth centuries.

The Art Institute owns prints by the Spanish artists Ribera,
Goya, Fortuny, Zuloaga, Picasso, Dali, Gris, Miró, Quintanilla,
the Mexican artists Posada, Manilla, Orozco, Anguiano, Arenal,
Bracho, Charlot, Chávez Morado, Dosamantes, Escobedo, Méndez,
Ocampo, Zalce, Mora, Pavón, Vázquez, and the Guatemalan artist
Mérida.

The Art Institute acquired in 1955 the famous Edward Gaffron
collection of ancient Peruvian art. It consists of some 750 objects
of earthenware, ceramics, wood, copper, silver, and gold. It was
assembled by the late Dr. Gaffron, who practiced medicine in Lima
for many years. It was exhibited in Berlin from 1912 to 1952.

The Ryerson Library has all of the publications of the Hispanic Society of America and a very full series of monographs on
all important Spanish painters.

In the Burnham Library of Architecture there are 100 or more
titles on various aspects of architecture in Spain.

Of the most important serials and periodicals, the libraries
currently receive 9 from Spain and Portugal and 20 from various
Latin American countries, and have in addition complete runs of a
number of periodicals no longer being published. Holdings are recorded in the Union List of Serials. The libraries have several
hundred titles on the art of Latin America, including a good representation of items in the bibliography entitled A Guide to the Art of
Latin America, edited by Robert C. Smith and Elizabeth Wilder.
There is an active program for the exchange of publications with
major art museums and societies in Spain, Portugal, and Latin
America.

Chicago Natural History Museum
(Formerly Field Museum of Natural History)
Roosevelt Road and Lake Shore Drive
Chicago 5

The Hispanic material in the department of anthropology of the Chicago Natural History Museum consists of 43,052 specimens from Southwestern United States; 18,828 specimens from Middle America, including the West Indies; and 22,970 specimens from South America. These include textiles, pottery, implements, sculpture, clothing, basketry, ornaments, and feathers.

The museum's anthropological expeditions have visited the following countries: Colombia (1922), Ecuador (1941), Guatemala (1928), Mexico (1894), Peru (1925, 1926, 1946). Expeditions have also been sent to the Southwestern United States in 1938, 1939, 1941, 1946, 1947, 1948, 1949, 1950, 1951, 1952, 1953, and 1954.

The staff of the department of botany has devoted much attention to exploring, collecting, and studying plants in many parts of Latin America. As a result, the herbaria, wood collection, and exhibits of the museum are replete with superb collections of specimens, widely used for research by the museum's botanists and others working in scientific institutions here and abroad. In order to facilitate the identification of these plants, the museum sent one of its botanists to Europe for the purpose of studying the early collections deposited there and of securing photographs of type and other historical specimens of tropical American plants. In consequence, the museum has now the largest collection of photographs of types of tropical American plants. Since many of the actual types were destroyed during World War II, this collection has attained a unique status as an irreplaceable center of documentation. The botanical exhibits (models) of economically important and other tropical American plants is unrivaled anywhere in the world.

Botanical expeditions sent out by the Chicago Natural History Museum have visited the following countries: Argentina (1912), Brazil (1912, 1926, 1927, 1929, 1935), Chile (1912, 1925), Costa Rica (1927, 1928), Cuba (1947, 1948, two expeditions in 1949, 1950, 1951, 1952, 1953, 1954), El Salvador (1946, 1947, 1948, 1949, 1950, 1951, 1954), Guatemala (1938, 1939, 1940, 1941, 1942), Honduras (1946, 1947, 1948, 1949, 1950), Mexico (1894, 1906, 1937, 1938), Nicaragua (1946, 1947, 1948, 1949, 1950), Panama (1923, 1927, 1928), Peru (1912, 1922, 1923, 1924, 1925, 1926, 1927, 1928, 1929, 1948), Venezuela (1941, 1942, 1944, 1945, 1953, 1954, 1955).

In the field of physical geology, mineralogical collecting exped

tions to Brazil were made in 1922 and 1923 by the late O. C. Far-rington. A similar expedition to South America was conducted by the late H. W. Nichols in 1926. In 1944 the eruptive stages of the famous Paricutín volcano in Mexico were studied by P. O McGrew and representative rock specimens were collected. Specimen collecting and studies of the post-eruptive stages of Paricutín were made by S. K. Roy in 1953. During the years 1950-51 and 1954, studies concerning physical features of the volcanoes and lacustrine sediments of El Salvador were conducted by S. K. Roy. This work was done in co-operation with the Tropical Institute of El Salvador.

In the field of vertebrate paleontology, expeditions to famous fossil-bearing strata of Argentina and Bolivia were conducted by E. S. Riggs from 1922 to 1926. Other important fossil mammals were collected in Honduras by P. O. McGrew in 1941-42. During 1952-53 and 1954, Bryan Patterson studied the extensive fossil collections in two major museums of Argentina. This study was sponsored by the Guggenheim Foundation.

Geological expeditions sent by the museum have visited the following countries: Argentina (1922, 1926, 1952, 1954), Bolivia (1924, 1926), Brazil (1922, 1923, 1926), Chile (1926), El Salvador (1950, 1954), Honduras (1941), Mexico,1895, 1944, 1953), Peru (1926), Uruguay (1926).

In zoology, some of the more important projects of the department have dealt with the southern half of South America, where the Marshall Field Expeditions of 1922-24 and 1926-27, and the Magellanic Expedition of 1939-40 concentrated their efforts under the direction of W. H. Osgood.

Following is a summary of the museum's expeditions in zoology to Latin America: Argentina (1922, 1926), Bolivia (1915), Brazil (1913, 1915, 1922, 1926, 1937), Chile (1922, 1939), Colombia (1911, 1948), Costa Rica (1908, 1910), Dominican Republic (1894), Ecuador (1929), El Salvador (1951), Guatemala (1903, 1906, 1933, 1948), Honduras (1923), Mexico (1901, 1903, 1933, 1945, 1948, 1951, 1952, 1953, 1954), Nicaragua (1903, 1906), Panama (1928), Paraguay (1926), Peru (1912, 1922, 1939, 1945, 1953), Uruguay (1922, 1926), Venezuela (1908, 1909, 1910, 1911, 1913, 1920, 1931).

Publications

Anthropological series:

Collier, Donald. Cultural Chronology and Change as Reflected in the Ceramics of the Viru Valley, Peru (1955).

Collier, Donald, and Murra, John V. Survey and Excavations in Southern Ecuador (1943), 108 pp.

Dorsey, G. A. The Arapaho Sun Dance (1903), 228 pp.

—. A Bibliography of the Anthropology of Peru (1898), 154 pp.

Holmes, W. H. Archeological Studies Among the Ancient Cities of Mexico. Part I. Monuments of Yucatán (1895), 138 pp. Part II. Monuments of Chiapas, Oaxaca and the Valley of Mexico (1897), 200 pp.

Kroeber, A. L. Proto-Lima: A Middle Period Culture of Peru (1954), 157 pp.

Laufer, Berthold. The American Plant Migration. Part I. The Potato (1938), 132 pp.

Martin, Paul S. Archaeological Work in the Ackmen-Lowry Area, Southwestern Colorado, 1937 (1938), 88 pp.

—. Lowry Ruin in Southwestern Colorado (1936), 216 pp.

—. Modified Basket Maker Sites, Ackmen-Lowry Area, Southwestern Colorado, 1938 (1939), 196 pp.

—. The SU Site. Excavations at a Mogollon Village, Western New Mexico, 1939 (1940), 98 pp.

—. The SU Site. Excavations at a Mogollon Village, Western New Mexico, Second Season, 1941 (1943), 174 pp.

Martin, Paul S., and Rinaldo, John B. Sites of the Reserve Phase, Pine Lawn Valley, Western New Mexico (1950), 177 pp.

—. The SU Site, Excavations at a Mogollon Village, Western New Mexico, Third Season, 1946 (1947), 110 pp.

—. Turkey Foot Ridge Site, A Mogollon Village, Pine Lawn Valley, Western New Mexico (1950), 162 pp.

Martin, Paul S., Rinaldo, John B., and Antevs, Ernst. Cochise and Mogollon Sites, Pine Lawn Valley, Western New Mexico (1949), 323 pp.

Martin, Paul S., Rinaldo, John B., and Bluhm, Elaine. Caves of the Reserve Area (1954), 228 pp.

Martin, Paul S., Rinaldo, John B., Bluhm, Elaine, Cutler, Hugh C., and Grange, Roger, Jr. Mogollon Cultural Continuity and Change. The Stratigraphic Analysis of Tularosa and Cordova Caves (1952), 528 pp.

Mason, J. Alden. Archaeology of Santa Marta, Colombia. The Tairona Culture, Part I. Report on Field Work (1931), 130 pp. Part II. Section I. Objects of Stone, Shell, Bone, and Metal (1936), 142 pp. Section II. Objects of Pottery (1939), 146 pp., 85 plates, 26 figures.

Thompson, J. Eric. Archaeological Investigations in the Southern Cayo District, British Honduras (1931), 148 pp.

—. Ethnology of the Mayas of Southern and Central British Honduras (1930), 191 pp.

Botanical series:

Ames, Oakes, and Correll, Donovan S.   Orchids of Guatemala
(1952-53), 2 vols.

Bartram, Edwin B. Mosses of Guatemala (1949), 442 pp.

Cuatrecasas, José. Contributions to the Flora of South America
(1950-51), 2 vols.

Dahlgren, B. E. Index of American Palms (1936), 456 pp.

Killip, Ellsworth P.   The American Species of Passifloraceae
(1938), 2 vols.

Macbride, J. Francis. Flora of Peru (in continuation, 1936—), 12 vols.

—. Spermatophytes, Mostly Peruvian (1929-31), 4 vols.

Millspaugh, C. F. Contributions to the Flora of Yucatán (1895-98),
3 parts.

—. Plantae Utowanae. Plants Collected in Bermuda, Porto Rico,
St. Thomas, Culebras, Santo Domingo, Jamaica, Cuba, the
Caymans, Cozumel, Yucatán and the Alacran Shoals. December,
1898,to March, 1899. Part I. Catalogue of the Species (1900),
110 pp. Part IA. Reconsideration of the Cyperaceae. Reconsideration of Cakile (1900), 23 pp.

—. Plantae Yucatanae (1903-4), 2 parts.

Rechinger, K. H. The North American Species of Rumex (1937), 152 pp.

Ruiz, Hipólito. Travels of Ruiz, Pavón, and Dombey in Peru and
Chile (1777-1788). Translated by B. E. Dahlgren (1940), 372 pp.

Sherff, Earl E. The Genus Bidens (1937), 2 vols.

—. Revision of the Genus Coreopsis (1936), 200 pp.

Standley, Paul C. Flora of Costa Rica (1937-38), 4 vols.

—. Flora of the Lancetilla Valley, Honduras (1931), 418 pp.

—. Flora of Yucatán (1930), 338 pp.

—. The Rubiaceae of Bolivia (1931), 88 pp.

—. The Rubiaceae of Colombia (1930), 175 pp.

—. The Rubiaceae of Ecuador (1931), 76 pp.

—. The Rubiaceae of Venezuela (1931), 146 pp.

—. Studies of American Plants (1929-40), 10 vols.

Standley, Paul C., and Record, Samuel J. The Forests and Flora
of British Honduras (1936), 432 pp.

Standley, Paul C., and Steyermark, Julian A. Flora of Guatemala
(in continuation, 1946—), 4 vols.

—. Studies of Central American Plants (1940-47), 7 vols.

Steyermark, Julian A., and collaborators. Contributions to the
Flora of Venezuela (in continuation, 1951—), 4 vols.

Williams, Llewelyn. Woods of Northeastern Peru (1936), 588 pp.

Yuncker, T. G. A Contribution to the Flora of Honduras (1938), 122 pp.

—. Flora of the Aguan Valley and the Coastal Regions near La Cieba,
Honduras (1940), 104 pp.

Historical series:

Curtis, W. E. The Authentic Letters of Columbus (1895), 106 pp.

Zoological series:

Cory, C. B., and Hellmayr, Charles E.   Catalogue of Birds of the Americas (1918-37), 10 vols.

Dickey, Donald R., and Van Rossem, A. J.   The Birds of El Salvador (1938), 610 pp.

Elliot, D. G.   A Check List of Mammals of the North American Continent, the West Indies and the Neighboring Seas (1905), 768 pp.

—. The Land and Sea Mammals of Middle America and the West Indies (1904), 2 parts.

Hellmayr, Charles E.   The Birds of Chile (1932), 472 pp.

—. A Contribution to the Ornithology of Northeastern Brazil (1929), 268 pp.

Hellmayr, Charles E., and Conover, Boardman.   Catalogue of Birds of the Americas (1904-48), 4 vols.

Meek, S. E.   The Fishes of the Fresh Waters of Panama (1916), 159 pp.

—. The Fresh-Water Fishes of Mexico North of the Isthmus of Tehuantepec (1904), 316 pp.

—. The Marine Fishes of Panama (1923-28), 3 vols.

Osgood, W. H.   The Mammals of Chile (1943), 268 pp.

Zimmer, John T.   Birds of the Marshall Field Peruvian Expedition, 1922-1923 (1930), 250 pp.

Miscellaneous:

Kroeber, A. L.   Archaeological Explorations in Peru. Part I. Ancient Pottery from Trujillo (1926). Part II. The Northern Coast (1930). Part IV. Cañete Valley (1937).

Martin, Paul S.   Archaeology of North America (1933), 122 pp.

O'Neale, Lila M.   Archaeological Explorations in Peru. Part III. Textiles of the Early Nazca Period (1937).

Thompson, J. Eric.   Archaeology of South America (1936), 160 pp.

—. The Civilization of the Mayas (1936), 104 pp.

Loyola University
Institute of Jesuit History
Chicago 26

The Institute of Jesuit History of Loyola University was established in June 1936, and has as its purpose to collect, organize, catalogue, and publish source materials pertaining to the history of the Society of Jesus in the two Americas. Many shorter articles have been published in Mid-America, a historical quarterly; longer works appear in the series of publications of the institute.

The effort is collaborative, and six historians are committed to the task, namely, W. Eugene Shiels, Raphael N. Hamilton, J. Manuel Espinosa, Joseph Roubik, Paul S. Lietz, and the director, Jerome V. Jacobsen, S. J. For the first years the concentration was upon the materials pertaining to the work of the Jesuits in the Mississippi Valley and its immediate approaches.

Before an extension of scope into the Hispanic American field could be made by the Institute, agreements were made with historians of other Jesuit provinces in both Europe and the Americas. The Monumenta Historica Societatis Jesu was being re-edited and amplified at Rome. The fifty-odd volumes have scarcely touched the archives pertaining to sixteenth-century Hispanic America, and consequently there is now in project a Monumenta Floridana and a Monumenta Mexicana, with a great likelihood of similar volumes for other places in South America. Again, the Archivum Historicum Societatis Jesu publishes semiannually the letters and documents from various archives of the Jesuits. Because of the wide dispersion and varied nature of the sources, collaboration was necessary to prevent duplication of effort and output.

The Loyola institute has collaborated with Herbert E. Bolton in publishing a series of works dealing with the progress of the Jesuits up the Pacific coast. Four Jesuits have worked out phases of the plan, Father Jacobsen taking the foundations of the order in New Spain, Father Shiels taking the first missionary martyr to the north, while Fathers Dunne and Bannon have been carrying the story to California.

Doctoral dissertations on Hispanic subjects and written under the direction of the institute include the following:

Daly, Robert W. "An Examination of Manuel Ugarte's Contribution to Hispano-Americanismo," 1949.
Lietz, Paul S. "Don Vasco Quiroga," 1938.
Lowery, Martin J. "The Economic Life of La Plata, 1622-1713," 1950.
Muller, Herman J. "Jesuit Writings of the Seventeenth and Eighteenth Centuries as a British Trade Stimulus," 1950.
Roemer, Beatrice Blum. "Foundations of the Jesuits in the Viceroyalty of Peru, 1568-1605," 1947.

Newberry Library
60 West Walton Street
Chicago 10

The Newberry Library, apart from its Edward E. Ayer and

William B. Greenlee collections, has not, as a part of its long-time policy, specialized in the field of Hispanic studies. The library in its general collections does have, however, some items which are of value to students specializing in Spanish, Portuguese, and Latin American cultures.

Items which will be cited below have been purchased or collected over a period of sixty-five years and, with the exception of the Bonaparte collection, were not acquired as full or as partial collections.

The library's holdings in the Hispanic field include many general works which are not exceptional in the fields of travel, history, and biography. The philological library of Prince Louis-Lucien Bonaparte, acquired by the library in 1901, has many unusual items in the field of linguistics and is rich in works relating to, or written in, Spanish and numerous dialects of that language. Especially important are the dictionaries and grammars. The Bonaparte collection is housed in the rare book room.

Some separate items which may be mentioned are:

Biblia Polyglotta, 6 vols. Alcalá de Henares: Arnaldo Guillén de Brocar, 1514-17. First polyglot edition of the Bible, produced in Spain under the patronage of Cardinal Francisco Jiménez de Cisneros.

Fourteen incunabula, representing ten Spanish presses in six Spanish cities.

Numerous manuscripts for the medieval and renaissance periods which are listed and described in de Ricci and Wilson, Census of Medieval and Renaissance Manuscripts in the United States and Canada. Those relating to church music are especially interesting.

The library has built up a fine collection of material on the Arthurian legend. One item of value to students in this field is a sixteenth-century Arthurian romance in Spanish, Demanda del Sancto Grial, 1st ed. (Toledo, 1515).

More information may be found in the following:

Butler, Pierce. A Check List of Fifteenth Century Books in The Newberry Library and Other Libraries of Chicago. Chicago: The Newberry Library, 1933.

Collins, Victor. Attempt at a Catalogue of the Library of the Late Prince Louis-Lucien Bonaparte. London: Henry Sotheran, 1894.

Harding, Jane. The Arthurian Legend. A Check List of Books in The Newberry Library. Chicago: The Newberry Library, 1933.

Probasco, Henry. Catalogue of the Collection of Books, Manu-
scripts, and Works of Art Belonging to Mr. Henry Probasco,
Cincinnati, Ohio (Oakwood, Clifton). Cambridge, Mass., 1873.
About 2,500 of these books were bought by the library in 1890.

Edward E. Ayer collection:

About sixty-five years ago Edward Everett Ayer (1841-1927),
a Chicago businessman, began to collect all available material concerning the North American Indian. He interpreted this motif in
the broadest sense and drew into his collection all works which he
considered had the slightest bearing, even indirectly, upon the
original subject. Beginning with the discovery of America and
the first contact of Europeans with the aboriginal peoples of America,
Mr. Ayer specialized in the collection of all available sources concerning the discovery, exploration, and colonization of the North
American continent. The scope of the collection is fully described
in the 1938 Handbook of the Newberry Library. The "cornerstone"
of the collection was William H. Prescott's Conquest of Mexico
and Conquest of Peru, and during Mr. Ayer's lifetime the gathering
of Hispanic material was confined chiefly to the American Southwest, Mexico, Central America, and Peru. Within the last twenty-
odd years, however, the field has been extended, in accordance
with Mr. Ayer's wishes, to cover the colonial history of South
America up to 1800.

The section of the collection which directly concerns Latin
America includes over 5,000 printed books, many original manuscripts, transcripts, maps, and illustrations. Among the printed
volumes are all important sources, many rare editions, and collections of various editions of early works and of all secondary
sources. Chronologically, the collection goes back to include the
pre-conquest history of the Indian and the history of Europe relating to the discovery of America. The Spanish discovery and exploration are, of course, of the greatest importance in this period
of American history. Mr Ayer was no less interested in the history of colonization. To supplement the printed works, 300,000
pages of transcripts of manuscripts in the archives of Seville,
Simancas, and Madrid, concerning Spanish colonization, were
added; and to enrich the collection of 300 original maps, about
1,200 photographs and photostats of manuscript maps from the archives of Spain, Portugal, France, and England have been secured.
The manuscript maps, over 300 in number, many of which pertain
to Spanish America, have been described by Clara A. Smith, List
of Manuscript Maps in the Edward E. Ayer Collection (Chicago,

1927). The collection of printed maps and atlases, including the famous Stevens-Ayer Ptolemy collection, is also extensive. But of more importance to the student than the printed works and the cartographical material are the manuscripts. These have been described by Ruth Lapham Butler, A Check List of Manuscripts in the Edward E. Ayer Collection (Chicago, 1937), pp. 119-221. The greater part of the manuscript collection relates to Mexico and the Spanish Southwest, little to South America. Though it is impossible to mention many manuscripts, a few of the more interesting ones are:

Avendaño y Loyola, Andrés de. Relacion de las dos entradas que hize a la conuersion de los Gentiles Itzaex (1695-96).
Sahagún, Father Bernardino de. Four works dating from 1574 to 1594.
Serra, Junipero. Diario (March 28 to June 30, 1769).
Taraval, Sigismundo. Historia de las Misiones Jesuitas en la California Baja desde su establecimiento hasta 1737.
Vélez de Escalante, Silvestre de. Derrotero y diario (1776-77).

There are also 3 unpublished Jesuit relations: that of 1615, written by Rodrigo de Cabredo; and those of the two following years, written by Nicolás de Arnaya.

Mention should also be made of the section of the Ayer collection concerning the Philippine Islands. It includes material on the Philippines during the Spanish period only. There is among it a notable collection of manuscript material. The more important manuscripts have been described in detail by Emma Helen Blair and James Alexander Robertson, The Philippine Islands, 1493-1803, 53 vols. (Cleveland, 1903).

The Philippine linguistic collection (1,154 items) has been listed in Doris Varner Welsh's Checklist of Philippine Linguistics (Chicago, 1950).

The Ayer collection is increasing its material in all of the above fields, with perhaps greater emphasis at present on Latin American history during the colonial period. A collection of 586 Philippiniana, manuscripts and printed works relating to the seventeenth, eighteenth, and nineteenth centuries, was added in 1954.

William B. Greenlee collection:

In 1937 Mr. William B. Greenlee presented to the Newberry Library his fine collection on the general history and literature of Portugal. The collection has grown rapidly and is today probably the best library in the United States on Portuguese history and

literature before 1820.   All phases of history have been included—
political, diplomatic, social, economic, ecclesiastical, artistic,
and colonial.   While some volumes are of great rarity, the chief
objective has been to provide a center of research materials rather
than a collector's paradise.

The books in the collection have been classified into eight
categories.   Following will be mentioned a few items from each
section to illustrate the richness of the whole collection.

Section I (periodicals, gazetteers, bibliographies, and collections of documents): Portugaliae monumenta historica, edited
by A. Herculano and J. J. da Silva Mendes Leal (Lisbon, 1856-97);
Alguns documentos do Archivo Nacional da Torre do Tombo acerca
das navegações e conquistas Portuguezas, covering the years
1416-1554 (Lisbon, 1892); Quadro Elementar das relações politicas
e diplomaticas de Portugal com as diversas potencias do mundo,
desde o principio da Monarchia portugueza até aos nossos dias, by
the Visconde de Santarem, 18 vols.   (Paris, 1842-76); the Corpo
diplomatico portuguez contendo os actos e relações politicas e
diplomaticas de Portugal com as diversas potencias do mundo
desde o seculo XVI até os nossos dias, edited in 15 vols. by Rebello
da Silva and others (Lisbon, 1862-1936); the Collecção dos tratados,
convenções, contratos, e actos publicos celebrados entre a coroa
de Portugal e as mais potencias desde 1640 até ao presente, edited
by Borges de Castro... Judice Biker, etc., in 45 vols. (Lisbon
and Coimbra, 1856-1921); Arquivo histórico de Portugal, 1932 to
date; Revista de Historia, edited by Fidelino de Figueiredo in 6
vols. (Lisbon, 1912-28); José de Almada, Tratados aplicáveis ao
Ultramar, 6 vols. and 2 vols. of maps (Lisbon, 1942-44); complete
(or nearly complete) files of such reviews as O Instituto (Coimbra,
1853 to date), Ocidente (Lisbon, 1938 to date), Olisipo (1938 to
date), Boletim de Agência Geral das Colónias (Lisbon, 1922 to date),
a complete file of the Boletim da Sociedade de Geographia de Lisboa,
and other more specialized serial publications such as the Boletim
da Direcção Geral dos Edifícios e Monumentos Nacionais (Oporto,
1935 to date) and the Bibliografia filológica portuguesa (Lisbon,
1935-45).   Archival publications are well represented by series such
as the Arquivo de Beja, 5 vols. (1944-49); the Arquivo Coimbrão,
10 vols. (1923-47); the Arquivo do distrito de Aveiro, 15 vols. (1935-
49); the Archivos dos Açores, 24 vols. (1878-1901), and many
others.

The bibliographical section is virtually complete; every
bibliography obtainable, new or old, on Portugal and her colonies,
is in the collection, as well as Barbosa Machado, Inocencio, and
all the old standard bibliographical authorities.

Section II (books of travel, social life, customs): The new
edition of António Caetano de Sousa's monumental História Genealógica da casa real portuguesa desde a sua origem até o presente
(originally published at Lisbon in 20 vols., 1735-49) is catalogued
in this section. In the section are also included all the standard
works on Portuguese art. Representative books are Luis Reis
Santos, Vasco Fernandes e os pintores de Viseu do século XVI
(Lisbon, 1946); Américo Cortez Pinto, Da famosa arte da imprimissão
(Lisbon, 1948); Joaquim de Sousa Leão, filho, Frans Post (Rio de
Janeiro, 1948); and the works of Reynaldo dos Santos and others,
as well as reprints of older books in the field such as Ramalho
Ortigão's Arte portuguesa, reprinted in 3 vols. (1943-47).

Section III (biography): Every good recent biography of
prominent Portuguese historical personages is included. A few
are D. Virginia Rau, D. Catarina de Bragança, Raínha de Inglaterra
(Lisbon, 1943); H. Raposo, D. Luisa de Gusmão, Duquesa e Raínha
(Lisbon, 1947); and J. E. Amaro, Francisco de Lucena (Lisbon,
1945).

Sections IV and V (special fields of Portuguese history and
general histories of Portuguese dynasties) and Section VI (local
history and description): All the standard Portuguese histories,
such as those by Fortunato de Almeida, História da Igreja em
Portugal, 8 vols. (Coimbra, 1910-24) and História de Portugal,
6 vols. (Coimbra, 1922-29), and the História de Portugal. Edição
Monumental, edited by Damião Peres, 8 vols. (Barcelos, 1928-
38) are available in the collection. In military history, attention
may be drawn to the História do exercito Portuguez by C. Ayres
de Magalhães, 23 vols. (Coimbra, 1902-32), and to some of the
more recent studies by Gastão de Mello de Matos, such as his
Memória sôbre o alcançe das armas usadas nos séculos XV a
XVIII (Lisbon, 1944); there is a complete set of the numerous
publications of the Academia Portuguesa da História, of which the
volumes dealing with the Restoration wars and diplomacy of the
years 1640-68 are particularly valuable. Mention may be made
of the Elementos para a história do Municipio de Lisboa, by Eduardo
Freire de Oliveira, which, with 2 index volumes (1942-43), totals
19 volumes (1882-1911). Other important items include A. Loureiro,
Os portos maritimos de Portugal, 8 vols. and atlas (Lisbon, 1904-
10), complete sets of the reprints of all the old chronicles of the
Houses of Burgundy and Aviz, and many of the publications of the
eighteenth-century Academia Real da Historia Portugueza.

The ecclesiastical history subsection is by far the richest
in old books (seventeenth and eighteenth centuries), all the standard

histories of the monastic orders and of the Church being on the
shelves. There are also about 40 of the Jesuit Relations and letters
dealing with their missions in the East, 1559-1677, mostly in French,
Latin, and Italian sixteenth- and seventeenth-century editions. Among
modern works in this field, particular attention should be paid to
Francisco Rodrigues, História da Companhia de Jesus na Assistência
de Portugal (Oporto, 1931——), and to Serafim Leite, História da
Companhia de Jesus no Brasil, 10 vols. (Rio de Janeiro, 1938-50).
There are also António de Silva Rego's Documentação para a história das missoes do Padroado Português do Oriente, India, 1499-
1542, 3 vols. (Lisbon, 1947), and his História das missões do
Padroado Português do Oriente, India (1500-1542) (Lisbon, 1949),
both of which series are being continued.

Section VII (colonial expansion) is extraordinarily rich in
modern works on the colonies and overseas expansion. The collection includes the great bulk of the historical publications of the
Agencia Geral das Colonias at Lisbon. All the publications of the
colonial governments and archives in this line are represented by
complete series, together with other similar publications. There
are also numerous foreign publications, such as the French Archives
Marocaines and the English Factories in India, 1618-1670, which
supplement the Portuguese records for the seventeenth century.
Mention may also be made of François Valentyn's invaluable Beschry-
vinge van Oud en Nieuw Oost-Indien, 8 vols. (Amsterdam, 1724-26),
C. W. Walckenaer's Histoire générale des voyages, 21 vols. (Paris,
1826-59), and C. Beccari's magnificent Rerum Aethiopicarum
scriptores, 15 vols. (Rome, 1903-17).

Section VIII (literature): Portuguese literature is well represented in the Greenlee collection. Particular attention has been
paid to the fifteenth, sixteenth, and seventeenth centuries.

In the spring of 1954 the library came into possession of a
collection of 1,000 leaflets, pamphlets, and booklets, dealing
mostly with Portuguese affairs and written in Portuguese, Spanish,
Latin, Italian, and French. They had originally been assembled
by Charles Chadenat, the antiquarian bookseller in Paris. Thanks
to their acquisition, the Greenlee collection has taken another step
toward becoming the foremost American repository of works on
Portuguese and Brazilian history. The various centuries between
the earliest imprint (1541) and the latest (1865) are unequally represented. The sixteenth century furnishes only 3 items, and the
nineteenth no more than a dozen or two. The output of the eighteenth
century is well represented and that of the seventeenth even better,
affording a good idea of the state of affairs in Portugal shortly be-

fore the restoration of independence from Spain in 1640 and during the war years that followed. Among the hundreds of relações are shipwreck stories, accounts of battles, and reports of royal births, weddings, and deaths. The news from overseas had to do not only with deeds of arms against the Dutch and the Mohammedan powers, but also with spiritual battles fought by the missionaries and their converts.

Most of the oratorical pamphlets are religious in character. The three sixteenth-century items previously mentioned were written by priests. Since the Chadenat purchase was made, a further lot of 50 pamphlets has been added to the collection. One of the rarities included in this latter group is a sermon preached by Father António Vieira in Bahia, Brazil, in the presence of the first, newly arrived viceroy of Brazil on July 2, 1640.

In addition to the relações and oratory, the collection includes examples of poetry and popular literature (the most interesting being stage plays), parliamentary speeches, polemical writings, and writings on scientific subjects.

For further information see "The William B. Greenlee Collection," by C. R. Boxer, in The Newberry Library Bulletin, Second Series, No. 6 (May 1951), pp. 167-78; and "Portuguese Pamphlets," by Gerald M. Moser, in the Bulletin, III, No. 7 (November 1954), pp. 206-15. A catalogue of the Greenlee collection was compiled by Doris Varner Welsh and published by the library in 1953.

University of Chicago
Library
Chicago 37

Owing to the location in Chicago of the excellent Ayer collection of manuscripts and rare books on the American Indian and his relations with the European (see Newberry Library), the library of the University of Chicago has not greatly stressed the colonial period in making its acquisitions on Latin America. The library does possess, however, the fundamental documentary collections dealing with the period—those published in Spanish America as well as in Spain. It also possesses a large number of secondary works: biographies of the explorers and conquerors, monographs on the conquest and colonial regime, and the like.

On the national period, the materials are more abundant. In the library will be found practically all of the published sources and secondary works bearing on the independence movement, as

well as a large number of the biographies and writings of a majority
of the many outstanding political leaders since 1830: Bernardo
O'Higgins, Diego Portales, Manuel Rosas, Carlos Antonio
López, José Artigas, Fructuoso Rivera, Gabriel García Moreno,
Tomás C. Mosquera, and many others. On the contemporary history of Latin America the collection is especially good, containing
practically all the Latin American government documents published
since 1929, and many compilations of national laws. Considering
the twenty republics separately, the library is best supplied with
materials on Colombia, Argentina, Mexico, the five republics of
Central America, Cuba, and Haiti. It possesses one of the best
collections on Colombia, Cuba, and Haiti to be found anywhere in
the United States. On the international relations of Latin America,
the library is also rich, containing practically all the collections
of treaties and of documents dealing with boundary disputes, a
large number of the reports of the ministers of foreign affairs of
the various countries, many of the best treatises, a considerable
collection of calendars and transcripts from the London Foreign
Office, and some microfilms from the U.S. National Archives.
The library also contains a bulk of materials on the economic history of Latin America since independence, including files of the
Stock Exchange Year Book and South American Journal.

In spite of the fact that the university draws largely upon the
resources of the Ayer collection and the Chicago Natural History
Museum in investigations of the Indians of America, its library
contains good collections on the Mayas and Aztecs, as well as valuable published materials on the Incas and Pueblos. In the field of
literature, the library possesses many of the Spanish American
anthologies and the collected works of a number of the individual
poets, as well as the leading works of several of the essayists and
novelists. In the field of geography, it contains a valuable collection of maps, fairly complete files of a large number of geographical
magazines in several languages, and many monographs.

John Herron Art Institute
Pennsylvania and Sixteenth Streets
Indianapolis

The John Herron Art Institute owns the following Hispanic
paintings:

Murillo (attributed to). "Boy Blowing Bubbles." Collections: the
Duke of Wellington, Apsley House; Mrs. Marshall Field, Washington, D. C.

Ortiz Echagüe, Antonio. "My Daughter in the Argentine."
Unknown, probably sixteenth century. "Crucifixion" (with Madonna
   on reverse side). Painting on copper.
Zuloaga, Ignacio. "The Philosopher."

     The Art Institute also owns prints by Goya, Picasso, Ricardo
de los Ríos, and Daniel Vierge, as well as 5 sketches by Joaquín
Sorolla y Bastida.

     Among the crafts represented may be mentioned textiles from
the fifteenth through the nineteenth centuries, 2 sixteenth-century
Hispano-Moresque plaques in gold lustre, and various lace and metal objects.

University of Notre Dame
Zahm South American Library
Notre Dame

     The Zahm South American Library consists of 1,500 volumes,
collected by the Rev. John A. Zahm while he was writing his books
on South America. The library is supplemented by a collection of
maps and photographs.

Davenport Public Museum
704 Brady Street
Davenport

     The Davenport Public Museum has fine archeological collec-
tions from Mexico, Central America, Panama, and Peru. The
Peruvian collection consists of approximately 400 objects assembled
by C. A. Ficke in 1911 during a trip to Peru. There are 96 specimens of beautifully colored pre-Inca pottery from the Nazca valley.
From other parts of Peru, there is a large collection of black and
of dull red modeled or molded pottery from the north coast, chiefly
from Ferrenafe, Chiclayo, and Trujillo. There are also representative specimens of various styles of pottery from the coast region
between Huacho and Pachacamac, and of pottery showing the Inca
influence. For a detailed description, see Edward K. Putnam,
"The Davenport Collection of Nazca and Other Peruvian Pottery,"
Proceedings of the Davenport Academy of Sciences, Vol. XIII
(1914).

Des Moines Art Center
Greenwood Park
Des Moines 12

The Des Moines Art Center has one major work by Goya, a full-length portrait of Don Manuel García de la Prada, which was painted about 1796. It was acquired for the Nathan Emory Coffin collection in 1953. In addition, the center has prints and drawings by Goya, Rufino Tamayo, Diego Rivera, and José Clemente Orozco.

Louisiana State University
Department of Archives
Baton Rouge

Following is a list of source materials in the Hispanic field in the Department of Archives of Louisiana State University:

Spanish colonial Louisiana:

New Orleans City Records, 1767-(1790-1836)-1877, 3,136 items. Official records of the city including ordinances, correspondence, licenses, bills. Records of that type for the Cabildo, 1769-1803. (Original minutes of the Cabildo and a translation and index prepared by the WPA are available in the Archives Department of the New Orleans Public Library.)

Papers of settlers in Louisiana under Spanish rule, chiefly land grants and surveys, especially in the Natchitoches area. Such items appear in numerous collections of papers of private individuals.

Pintado Papers, 1771-(1779-1818)-1909, 11 volumes. Spanish land grants and surveys made by Spanish colonial surveyors. A typewritten translation with index, prepared by the Survey of Federal Archives in Louisiana, is also available.

Public records pertaining to Spanish Louisiana in state and parish offices in Baton Rouge, such as the 19th Judicial District Court and the State Land Office, have been transcribed or translated and indexed by the Survey of Federal Archives in Louisiana. The bulk of these records pertain to land, but include succession papers, civil and criminal litigation, slave sales, and business and marriage contracts. Copies of the Survey of Federal Archives volumes are in the Department of Archives, at Tulane, and in Washington, D.C.

Mexico:

Billaud (family) papers, 1845-66, 11 items. Includes a letter of

1866, written from Monterrey, Mexico, containing references
to Mexican political and military matters during the occupation
of Maximillian.

Farno (Henry) papers, 1837-61, 6 items. Includes typewritten
copies of 2 letters of Colonel Henry Farno, United States Army,
written during the period of the Mexican War: one from San
Antonio, Texas, and another from Parras, Mexico, where
Farno, in command of a wagon train, made camp.

Hazard (Joseph P.) letter, 1847, expresses sentiment in New
Orleans against the Mexican War.

Hennen-Jennings papers, 1803-(1850-70)-1918, 216 items and 26
volumes. Includes letters from Pierre Soule, written in 1857
from Mexico.

Moro (Don José de Ortega) letter, 1772, 1 volume. Letter (in
Spanish) written by José de Ortega Moro, counselor to Don
Francisco Fabian y Fuero, Bishop of Puebla, Mexico, to a
Mother Superior of a convent in Puebla. The letter criticizes
the practices of the nuns in the convents of Mexico and the local
clergy who do not favor the reform promoted by the Bishop.
In the back of the book are comments by the owner of the letter.

Morris (Mrs. Thomas H.)—Sibley (Mrs. Mary W.) papers, 1846-
(1846-79)-1910, 93 items (also bound typed copy). Includes a
letter written from Matamoros, Mexico, February 18, 1865,
describing the trip through the lower part of Texas, the town
of Matamoros, business conditions, and the attitude of businessmen who were not desirous of a peace being signed.

Ocampo (Don Sebastián de) manuscript, 1800, 1 volume. Manuscript (in Spanish) of funeral orations given annually in the city
of Cuernavaca by Don Sebastián de Ocampo, a native of Real
del Fazco.

Riva (Francisco de la), papers, 1793-1805, 77 items. Consists
of letters in Spanish, chiefly to de la Riva, concerning agriculture, Indians, and social and economic conditions in Mexico.

Ruiz (José Antonio and J. Ovidio) papers, 1820-(1910-20)-1920,
16 items. Consists of land grants, maps, and inventories of
property in Mexico (in Spanish).

Sale of the Office of Regidor manuscript, 1793, 1 volume. Manuscript volume (in Spanish) of the sale of the office of Regidor
in Puebla, Mexico, formerly held by Juan de Zarate y Vera,
to Antonio de Ojeda y Estrada. Transcription and translation
by Alicia de Jongh, "Sale of the Office of Regidor Juan de
Zarate in Puebla, Mexico, 1793." (Master of Arts thesis,
Louisiana State University, 1945.)

Taylor (Zachary) papers, 1846, 2 items. These papers include a dinner invitation written from Camargo, Mexico, to Theodore Lewis, September 4, 1846; and a broadside signed by Taylor, entitled Proclamación por el General Comandante del Ejército do los Estados Unidos de América, a la Nación Mejicana.

Tureaud (Benjamin) papers, 1805-(1848-1880)-1932, 3,332 items and 88 volumes. Papers during the period 1804-45 include some pertaining to the activities of the Phoenix Company of Louisiana in the Mexican War.

Wilson (Henry) papers, 1779-(1804-20)-(1835-48)-1885, 335 items and 16 volumes. Official papers of Henry Wilson, an army officer who served in the Seminole War and the War with Mexico. Includes a copy of a letter from General James Wilkinson disclosing plot of certain citizens of the United States to capture Baton Rouge and the Province of Mexico, December 6, 1806, and an eyewitness account of the entrance of the United States forces into Monterrey.

Nicaragua:

Miscellaneous lottery collection, 1891-1903, 3 items. Broadsides issued by the Little Havana Lottery Company, Nicaragua Lottery, and Delaware State Lotteries, announcing numbers drawn and prizes awarded.

Rozet (George H.) correspondence, 1856, 1857, 2 items. Letter of James Guthrie, Secretary of the Treasury, to George H. Rozet, special inspector of the customs of the United States, residing at San Juan del Sud, State of Nicaragua, outlining his duties as customs officer and stating the compensation he will receive, 1856. Letter of Henry Dickson, written from West Philadelphia to Rozet, giving information concerning conditions in Nicaragua immediately before General William Walker, American filibusterer, was forced to leave the country, 1857.

Cuba:

Brown (James) papers, 1764-(1804-10)-1811, 95 items (bound typewritten copies available). Includes letters of J. Gimbul, Havana, 1805, pertaining to shipping and ship insurance.

Miscellaneous lottery collection, 1891-1903, 3 items. Broadsides issued by the Little Havana Lottery Company, Nicaragua Lottery, and Delaware State Lotteries, announcing numbers drawn and prizes awarded.

Panama:

Chambers (Rowland) diaries, 1849-63, 7 volumes. Diaries and journals of Dr. Rowland Chambers, itinerant dentist of Vicks-

burg, Mississippi. The early diaries record a trip from St.
Louis to Panama City by way of New Orleans, Chagres,
Gorgona, and Cruces. Chambers practiced dentistry in Panama
City for a year and in 1851 returned to Natchez.

Louisiana State Museum
Jackson Square
New Orleans

The Louisiana State Museum contains a variety of manuscripts related to the Spanish and French period in Louisiana,
including original Spanish and French documents from the year
1723. In addition, there are various broadside manuscripts and
other material relating to the Louisiana Purchase in 1803. The
miscellaneous material related to the Spanish period includes
miniatures and broadsides. The Cabildo was the seat of the government in Louisiana during the Spanish occupation, and a variety
of objects relate to this era. For all inquiries, write to Lester
B. Bridaham, 616 Pirates Alley, New Orleans 16.

Tulane University
Middle American Research Institute
New Orleans

The Middle American Research Institute of Tulane University, established in 1924 through the generosity of Mr. Samuel
Zemurray, is devoted primarily to research, education, and public
service related to Middle America, including Mexico, Central
America, and the West Indies. It has sent many expeditions to
Middle America, these ranging from simple reconnaissance to
intensive work in agronomy, archeology, art, biology, physical
anthropology, ethnology, geography, bibliography, history, motion
pictures, linguistics, and sociology.

The institute has recently embarked on a long-term program
of co-ordinated area research in the social sciences. Field work
in archeology, social anthropology, sociology, geography, history, and political science has already been initiated, and it is
planned to bring to bear on common problems and concepts of
human relations the combined resources and approaches of these
and other disciplines. Results will appear as research monographs
by individual staff members and jointly authored works of collaboration.

The Middle American Research Institute publishes three

series of reports. The first is the regular book-size series of major publication, 15 volumes of which have appeared as of 1951, with more in press and in preparation. The second series published by the institute, Middle American Research Records, consists of separate monographs, papers, and articles issued at irregular intervals; up to 1951, 16 of these had been published and more are in preparation. The third is the Miscellaneous Series, which includes administrative reports, museum guides, library listings of special collections, and other releases.

In the field of public service, the institute maintains an information service and an audio-visual education program. It provides maps, photographs, and bibliographies, and prepares reports on Middle American subjects to individuals and institutions requesting them; during the past few years this service has gone out to an average of thirty states and sixteen foreign countries each year. Furthermore, the institute's museum sends loan exhibits to many museums each year, and distributes motion pictures, including its own film, Middle America, in sound and color.

Qualified students and research scholars are provided study space at the institute and may use its extensive catalogue, photographic, and site-file collections for their studies. Lectures, art exhibits, motion pictures, and special programs are held at the request of civic and social organizations.

In 1942, the institute's museum gallery was remodeled and modernized. Its museum collections are chiefly archeological, ethnological, and historical.

The institute's Index of Maya Ruins contains bibliographical, geographical, and archeological information on all known and reported ruins in the Maya area. A map based on this information is distributed at cost to interested individuals and institutions.

The Middle American Research Institute's library is one of the finest of its kind in the world. Its nucleus was the William E. Gates collection, particularly rich in linguistic material; to this nucleus have been added the library of Dr. Rudolph Schuller, renowned German scholar and historian, the Pepper collection, providing much marginal material on the United States Southwest and northern Mexico, the Frederick L. Hoffman collection, the Sedley J. Mackie collection, and the Fayssoux collection, all of which have contributed many thousands of books, reprints, articles, manuscripts, and other documents of general as well as specialized interest. A large collection of material from Mexican archives, dating from the Spanish conquest to 1825, was added in 1932-33. Library collections have been kept up to date in recent years with the aid of generous grants from the Rockefeller Foundation and the Carnegie Corporation.

Outstanding items in the library collections are: the Codex Tulane, a complete Mixtec pictorial manuscript, painted in colors on a twelve-foot strip of white deerskin; the Cortés Laws, manuscript of the first laws drafted and promulgated on the American mainland, dictated and signed by Hernando Cortés in 1524; the William Walker papers relating to the famous filibuster campaigns in Nicaragua; and viceregal administrative manuscripts from 1493 to 1865.

The Middle American Research Institute takes an active part in the expanded program of Latin American studies at Tulane, made possible by a five-year grant of the Carnegie Corporation, shared by Tulane University, Vanderbilt University, and the universities of Texas and North Carolina.

Baltimore Museum of Art
Wyman Park
Baltimore

The Baltimore Museum of Art owns the following Hispanic objects:

Painting—"Figure Study, " by Mariano Fortuny.

Graphic art—lithographs and drawings by Federico Castellón, Jean Charlot, Goya, José Clemente Orozco, Picasso.

Ceramics—twelfth-century Spanish dish; a pottery figurine from Usumacinta Valley, Guatemala; 9 pieces of Peruvian pottery of the Chimbote Chimu culture, colors red and black [see H. Doering, The Art of Old Peru (London: Ernest Benn, 1924), p. 55].

Textiles—some fine Spanish Renaissance lace; a Spanish embroidered banner, green and gold threads on white silk, forming a portrait of María Luisa de Borbón, dated 1803.

Jewelry—90 Spanish eighteenth-century pieces; about 15 Spanish and Portuguese nineteenth-century items.

Miscellaneous—a seventeenth-century Spanish gilt mirror, 3 Spanish swords, and an eighteenth-century silver spice cellar with hall marks on bottom and engraving on top.

Walters Art Gallery
Baltimore

The Walters Art Galley possesses the following Hispanic
paintings:

Catalonian, thirteenth century. Altar frontal: "Christ in Majesty"
   with scenes from the "Life of St. Martin."
Fortuny, Mariano, "Hindoo Snake Charmers," oil on canvas; :
   "An Ecclesiastic," oil on panel; "Arab Fantasia," oil on
   canvas; and water colors—"The Rare Vase," "The Mendicant,"
   "Don Quixote," "Café of the Swallows," and "Faithful Friends."
Goya (attributed to). "Portrait of General Ricardos," oil.
Greco, El (manner of). "St. Francis in Ecstasy," oil.
Jiménez y Aranda, José. "Boutique of Figaro," oil on panel.
Lucas, Eugenio. "The Procession," oil.
Madrazo, Raimundo de. "Coming Out of Church," oil.
Master of Arguis. "Triptych with Four Saints," tempera on
   panel; center once contained sculpture; possibly as late as 1460.
Murillo. "The Immaculate Conception," oil.
Murillo (?). "Holy Family with Two Rustics and Angels," oil.
Ribera. "St. Jerome in Penitence," oil.
Ribera (school of). "The Good Samaritan," oil.
Rico, Martín. "Gathering Oranges, Toledo," oil; "Venice," oil;
   "View of La Tour St. Jacques, Paris," ink drawing; and water
   colors—"Fisherman, Seville," "A Spanish Garden," and
   "Seville."
Spanish School, sixteenth century. "Boy Holding a Falcon," oil
   on canvas; "Portrait of a Young Man," oil on panel; "Portrait
   of Dom Ferdinand de Ruis."
Spanish School, seventeenth century. "Cavalrymen and Battle
   Scene"; "Boy Musicians"; "Temptation of St. Anthony";
   "Two Holy Women, a Monk and Three Angels in a Landscape";
   "The Sacrificial Lamb" (Symbol of the Redeemer); "Guardian
   Angel."
Valencian School, fifteenth century. "Madonna and Child," tempera
   on panel.
Villegas, José. "Cairo—The Slipper Merchant," oil; "Poultry
   Market—Tangiers," oil on panel.
Zamacois, Eduardo. "Spain, 1812—French Occupation," oil on
   panel; "Waiting at the Church Porch," water color.

Hispanic sculpture and crafts in the gallery include a pair
of Visigothic earrings and fibulae; 2 Romanesque capitals; about
6 pieces of Gothic enamel and metal work; a Gothic silver niello

cross; a stone Gothic relief from Marciac, fourteenth century;
Gothic door knockers; 1 Spanish ivory, thirteenth century; several
Spanish-Portuguese ivories, sixteenth to eighteenth centuries;
a Catalan brass casket, fifteenth century; about 15 pieces of
Hispano-Moresque gold work and enamel; about 12 pieces of
Hispano-Moresque ware, fifteenth to seventeenth centuries; about
6 pieces of Renaissance metal work; Renaissance embroideries;
about 6 Renaissance wood carvings; Baroque ivories; Spanish-
Portuguese colonial ivories, seventeenth to eighteenth centuries;
1 sixteenth-century tile; 11 swords and daggers, sixteenth and
seventeenth centuries; Indo-Portuguese ivories.

Manuscripts:

See S. de Ricci and W. J. Wilson, Census of Medieval and
Renaissance Manuscripts in the United States and Canada (New
York, 1935), I, 757-856 (MSS 155, 322, 400, 554, 555).
See Henry Walters, Incunabula Typographica, 1460-1500 (Baltimore,
1906), pp. 119, 354, 462.

Post-Incunabula:

Antonio, D. Nicolao. Bibliotheca Hispano sive Hispanorum, 2
vols. (Rome, 1672); armorial binding of Pope Pius VI (Giov.
Angelo Braschi, pope 1775-99); from library of Duke Thomas
Vargas Macciucca.
Commentarios de Cayo Julio Cesar: dedicados a la S. C. C. M.
del Emperador y Rey Mestro Señor (Alcalá, 1529).

Boston Public Library
Ticknor Collection
Boston 17

The Boston Public Library received the Ticknor collection
of Spanish and Portuguese literature in April 1871, subsequent
to the death of George Ticknor, one of the founders of the library
and a member of its board of trustees for fourteen years. The
collection consisted of 3,907 volumes. Mr. Ticknor also bequeathed to the library the sum of $4,000 to form a trust fund,
the income of which was to be spent on the purchase of books of
permanent value and authority in the Spanish and Portuguese languages. Through expenditure from the fund the collection has
been augmented until today it now includes some 7,500 volumes.

In accordance with the terms of the donor's will, the books
in the collection, whether originally bequeathed to the library or
later acquired through purchase from the trust fund income, are

kept together in the Rare Book Department. None of the books
may be sold, exchanged, or loaned. Photostat and microfilm
facilities are available.

The larger part of the original collection was assembled
by Ticknor preparatory to his writing his three-volume History
of Spanish Literature, which upon its publication in 1849 was
hailed as the first comprehensive history of Spanish literature.
It was translated into Spanish, French, and German.

Ticknor began collecting in 1818; the largest part of the
collection was acquired between 1838 and 1852. He had the assistance of vigilant agents on the continent who brought to his attention the availability of items valuable for his purposes. In one
year alone he authorized the purchase of 1,295 items, but was
successful in securing less than 300 of them. Literary friends,
especially D. Pascual de Gayangos, a member and later president
of the Spanish Academy, helped him. Many of the books he acquired
belonged to such men as Iriarte, the Comte de Puymaigre, Ferdinand Wolf, and Robert Southey.

Ticknor's original collection was remarkable in all fields,
yet strongest in history and general literature (poetry, theater,
and libros de entretenimiento). Many of the items are rare, some
are unique. The collection includes 15 incunabula representing
seven cities—Seville, Burgos, Saragossa, Zamora, Salamanca,
Barcelona, and Pamplona. The collection is most extensive in
sixteenth- and seventeenth-century books. Among some of the
interesting items are a copy of La Celestina (Seville, 1502);
the Complutensian Bible printed by Brocar in 1514-17; the Decadas
de Tito Livio (Saragossa, 1520); the Amadis de Gaula (Venice, 1533);
Garcilaso de la Vega, Obras (Barcelona, 1543); Las Casas, Brevissima
relacion de las Indias (Seville, 1552); Don Juan Manuel, El Conde
Lucanor (Seville, 1575); Montemayor, Diana (printed at Valencia
at an uncertain date, but not later than 1559); and La Vida del
Lazarillo de Tormes (published in 1554 at Antwerp, where so many
of the early Spanish books were produced). There are four editions
of the Cancionero General, the earliest a copy of the important
third edition of 1517. Of sixteenth-century Valladolid crónicas
alone, there is a complete set. In first editions of Cervantes, Lope
de Vega, Tirso de Molina, Calderón, and the other great figures
of the first half of the seventeenth century, the collection is so
rich that their bare enumeration would be beyond the scope of this
note. Only one item will be singled out: the complete autograph
manuscript of Lope de Vega, El Castigo sin venganza, signed by
the author on the first day of August, 1631.

A 476-page catalogue of the books in the collection, including other Spanish and Portuguese books in the library, was published by the trustees of the library in 1879. The catalogue was begun by William A. Wheeler. The final editing and annotating was done by James Lyman Whitney. Many of these annotations are from Ticknor own manuscript notes in the books themselves.

Various lists of the contents of the collection have appeared in the Bulletin of the Library and its successor, More Books. These are:

January 1881. A list of manuscripts in Spanish.
August 1884. A list of Spanish grammars and dictionaries.
July 1890. A list of the dramas of José and Miguel Echegaray.
April 1891. A list of modern Spanish and Portuguese biography, fiction, and poetry.
January 1896. A chronological index to historical fiction in Spanish and Portuguese.
October 1921. A description of the Ticknor Library.
December 1926. A bibliographical study of first and rare editions of Cervantes and Lope de Vega.
April 1937. An article on the Chronicles of Spain.
October 1942. An article, "George Ticknor, Lover of Culture."
September 1943. An article, "Marvellous Travels of Don Pedro."
December 1947. An article, "The Quarter-Centenary of Cervantes.

Isabella Stewart Gardner Museum
Fenway Court
Boston 15

The Isabella Stewart Gardner Museum possesses the following objects of Hispanic interest:

In its Spanish Cloister: an arched Romanesque stone door-way of the eleventh or twelfth century, either Spanish or Southern French.

In the Spanish Chapel: a sixteenth-century altar frontal of Spanish drawnwork; a tomb relief of a knight in armor, second half of the fifteenth century, said to represent a member of the Maldonado family of Salamanca; and Zurbarán, "Madonna and Child."

In the cloister itself: seventeenth-century Mexican wall tiles from Atlixco; and Sargent's "El Jaleo."

Other Hispanic works to be mentioned are:

In the East Cloister: a Spanish stone escutcheon, with the arms of Emperor Charles V.

In the Raphael Room: a triptych, "The Madonna and Child," "Saint George," and "Saint Martin," from the studio of Jaime or Pedro Serra (formerly in the collection of Emile Gavet). Also a Spanish or Italian sixteenth-century velvet cope.

In the Tapestry Room may be found:

Bermejo, Bartolomé. "Santa Engracia." Probably painted for the Church of Santa Engracia at Saragossa. Collection: Somzée.
García de Benabarre, Pedro. "St. Michael."
Gothic-arched stone window, Spanish, late fourteenth or early fifteenth century.
Gothic stone windows, Spanish or South Italian, fifteenth or sixteenth century.
Iron pulpit, Spanish or French Gothic, fourteenth or fifteenth century.
Velázquez (based on the portrait by). "Pope Innocent X," 1644-55. Collection: Prince Brancaccio, Rome.

In the Dutch Room are shown:

Moro, Antonio (Anthonis Mor). "Mary Tudor, Queen of England." Painted at the time of the betrothal of the Queen to the future Philip II of Spain. Presented by Queen Mary to her Master of the Household, Sir Henry Jerningham. From his house, Costessy Hall, Norfolk.
Pourbus, Frans, the Younger. "Isabella Clara Eugenia of Spain, Archduchess of Austria," 1566-1633.
Zurbarán. "A Doctor of Law at the University of Salamanca."

In the Titian Room are old Dutch, German, Spanish, and Italian glass. Also the following paintings:

Coello, Alonso Sánchez. "Juana of Austria [1537-73] with Her Niece Margaret (?) [1567-1633]."
Titian. "The Rape of Europa." This picture, painted for Philip II of Spain, was to have been part of the dowry had the marriage of Charles I to the Infanta María, daughter of Philip III, taken place. It went to France, possibly as part of the dowry of the Infanta María Theresa, daughter of Philip IV, who was married to Louis XIV, and it eventually entered the Orleans collection. When this was sold, it went to the Berwick collection in England and was afterwards purchased by Lord Darnley, who hung it at Cobham. Rubens made a copy of it, which hangs in the

Prado at Madrid, and wrote while copying it that to him it was the first picture in the world.

Velázquez. "Philip IV." Collection: Bankes, at Kingston Lacy.

In the Long Gallery are a Spanish Gothic processional cross, said to have come from the Cathedral of Burgos; and a silver hanging lamp from a Spanish convent. The legend on the latter reads, DIO ESTA LAMPARA DONA YSABEL DE PERNIA Y MONTOYA MONJA Y DONA ANA DE SOTO Y MONTOYA EL ANO 1602 PESA DOZE MARCOS Y DE HECHVRA 24 DVCADOS ES TODO MIL Y 40 REALS.

In the Gothic Room are: an eagle in wrought iron mantling the arms of Isabel la Católica of Spain (1451-1504), from the Church of San Juan de los Reyes, Toledo; a fifteenth-century Spanish Gothic chest; a pair of Spanish fifteenth-century wrought-iron torchères, with the arms of a bishop of Toledo; a thirteenth- or fourteenth-century Spanish wheel window.

On the third-floor stair hall are a Spanish sixteenth-century painted wood relief of Saint Peter Martyr; a Corpus from a deposition, twelfth-century Catalan; and a pair of carved doors with scenes from the life of Christ, Spanish or French fifteenth century.

Museum of Fine Arts
Boston 15

There are 33 significant Spanish paintings in the collection of the Museum of Fine Arts:

Andalusian School, fifteenth century. "Flight into Egypt," panel.

Bayeu, Francisco (attributed to). "Portrait of a Young Man," canvas.

Catalan School, fifteenth century. "St. Martin and the Beggar," panel.

Fortuny, Mariano, "The Antiquaries," canvas.

Goya. "Portrait of Unknown Man in a Brown Coat," canvas; "Manuel García," canvas; "Spain, Time and History" (sketch for the painting in Chicago), canvas.

Greco, El. "Portrait of Fray Félix Paravicino," canvas; "St. Dominic," canvas.

Lucas, Eugenio. "A Street Brawl," canvas.

Marzal de Sas, Andrés. "Virgin and Child," panel.

Menéndez, Luis. "Still Life: Bread, Bacon and Vegetables," canvas; "Still Life: Melon and Pears," canvas; "Still Life: Fruit and Flowers," canvas.

Ribera. "St. Jerome," canvas.

Ruiz de la Iglesia, Francisco Ignacio. "Immaculate Conception," canvas.

Soria, Martín de. "Retable with St. Michael and St. Anthony, "
  panel; "Retable of St. Peter, " panel.
Sorolla. "The Paseo del Faro, Biarritz, " canvas.
Twelfth-century apsidal fresco from the Church of Santa María
  de Mur in northwest Catalonia, representing "Christ in Majesty, "
  "Evangelists, " "Apostles, " "Visitation, " "Nativity, " "Adora-
  tion, " etc.
Twelfth-century frescoes from the Church of San Baudelio de
  Berlanga in Castile—"The Last Supper, " "The Resurrection. "
Valencian School, fifteenth century. "Coronation of the Virgin, "
  panel; "Virgin and Child, " panel.
Velázquez. "Don Baltasar Carlos and His Dwarf, " canvas; "Luis
  de Góngora y Argote, " canvas.
Velázquez (studio of). "The Infanta María Teresa, " canvas; "Philip
  IV, King of Spain, " canvas.
Zuloaga. "My Uncle Daniel and His Family, " canvas; "Castilian
  Landscape, " canvas.
Zurbarán. "St. Francis, " canvas; "St. Thomas, " canvas; "St.
  Cirillo, " canvas.

Among works of Hispanic interest in the Print Department,
the following books should be mentioned:

Díaz Morante, Pedro. Nueva arte de escrevir, Parts I-IV, Madrid,
  1616, 1624, 1628, 1631.
Goya. "Los Caprichos, " Madrid; "Disasters of War, " Madrid,
  1863.
Livy. Las Quatorze decadas di Tito Livio, Saragossa, 1520.
Missale Romanum. Lisbon: M. Manescal da Costa, 1764. Bound
  with Missae propriae sanctorum (Lisbon, 1773).

Artists represented in the Print Department are: I. Aguirre,
Blas Amettler, R. Anguiano (10), J. Arellano Fischer (8), A.
Beltrán, R. Bordallo, A. Bracho, I. A. Carmona, M. S. Carmona,
Antonio Casanova, J. Castellanos, F. Castellón, J. Charlot (17),
J. Chávez Morado, M. Covarrubias, Pedro Díaz Morante (19 wood-
cuts), F. Dosamantes (6), T. L. Enguidanos, J. Escobedo, Esquivel
de Sotomayor, R. Estevez, Ferdinand of Saxe-Coburg Gotha (King-
Regent of Portugal), Mariano Fortuny (13), F. García Bustos, A.
García Sanz, Joas Glamma Stroberle, Goya (216, including 4 litho-
graphs), J. F. G. Llanta, Tomás López, F. de Madrazo, Stefano
Magiore, J. de Méndez, L. Méndez, C. Mérida (14, and 4 stencils),
J. Molina, F. Mora, I. Ocampo, P. O'Higgins, Orozco, Ortega,
F. Castro Pacheco, Cayetano Palmaroli, Picasso, J. G. Posada,
A. Pujol, G. Francisco de Queiroz, Ribera (11), Ricardo de los
Ríos, Carlos Luis Rivera, D. M. Rivera (8), J. Sabogal, Fernando
Selma (21), G. Spagnolo, R. Tamayo, B. Vásquez, A. Villagra, A. Zalce.

Spanish holdings in the Decorative Arts Department include 23 fragments of leather, and several pieces of metal, including a lectern and 2 candlestands. Also the following:

Architectural detail: Romanesque portal of stone (fine sandstone), twelfth to thirteenth century; capital of pink marble from the cloisters of San Miguel de Cuxa, twelfth century.

Arms and armour: 1 composite suit of armour, last quarter of fifteenth century.

Ecclesiastical ornaments: pyx of bronze or copper; 3 chalices; reliquary; and 2 patens (all Spanish colonial).

Furniture: walnut vargueño; choir stall, fifteenth century; walnut table; chest, sixteenth century.

Glass: 38 pieces (several have sometimes been called Venetian), none of which are on exhibition.

Ivory: plaque of Death of St. Aemilianus, ca. 1070; 6 figures of Christ on crucifix; figures of Christ, saints, John the Baptist, Madonna, head of monk, man.

Pottery: 20 pieces (unknown factory); 2 Andújar; 4 Buen Retiro; 3 Granada; 4 Seville; 8 Talavera; 1 Valencia; glazed and decorated bowl, probably Talavera, ca. 1700.

Sculpture: jet statue of St. James, fifteenth century; alabaster statues of St. Simon Zelotes, St. John, and St. Bartholomew, School of Gil de Siloé, ca. 1500; reliquary bust of St. Barbara; Virgin, polychromed wood, signed Juan de Córdoba, 1475; part of a retable from Anglesola, Lérida, Catalonia, ca. 1320; wooden figure of apostle, early thirteenth century; marble relief, Adoration of the Kings, School of Burgos, 1525-30; alabaster bust of a man, early sixteenth century; polychromed wood figure of St. Anthony, early fifteenth century; tomb figure, fourteenth century.

Woodcarving: Hispano-Moresque intarsia casket, fourteenth to fifteenth century.

Among Portuguese objects in the decorative arts are one walnut table, a silver pendant and silver clasp, pottery and tiles from the Azores (not on exhibition), and 2 shaving basins with ewers.

As to Spanish textiles, there is an unusually fine collection of fragments of silk, and silk and gold weaving, dating from the thirteenth through the fifteenth century, woven by Arabs in Spain or showing Arabic influence. There are approximately 22 pieces of this type, including the fragment of the shroud of Don Felipe, son of San Fernando, who died in 1252, which is illustrated by Julius Lessing on plate 124c of his Gewebesammlung zu Berlin.

There are also fragments of four different designs in silk and gold weaving from the thirteenth century vestments once in Lérida Cathedral.

Spanish brocades, velvets, and damasks from the fifteenth through the eighteenth century are represented. Some have distinctive Spanish designs, others may only be presumed to be Spanish, since they appear to be Spanish copies of Italian and French weavings.

Spanish lace and embroidery, including peasant embroidery of the eighteenth century, are adequately represented. There is one knotted Spanish rug of the sixteenth century and two fragments of rugs of the same peiod, but no Spanish tapestries in the collection.

Carnegie Institution of Washington
Department of Archaeology
10 Frisbie Place
Cambridge 38

The Section of Aboriginal American History operated as a part of the Division of Historical Research from 1930 through 1950, when this division was abolished as a result of economic stringencies. The work in archeology was then organized into the present Department of Archaeology. The section, and later the department, has concerned itself with studies relating to the rise of native civilizations in the New World, its two principal fields being the Maya area in Mexico and Central America, and the Pueblo area of southwestern United States. The primary excavations have been carried out at Mayapán in Yucatán. There have also been archeological surveys in Tabasco and western Campeche, along the eastern and northern coasts of Yucatán, and several lesser explorations to various points in the peninsula. The work in the American Southwest is about to be abandoned. While the early work of the Carnegie Institution in these fields was purely archeological, a fact that still is mainly true of the work carried on in the Pueblo region, there has developed a program of investigation amounting to a general scientific survey of the Maya area.

The department is engaged in studying the career of the Maya Indians from the earliest times to the present. Its primary objective is, of course, to learn the facts of Maya history. As an aid in this endeavor, it is also working on the language, ethnology, and physical anthropology of the modern Maya. At the same time an attempt is being made to gather data regarding the environment

in which these people have lived and are living. The program of
the department, therefore, falls naturally into two parts, the one
concerning itself with events and social conditions, the other with
the ecology of the area in which those events took place and those
conditions arose. The ultimate aim of the research is to paint, in
the light of these two categories of information, a true historical
picture.

The framework, so to speak, of the program is provided
by the archeological investigation, which covers the pre-Columbian
period; and by documentary research, dealing with the four centuries that have elapsed since the discovery of Yucatán. Both
endeavors have perfectly definite objectives, the reconstruction
of sequent phases of Maya history. The environmental studies,
as well as those in linguistics, ethnology, and physical anthropology,
serve to illumine and render interpretable the findings of excavator
and archivist. The direction which they must take is, therefore,
to some extent dependent upon current needs of the central historical investigation. Furthermore, this group of projects is being
carried out, for the most part, by associated or co-operating
scholars, rather than by staff members. This necessitates a certain degree of opportunism in developing the nonhistorical elements
of the program; but it permits utilization, even if only intermittently,
of the services of a greater number of expert specialists than could
well be mobilized by the Carnegie Institution or any other single
agency. In spite, then, of its many administrative difficulties and
of the evident danger of diffusion of effort, it seems that a co-
ordinated investigation of the sort which the department is attempting to make is the most effective method for attacking with limited
funds and personnel the complex problems of Maya history.

Harvard University
Botanical Institutions
Cambridge 38

At Harvard University there are three great botanical li-
braries and three great herbaria, all rich in North and South Ameri-
can material. These are the Gray Herbarium in Cambridge, the
Farlow Reference Library and Herbarium in Cambridge, and the
Arnold Arboretum, herbarium and library, formerly in Jamaica
Plain, now in Cambridge.

The Gray Herbarium consists of flowering plants, ferns,
and fern allies from all parts of the world and is particularly rich
in historical material from various parts of Mexico, the West

Indies, Central America, and South America. There are about 1, 300, 000 sheets in this herbarium, many of them with two or more collections on the same sheet. It is one of the most important depositories of historical specimens in North and South America. Its library contains over 45, 000 bound volumes and pamphlets. Among members of the staff, research is in progress on the flora of Bolivia, the West Indies, northeastern Mexico, and southeastern United States. They are doing active monographic work on the Cruciferae, Iridaceae, and Leguminoseae of the western hemisphere.

The Farlow Reference Library and Herbarium is devoted to the cellular cryptogams, that is, the mosses, hepatics, lichens, fungi, and algae, and thus does not duplicate the resources of the Gray Herbarium. The collection contains over 1, 000, 000 specimens and is particularly rich in historical material because of the acquisition, from time to time, of important personal collections of various specialists. Its library contains about 39, 000 volumes and pamphlets.

The Arnold Arboretum is an institution dedicated to the study of woody plants. In addition to approximately 7, 000 different species and varieties of trees, shrubs, and woody vines in actual cultivation in its extensive grounds in Jamaica Plain, its herbarium contains about 650, 000 sheets of mounted specimens from all parts of the world. Its library contains about 62, 000 volumes and pamphlets and about 20, 000 photographs. In 1954, the Gray Herbarium and the herbarium and library of the Arnold Arboretum were moved to a central new building connected to the building of the Farlow Herbarium on one end and the Museum of Comparative Zoology building on the other. Thus the resources of these three institutions have been brought together in a single location with fine modern research facilities.

The Atkins Garden and Research Laboratory at Soledad, Cienfuegos, Cuba, is devoted primarily to research in tropical agriculture, horticulture, and economic botany. It comprises more than 200 acres of land devoted in part to permanent plantings of tropical economic and ornamental species and in part to experimental plantings of tropical agricultural and horticultural crops. There are limited facilities for outside students and scientists who may wish to carry out research in a tropical area.

The botanical libraries, mentioned above, of the independent research institutions affiliated with the Faculty of Arts and Sciences are supplemented by the great resources of the Harvard College

Library and the important biological library in the Museum of Comparative Zoology. These unique library facilities have been built up over a long period of time, and the result is that the botanical library resources at Harvard University are scarcely equaled anywhere in North and South America.

The herbarium facilities are also unique, containing as they do many thousands of types on which original descriptions were based and other material intensively studied by several generations of botanists. Further, they contain numerous important sets of duplicate specimens representing species collected by various botanists in Europe and in South America, particularly historical collections made in Mexico, Central America, the West Indies, and various parts of South America.

Harvard University
Division of Fine Arts and Fogg Museum of Art
Cambridge

The Division of Fine Arts at Harvard University has been a leading center of research on Spanish art. Under the guidance of Professor Emeritus Chandler R. Post and the late Professor Arthur Kingsley Porter, whose personal contributions to the study of Spanish painting and Spanish Romanesque sculpture have been epoch-making, a considerable number of scholars have been trained in the Spanish field. In connection with the publications of Professor Post, Professor Porter, and their pupils, the research materials in the Widener Library and the Fogg Museum of Art have been augmented with the intention of making them as complete as possible. All obtainable studies and source books relating to Spanish art have been, and continue to be, added to the resources of the library. The library possesses complete files of scholarly periodicals published in Spain, such as: Archivo Español de Arte y Arqueología and the Boletín de la Sociedad Española de Excursiones. It also subscribes to the local bulletins published by museums and provincia societies, such as: the Boletín de la Comisión Provincial de Monumentos Histórico-Artísticos de Burgos, Boletín de la Sociedad Castellonense de Cultura, Boletín de la Comisión de Monumentos Históricos y Artísticos de Navarra, and Boletín del Museo de Bellas Artes de Cádiz.

The photographs of Spanish art, housed at Harvard in the Fogg Museum library, number over 60, 000 the largest and most comprehensive photograph collection in any institution. They have been purchased systematically from the leading Spanish photog-

raphers, and many monuments have been photographed on special
order for the publications of Professor Post and his students. The
photographers Mas and later Gudiol from Barcelona have made
expeditions to many Spanish provinces under the joint auspices of
the Fogg Museum library, the Frick Library of New York, and
the Institute of Fine Arts of New York University. Monuments
have been photographed in great detail. As a result of the civil
war in Spain and the consequent destruction, this collection of
photographs in the Fogg Museum library acquires an increasing
historic value. Material here assembled is unique and invaluable.
See "The Collection of Spanish Photographs in the Fogg Museum,"
Bulletin of the Fogg Art Museum, V (1935), 12-15,

A considerable number of original works of Spanish art have
been added to the collection of the Fogg Museum within the past
few years, coincident with the growth of research in the Spanish
field. Paintings, sculptures, prints, and ecclesiastical embroideries are included in the collection. The print room contains
sets of Goya's "Caprichos," "Proverbios," and "Tauromaquia."
Of the 15 paintings, it will suffice to mention only the outstanding
masterpieces. El Greco's small canvas representing "Christ
Driving the Money Changers from the Temple" is related to pictures of the same subject in the Frick Collection of New York and
the National Gallery of London. Murillo's "Holy Family," with
its full rich blues and reds, must be ranked among the best productions of the master's brush. A picture, likewise of first rank
qualitatively, is Ribera's "St. Jerome in Penitence." Pleasing
works of the late Gothic period are Juan de Burgos' signed "Annunciation," and the "Purification" from the school of Valladolid.

The Romanesque and Gothic sculptures in the Fogg Museum
are no less important than the paintings. Historically the most
interesting is the column carved in relief with the figures of St.
Simon, St. Judas Thaddaeus, and St. Matthias, which was originally
a part of the altar placed in the early twelfth century over the grave
of St. James in the great pilgrimage church of Santiago de Compostela. The two companion pieces belong to the Museo Arqueológico in Madrid. Worthy of special mention are the Romanesque
Virgin in wood from Tahull, the two fine capitals from Sta. María
de Alabanza inscribed with the date 1185, and a double capital from
Sta. María de Aquilar de Campoo. The sepulchral effigy in wood
of Don Diego García (d. 1288) is not only rare, but is aesthetically
a masterpiece of Spanish Gothic sculpture, and was fittingly presented as a memorial to Professor Porter.

The Fogg Museum possesses the following Spanish objects.

Paintings:

Borrassá, Luis. "St. Barbara and St. John the Baptist," tempera on panel. See C. R. Post, A History of Spanish Painting, V (Cambridge, 1934), pp. 261-64; F. R. Grace, Fogg Museum Bulletin, March 1934.

Burgos, Juan de. "Annunciation." See Fogg Art Museum, Collection of Medieval and Renaissance Paintings (Cambridge, 1919), pp. 246-48; C. R. Post, op. cit., III (1930), 292-96.

Campaña, Pedro (Peter de Kempener, attributed to). "Holy Family and Annunciation," triptych, oil on panel. Central panel: Holy family with infant St. John and two kneeling angels. Left wing: Angel. Right wing: Virginia Annunciate.

Cano, Alonso (attributed to). "Madonna and Child with St. John the Baptist," oil on canvas.

Catalonian, thirteenth century. "Bishop Saint and Scenes from His Life" (?), antependium.

Fortuny, Mariano. "Courtyard at Alhambra," oil on canvas; "Standing Woman in Peasant Costume," water color; "Two Moroccan Women," water color.

Goya (attributed to). "Portrait."

Greco, El. "Christ Bearing the Cross," oil on canvas.

—. "Christ Driving the Money Changers from the Temple," oil. See Legendre and Hartmann, El Greco (Paris, 1937), Pl. 160; A. L. Mayer, El Greco (Munich, 1926), No. 52.

Hearst Master. "Nativity, Madonna and Child, Crucifixion, Christ Enthroned," retable, oil on panel. See C. R. Post, op. cit., VIII (1941), 259.

Hispano-Flemish, fifteenth century. "St. Christoper." See C. R. Post, op. cit., IV (1933), 193-96; VII (1938), 862-63.

—. "The Purification," panel, School of Castile. See C. R. Post, op. cit., IV (1933), 418-28; V (1934), 182, 194.

Juni, Juan de (attributed to). "St. Peter and St. Paul," diptych, oil on panel.

Master of St. Ildefonso. "St. Christopher," oil on panel.

Master of St. Mark. "Nativity," triptych, panel.

Miró, Joan. "Study for the Mural at the Harvard University Graduate Center," tempera and ink.

Moguer Master. "St. Peter." See C. R. Post, op. cit., X (1950), 110.

Murillo. "Holy Family," oil.

Pantoja de la Cruz. "Portrait of Philip III."

Ribera.   "St. Jerome, " oil on canvas.   See C. R. Post, Fogg
Museum Notes, June 1932.
Soria, Martín de.   "Madonna and Child. "   See C. R. Post, His-
tory of Spanish Painting, VIII (1941), 368.
Sorolla y Bastida.   "Landscape. "
Spanish School, fifteenth century.   "Dedication of a Church to
St. Michael, " tempera on panel.
Spanish School, seventeenth century.   "Still Life, " oil on canvas.
Twelfth- or early thirteenth-century Romanesque fresco of a half-
beast-half-bird, coming from the chapter house of the monastery
of San Pedro de Arlanza. See C. R. Post, op. cit., IV (1930),
189-94.
Vargas, Luis de.   "Annunciation, " oil on panel.

   Sculpture:

Spanish, twelfth century.   Virgin from Tahull; wood.   See A. K.
Porter, "The Tahull Virgin, " Fogg Art Museum Notes, II (1931),
No. 6; A. K. Porter, Spanish Romanesque Sculpture, II (Flor-
ence, 1928), p. 13, Pl. 71.
——. Romanesque capital from Abbey of Santa María de Alabanza,
Palencia; stone; dated 1185.   Right: two saints with double cross.
Principal face: Christ with angel, eagle, lion, and ox.   Left:
two saints, one with staff.   Top: detachable, with leaf scroll
and Latin inscription.
——. Romanesque capital from Abbey of Santa María de Alabanza,
Palencia; stone; dated 1185.   Principal face: two female figures
and angel before table on which is a Latin inscription (three Marys
at the Tomb).   Left: saint with mattock on shoulder.   Right:
female saint.   Abacus: detachable, leaf scroll and Latin in-
scription.   See A. K. Porter, "The Alabanza Capitals, " Fogg
Art Museum Notes, II (1927), No. 3; A. K. Porter, Spanish
Romanesque Sculpture, II, p. 32, Pls. 103-4.
——. Saint; wooden applique; traces of polychromy, green and red;
mounted on black velvet.
——. Column from the Monastery of San Pelayo de Antealtares in
Santiago de Compostela; marble.   Representations of the apostles
Simon, Matthias, and Judas, in relief.   See A. K. Porter, op.
cit., II, pp. 4-8, Pl. 59; Fogg Art Museum Bulletin, March
1934.
——. Romanesque figure of Christ from Santa Marta de Tera; in
relief.   See A. K. Porter, op. cit., I, p. 62, Pl. 29.
Spanish, thirteenth century.   Double capital from Santa María
de Aquilar de Campoo, Palencia; stone.   See Fogg Museum
Bulletin, March 1934.

—. Impost block from Santa María de Aquilar de Campoo, Palencia; stone.

—. Sepulchral monument of Don Diego García; wood. See F. B. Deknatel, Fogg Museum Bulletin, March 1937.

Spanish (?), sixteenth century. Half-length figure of a man; wood.

Spanish (?), sixteenth century (?). St. John and Virgin; ivory.

Spanish, sixteenth century. Large reredos with sculptured figures; carved wood polychrome.

Spanish, seventeenth-eighteenth century. Two doors; wood, in entrance to Great Hall, Fogg Museum.

Drawings:

In the way of original material the collection of the Fogg Museum of Art is richer in Spanish paintings and sculpture than in drawings; however, the Goya sketches are among the finest in the United States.

Fortuny, Mariano. "Study for the Battle of Tetuán" (painting in the Barcelona Museum), black and white chalk on grey paper.

Goya. "Woman Knitting," pen and ink with brush and wash.

—. "Manola et Novio" (recto), "La Jeune Mère" (verso), pen and ink with brush and wash (drawings on both sides of sheet).

—. "You Make a Mistake if You Seek to Get Married" (A Beggar), pen and ink with wash. Gift of Meta and Paul J. Sachs.

Picasso. "Portrait of Fonte," charcoal, black, blue, and yellow wash on cream-colored paper. Gift of Meta and Paul J. Sachs. See Mongan-Sachs, Drawings in the Fogg Museum of Art, I (Cambridge, 1946), No. 739, p. 402; II, Fig. 398.

—. "Study After Guernica—1937," pen and ink with water color.

Prints:

Goya. Complete set of "Los Caprichos," 1st ed.

—. Complete set of "Los Desastres de la Guerra," including several early proofs.

—. Set of "Los Proverbios," 1st issue (Madrid, 1863).

—. Set of "La Tauromaquia," 2d ed. (Madrid, 1855).

Textiles:

Ecclesiastical embroidery. "The Visitation," Spanish (?) ca. 1400

—. "Birth of the Virgin, Presentation, Nativity and Crucifixion," Spanish (?) ca. 1400.

—. "Meeting of Joachim and Anna," Spanish (?) ca. 1400. See Fogg Museum Bulletin, January 1932, pp. 33-39.

Brief list of publications:

Conant, K. J. The Early Architectural History of Santiago de
Compostela. Cambridge, 1926.
Cook, W. W. S. Pintura e imaginería románicas. Madrid, 1950.
Darby, D. F. Francisco Ribalta and His School. Cambridge,
1938.
Hersey, C. K. The Salamantine Lanterns. Cambridge, 1937.
Kuhn, C. L. Romanesque Mural Painting of Catalonia. Cambridge,
1930.
Porter, A. K. Romanesque Sculpture of the Pilgrimage Roads, 10
vols. Boston, 1923.
—. Spanish Romanesque Sculpture, 2 vols. Florence, 1928.
—. The Writings of A. Kingsley Porter, a Bibliography, compiled
by Lucy Kingsley Porter. Cambridge, 1934.
Post, C. R. A History of Spanish Painting, 11 vols. Cambridge,
1930-53.
Rowland, B. J. Jaume Huguet. Cambridge, 1932.
Wethey, H. E. Gil de Siloé and His School. Cambridge, 1936.

There are also numerous magazine articles in Art Bulletin,
Gazette des Beaux-Arts, and others, available through the Art
Index.

Harvard University
Harvard College Library
Cambridge

Latin America

The collection of works on the various aspects of Latin
America in the Harvard College Library now numbers about 46,000
volumes and pamphlets. Here, as in other branches of Americana
in the library, the early works on the discovery, exploration, and
conquest are well represented. These are classified with United
States history, except when they relate to a particular Latin American country. As a tercentenary gift, the library received from
the Bodleian Library the Columbus letter: Epistola de insulis
nouiter repertis (Paris, 1493). A list of some of the early books
to be found in the Latin American collection follows below. Many
rare volumes were secured with the Ebeling library in 1818 and in
the Prescott bequest in 1859, but the greater part of the collection has been acquired within the last three decades. Additions
were made in 1906 and 1909 by means of gifts from Enrique de
Cruzat Zanetti, for the purchase of books on Cuba. In 1906,
there was also received from Rear Admiral John G. Walker a

notable collection of works relating to the Panama Canal and to the history and construction of great canals generally, a collection made by W. Cameron Forbes. Special attention to the Spanish-American War and the Panama Canal is also found in the Theodore Roosevelt collection, formerly located in New York but presented by the Roosevelt Memorial Association in 1943. In 1909, Professor Archibald Cary Coolidge and Clarence Leonard Hay, of Washington, presented to the library the private collection of the late Luis Montt, of Santiago, Chile. Señor Montt was long the librarian of the Biblioteca Nacional, and his own library was particularly rich in broadsides, newspapers, and periodicals, as well as in books and pamphlets on the politics of his country during the past century. In 1913-14, Walter Lichtenstein, then librarian of Northwestern University, visited the countries of South America on behalf of several American libraries. Through his trip, the Harvard library obtained besides many miscellaneous works, a large portion of the private libraries of Manuel Segundo Sánchez, librarian of the National Library of Venezuela and author of the Bibliografía venezolana, and of Donato Lanza y Lanza of La Paz, Bolivia, as well as the whole of that of Blas Garay of Asunción, Paraguay, and an almost complete collection of statutes of all the South American countries (for the Harvard Law School Library). In 1915, Julius Klein spent several months in Brazil, Argentina, and Uruguay on a traveling fellowship, and purchased some 2, 000 volumes and pamphlets. Finally, in 1917, Thomas Barbour, of the Harvard University Museum, aided Harvard in securing a collection of about 2, 000 volumes and pamphlets on Cuba, formed by José Augusto Escoto, of Matanzas, librarian of the provincial library at Matanzas. From 1918 to 1926, purchases from the Escoto library added about 2, 500 volumes. This total was further increased by many gifts from Señor Escoto, and by the gift in 1932 of about 1, 000 items from Thomas Barbour.

The Harvard collections attempt to cover as far as may be the history, geography, politics, economics, and the literature of the various countries. Special effort has been made to secure sets of periodicals and society publications, and the collection of these comprises about 3, 000 volumes. There is also about the same number of official documents. For many of the countries, especially Chile, Venezuela, and Bolivia, the collections of political pamphlets and broadsides are large and important.

A characteristic of this section of the library is the remarkably even development it has undergone, so that all countries have some representation. The Argentine collection is probably the strongest, although those of Chile, Venezuela, Bolivia, and Brazil are im-

ortant. The collection on Mexico, while by no means complete,
s nevertheless extensive. Cuba is also well represented both as
o its history and literature. The Escoto library, which serves as
ts foundation, contains some documentary material and a number
of manuscripts.

The collection relating to Latin American history and politics
now contains about 30, 200 volumes and pamphlets, while belles-
ettres from the same region comprise approximately 11, 000 vol-
imes and pamphlets. The greatest strength probably lies in Chilean
literature, especially poetry. An interesting collection of Fernández de Lizardi material has been added to Mexican literature. Much
of the general strength in different collections is due to the continued
gifts of national libraries in their respective countries.

Following are examples of early books in the Latin American
collection:

Anghiera, Pietro Martire d'. De nuper sub D. Carolo repertis
insulis simulaz incolarum moribus. Basel, 1521.
Apollonius, Levinus. De Peruuiae... inuentione. Antwerp, 1566.
___. De Peruuiae... inuentione. Antwerp, 1567.
Cieza de León, Pedro de. Parte primera de la chronica del Peru.
Antwerp, 1554.
Cortés, Hernando. Praeclare de Ferdinâdi Cortesii de Nova Maris
Oceani Hyspania narratio. Nûremberg, 1524.
___. Ferdinâdi Cortesii von dem Newen Hispanien. Augsburg, 1550.
Federmann, Nikolaus. Indianische historia. Hagenau, 1557.
Fernández, Diego. Primera y segunda parte de la Historia del
Perú. Seville, 1571.
Keymis, Lawrence. A Relation of the Second Voyage to Guiana...
in 1596. London, 1596.
López de Gómara, Francisco. Historia de Mexico. Antwerp: J.
Bellero, 1554.
___. Historia de Mexico. Antwerp: J. Steelsio, 1554.
___. Historia del illustriss. et valorosiss. capitano Don Ferdinando
Cortes, marchese della Valle, et quando discoperse et acquisto
la Nuova Hispagna. Rome, 1556.
___. La Historia general de las Indias. Antwerp, 1554.
___. The pleasant Historie of the conquest of the West India. London,
1578.
___. The pleasant historie of the Conquest of the West India. Lon-
don, 1596.
Philip II. Provisiôes, cedulas, instruciones de su Magestad...
pa... governaciô dsta Nueva España. Mexico, 1563.
Raleigh, Sir Walter. The Discoverie of the large, rich, and
bewtiful Empyre of Guiana. London, 1596.

Saavedra Guzmán, Antonio de. El Peregrino Indiano. Madrid, 1599.
Spain—Consejo real de las Indias. Libro primero [-segundo] de
provisiones. Madrid, 1596.
—. Ordenanzas reales del Conseio de las Indias. Madrid, 1585.
Xeres, Francisco de. Libro primo de la Conquista del Peru.
Venice, 1535.
Zárate, Augustín de. Historia del descubrimiento y conquista del
Peru. Antwerp, 1555.
—. Historia del descubrimiento y conquista de las provincias del
Peru. Seville, 1577.
—. Le historie del Sig. Agostino di Zarate contatore et consigliero
dell' imperatore Carlo V. Dello scoprimento et conquista del
Peru. Venice, 1563.
—. De wonderlijcke ende warachtighe historie vant coninckrijck
vã Peru. Antwerp, 1573.
Zurita, Ferdinandus. Theologicarum de Indis quaestionum
enchiridion primum. Madrid, 1586.

Portuguese History and Literature

The Portuguese collection includes some 10, 000 volumes and
pamphlets. It has had its greatest growth since 1922 through the
continuous accumulation of the books presented by John B. Stetson,
Jr., in memory of Aleixo de Queiroz Ribeiro de Sotomayor d'
Almeida e Vasconcellos, Count of Santa Eulalia. The most important of these gifts was the entire library of Fernando Palha, historian and member of the Academy of Sciences of Lisbon. This
library of some 6, 700 volumes and pamphlets covered the whole
field of Portuguese history and literature, and contained many
early works of the greatest rarity. Besides these books, it has a
good deal of material in other languages, especially Spanish. A
catalogue of the Palha library was printed in Lisbon in 1896.

The collection of Portuguese history is strong in the publications of learned societies, periodicals, and documentary material, including several early local constitutions and other books
of extreme rarity. It includes a good set of the Gazeta de Lisbõa,
beginning in 1715. There is a considerable number of political
pamphlets of the seventeenth, eighteenth, and nineteenth centuries.

In literature, the Palha library, together with individual gifts
of Mr. Stetson, has made the collection particularly strong for all
periods. There are many rare editions—a few said to be unique.
The Camoes collection of over 1, 000 volumes is unusually complete and includes many early and rare editions from the Monteiro
and Palho libraries.

There were many manuscripts in the Palha library, the most important of these being a series of letters, 372 in number, of John III of Portugal (1521-37). They were edited by Professor J. D. M. Ford and published by the Harvard University Press in 1931. In addition, there were 175 letters by his queen, Catherine, and other members of the court. These were edited by Professor Ford and L. G. Moffatt and published by the Harvard University Press in 1933.

Other noteworthy parts are a special collection of 500 plays; a group of so-called autos, one of the most popular forms of the early Portuguese theater; and eighteenth-century anonymous humorous and satirical writings. For modern literature, Mr. Stetson's purchases have procured an unusually complete collection.

Spanish History and Literature

The collection of Spanish history and literature includes about 28,000 volumes and pamphlets. The history section contains many government documents, a good number of historical periodicals, treatises on constitutional history, and a number of political pamphlets and broadsides. Although, since the Prescott bequest in 1859, the library has not had the opportunity of acquiring unusual and outstanding collections in this field, many important early books have found their way to the library's shelves. The following titles serve as examples:

Arredondo y Alvarado, Gonzalo. Castillo inexpugnable defensorio d̃ la fee. Burgos, 1528.

Bleda, Jaime. Cronica de los Moros de Espana. Valencia, 1618.

Carbonell, Pere Miguel. Chroniques de Espaya que tracta del nobles e invictissimo Reys dels Gots. Barcelona, 1547.

Castile. Ordenaças reales de Castilla. Burgos, 1528.

Chronica del famoso cavallero Cid Ruydiez Campeador. Burgos, 1593.

Gómez de Ciudad Real, Alvaro. El Vellocino Dorado y la historia de la ordẽ del Tuson. Toledo, 1546.

Marineus, Lucius. Cronica Daragon. Valencia, 1524.

——. Obra... de las cosas memorables de España. Alcalá de Henares, 1539.

Medina, Pedro de. Libro de grandezas y cosas memorables de España. Seville, 1549.

Pérez de Guzmán, Fernando. ...Cronica del serenissimo Rey Don Juan el segundo. Logroño, 1517.

Pragmaticas del reyno, Las. Seville, 1520.

Quadernos de las cortes que Su Magestad de la emperatriz y reyna

tuvo en la ciudad de Segovia, 1532. Jũtamẽte cõ las cortes q̃
Su Magestad del emperador tuvo en la villa de Madrid, 1534.
Madrid, 1535.

Rades y Andrada, Francisco de. Chronica de las tres ordenes
y cavallerias de Sanctiago, Calatrava y Alcantara. Toledo,
1572.

Rodríguez de Almela, Diego. Valerio de las hystorias scolasticas
de la sagrada scritura y de los hechos d'España. Nuevamẽte
corregido. Seville, 1536.

Sánchez de Tovar, Fernán. Chronica del muy esclasecido Principe
y Rey Don Alonso. Y ansimismo al fin deste libro va encorporada
la Chronica del rey Don Sãcho el Bravo. Valladolid, 1554.

Local history has been well developed, especially the Catalonian section, which includes some seventeenth-century pamphlet material, and works on the separation question. There is
a good series of fueros, or statutes, of various places. In 1859,
William Hickling Prescott bequeathed the collection of books that
he had made for the preparation of his History of Ferdinand and
Isabella. It consisted of 282 volumes of printed books and 5 folio
volumes of manuscripts. Beginning with this reign, and continuing
through the reign of Philip II, the collection is especially strong.
In recent years an effort has been made to gather material for the
period of the Primo de Rivera dictatorship, the revolution of 1931,
and the civil war of 1936 to 1939.

The literature section was recently enriched by the Carl
T. Keller collection of Don Quixote. This outstanding collection
of the Cervantes classic now amounts to over 750 editions, representing forty-seven languages. There are approximately 225
editions of the Spanish text, including three 1605 editions (Sune Benages
5, 6, 7), 200 editions in English, and 100 editions in French.
The Cervantes collection is also strong in modern critical material.

In its collection of early printed books, the library has 17
Spanish incunabula. There is a fair sprinkling of works printed
in the sixteenth and seventeenth centuries. The writings of the
novelists and dramatists of the last sixty years or more are well
represented. Nineteenth-century plays in the pamphlet collection
number over 5,000 with about two-thirds of these in a series of
collective bound volumes, arranged alphabetically.

An important addition was made in 1933 by the purchase of
a collection of over 10,000 broadside poems both in Spanish and
Catalan. These verses, known in the former language as gozos
and in the latter as goigs, are in praise of the Virgin or of some saint.

They date from early in the seventeenth century to the present day, and were printed not only in Madrid and Barcelona but in many provincial towns.

While the division of Catalan literature is not large, it is representative.

Harvard University
Harvard Law School Library
Cambridge 38

In May 1898, Edward Henry Strobel was appointed Bemis Professor of International Law in the Harvard University Law School. Professor Strobel had been American minister to Ecuador and later minister to Chile, and by his aid, in 1899, the library was enabled to make contacts with various persons in the diplomatic service in South America, who procured for it a few outstanding South American law books, mainly treatises and codes. These volumes formed the nucleus around which has grown the present Latin American collection.

The collection is designed to cover the whole field of law, particular emphasis being laid upon the acquisition of primary sources, laws passed by law-making authorities, and decisions of the courts. The memorias of the various ministers, with the exception of those of the Minister of Foreign Affairs, are poorly represented here. Their decretos, however, are quite generally included in the volumes of session laws.

In addition to the documentary material mentioned above, the library possesses about 1,500 volumes dealing with South American boundary disputes and arbitrations.

Detailed information about the collecton follows:

South America

General:

1493, May 4.   Bull of Alexander VI dividing the territories of the New World between the sovereigns of Spain and Portugal. The library apparently has no separate; it may be found in Cherubinus, Bullarium sive collectio Constitutionum (Rome, 1586), I, p. 134.

Of the colonial period, the library has:

1627.   Ordenanzas del tribunal del consulado de esta ciudad y reynos del Perú, Terra firme y Chile...1627 (Lima, 1680 and 1820).

1685. Ordenanzas del Perú...recogidas y coordenadas por Thomas de Ballesteros (Lima, 1685).

1752. Ordenanzas del Perú...recogidas y coordenadas por Thomas de Ballesteros. Nuevamente añadidas las ordenanzas que para el nuevo establecimiento del tribunal de la sta. cruzada, hà dispuesto, y mandado observar...Joseph Antonio Manso de Velasco, conde de Super-Unda (Lima, 1752).

1782. Real ordenanza para el establecimiento é instrucción de intendentes de exército y provincia en el vizreinato de Buenos Aires año de 1782 (Madrid, n. d.)

1807, November 29. The prince regent of Portugal (later John VI) accompanied by the queen and the great officers of state, fleeing from the armies of Napoleon, departs for Brazil.

1808, March 7. Seat of Portuguese government established at Rio de Janeiro. The library has Collecção das leis brasileiras desde a chegada da corte ate a epoca da independencia, 1808 á 1816, 2 vols. (Ouro Preto, 1834-35).

1809, August. First junta set up at Quito in the viceroyalty of New Granada. The library apparently has nothing of this period.

1810. The government of the Viceroy Cisneros at Buenos Aires, representing the Napoleonic regime in Spain, is overthrown by a local revolutionary movement begun on May 10, and a junta provisoria gubernativa installed. The library has Registro oficial de la República Argentina que comprende los documentos espedidos desde 1810 hasta 1873. Publicación oficial, 6 vols. (Buenos Aires, 1879-84).

1810, July. Local government at Valparaíso overthrown. On September 18, an independent government was established by the revolutionists for Chile (heretofore a captain-generalcy under the viceroy of Peru). The library has Boletín de las leyes i decretos del gobierno, 1810-1814 (Santiago de Chile, 1898); also continuations to date.

1810, December. The Republic of Cundinamarca was established at Bogotá. The library has the constitution of 1811, but only in a general collection of constitutions.

1811, March. Meeting of the first congress of Venezuela. On account of the approach of the royalist troops under Monteverde in April 1812, and the subsequent restoration of the Spanish, no further sessions were held. This congress proclaimed the independence of Venezuela and framed the first constitution (see below). No known copy exists of the records of the proceedings of the first session. The libro de actas of the second session now preserved in the state archives has been officially reproduced in the following volume, which the library has: El

Libro nacional de los venezolanos: actas del congreso constituyente de Venezuela en 1811 (Caracas, 1911).

1811, July 5.   The Declaration of Independence was adopted by
the representatives of the united provinces of Caracas, Cumaná,
Barinas, Margarita, Barcelona, Mérida, and Trujillo, forming
the Confederación Americana de Venezuela.   The library has
this declaration in Interesting Official Documents Relating to
the United Provinces of Venezuela... in Spanish and English
(London, 1812). Also in El Libro nacional (see above).

1811, November 17. Act of Federation. A union of the provinces
of Antioquia, Cartagena, Neiva, Pamplona, and Tunja to form
the United Provinces of New Granada. The library has this in
a collection of constitutions.

1811, December 21. Federal constitution for the states of Venezuela.
Of this constitution, 120 copies were ordered to be printed by
the congress. The library has Constitución federal para los
Estados Unidos de Venezuela hecha por los representantes de
Margarita etc... reunidos en congreso general (Caracas, 1812).

1812, June 14. Constitution of Cartagena de Indias. The library
has Constitución del estado de Cartagena de Indias sancionada
en 14 de junio del año de 1812 (Cartagena, n. d.).

1812, October 27. Reglamento constitutional provisorio (Chile).
On the reconquest of Chile shortly after by the Spanish viceroy of Peru, this regulation became of no effect. The library
has it in the Boletín.

1813, August. Bolívar enters Caracas and is reinvested with
dictatorial power over Venezuela by an assembly of notables
which he convokes. This power was to last until a union of
New Granada and Venezuela was brought about, but Bolívar
was soon obliged to flee to New Granada by the return of the
royalist forces.

1814. Dr. Francia named dictator of Paraguay.

1816, July 9. Declaration of Independence of the United Provinces
of La Plata (Provincias Unidas del Río de la Plata). The library has it in the Registro oficial, I, p. 366. Also an English
translation (see below—1819, April 22) and an 1817 edition in
Spanish.

1818, January 1. Proclamation of the independence of Chile by
the head of the state, Bernardo O'Higgins. The library has it
in the Boletín de las leyes.

1818, August 18. Provisional constitution of Chile published.
The library has it in the Boletín.

1819, February 15. Second congress of Venezuela convened at
Angostura. For the first congress, see March 1811.

1819, April 22. Constitution of the United Provinces of South
America sanctioned and ordered to be published. The library
has: Constitución de las Provincias Unidas en Sud América
sancionada y mandada publicar por el soberano congreso general
constituyente en 22 de abril de 1819 (Buenos Aires, 1819); and
Constitution of the United Provinces of South America...together
with the Declaration of Independence... Translated by William
Walton (London, 1819).

1819, August 7. Battle of Boyacá. The victory of the revolutionists
ended the Spanish power in New Granada. Following his victory, Bolívar left for Venezuela to report to the congress there.

1819, December 17. Fundamental law uniting the republics of
Venezuela and New Granada to form the new republic of Colombia. The library seems to have no separate; it may be found
in Cuerpo de leyes, I (see below—1821, May 6).

1820. Congress of Angostura.

1820. The city of Guayaquil erects a junta and declares its independence. The library apparently has nothing of this period.

1821, February 12. Provisional regulation of Huaura (Peru).
The library has it in Colección de los reglamentos (see below—
1821, October 8).

1821, May 6. First congress of Colombia meets. The library
has Cuerpo de leyes de la república de Colombia, comprende
la constitución y leyes sancionadas por el primer congreso
general, I (Bogotá, 1822; London, 1825; Caracas, 1840).

1821, July 15. Independence of Peru declared at an assembly of
citizens; publicly proclaimed on July 28.

1821, August 3. Proclamation of San Martín, assuming the supreme
power in Peru as Protector. The library has it in Colección
de leyes, I (1831) (see below—1821, October 8).

1821, August 30. Constitution of Colombia (Great Colombia) promulgated. The library has Constitución de la república de
Colombia (Rosario de Cúcuta, 1821).

1821, October 8. Provisional constitution for Peru promulgated.
The library has this in Colección de los reglamentos expedidos
por el Protector de la libertad de Peru (San Martín) (Lima,
1821). The library also has Colección de leyes y decretos
sancionados desde la jura de la independencia (1821-25), 2 vols.
(Lima, 1825-26); and Colección de leyes, decretos y órdenes
publicadas en el Perú desde su independencia en el año de 1821,
13 vols. (Lima, 1831-54). The library lacks Colección ó
catálogo de leyes, decretos, reglamentos y instrucciones dictadas
desde el año de 1820 hasta el de 1830, I-II (1820, 1824-25,
1831).

1822, May. Quito taken by the revolutionary forces and a union
with Venezuela and New Granada agreed upon by an assembly
of prominent citizens.

1822, July. Proclamation of Bolívar annexing Guayaquil to
Colombia.

1822, July 6. Treaties of union and federation signed at Lima.

1822, September 7. Independence of Brazil declared by Dom
Pedro (heir to the crown of Portugal).

1822, September 20. First constitutional congress of Peru (Primer
Congreso Constituyente del Perú) installed.

1822, October 12. Pedro proclaimed constitutional emperor of
Brazil.

1822, October 23. Constitution of Chile promulgated. The library
has Constitución política del estado de Chile promulgada el 23
de octubre de 1822 (Santiago? Imprenta del Estado, n. d.).
Owing to the disturbed internal condition of the nation, this
constitution was followed in rapid succession by three others
in 1823, 1828, and 1833. Editions of 1823 and 1833 are in the
Law Library.

1822, December 17. "Bases de la Constitución Política de la
República Peruana" promulgated. The library has it in
Colección de leyes y decretos, II (see—1821, October 8).

1823, May. Constitutional assembly meets at Rio de Jameiro to
draft a constitution for Brazil but is dissolved by the emperor
in November.

1823, July 25. Revolutionary army enters La Paz but is soon
driven out by the Spanish forces.

1823, November 12. Constitution sanctioned by the Primer Congreso Constituyente of Peru. The library has an official edition
printed in Lima (without date).

1823, November 26. Commission of ten meets to frame a constitution for Brazil. The draft was prepared by Carneiro
de Campos.

1824, February 10. Peruvian congress dissolved and Bolívar
named dictator.

1824, March 25. Constitution for Brazil promulgated. The library lacks an original edition but has Constituição politica do
imperio do Brazil (Lisbon, 1826).

1825, February 9. Decree of General Sucre calling a congress
for Upper Peru. The library has it in Colección oficial (see
below—1825, August 6).

1825, April 25. Division of the Peruvian army under Miller (an
English veteran) enters Potosí.

1825, May 16. Decree of Bolívar confirming the decree of Sucre calling a congress for Upper Peru. The library has it in Colección oficial (see below—1825, August 6).

1825, June 14. Provisional government installed for the Provincia Oriental del Río de la Plata. The library has: Colección legislativa de la República Oriental del Uruguay (Montevideo, 1876), I (covering the period 1825-52) and II-XXX (1852-1907); and Compilación de leyes y decretos 1825-1930, 58 vols. (Montevideo, 1930).

1825, August 6. Congress for Upper Peru meeting at Chuquisaca (Sucre) declares the independence of Upper Peru. The library has it in Colección oficial de leyes, ordenes, resoluciones que se han expedido para el régimen de la República Boliviana 1825 y 1826, I (Paz de Ayacucho, 1834). This is apparently not the first publication of its kind, as on the title page there is the following note: "En esta colección se han suprimido algunas disposiciones contenidas en la antigua." The library also possesses another edition of Colección oficial...1825 y 1826 (La Paz, n.d.), which includes the constitution of November 19, 1826 (see below). The library has a Registro oficial for 1826-29 (see below).

1825, August 11. Name of the new republic of Upper Peru changed to República Bolívar in honor of the "liberator"; later, to República de Bolivia. The library has Registro oficial de leyes, decretos y ordenes del gobierno, 47 nos. (Chuquisaca, 1826-29).

1825, August 25. Declaration of independence from Brazil and Portugal by the House of Representatives of the Provincia Oriental del Río de la Plata. By a decree of the same date the Provincia Oriental was annexed to the United Provinces of the Río de la Plata. The library has both of these in Colección legislativa (see—1825, June 14).

1826, November 19. Constitution of Bolivia promulgated. The library apparently lacks the first printing but has Constitución de la República Boliviana, reimpresa de orden del supremo gobierno en Chuquisaca en 30 de mayo de 1827 (Chuquisaca, 1827).

1828, August 27. Treaty between Brazil and the United Provinces renouncing all rights to Montevideo Province and providing for the formation of an independent state (Uruguay). The library has this in Colección legislativa (see—1825, June 14).

1829, September 10. First constitution for Uruguay framed. The library has Constitución de la República Oriental del Uruguay, sancionada por la asamblea general constituyente y legislativa el 10 de septiembre de 1829 (Montevideo, 1829).

1830. The departments of Venezuela and Ecuador having with-
drawn from the union, the republic of Great Colombia is dissolved and the independent republics of New Granada, Ecuador,
and Venezuela formed.

1830, September 22. New constitution for Venezuela promulgated.
The library has: Constitución del estado de Venezuela (Valencia,
1830), and Constitución y demás actos legislativos sancionados
por el congreso constituyente de Venezuela en 1830 (Caracas,
1832).

1830, September 23. Constitution of the state of Ecuador promulgated. The library has no separate; it may be found in
Actas del congreso ecuatoriano de 1831, precedidas de una
introducción historica, por Francisco Ignacio Salazar (Quito,
1888). The library apparently has no session laws of the new
government before 1835.

1831, November 17. Ley fundamental del estado de la Nueva
Granada. The library has this in Colección de las leyes dadas
por la convención constituyente del estado de la Nueva Granada
en las sesiones de los años 1831 y 1832 (Bogotá, n.d.).

1832. Constitution of New Granada. The library has this in
Constitución del estado de la Nueva Granada, dada por la
convención constituyente en el año de 1832 (Bogotá, 1832).

1869, September 10. Acta de instalación del Gobierno Provisorio
de la República del Paraguay. The library has this in Rejistro
oficial del gobierno provisorio de la república del Paraguay,
años de 1869 y 1870 (Asunción, 1871). Of the period of the
dictators José Gaspar Rodríguez de Francia, Carlos Antonio
López, and Francisco Solano López (from 1814 to 1869), the
library has only Repertorio nacional (año de 1843), 21 nos.
(Asunción: Imprenta de la República, 1843). This volume
contains decrees of Carlos Antonio López.

1870, November 18. Constitution of Paraguay sanctioned by the
convention. The library has no early edition but has Rejistro
oficial del gobierno provisorio de la república del Paraguay,
años de 1869 y 1870 (Asunción, 1871).

1903, November 3. Panama revolts and declares its independence.

1904, February 15. Constitution for Panama sanctioned. The
library has: Constitución de la república de Panamá (Panama,
1904); and Leyes expedidas por la convención nacional constituyente de la república de Panamá en 1904 (Panama, 1912).

Argentine Republic:

The library has the first constitution of 1819 and the session
laws as contained in the Registro oficial, from 1810 to 1873; also

the Registro nacional, from 1851 to 1911, and for the year 1938. The Registro is a complete publication containing both leyes and decretos. The library also has Colección legislativa. ...Leyes nacionales sancionadas por el congreso from 1914 to date; and Colección completa de leyes nacionales, which contains the session laws (leyes only) from 1852 to 1925, completely reprinted. There is also Leyes nacionales clasificadas y sus decretos reglamentarios in 18 volumes, containing the session laws in classified form to 1934, with supplementary annual volumes to date. The Anales de legislación Argentina, 1941 to date, contain important national and provincial laws. Of the official gazette Boletín oficial de la República Argentina, the library has 1912-13, 1929-44, and 1946 to date.

In addition to the session laws there is a good lot of the various codes, compilations of laws of general interest (leyes usuales), and collections of treaties. The library has the decisions of the supreme court, the federal courts of appeal, and the courts of the capital (as far as they have been published) from the installation of these tribunals.

With the exception of the memorias of the minister of foreign affairs, documentary material of an administrative nature is incomplete.

Argentine Republic—Provinces:

Buenos Aires: A good collection of sessional legislation (leyes and decretos) from 1810 to date, some compilations, a fair collection of codes of procedure, and the reports of the supreme court of the province from 1810 to date (as far as published).

Catamarca: The constitution, and the Boletín oficial y judicial from 1948 to date.

Córdoba: The constitution, procedural codes, and a good collection of legislation from 1810 to date; also several collections of the decisions of the local tribunals.

Corrientes: A few procedural codes and a collection of decisions of the tribunales superiores from 1896 to 1901.

Entre Ríos: The constitutions of 1822 and 1933, collections of laws 1821-95, an official compilation (Recopilación de leyes) of recent date, and some procedural codes. Also the reports of the superior tribunal from 1938 to date.

Jujuy: A few laws and codes; no reports.

La Rioja: A few early laws (1854-75).

Mendoza: A good collection of the session laws from 1860 to

1914; also some compilations and procedural codes. A number
of reports of decisions, including Jurisprudencia de Mendoza,
1939-47.

Salta: The library has the constitutions of 1855 and 1906, and
Recopilación general de leyes de la provincia de Salta y sus
decretos reglamentarios, which contains the session laws from
1855 to 1935. Session laws as well as reports of decisions are
published in the Boletín oficial de la provincia, which began in
1908, and which the library receives currently.

San Juan: Very little.

San Luis: Very little.

Santa Fé: Publication of the laws from 1815 is in progress, but
at present the publication is suspended. The last volume in
the library is for the year 1891 (published in 1928). Recent
compilation of laws and codes. Reports of decisions of the
supreme court from 1892-97 and 1922 to date.

Santiago del Estero: Very little.

Tucumán: A collection of session laws (leyes and decretos) from
1852 to 1909, fairly recent editions of the procedural codes,
and decisions of the supreme court from 1925 to 1944.

In addition to the above, the library has about 900 books and
pamphlets covering all fields of Argentine law, and nearly 550
volumes of periodicals.

Bolivia:

In addition to the text of 14 different constitutions, the library has the session laws (leyes and decretos) from 1825 to date;
also fairly recent editions of the codes and collections of treaties.
Decisions of the courts from 1858 are contained in the Gaceta
judicial, which the library has from its beginning. There is very
little from the departments and provinces. About 50 legal treatises
are in the library and 3 general legal periodicals, in addition to
the Gaceta mentioned above.

Brazil:

The library has a number of editions of the various constitutions, and a complete collection of the session laws of Brazil
from 1808, as well as recent editions of the codes. Decisions of
the Supremo Tribunal are to be found in Revista do supremo tribunal federal (1914-25), Jurisprudencia. Supremo tribunal federal
(1932-43), and Jurisprudencia (1941-45); and decisions of the courts
generally in O direito (1873-1913), Revista de direito civil, commercial
e criminal (1906-45), Revista de jurisprudencia brasileira (1928

to date), and in a few other series. Of the official gazette, Diario oficial, the library has volumes from 1823 to 1832, and from 1934 to date, the latter run with some gaps.

Brazil was originally divided into provinces which became states in 1891. Of these provinces and states, the library has:

Acre: A few decisions only.

Alagôas: A compilation of laws, 1835-72. Session laws from 1888 to 1932. Decisions of the Tribunal Superior, 1904-10.

Amazonas: The constitution of 1935. Laws from 1852 to 1927. After 1927, session laws are published only in the Diario, which the library does not have. Decisions of the Tribunal Superior from 1894 to 1934.

Bahia: The constitutions of 1891 and 1935. Laws from 1901 to 1937. Reports of decisions 1894-1903 and 1932-34.

Ceará: Laws from 1894 to 1938. No decisions.

Espírito Santo: 5 constitutions. Laws from 1899. Reports of the Tribunal Superior, 1920-25.

Federal District: Some procedural codes. Municipal laws, 1893-1921.

Goiás: Three constitutions. Laws from 1892 to 1930.

Maranhao: Laws from 1900. No decisions.

Mato Grosso: Mainly the Diario oficial, 1944 to date.

Minas Gerais: The constitutions of 1891 and 1936. Laws from 1891. Some procedural codes. Reports of decisions from 1904 as contained in Revista forense.

Pará: The constitutions of 1891 and 1935. A few laws and reports of decisions.

Paraiba: The constitution of 1935. Some procedural codes. Laws from 1892. Decisions from 1907 as contained in Revista do foro, 1907 to date.

Paraná: The constitutions of 1892 and 1935. A fairly complete collection of laws and decrees from 1890 (decretos to 1928, leis to 1929). Reports of decisions are contained in Paraná judiciario, which the library has.

Pernambuco: The constitutions of 1930 and 1935. Leis and decretos from 1924 to 1940, and a number of separate laws, as well as of codes of procedure. Eight volumes of decisions.

Piauí: The constitutions of 1892 and 1935. Laws and decrees from 1889 to 1946.

Rio de Janeiro: Laws and decrees from 1889 to 1912, but not complete. Decisions of the courts as contained in Relatorio do Tribunal (1905-29) and Boletín judiciario (1932 to date).

Rio Grande do Norte: The constitutions of 1907 and 1947. <u>Actos</u>
  <u>legislativos e decretos</u> (1889-1947), issued in two parts: <u>Leis</u>
  and <u>Decretos</u>.
Rio Grande do Sul: The constitutions of 1891, 1935, and 1947.
  Laws and decrees from 1890 to 1941. A few procedural codes.
  Reports and decisions as contained in <u>Decisões do superior</u>
  <u>tribunal</u> (1895-1928); also <u>Revista jurídica</u> (1953 to date).
Santa Catarina: The constitution of 1935. Laws from 1835 to 1929.
  Reports of decisions as contained in <u>Jurisprudencia do superior</u>
  <u>tribunal</u> (1891-98, 1911-20, 1953 to date).
São Paulo: The constitutions of 1891 and 1935. Laws and decrees
  from 1892 to date. Reports of decisions as contained in <u>Gazeta</u>
  <u>jurídica</u> (1893-1907), <u>São Paulo judiciario</u> (1903-14), and <u>Revista</u>
  <u>dos tribunaes</u> (1912 on).
São Pedro: Very little.
Sergipe: The constitutions of 1901 and 1935. Laws and decrees
  from 1889 to 1924. Reports of decisions as contained in <u>Sergipe</u>
  <u>judiciario</u> (1828-30).

The library has over 900 volumes of legal periodicals of
Brazil, and about 600 treatises.

Chile:

In addition to the constitutions already mentioned, the library
has various editions of the constitution of 1925, the latest dated
1946, including the reforms of 1943. There is a good collection
of codes, some of them fairly recent editions. Reports of decisions
are to be found in <u>Gaceta de los tribunales</u> (1841 to date). The
library possesses about 150 legal treatises and over 100 volumes
of legal periodicals.

Colombia:

Of the Spanish regime before the Act of Union in 1811, there
is nothing in the library. There is very little material of the United
Provinces of New Granada, which was founded in 1811 by a union
of the provinces of Antioquia, Cartagena, Neiva, Pamplona, and
Tunja.

The library possesses a good collection of official material
beginning with the Republic of Colombia (Great Colombia) in 1819
and continuing to date. Session laws start with 1821 and are nearly
complete, although the form in which they appear varies greatly.
In 1924, there was started a republication of the laws entitled
<u>Codificación nacional de todas las leyes</u>, the volumes of which are
being received as issued. The library has <u>Diario oficial</u> from 1864.

Reports of decisions of the supreme court from 1887 are to be found in Gaceta judicial.

Great Colombia was divided in 1830 to form the independent republics of New Granada, Ecuador, and Venezuela. New Granada was again divided into many provinces, which later became states. Of the period from about 1855 to 1886, when the states were sovereign with their own legislative assemblies, the library has many laws and codes, notably of Antioquia, Bolívar, Cauca, Cundinamarca, Magdalena, Panama, and Santander. The library possesses judicial decisons of some of these.

In addition to the above, there are in the library about 300 legal treatises and 200 volumes of periodicals.

Ecuador:

The library has 13 constitutions. There is a broken collection of laws and decrees from 1835 to 1931, and a representative collection of codes, some fairly recent. The set of the official gazette (Registro oficial) is quite complete from 1905. The library also possesses reports of decisions of the supreme court from 1902 as contained in the Gaceta judicial, and has about 60 volumes of periodicals, and a few treatises. Very little from the provinces.

Panama:

Of the state and department of Panama, the library has a broken set of the session laws from 1860 to 1900; of the republic, the constitutions of 1904, 1941, and 1946, and a nearly complete run of session laws from 1904 to date, as well as the Gaceta oficial from November 14, 1903. There is also a fair collection of the codes. Decisions of the courts are to be found in the Registro judicial (1892-1903, 1903-43, 1943-46 incomplete). About 25 legal treatises. No periodicals.

Paraguay:

The library has a few decrees of the dicatator Carlos Antonio López as contained in Repertorio nacional (1843); the constitution of 1870 in a printing of 1890, and those of 1925 and 1940; also session laws for the period 1869 to date in the Registro oficial, with some gaps. The library has the Gaceta oficial from 1936 to date, with some gaps. The collection of codes is moderately good. Decisions of the courts are to be found in Boletín de los tribunales (1920-22, 1931-32, 1939), which from 1922 to 1931 was incorporated in the Diario oficial (1918-34). About 35 volumes of treatises; 20 volumes of periodicals.

Peru:

The library possesses a few ordinances of the vice-regal
period.   There are numerous editions of the several constitutions.
The collection of session laws of the republic commences in 1821
and, in one form or another, is fairly complete to date.   The collection of codes is an exceptionally good one.   There is also a large
collection of laws on specific subjects.

There is in the library a fairly good number of decisions of
the courts as reported in various periodicals.   Among them are the
following: El Republicano (1835-46), Gaceta judicial (1858-59),
Repertorio judicial (1864-65), Diario judicial (1890-1925), Anales
judiciales (1877-78, 1906 to date), Revista de los tribunales (1931-
48), and Revista de jurisprudencia peruana (1943 to date).

The library has the official gazette, El Peruano, from 1838
to date, with a few gaps.

Peruvian governmental material comprises, in addition to
laws and decisions, documents of various departments; for example,
memorias of the Ministerio de Justicia, the Ministerio de Fomento,
the Ministerio de Gobierno y Policía, and the Ministerio de Relaciones
Exteriores, also memorias of the various courts of justice.   With
the exception of the reports of the Ministry of Foreign Affairs, the
library does not have as much of the same nature for the other Latin American countries.

Including students' theses, the library possesses about 600
volumes and pamphlets on Peruvian law, and 100 or so volumes
of ordinances of cities.   It also has about 500 volumes of periodicals.

Uruguay:

The library has various editions of the constitutions of 1830,
1919, 1934, and 1942.   Session laws (leyes, decretos, y resoluciones)
are found in Colección legislativa (1825-1907); also in Compilación
de leyes y decretos (1825-1930) and Registro nacional (1908 to
date).   There is a very good collection of the various codes.   The
library has the Diario oficial from September 1905.

Decisions of the courts are found in Jurisprudencia uruguaya
(1928 to date), Beltrán, Fallos de la alta corte de justicia (1908-
9), Boletín judicial (1919-23), Revista de derecho, jurisprudencia
y administración (1894 to date), and in the Diario oficial.   There is
also Jurisprudencia: Colección Abadie Santos, a digest of decisions

from 1907 to (so far) 1941, publication of which began in 1930 and continues to date.

The library possesses a good collection of treatises and some 300 volumes of periodicals.

Venezuela:

The Law School has 19 constitutions of Venezuela, dating from the first in 1811 (printed in 1812) to 1953, and the session laws (leyes, decretos, etc.) in various editions, almost complete from 1830 to date. There is also a very good collection of the codes. Reports of decisions of the Alta Corte Federal (1870-1903), the Corte de Casación (1881-1903), the Corte Federal y de Casación (1904-29), and the Corte de Jurisprudencia (1924-49) are found in the memorias of the respective courts. There is also the Gaceta oficial from 1923 to date.

The library possesses also material for the following states, territories, and districts: Los Andes, Anzoátegui, Apure, Aragua, Barcelona, Barquisimeto, Bermúdez, Bolívar, Carabobo, Caracas, Cojedes, Colón, Cumaná, Delta-Amarcuru, Falcón, Guárico, Guayana, Lara, Maracaibo, Mérida, Miranda, Nueva Andalucía, Nueva Esparta, Portuguesa, Ribas, Sucre, Táchira, Trujillo, Zamora, Zulia, and the Federal District.

In addition to the above, there are in the library about 150 treatises and 100 volumes of periodicals.

Central America

The five republics of Central America (Costa Rica, Guatemala, Honduras, Nicaragua, and El Salvador) in the viceregal period formed parts of the captaincy-general of Guatemala. After the revolution in 1821, all or a part of these republics were successively united to the Mexican Empire of Iturbide (1821-22) or, with intervening periods of complete independence, associated to form the various Central American Federations, namely, in 1823-39, 1842-45, 1895-98, and 1921-22. There is nothing in the library of the viceregal period.

The library has a copy of Facsímil del Acta de independencia, September 15, 1821, published in 1954. Of the first federal period (1823-39), the library has Constitución de la república federal de Centro-América, dada por la asamblea nacional constituyente en 22 noviembre de 1824, plus 54 separate laws; of the second federation (1842-45), Pacto de la confederación Centro-Americana (Imprenta del E[stado] a cargo de José María Sánchez, 1842).

Of the third federation (1895-98), to which only the states of Honduras, Nicaragua, and El Salvador belonged, the library has Constitución política de los Estados Unidos de Centro-América y
decretos de la asamblea constituyente (Tegucigalpa, 1898); the
constitution is also contained in La Gaceta: periódico oficial de
estado de Honduras, XXII, pp. 425-31. Of the fourth federation
(1921-22), the library has Pacto de unión de Centro-América,
celebrado en San José de Costa Rica, el 19 de enero de 1921
(Tegucigalpa, n. d.); Constitución política de la República de
Centro-América (Tegucigalpa, 1921), 2 printings; and the same
constitution printed in Guatemala (1921) and El Salvador (1921).

Costa Rica:

The library has the constitutions of 1847 with reforms of
1848, 1859, 1869, 1871, 1917 (in several editions incorporating
amendments), and 1949; a complete collection of the session laws
from 1824 to date; also recent editions of the codes. Reports of
decisions of the court of cassation are here from 1888, and memorias
of the Secretaría de Relaciones Exteriores from 1885 to 1936.
It has also about 20 legal treatises and about 40 volumes of periodicals.

Guatemala:

The library has 7 different constitutions of Guatemala. The
session laws are to be found in the Recopilación de las leyes (1871-
1946); also in the various official gazettes of which the library
possesses a very good collection, almost complete from 1841 to
date. There is in addition a very good collection of codes.

Reports of decisions of the courts are to be found in Gaceta
de los tribunales (1881 to date), which the library has complete.
It also contains 35 volumes of legal periodicals of a general nature,
about 45 treatises, and almost 100 theses, though these are of
little consequence.

Honduras:

The library has 5 constitutions, and Decretos del congreso
nacional (1885, 1896-1903, 1924 to date). La Gaceta is to be
found from 1876 to date; also several codes but few (1940, 1944)
very recent editions. Decisions of the courts are to be found in
La Gaceta; also in the Gaceta judicial (of which the library has
scattered volumes for 1895-1923) and in the Revista judicial (1904-
7). There is only a handful of treatises and about 12 volumes of
periodicals other than those already mentioned.

Nicaragua:

There are 6 constitutions in the library. Of session laws, there are Decretos y acuerdos de la administración constitucional del... Tomás Martínez (1857-61), and a broken run of Colección de decretos legislativos promulgados (1857-1919). Session laws are also contained in La Gaceta (1913 to date). There is a fair collection of codes, the only recent ones, however, being the civil codes, the commercial code, criminal code, labor code, and mining code. There are a number of separate laws. Decisions of the courts are contained in Boletín judicial (1913-45). The library has the memorias of the Recaudador General de Aduanas from 1911 to date. There are about 30 treatises and 7 volumes of periodicals.

El Salvador:

The constitutions of 1864, 1883, 1886, 1939, and 1950 are in the library. Session laws from 1880 are contained in Anuario de legislación (1880-1908, 1913-16), Repertorio de legislación (1911-12), and Diario oficial (1907 to date). The collection of codes is fair. Decisions of the courts will be found in Revista judicial (1901 to date). There are some twenty treatises and a half dozen volumes of periodicals.

Mexico

After the conquest, the territory which is now Mexico was ruled by audiencias until 1535, when the viceroyalty of New Spain was established. This viceroyalty at one time included the Spanish dominions in the New World from Guatemala to Vancouver Island, as well as the island of Santo Domingo.

Of the viceregal period, the library has the following collection of laws commonly known as the Cedulario de Puga: Philippus hispaniarum et indiarum rex. Prouisiones, cedulas, instrucciones de su magestad, ordenanças de difuntos y audiencia para la buena expedición de los negocios y administración de justicia y gouernación de esta Nueva Espana, y para el buen tratamiento y conseruación de los Indios desde el ano de 1525 hasta esta presente de 63 (Mexico, 1563). The law school has the reprint of 1878-79 and a facsimile published in 1945, but an original is in the Harvard College Library. This is the first important legal publication in the New World.

Although in a measure the viceregal authority in Mexico did not end until August 24, 1821, when Juan O'Donojú (the last viceroy) confirmed the independence of Mexico, the revolution actually began in 1810.   In 1813, the revolutionary leader José María Morelos convoked a congress, and a constitution was drafted and sanctioned by the congress on October 22, 1814.   The library has Decreto constitucional para la libertad de la América Mejicana, sancionada en Apatzingan a 22 de octubre de 1814 (2d ed., Imprenta Nacional, 1815; 3d ed., Moreno Hermanos, 1821).

Shortly after, however, Morelos was taken prisoner by the royalists and, notwithstanding the protests of the congress, then in session, was tried and executed.

On February 24, 1821, by agreement between the revolutionary leaders Agustín de Iturbide and Vicente Guerrero, the "Plan of Iguala" was proclaimed as the basis of a new state.   Congress assembled on February 24, 1822 and elected Iturbide emperor.   He was crowned July 21, 1822.   The library has Colección de los decretos y ordenes que ha expedido la soberana junta provisional gobernativa del Imperio Mexicano, desde su instalación en 28 de setiembre de 1821 hasta 24 de febrero de 1822 (Mexico, 1822).

The empire was short-lived.   Iturbide was compelled to abdicate on April 19, 1823 and, upon his return from Italy to which he had been exiled, was arrested and executed (July 1, 1824).   Meantime a new congress had been installed on February 24, 1822, and a new constitution presented and adopted on October 4, 1824.   The library has the following:

Acta constitucional presentada al soberano congreso constituyente por su comisión el dia 20 de noviembre de 1823.   Mexico: Imprenta del Supremo Gobierno en Palacio, n. d.
Colección de los decretos y órdenes del soberano congreso constituyente mexicano, desde...5 de noviembre de 1823 hasta 24 de diciembre de 1824, en que cesó.   Mexico, 1825.
Colección de los decretos y órdenes del soberano congreso mexicano, desde su instalación en 24 de febrero hasta 30 de octubre de 1823 en que cesó.   Mexico, 1825.
Constitución federal de los Estados Unidos Mexicanos sancionada por el congreso general constituyente el 4 de octubre de 1824.   Mexico: Imprenta del Supremo Gobierno, 1824.

In addition to these, there are the constitutions of 1836, 1843, 1847, 1857, and 1917; there are many editions of the last two.

The law library has a few compilations of laws of the viceregal period and the session laws practically complete from the beginning of the republic.   Many of these are in several editions.   The library has also a very good collection of the federal codes and many separate laws and collections of laws on particular subjects.

Reports of decisions of the courts are here from an early period. The current series (Semanario judicial de la federación) started publication in 1871. The official gazette (under various names) is fairly complete from 1841. Other government documents with the exception of the reports of the Ministry of Foreign Affairs, are fragmentary.

Mexico—States:

Aguascalientes: Several editions of the constitutions of 1868 and 1917, and a few codes and separate laws.

Baja California: An incomplete set of the official gazette to 1882.

Campeche: The constitutions of 1862 and 1917; a few codes and laws, some quite recent.

Chiapas: The constitutions of 1826, 1858, 1893, and 1921; a few codes and laws, some fairly recent.

Chihuahua: The constitutions of 1858, 1887, and 1921, the last two in several editions; some early session laws; a few codes.

Coahuila: The constitutions of 1852, 1869, and 1882, the last named in a number of editions incorporating amendments; a number of laws and codes, including several of quite recent date.

Coahuila and Texas: An early constitution.

Colima: The constitutions of 1882 and 1917. Colección de leyes, 1857-1906. A few codes and separate laws; odd volumes of the government gazette (1906-12).

Durango: The constitutions of 1846, 1863, 1887, and 1916; session laws for 1827-33, 1865, 1877-1914; also the official gazette under various names from 1850 to 1922, somewhat incomplete; a number of codes and separate laws.

Federal District: A large number of codes, including recent editions: some collections of laws and many separate laws. Boletín oficial del consejo superior de gobierno (1903-10); also Anales de jurisprudencia (1933 to date), containing reports of decisions.

Free State of the West: Constitution of 1825.

Guanajuato: The constitutions of 1826, 1861, and 1917, the last two in several editions incorporating amendments; session laws from 1824-88, 1921-22; a fair collection of codes; and some separate laws.

Guerrero: The constitutions of 1851, 1862, 1874, 1880, and 1917; a few codes and separate laws.

Hidalgo: The constitutions of 1870, 1894, and 1920; session laws from 1869 to 1920. Periódico oficial (1869-1927, not quite com-

plete; a few codes. Also La Tribuna: periódico parlamentario
y judicial (1873-93, 1918-21), containing reports of decisions.
Jalisco: Constitutions of 1824, 1857, 1906, and 1917; session laws
from 1823 to 1910. El Estado de Jalisco (official journal containing reports and laws) from 1876 to 1920, and two other official
journals, El País (1860-64, 1866-69) and El Imperio (1864-65).
A good number of codes and some separate laws; and El Litigante
(1881-99), containing reports of decisions.
Mexico: Constitutions of 1827, 1861, 1870, and 1917; session laws
from 1824 to 1911; a fair collection of codes and a number of
separate laws.
Michoacán: Constitutions of 1825, 1858, and 1917 (several editions
of the last two); session laws from 1824 to 1912; several recent
codes and a few separate laws.
Morelos: Constitutions of 1870, 1871, 1878, 1888, and 1898; session
laws from 1869 to 1898; a number of codes and separate laws.
Nayarit: The constitution of 1918; the criminal code, 1947; a few
laws; Periódico oficial (1927 to date).
Nuevo León: Constitutions of 1825, 1878, and 1917; session laws
from 1824 to 1830, 1867 to 1906; a good lot of recent codes.
Nuevo León and Coahuila: Constitution of 1857.
Oaxaca: Constitutions of 1825, 1857, and 1922; session laws from
1823 to 1910; short runs of three early official gazettes (La
Democracia, 1856-58; El Regenerador, 1872-76; La Victoria,
1876-77); and Vols. XXII-XXXIV (1902-14) of the current
Periódico oficial del gobierno; a fairly good lot of codes.
Puebla: Constitutions of 1825, 1861, 1880, 1883, 1892, 1894, and
1917; session laws for 1824-35, 1846-49, 1879, 1886-89, 1894-
95, 1903-8, 1916; an incomplete set of the Periódico oficial
(1873-1915); a fairly good collection of codes.
Querétaro: Constitutions of 1825, 1869, 1879, and 1917; a few
odd volumes of laws and a few codes.
San Luis Potosí: Constitutions of 1826, 1857, 1861, 1917, and 1943;
2 volumes of early laws (1824-35), and a few codes of recent
date.
Sinaloa: Constitutions of 1861, 1880, 1894, 1917, and 1922; a few
volumes of laws and several codes.
Sonora: The constitution of 1831 as reformed in 1848, the constitution of 1861 in several editions with later reforms, and the constitution of 1917; very few laws; some recent codes; 1 volume of
an official gazette, La Constitución (1902).
Tabasco: Constitutions of 1825, 1857, 1883, 1890, and 1919; a
volume of session laws for the period 1824-50; several quite
recent codes.

Tamaulipas: Constitutions of 1825, 1871, 1920, and 1921; no
session laws; some quite recent codes.

Tlaxcala: Constitutions of 1849, 1868, 1891, and 1918; session
laws from 1857 to 1885; the official gazette, El Estado de Tlaxcala:
órgano oficial, and continuation (1887-1910); a few codes.

Vera Cruz: Constitutions of 1825, 1857, 1871, 1873, 1917, and
1932; session laws from 1824 to 1919; a good collection of codes.

Yucatán: Constitutions of 1841, 1862, 1870, 1905, and 1918; session
laws from 1823 to 1911; the official gazette under various names
from 1877 to 1896; a good collection of codes.

Zacatecas: Constitutions of 1825, 1832, 1852, 1857, 1869, 1910,
1918, 1921, and 1944; session laws from 1867 to 1904, not
quite complete; a few codes and a number of separate laws.

In addition to the above, the library contains about 500
volumes of Mexican legal periodicals and about 1,000 volumes and
pamphlets of legal content.

West Indies

Cuba:

The Law School has constitutions of 1897 (royal decree of
the king of Spain), 1901, 1902, 1927, 1928, 1934, 1935, and 1940.
The session laws (leyes y decretos) are in the library from 1854,
with a few earlier, through 1926, as is also the section on legislation
of Jurisprudencia al día from 1931 to date. There is a good collection of the codes in recent editions, and many separate laws. Decisions of the courts are contained in the following periodicals:
Jurisprudencia al día, 1912 to date; Jurisprudencia del tribunal
supremo, to 1913; and Repertorio judicial, 1925 to date. The library has also about 650 books and pamphlets dealing with Cuba
and its laws, and some 75 volumes of legal periodicals.

Dominican Republic:

There are in the library the constitutions of 1844 (as printed
in 1847), 1875, 1896, 1906, 1908, 1924, 1929, 1942, and 1947.
The library has Colección de leyes, decretos y resoluciones (1844-
1916, continued to date in another form); also an incomplete set of
the official gazette, issued under various titles, from 1866 to date.
Fairly recent editions of the various codes are to be found and reports of decisions of the supreme court from 1910 as contained in
Boletín judicial; also a few volumes of decisions of the courts of
appeal of Santo Domingo and La Vega. There are about 20 volumes
of periodicals and a few treatises.

Haiti:

The library has 18 constitutions, from the 1816 revision
of the constitution of 1806 (printed in 1818) to the constitution of
1950. It has also the session laws as contained in Recueil général
des lois (1804-45), Recueil des actes (1887-1904), and Bulletin des
lois (1870-86, 1891, 1916-36, 1941 to date). Of Le Moniteur,
journal officiel, which began in 1846, the library has a nearly complete run from 1873 to date. The library possesses nothing for the
period 1846-69. It has a good collection of codes, including some
recent ones. Decisions are to be found in Bulletin officiel du dé-
partement de la justice (1906-14) and in a few other volumes which
the library has. There is one periodical, Revue juridique de Haïti
(1945); and the library has about 50 legal treatises.

Harvard University
Museum of Comparative Zoology
Cambridge

The fauna of Central and South America is represented
by a great wealth of material in the Museum of Comparative Zoology
at Harvard University. There are many thousands of mammals,
birds, reptiles, amphibians, and fishes, the most famous single
collection being perhaps that of the fishes from the fresh waters of
Brazil made by Professor Agassiz and a group of young assistants,
greatly aided by the Emperor, Dom Pedro, during the period of the
American Civil War. Although many papers have been based upon
the results of this expedition, the material has not as yet been fully
classified and described.

Among the invertebrates, naturally, the insects are most
abundantly represented. The last important item in this connection
to have been received was the Herbst collection of insects from
Chile, especially rich in bees and wasps. Many expeditions have
helped the museum's representation of marine invertebrates. The
Hassler expedition (1872-73) circumnavigated South America, and
Alexander Agassiz's explorations of the Caribbean Basin on the
Wild Duck, the Bib, and the Blake (three cruises) have made the
marine representation of forms inhabiting the Caribbean Basin one
of the most important in the world. More recently the research
ship Atlantis and the research yacht Utowana have worked about the
coasts of Cuba and both coasts of Central America. The collections
made by the Albatross while in charge of Agassiz, and the shore
collections of other investigators have enriched the representation
of both shallow-water and deep-sea life of the west coast region,

from Panama Bay to Chile. In addition to a very large collection
of land and freshwater shells from all of South America, there are
many species of mollusks from the West Indies, particularly from
the island of Cuba. Half of the famous Carlos de la Torre collection
of Cuban land shells has recently been transferred to this museum.

It would be impossible to catalogue the individual collections
which have been given to the museum or those that have been made
by expeditions sponsored by the museum, without writing a book on
the subject. It may, however, be pointed out that the fauna of El
Salvador is not particularly well represented, nor is that of Venezuela, although the museum has some material from both of these
countries. A student interested in the fauna of the other states
would find, in most cases, reasonably good synoptic representations
of their animal life and, in the case of very many of these states,
perhaps the most nearly complete representation to be found in any
museum for many groups of the animal kingdom.

References: Notes Concerning the History and Contents
of the Museum of Comparative Zoology (by members of the staff),
1936, 89 pp. For a list of the great number of the museum's publications referring to Latin America, see the Revised Price List
of the Publications of the Museum of Comparative Zoology, 1859-
1950, and the supplementary Price List, 1950 to date.

Harvard University
Peabody Museum
Cambridge

The Peabody Museum contains two large halls filled with
collections from Middle America, in addition to space given to
collections from the West Indies. The museum is especially rich
in archeological material from the Maya area, with special emphasis on the ruins of Copán, Honduras, the Ulloa Valley, and
various Yucatán ruins, particularly those of Chichén Itzá. It has
models and casts of many of the altars and stelae from Piedras
Negras and Yaxchilán. The museum is rich in collections from
southern Central America, including Costa Rica, Nicaragua, and
Panama. The ethnological collections from Middle America are
represented by extensive collections of textiles from Guatemala
and a very important mass of materials from the Lacandones.
South America is represented both archeologically and ethnologically
by extensive collections, especially from Colombia and Peru.

Facilities are given to scholars to work in the museum

laboratory upon Latin American collections, not only those on exhibition but also those in storage.

The library of the Peabody Museum has an extensive collection of books on Hispanic America. It contains a number of old and rare books on Central America with emphasis on archeology, ethnology, and linguistics. It also possesses 13 volumes of manuscripts by Adolph Francis Bandelier, copied from ancient documents on the early history of Mexico, Santa Fe, and New Mexico. About 1888, Charles Pickering Bowditch's visit to a number of ruins in Central America kindled an enthusiasm which led to a long series of benefactions. His interest and generosity, which now continue through his legacy, have made possible a professorship, a fellowship, and expeditions, research, and publications in the field of Middle American archeology. During his lifetime he not only gave the library all the available reproductions of Maya and Mexican codices, but had several in European libraries copied in colors. There are over 250 volumes in the Bowditch-Gates collection of photographs, and photostats of practically every unpublished manuscript or unique book in the various Maya dialects and others in the languages of Mexico. In 1946, the library received the personal collection of Philip Ainsworth Means, author of Ancient Civilization of the Andes, consisting of 1,377 volumes and pamphlets relating to South America. The library owns several important original manuscripts including a post-Columbian Mexican codex, one in Testerian writing, and the Xiu probanzas in the Maya language, dating from 1608. Purchases in this field have been continued, with the result that the Peabody Museum library has unquestionably attained pre-eminence in Central American anthropology.

The card catalogue, an excellent bibliographical tool for the research student in the study of archeology, anthropology, and ethnology, contains some 303,000 entries, indexing the entire collection of 56,000 periodicals, books, and pamphlets. This catalogue is remarkable for the fact that it indexes periodical articles according to author and subject; the subject cards are filed in a separate section, arranged mainly under geographical or tribal names, subdivided by topics.

Smith College
Museum of Art
Northampton

The Museum of Art possesses the following Hispanic paintings:

Goya. "Self Portrait, " oil on canvas; not signed or dated; probably painted between 1808 and 1813. Collections: Mrs. A. B. Blodgett acquired it at the Baroilhet sale in 1872 and retained it until her death around 1928; disposed of then by Miss Eleanor Blodgett. See: Art Bulletin (March 1931), pp. 5-10, represented as frontispiece and on p. 11; Antiquarian (March 1931), represented p. 32; Parnassus (January 1931), represented on front cover; Smith College Museum Bulletin (1931), pp. 2-13, represented on front cover; ibid. (1932), represented on p. 3. It is interesting to compare this "Self Portrait" with those at the Prado and the Academia de San Fernando in Madrid—the latter dated 1815.

Gris, Juan. "Still Life, " oil on canvas; pieces of paper pasted on the canvas form part of the design; on newspaper scrap in center appears "Le Jou..."; in scrap at left, "Les Villes soeurs. "

__. "Still Life, " oil on canvas; playing cards in lower center; at center right are painted the letters "Le Jo..."

__. "Abstraction, " oil on canvas; colors—blue, green, yellow, brown, and black; certain areas in solid color, others covered with dots and wavy lines.

__. "Still Life—Abstraction, " oil on canvas; painted on are the letters "L...ournal"; colors—gray, purple, lavender, green, blue, brown, and black.

__. "Still Life, " oil on canvas; colors—blue, brown, gray, white, lavender, and black; painted on are the letters "Rhum. "

Picasso. "Abstraction—La Table, " oil on canvas; in values of gray, blue, fawn, and green, with touches of terra cotta; painted in 1920. Collections: Valentine Dudensing. See: Smith College Museum Bulletin (May 1933), pp. 1-6, represented on p. 2; Art Digest (March 1, 1933), p. 29; American Magazine of Art (April 1933), p. 208; Atelier (April 1931), p. 415 of Vol. I.

Sorolla y Bastida. "Spanish Landscape, " oil on canvas.

As to Hispanic prints in the Museum, there are:

Goya. "Self Portrait. " Plate I of Los Caprichos.

__. "Ya tienen asiento. " No. 26 from Los Caprichos.

__. "Las rinde el sueño. " No. 34 from Los Caprichos.

Picasso. "Toilette de femme. " Also known as "La Famille de l'arlequin. " Made in 1905; not signed or dated. Reproduced in Raynal, Picasso, as B. under Etchings (no page numbers in that section), and as No. 15 in Bernhard Geiser, Picasso, Peintre-Graveur.

Ribera. "St. Jerome in the Desert, " signed etching. From the T. J. Thompson collection (Fagan 504).

__. "Pietà, " signed etching.

The museum also owns a crucifix, not signed or dated, attributed to Gregorio Hernández (early seventeenth century). The ivory figure is by now a deep creamy tone shading to brown. Both arms are mended—they had been severed at the shoulder, one crack extending over left shoulder. See Chandler R. Post, History of European and American Sculpture, II, p. 72; and B. Bevan, Burlington Magazine Monograph on Spanish Art, p. 97.

Berkshire Museum
Pittsfield

Spanish paintings in the Berkshire Museum include the following:

Carreño de Miranda, Juan. "Portrait of Eleonora Toletana," oil on canvas, seventeenth century. Gift of Zenas Crane, 1906.

González, Bartolomé. "Duchess of Modena," oil on canvas, early seventeenth century. From the collection of Benito Cabrera, Valladolid, Spain. Gift of Zenas Crane, 1913.

Murillo. "St. Francis," oil on canvas. From the collection of Martin Colnaghi, London. Gift of Zenas Crane, 1915.

Pons, Juan. "Adoration of the Magi," oil, transferred from wood to canvas; signed and dated—Johannes Pontis 1477. Painted to be the center or one of the principal compartments of a retable. Formerly in the collection of Asher Wertheimer, London. Gift of Zenas Crane, 1913.

Unknown, seventeenth century. "Portrait of Philip IV of Spain," oil on canvas. Deposited by Mrs. Winthrop Murray Crane, 1931.

Wellesley College
Library
Wellesley

The Wellesley College Library possesses a notable collection of Hispanica, of especial interest being the splendid collection of photographs acquired from the library of the late Foulché Delbosc and consisting of 8 folio volumes, each of which contains from 70 to 90 photographs of varying size. These cover not only art and architecture, but fiestas, regional customs, and historical scenes. The collection was made in 1884.

The rare book collection contains a number of Spanish manuscripts: an antiphonarium written in Spain, fifteenth century; a grant of mining right to Francisco de Sotomayor, Count of Belalcaçar, signed by Charles V at Worms, March 6, 1521; carta de hidalguía, granted by Charles V to Ipólito de Salas, of Valladolid, 1549; carta de hidalguía, granted by Philip II to de Moya, 1564; regulations of a Spanish hospital, apparently at Palencia, sixteenth century; a photostatic edition of the manuscript of the Cid (about 1140), published by the city of Burgos, signed by the mayor (one of 638 copies). The book collection contains 2 incunabula: Alfonso X el Sabio, Tabulae astronomicae (Venice: Ratdolt, 1483); and Rabbi Abraham Aben, or Ibn Ezra, Liber de nativitatibus (Venice; Ratdolt, 1485). Also included are several books printed in Spain in the sixteenth and seventeenth centuries, and many in the eighteenth century; the Biblia de la Casa de Alba, printed 1920-22, was inscribed and presented by the Duke of Alba in 1929.

An important gift has been received from Miss Alice H. Bushee, Professor of Spanish, Emeritus, of printed books and photostat copies of all known editions of Gabriel Téllez (Tirso de Molina, pseudonym), La Prudencia en la mujer (except that published by Teresa de Guzmán in Madrid, two copies of which are to be found in the nearby Ticknor Collection of the Boston Public Library).

Besides the volumes in the library, Professor Ada M. Coe has a valuable private collection of seventeenth- and eighteenth-century editions of Golden Age plays (comedias sueltas), many of which are not commonly found elsewhere. Professor Coe also has the first series of the Memorial Literario, Instructivo y Curioso de la Corte de Madrid (1784-97); this file is more complete than those in the Biblioteca Nacional, Hermeroteca, and Palacio Nacional of Madrid, not to mention those in the United States and Canada.

American Antiquarian Society
Worcester

The American Antiquarian Society contains a representative collection of some 15,000 volumes of history and travel relative to Latin America. There is a good collection of the artes and diccionarios from the Medina of 1555 to the end of the eighteenth century.

The society possesses an especially good collection of Mexican history, newspapers, almanacs, and early imprints, and what is probably the largest collection of the newspapers and almanac of the West Indies, with examples of printing from practically every island in which printing has been introduced. There are excellent collections of the earlier publications on the antiquities of Central America and of the history of the Bermudas, as well as very good early newspaper files from Bolivia, Chile, and Guatemala. The

ociety's collection of West Indian newspapers is listed in a "List
f Newspapers of the West Indies and Bermuda, " by Waldo Lincoln,
rinted in the proceedings of the society for April 1926, although a
onsiderable number of additions have been made to the collection
ince that date.

Worcester Art Museum
Worcester 2

The Hispanic objects in the Worcester Art Museum include paintings, drawings, sculpture, and minor arts. They have
been gradually acquired since the founding of the museum in 1896.
Every period from the fifteenth to the twentieth centuries is represented by Spanish paintings, which include "Saint Bartholomew"
by an unknown master of the fifteenth century and "The Entry into
Jerusalem, " by Domingo Valls. Among the seventeenth-century
paintings are works by Ribera, Alonso Cano, and El Greco, while
the nineteenth century is represented by Goya's "Portrait of Don
Fray Miguel Fernández. "

Early Spanish sculpture in the museum includes a twelfth-
century Catalan capital and a thirteenth-century Leonese crucifixion
group of three figures in polychrome wood. A wooden "Mater
Dolorosa" from the Cathedral Treasury of León is of the fourteenth
century, and the museum also has 4 alabaster plaques attributed to
Pablo Ortiz.

The minor arts collection includes ceramics (notably an
Hispano-Moresque lustre plaque of the sixteenth century), some
woodwork and ironwork, and Spanish textiles of the fourteenth to
the eighteenth centuries.

Latin American objects in the Worcester Art Museum
include Peruvian textiles, some nineteenth-century Argentine lace,
various potteries and wrought-iron work, and pencil drawings by
Diego Rivera.

Of interest in the museum library's collection are photographs of Catalan painting, sculpture and minor arts, and books on
pre-Romanesque Catalan art.

The museum's Catalogue of Paintings and Drawings and
the Guide to the Collections of the Worcester Art Museum contain
descriptions of some of the Hispanic objects. The museum Bulletins, published monthly October through May, generally have a
description of each object as it is acquired. Other publications of

the museum consist of the Annual, the Annual Report, and catalogue of the current exhibitions.

Following is a list of the Hispanic paintings in the museum

Cano, Alonso. "Christ Bearing the Cross," oil on canvas; signed.

Carmona, Manuel Salvador. "Child Asleep in a Chair," red chalk drawing.

González y Serrano, Bartolomé. "Portrait of a Young Noblewoman," oil on canvas.

Goya. "Portrait of Don Fray Miguel Fernández," oil on canvas; signed lower right.

Greco, El. "The Magdalen," oil on canvas; signed lower left.

Murillo (attributed to). "Santa Rosa di Viterbo," oil on canvas.

Ribera. "The Astronomer," oil on canvas; signed at the right.

Unknown, twelfth century. Catalan altar frontal; tempera on wood panel. Originally in a Pyrenean parish church.

Unknown, School of Valencia, second quarter of fifteenth century. "Saint Bartholomew," tempera on panel.

Unknown, fifteenth century (ca. 1470). Triptych of the Madonna: center section, "Madonna and Child with Donor and Saints," "Crucifixion" above; left wing, "Annunciation" above, "Adoration of the Shepherds" below; right wing, "Coronation of the Virgin" above, "Adoration of the Magi" below; tempera on panel.

Valls, Domingo. "Entry into Jerusalem," tempera on panel.

Hispanic sculpture in the museum includes:

Catalan, twelfth century. Stone capital from the monastery of San Pere de Roda. Shows influence of the classic traditions in the Catalan Ampurias.

Leonese, thirteenth century (late). Wooden crucifixion group, consisting of The Christ, Mary the Mother, and St. John; from the convent of Santa Clara, village of Campos, province of Palencia.

Leonese, fourteenth century. "Mater Dolorosa" from the Cathedral Treasury of León.

Martins, Maria. "Aioka," bronze; twentieth century, Brazilian.

Ortiz, Pablo. Five alabaster plaques, sixteenth century, from base of tombs at the Victoria and Albert Museum, which have similar reliefs.

The museum also owns a sixteenth- or seventeenth-century Spanish chest covered with velvet, and a seventeenth-century set of 3 carved walnut benches (Catalan).

In addition, there are 4 lithographs of a Bordeaux bull-

ight (1825) series by Goya, and prints by the Mexicans Dosamantes
8), Méndez, Orozco, and Siqueiros.

University of Michigan
William L. Clements Library
Ann Arbor

The William L. Clements Library is a collection of
are source materials illustrating the history of the Americas.
The library is divided into several sections, with about 60,000
printed books, approximately 500,000 manuscript items, several
housand maps printed before 1800, and a large and representative
collection of prints. In addition there is a considerable collection
of eighteenth-century newspapers, including those of Mexico. Bulle-
ins of special exhibits, Peckham's Guide to the Manuscript Division, and works by the director, Randolph G. Adams, survey the
contents of the library, although incompletely.

In the book division are hundreds of reports of the early
voyagers of all nations, a number of sixteenth-century Mexican
imprints, including the Breve Doctrina, early Peruvian and Para-
guayan imprints, and a particularly complete group of books and
pamphlets relating to Mexico in the early days of the independence
period. Among secondary materials must be mentioned the extensive library of the great Americanist, Henry Vignaud.

The manuscript division, particularly in recent years,
has added heavily to its holdings in the field of Mexican history.
It already contained the great bulk of the British headquarters papers,
reflecting the story of the North American revolution from the British
side. In these are found the reports of the conflict with the Spanish
American peoples, including the boundary settlements. In Lord
Shelburne's papers also are the "Asiento Papers," which detail
the inner workings of the slave trade and the breakdown of the Haps-
burg monopoly.

The Shelburne papers also contain intelligence reports
from British agents throughout the world, documents on the English
logwood-cutting enterprises in Honduras and Campeche, the trade
with the West Indies, and the conduct of foreign relations between
Britain, Spain, and Portugal. The colonial and commercial rivalry
with Spain is reflected in these papers and reports, as is the course
of events which led up to Spanish participation in the North American
revolution.

The papers of the British commanders-in-chief in the

course of the revolution include much material on the several collisions with Spanish interests and arms, especially in Florida.

Numbers of items in the Phillips collection, and similar scattered material from other sources, throw light on widely separated aspects of South American culture, from Mariano Moreno on the Río de la Plata, to the viceroys of Peru. But the widest coverage is provided in the area of New Spain. Here virtually every viceroy is repre sented by at least a few documents. The silver trade from the mining center of Zacatecas is well covered by a long series of items. From the period of the North American revolution comes the instrucciones left for the then-active viceroy.

In the period of the independence movement in Mexico there is much of interest. A series of contemporary reports document the Hidalgo rising, including an eyewitness report of his death. There is also Agustín Iturbide's deposition as to one of the numerous anti-Spanish plots, and a considerable amount of material from the pens of Morales, Rayón, and the other principal leaders of the independence movement. Both sides are represented in the Wars of the Reform, but a particular treasure is Porfirio Díaz' personal correspondence for the year 1867, the time that saw his military star at its highest peak and culminated in the recapture of Puebla.

Detroit Institute of Arts
Detroit 2

The Detroit Institute of Arts possesses the following Hispanic paintings:

Andreu, Mariano. "The Bathers"; "Spanish Dancer"; "Still Life."
Goya. "The Cardinal," water color.
Greco, El. "St. Francis in Ecstacy" (XIII,* January 1932).
Murillo. "Martyrdom of St. Andrew"; "St. Francis of Assisi";
    "Jacob and Rachel"; "Immaculate Conception" (II, January 1908);
    "The Flight into Egypt."
Ribera. "Bust of an Old Man"; "St. Jerome in the Desert."
Velázquez. "Portrait of a Man" (XI, November 1929; Pantheon,
    July 1929).
Zurbarán. "Portrait of a Girl" (The Arts, XIII, March 1928).

Among the prints, there are:

Bueno, León. "Pastorcita."

*Unnamed references are to the Bulletin of the Detroit Institute of Arts. See also Detroit Institute of Arts, Catalogue of Painting

Fortuny, Mariano. "Arabs Seated"; "Kabyle Mort"; "Zamacois."
Goya. "Bacchus Crowning a (Drunkard) Soldier," etching dated 1778.
Picasso. "Two Nude Figures"; "Visage."
Ribera. "St. Jerome"; "St. Jerome Reading"; "St. Bartholomew";
"St. Peter Repenting his Sin"; "The Poet"; "Bust of a Very Ugly
Man."

As to sculpture, the institute owns an early thirteenth-
century stone head of a bearded saint (IX, February 1928); a thirteenth-century madonna and child of polychromed wood; a fourteenth-
century carved marble water vessel; a sixteenth-century madonna
and child of polychromed stone (VII, No. 4); Alonso Cano's Pietà,
painted terra-cotta sculpture (VII, No. 4); and Manuel Martínez
Hugue's bronze nude (Exhibition of Contemporary European Sculpture, Society of Arts and Crafts, Detroit, March 25 to April 10,
1935).

The institute also owns a sixteenth-century walnut console
representing a reclining male figure; a late fifteenth- or early sixteenth-century wooden panel, old polychrome; 5 carved walnut arm-
chairs, sixteenth to eighteenth century; a seventeenth-century brazier;
a sixteenth-century cabinet (V, January-February, 1924); 2 inlaid
chairs in Moorish style, possibly Portuguese, eighteenth to nineteenth
century; a sixteenth-century chest of drawers, oak inlaid with bone;
a seventeenth-century chest; a seventeenth-century walnut table;
fourteenth-century painted choir stalls from Astudillo; and a Spanish
altarpiece, third quarter of fifteenth century.

There are also the following ceramics: a fifteenth-
century fragment, lustre (5 pieces); 4 eighteenth-century vases,
Talavera ware invested with green glaze; a fourteenth-century pottery plate; a Hispano-Moresque fifteenth-century bowl; and 2 polychrome tiles.

Minneapolis Institute of Arts
201 East Twenty-Fourth Street
Minneapolis 4

Following is a list of the Spanish paintings in the Minneapolis Institute of Arts:

Coello, Alonso Sánchez. "Portrait of a Lady Holding a Dog."
Goya. "Self Portrait with Doctor Arrieta," 1820. Presented by
the artist as a gift to his physician; it later appeared in private
collections in Madrid and Paris, and was purchased by the institute in 1953.

Greco, El. "Christ Driving the Money Changers from the Temple, " 1571-76.
__. "El Espolio, " 1579.
__. "Portrait of a Spanish Noble" (sometimes known as "A Man with Beard" or "Bildnes eines Hidalgo").
Lucas, Eugenio. "The Bull Fight. "
Murillo (attributed to). "The Pilferer Alarmed. "
Ribera, José. "St. Anthony the Hermit. "
Sorolla. "On the Beach, " 1906.
Zuloaga. "Pepita. "
Zurbarán. "Maria Sewing. "

The institute also has extensive collections of pre-Columbian art, both Mexican and Peruvian.

University of Minnesota
Bibliography of Professor Raymond L. Grismer
Minneapolis

In 1933, Professor Raymond L. Grismer, with the aid of two graduate students, Joseph Edward Lepine and Richard Hubbell Olmsted, published a tentative volume of bibliography entitled A Bibliography of Articles on Spanish Literature.

The new venture in the field of bibliography received so much favorable comment that Mr. Grismer continued it alone— his former collaborators had accepted positions in other parts of the country. The result was a volume of bibliography, published in 1935, with entirely new material, and entitled A Bibliography of Articles and Essays on the Literatures of Spain and Spanish America.

These 2 volumes consist of 750 pages of bibliography, and list essays and articles culled from over 1, 100 magazines, journals, and other collections of studies. Books, too, are listed if they are reviewed in some periodical. The work has been continued since the publication of the 2 tentative volumes, with books and manuscripts included in addition to the articles. Seven volumes (A-Ci) have been published, with 17 volumes (Ci-Zz) ready for publication.

A by-product of this bibliography is a Reference Index to Twelve Thousand Spanish-American Authors. In filing articles on writers of South America, the compilers of the bibliography found it necessary to keep a list of authors for quick reference. This list, with some additional work on it, has reached such proportions that it includes approximately 12, 000 authors. The full name of the author is given with his dates, if known, the name of the country

with which he is most closely identified, and references to studies
about him.

University of Minnesota
Library
Minneapolis 14

The James Ford Bell collection, which since October 20, 1953
has been housed in a special room in the University of Minnesota Library, is a collection of materials related to the history of commerce,
particularly the fifteenth- to eighteenth-century period. This subject
interest encompasses the search for trade routes in all parts of the
world, the seeking of new lands, new materials, and new markets.
Since Spain and Portugal were in the forefront of this expansion of
European commerce, it is natural that the collection should include
considerable material related to their colonial and commercial efforts.

As background for the age of discovery, the Bell collection
has a number of rare works which were used by scholars and navigators of the late fifteenth and early sixteenth centuries. Among
these are the Cosmographia of Ptolemy, 1482; Caxton's translation
of the Mirrour of the World, 1481, and the Polyhistor of Solinus in
its 1475 edition; the Cosmographi geographia of Pomponius Mela,
1482; a 1491 edition of the Meteorologica of Aristoteles; and the 1485
edition of Sacro Bosco's Sphaera Mundi.

The collection includes a number of collected voyages, many
of which contain material directly descriptive of Hispanic commercial
and colonial enterprises. Among these are Montalboddo's Paesi
Nouvamente Retrovati in several editions, including that of 1507;
the Decades of Peter Martyr in several editions, including that of
1511; Simon Grynaeus' Novus Orbis, 1532; Ramusio's Delle Navigationi et Viaggi, 1556-88; Richard Hakluyt's Principall Navigations, 1589, and the supplementary Pilgrimes of Samuel Purchas,
1625; the Great Voyages and Small Voyages published by the De Bry
family, 1590-1630; and a considerable part of the series of voyages
and travels published by Levinus Hulsius in Frankfort between 1598
and 1650.

With respect to works devoted entirely to Portuguese commercial and colonial history, the collection is developing rapidly
and includes, among the more outstanding works, the following items:

the 1424 nautical chart, recently discovered, and believed to represent the New World cartographically for the first time; an instruction book for sailing from Lisbon to Calicut, including the first
printed map of the Cape of Good Hope route; a newsletter purporting
to be the copy of a letter from the king of Portugal to the king of
Spain, which describes the first four commercial voyages from
Portugal to India, mentioning for the first time in print the discovery
of Brazil; Vespucci's Mundus Novus, 1504, as well as several other
editions of this work. Four of the great chronicles of the Portuguese
Empire are in the collection, namely, João do Barros' Asia, 1552-
1616; Couto's Decades, 1602-73; Castanheda's Historia do descobrimento
e conquista da Inda, 1552-61; and Goes' Chronica do... Rei Dom
Emanuel, 1566-67.

The early Spanish explorations and conquests are represented
in the following works: the Columbus letter, 1493; Martin Waldseemüller's Cosmographia Introductio, 1507, with the accompanying
unique globe map of the same year; the first edition of De Moluccis
Insulis, 1523, describing Magellan's voyage around the world;
Benzoni's Histoire nouvelle du Nouveau Monde, 1579; the Relacion
del viaje of the Nodal brothers, who made the first Spanish exploration around Cape Horn in 1620; Cristobal de Acuña's Nuevo desco-
brimiento del Gran Rio de la Amazonas, 1641; and Herrera's Historia general, 1601-15. Two works reflecting Spanish interest in
the East are the Conquista de las Islas Molucas, 1609, by Argen-
sola; and Gomes Solis' Discursos sobre los commercios de las
Indias, 1622.

Among other descriptions of South and Central America's
non-Hispanic explorers are those of Thevet, Claude d'Abbeville,
Jean de Léry, and Walter Bigges. The collection contains a number of pamphlets relating to the Dutch West India Company, and
also many works pertinent to the development of the Darien Colony
by the Scots.

As collateral material to these sources, the collection contains editions of Ptolemy from 1508 to 1545; general geographies
by Thevet, Sebastian Frank, Sebastian Munster, and others; and
atlases by Mercator, Ortelius, Blaeu, Speed, Wytfliet, and other
leading cartographers of the sixteenth and seventeenth centuries.

Mr. John Parker is preparing a descriptive list of additions
to the 1951 catalogue of the James Ford Bell collection, of which
he is curator.

In addition to the above materials, the university library
has among its general collection the following items:

The Spanish Cortes' Diario de sesiones for 1823, 1838-39, 1847-60, 1865-71, 1873-74, 1876-91, 1893-96, 1898-1911, 1914-18.
Cronica general de España. This is a fifteenth-century manuscript in more than 200 leaves. Its authorship is usually attributed to Alfonso X, King of Castile and León.

Walker Art Center
1710 Lyndale Avenue South
Minneapolis 5

The Hispanic paintings, all oil on canvas, in the T. B. Walker collection, now part of the Walker Art Center, are as follows:

Espinosa, Jerónimo Jacinto. "Diogenes with his Lantern."
Llorente, Bernardo Germán de. "St. Rose of Lima."
Lucas the Elder, Eugenio. "Spanish Woman in Maja Costume."
Márquez de Velasco, Esteban. "The Nativity with Angels."
Murillo. "St. Augustine Washing Christ's Feet."
Núñez de Villavicencio, Pedro. "Portrait of the Archbishop Spinola."
Pantoja de la Cruz, Juan. "A Lady of the Court of Philip III."

William Rockhill Neson Gallery of Art
and
Mary Atkins Museum of Fine Arts
Kansas City 2

The following Spanish paintings are included in the gallery's collections:

Cano, Alonso. "St. Lawrence," oil on canvas, dated 1638.
Carreño de Miranda, Juan. "Portrait of Doña Mariana of Austria," oil on canvas.
Goya. "Portrait of Don Ignacio Omulryan y Rourera," oil on canvas, signed and dated, 1815.
Greco, El. "Crucifixion," oil on wood.
__. "The Penitent Magdalene," oil on canvas.
__. "Portrait of a Trinitarian Monk," oil on canvas, signed, 1604-10.
Lucas, Eugenio. "Bullfight," oil on canvas.
Morales, Luis de. "Ecce Homo," oil on panel.
Murillo. "The Little Conception," oil on canvas.
Nicolau, Pedro, and Marzal de Sas, Andrés, Circle of. Altarpiece to the Virgin, tempera on wood, ca. 1425.
Picasso. "Gardens at Vallauris," oil on canvas, 1953.

Sánchez-Perrier, Emilio. "View of Alcalá, " oil on panel.
Solana, Nicolás. "Angel, from the Death of St. Catherine, "
 tempera on panel, first half of fifteenth century.
Torralba Master. "Descent from the Cross and the Entombment, "
 tempera on panel, fifteenth century.
Valdés Leal, Juan de. "St. Anthony Abbot, " oil on canvas.
—. "St. Andrew with Scenes of His Life, " oil on canvas.
Velázquez. "St. Peter, " oil on canvas, ca. 1620.
—. "Portrait of Mariana, Queen of Spain, " oil on canvas.
Velázquez, School of. "The Bacchante, " oil on canvas.

  Other Spanish holdings include:

Sculpture: limestone apostle relief, eleventh century, from Vich;
 gray slate tomb slab with figure of a man, fourteenth century;
 gray slate tomb slab with figure of a woman, fourteenth century;
 kneeling figure of an angel, alabaster, fourteenth to fifteenth
 century; carved wood group, polychromed, representing the
 Last Supper, fifteenth century; alabaster statue of St. Thomas,
 fifteenth century; stone coat of arms of Aras family, Aragon,
 ca. 1580; marble coat of arms, late sixteenth century; and
 another marble coat of arms from the sixteenth century.
Prints: Goya's aquatint series, "Los Caprichos" (complete set),
 "Los Desastres de la Guerra" (complete set), and 5 aquatints
 in the bullfight series; Picasso's etching and aquatint, "The
 Lies and Dreams of Franco, " Jan. 8, 1937 (2 prints); and Ribera's
 etching, "The Poet. "
Pottery: Hispano-Moresque gold lustre plate, fifteenth century.
Furniture: extensive collection of objects from the sixteenth and
 seventeenth centuries.

   City Art Museum of St. Louis
   Forest Park 5

  The City Art Museum of St. Louis contains a small but
comprehensive collection of Hispanic material. Probably the most
important item is a composed room of the late fifteenth century with
fine frieze and archway of carved stucco arabesque, artesonado
coffered wooden ceiling, and immense sobrepuesta wooden doors.
Decorative arts of this period or earlier are represented by a
Hispano-Moresque compartment rug, 3 majolica plates, and by an
ivory carving of the thirteenth to fourteenth century. Slightly later
are a wrought-iron bolt, 4 embossed silver plaques, and an openwork
silver platter; a gilt clock, helmets, rapiers and other weapons,
and a magnificent scales from the old Madrid mint, as fine an ex-

ample of a carved and gilded steel utensil as is to be found anywhere.
A silver-gilt chalice in strongly German style was presented to the
museum by a gentleman who purchased it in Spain. It bears a mark
which may have been that of the Barcelona goldsmith Francesch
Torres (admitted, 1543). From the early sixteenth century is an
alabaster reredos in relief with representations of the Visitation,
the Nativity, and the Adoration. An enameled boss from a sixteenth-century horse trapping, a polychrome statuette of Santiago
Matamoros, a pair of wrought-iron candlesticks, a specimen of
rich brocade, 5 chairs, and a vargueño also date from the sixteenth
to eighteenth century.

Of Spanish painting, the museum contains a fine example
of El Greco ("Saint Paul"), 2 Zurbaráns ("A Franciscan Monk"
and "Still Life"), a Ribera, an Antonio Moro, a Murillo, and a
very early Goya self-portrait. Of the modern Spanish and Latin
American artists, the museum has paintings by Casanova y Estorach,
Sorolla, Zuloaga, a water color and an oil by Orozco, 2 water colors
by Rivera, and 3 oils by Picasso. Prints include numerous examples
by Goya, Picasso, and Orozco.

The museum has examples of Hispanic American pottery,
South American silver, pre-Columbian gold, and Mexican clay
and stone sculpture, as well as a collection of santos and a fine
set of Portuguese pistols and accessories made by Iacinto Xavier
in 1799.

The museum also exhibits an unusually fine group of Peruvian and Mexican pottery belonging to the St. Louis Branch of the
Archaeological Institute of America, including 1 anthropomorphic
vase which is considered unique. The museum owns a number of
early textiles from Peru and later ones from Guatemala.

Missouri Historical Society
Jefferson Memorial Building
St. Louis 12

The Missouri Historical Society was established in 1866
to preserve and make available for research the books, newspapers,
manuscripts, and museum objects relating to the history of St.
Louis, Missouri, and the Louisiana Purchase area. St. Louis
was so closely allied with the westward expansion of the nation and
with exploration, travel, and trade in the Far West, the Southwest,
and Mexico, that the society has always had a deep interest in
Spanish American history, and its collections contain much information relating to that subject.

Books, pamphlets, some newspapers, maps, photographs, and prints relating to Hispanic American subjects are included in the general library collection, although the section of books and pamphlets relating to Central and South America are unimportant. Of interest is a small collection of New Orleans imprints (1770-1804) and a partial file of the Santa Fe Republican (Sept. 10, 1847—April 2, 1848; and in photostat the issues for May 3, 1948—Sept. 23, 1848).

The society's museum collection includes 45 pre-twentieth-century pottery jars and baskets produced by Indians in New Mexico and Arizona; original portraits and photographs of portraits of officials, trappers, and traders during the Spanish colonial period in Louisiana and the period of trade and expansion to the Southwest; some Spanish arms of the colonial period; and a large collection of objects brought from Mexico by the Mexican War veterans. Among the latter are: a bronze cannon used in the defense of the Alamo; 2 bronze cannon cast in Spain about 1725 and originally used in the Texas missions of Concepción and San José; a Mexican serape of the 1840's or earlier; Mexican lance blades; a brass helmet and cuirass used by Mexican cavalrymen; and a "skull and crossbones" flag (white paint on black cloth), captured from Mexican troops during the Battle of Sacramento.

The society's manuscript holdings include a very considerable group of documents relating to the civil history of Upper Louisiana during the colonial period, the fur and Indian trade, travel and exploration, and family data. A second group deals with Anglo-American expansion to the Southwest and with the Mexican War. The manuscript collection is arranged in various subcollections, usually named for the subject with which they are chiefly concerned, or for the donor. All these collections have been catalogued and most of them have been indexed.

Hispanic American materials are scattered through many of the manuscript collections, but those which deal principally with this subject are briefly listed below. No attempt has been made here to include any list of the manuscripts dealing with the Mexican War period, as the holdings on this subject are very considerable and are scattered through many collections.

The Pierre Chouteau collection contains letters relating to the history of colonial Missouri. They are mainly letters from the governors of Louisiana Territory stationed at New Orleans to the lieutenant-governors of Illinois. They cover the period from 1796 to 1807. Following is a brief analysis of them, with the names of the senders.

Box 1:

Env. 1.   Juan Morales, 75 letters, April 1796 to 1804.
Env. 2.   Baron de Carondelet, 13 letters, August 1796 to 1797.
Env. 3.   Manuel Gayoso de Lemos, 15 letters, August 1796 to 1799.
Env. 4.   Don Carlos Howard, 4 letters, April 6, 1797 to July 10, 1807.

Box 2:

Env. 5.   R. de López y Augusto, 13 letters, January 10, 1800 to
May 16, 1801.
Env. 6.   Marqués de Casa Calvo, 14 letters, June 1800 to July 1,
1806.
Env. 7.   Don Manuel de Salcedo, 13 letters, August 27, 1801 to
May 3, 1803.
Env. 8.   William Henry Harrison, photostatic copies of 3 letters
from the Tullach Collection, in English, dated Vincennes, Indiana,
August, March, and November, 1803.
Env. 9.   Juan Gautier, 1 letter, July 6, 1798.
Franco Bouriony, 1 letter, September 6, 1799.
Cayetano Valdés, 1 letter.
Manuel G. Moro, 2 letters, February 24 and July 13, 1804.
Agustín Grande, 2 letters, May 5, 1804.
Santiago de St. Vrain, 2 letters, November 25, 1804.
Benjamin Fooy, 1 letter, December 29, 1805.
Manuel Arzaro, 1 letter, November 26, 1805.

The society also has the following:

Archives of the Indies (1768-91). Photographic copies (2,989) of
documents in the Archives of the Indies, Spain, copied from the
file in the Carnegie Institution. Official dispatches from the
Spanish governors of Louisiana to their immediate superiors,
the captains general at Havana.
Chouteau (1753-1880). Approximately 10,000 manuscripts. Letters,
accounts, and account books of the various members of the Chouteau
family of St. Louis and their relatives. Particularly important
for information relating to the early fur trade in the West.
Clark, George Rogers (1766-1799). The collection includes some
documents relating to Clark's contacts with Spanish officials
during the American Revolution, and following. Also a pen-
and-ink sketch of Governor de Lemos' galley.
DeLassus-St. Vrain (1544-1909). About 1,000 manuscripts of the
DeLassus family. The most important part of the collection
deals with the period when Don Carlos DeLassus was lieutenant-
governor of Upper Louisiana.

Díaz, Porfirio (1879-1906). Six manuscripts relating to consular matters and land transactions.

Jefferson, Thomas (1763-1826). About 1,000 manuscripts, including correspondence with Don Carlos Martínez d'Yrujo, Baron de Carondelet, and others.

Lisa, Manuel (1772-1820). One hundred fifty-eight manuscripts.

Louisiana Purchase and Transfer (1803-5). Approximately 30 manuscripts and 40 photographic copies of documents relating to the purchase and transfer of Louisiana, including one of the six original copies of the document transferring Upper Louisiana from Spain to France (1804).

Missouri Archives of the Spanish Period (1766-1804). Many thousands of manuscripts representing the official records which were left in the five Missouri districts following the transfer of Louisiana. The collection contains most of the papers for the districts of St. Louis, St. Charles, Ste. Genevieve, and New Madrid, with a few scattered documents from the files of the district of Cape Girardeau.

Mun, Jules de (1780-1859). One hundred fifty-four manuscripts, including the journal of his trip to Mexico (1815).

Santa Fe (1807-1900). About 200 manuscripts (and a large collection of typescript copies) relating to early American expeditions to the Southwest.

Sappington, Dr. John (1808-1900). Numerous manuscripts (2,727), including data on the Santa Fe trade, the annexation of Texas, and the Mexican War.

Soulard, Antoine (1766-1875). Over 100 manuscripts relating chiefly to Soulard's work as surveyor-general of Upper Louisiana during the closing years of the Spanish period.

Spanish Lieutenant-Governors (1770-1804). Nine documents representing autographs of the lieutenant-governors of Upper Louisiana during the Spanish period.

Stoddard, Amos (1798-1804). Fifty manuscripts, the most important part concerning Stoddard's assignment as French and American commissioner to receive Upper Louisiana from the Spanish authorities.

Texas (1822-69). Eighty-five manuscripts and some typescript copies, chiefly letters written by Stephen F. Austin, Sam Houston, Anson Jones, Ashbel Smith, M. B. Lamar, General Waddy Thompson, and Joseph C. Higgerson. Other Texas material is scattered through collections unlisted here, particularly the Moses Austin Letters.

Valle (1773-1917). About 1,000 documents relating to the Valle and other early families of Ste. Genevieve.

Waldo, Dr. David (1832-80). Twenty-two manuscripts relating
chiefly to the Waldo family and the Santa Fe trail.

Joslyn Art Museum
2218 Dodge Street
Omaha 2

The Joslyn Art Museum owns 2 Spanish paintings: "Portrait
of the Marquesa de Fontana" by Goya; and "St. Francis in Prayer"
by El Greco. There are also examples of seventeenth- and eighteenth
century ceramic tiles and pottery.

As to Latin American collections, the museum has a good
study collection of pre-Incaic textiles, in addition to examples of
Peruvian pottery (mostly Mochica, Nazca, and Chimu).

Dartmouth College
Library
Hanover

On the walls of a reading room in Baker Library, Dartmouth
College, are frescoes by José Clemente Orozco, painted during
1932 to 1934. He called the theme of the frescoes "The American
Idea." The first panels represent the migration of Mongolian types
throughout the continent; then are shown elements of Mexican culture at the time of the Spanish conquest; the legend of Quetzalcoatl,
the blue-eyed white god, is pictured on the west wall; Spanish
American and North American social and political histories are
shown in alternate panels on the east wall; then comes a panel
picturing twentieth-century mechanical gadgets; and finally "Modern
Migration," showing a risen Christ standing beside a fallen Cross.

Following is a bibliography:

Benson, E. M. "Orozco at Dartmouth College," The Nation, Nov.
8, 1933, pp. 546-47.
—. "Orozco in New England," American Magazine of Art, Oct.
1933, pp. 443-49.
Dickerson, Albert I., ed. Orozco Frescoes at Dartmouth.
Mumford, Lewis. "Orozco in New England," The New Republic,
Oct. 10, 1934, pp. 231-35.
Orozco at Dartmouth—A Symposium. Hanover: The Arts Chap-
books No. 4, 1933.
Watts, Harvey M. "Dartmouth and American Civilization," Art
Digest, Sept. 1, 1934, p. 5.

The Dartmouth College Library has a noteworthy Spanish
drama collection.

Princeton University
Art Museum
Princeton

The Princeton Art Museum possesses the following Hispanic paintings:

March, Miguel. "The Poultry Seller," sixteenth century.
Perea Master. "Magdalen's Last Communion."
Unknown, late fifteenth or early sixteenth century. "Head of
   Christ."
Villarroya Master. "St. Michael at Last Judgment," tempera on
   panel; about 1450.
Zurbarán. "St. Francis."

There is also an early sixteenth-century Italo-Hispanic manuscript—miniature on vellum, a Pietà with two angels. Of sculpture, there is a polychromed wood martyr saint, over life size, from the seventeenth century. In addition, the museum has drawings by Ribera, Fortuny, Picasso, Alenza, Luis Quintanilla, Juvara, Roig, and Juan de las Ruelas; and prints by Fortuny, de los Ríos, Goya, and Picasso.

NEW MEXICO AND ARIZONA

Spanish Missions

Select bibliography:

Alegre, Francisco Javier. Historia de la Compañia de Jesús en
   Nueva-España, 3 vols. (Mexico City, 1841).
Arricivita, Juan Domingo. Crónica Seráfica y Apostólica del
   Colegio de Propaganda Fide de la Santa Cruz de Querétaro en
   la Nueva España (Mexico, 1792).
Baldwin, Percy M. "Fray Marcos de Niza's Relación," New Mexico
   Historical Review, I (1926), 193-223.
Bancroft, Hubert Howe. History of Arizona and New Mexico,
   1530-1888 (San Francisco, 1888).
Benavides, Alonso de. Memorial (1630); translated by Mrs. Edward
   E. Ayer and annotated by F. W. Hodge and C. F. Lummis
   (Chicago, 1916); Revised Memorial of 1634 (Albuquerque, 1945).
Bloom, L. B. "Barreiro's Ojeada sobre Nuevo México," New
   Mexico Historical Review, III (1928), 73-96, 145-78.
Bolton, Herbert E. Coronado on the Turquoise Trail; Knight of
   Pueblos and Plains (Albuquerque, 1949).
—. Kino's Historical Memoir of Pimería Alta, 2 vols. (Cleveland,
   1919).

__. "The Mission as a Frontier Institution in the Spanish American Colonies," American Historical Review, XXIII (1918), 42-61.

__. The Padre on Horseback (San Francisco, 1932).

__. Spanish Exploration in the Southwest, 1542-1706 (New York, 1916).

Coues, Elliott. On the Trail of a Spanish Pioneer: The Diary and Itinerary of Francisco Garcés...1775-1776, 2 vols. (New York, 1900).

Engelhardt, Padre Zephyrin (Charles Anthony). The Franciscans in Arizona (Harbor Springs, Mich., 1897).

__. The Franciscans in New Mexico (Harbor Springs, Mich., 1899).

Forrest, Earle R. Missions and Pueblos of the Old Southwest (Cleveland, 1929).

Hackett, Charles Wilson. Historical Documents Relating to New Mexico, Nueva Vizcaya and Approaches Thereto, to 1773, 3 vols. (Washington, D.C., 1923-37).

__. "The Revolt of the Pueblo Indians of New Mexico in 1680," Texas State Historical Association Quarterly, XV (1911), 93-147.

__. Revolt of the Pueblo Indians of New Mexico and Otermin's Attempted Reconquest, 1680-1682, 2 vols. (Albuquerque, 1942).

Hallenbeck, Cleve. Alvar Nuñez Cabeza de Vaca: The Journey and Route of the First European to Cross the Continent of North America, 1534-1536 (Glendale, Calif., 1939).

Hammond, George P. Coronado's Seven Cities (Albuquerque, 1940).

__. Don Juan de Oñate and the Founding of New Mexico (Santa Fe, 1927).

__. "Pimería Alta after Kino's Time," New Mexico Historical Review, IV (1929), 220-38.

Hammond, George P., and Goad, Edgar F. The Adventure of Don Francisco Vásquez de Coronado (Albuquerque, 1938).

Hammond, George P., and Rey, Agapito. Don Juan de Oñate, Colonizer of New Mexico, 2 vols. (Albuquerque, 1952).

__. Expedition into New Mexico Made by Antonio de Espejo, 1582-1583, as Revealed in the Journal of Diego Pérez de Luxan (The Quivira Society, Vol. I, Los Angeles, 1929).

__. The Gallegos Relation of the Rodríguez Expedition to New Mexico (Santa Fe, 1927).

__. Narratives of the Coronado Expedition, 1540-1542 (Albuquerque, 1940).

__. Obregón's History of the 16th Century Explorations in Western America (Los Angeles, 1928).

Hewett, Edgar L. Ancient Life in the American Southwest (Indianapolis, 1930).

Hodge, Frederick Webb. Handbook of American Indians North of Mexico, 2 vols. (Washington, D.C., 1907-10).

___. History of Háwikuh, New Mexico, One of the So-called Cities of Cíbola (Los Angeles, 1937).

Hughes, Anne E. The Beginnings of Spanish Settlement in the El Paso District (Berkeley, 1914).

Keleher, William A. Turmoil in New Mexico, 1846-1868 (Santa Fe, 1952).

Lockwood, Francis C. Story of the Spanish Missions of the Middle Southwest (Santa Ana, Calif., 1934).

Maas, P. Otto. Misiones de Nuevo Méjico. Documentos del Archivo General de Indias (Sevilla) publicados por primera vez y anotados (Madrid, 1929).

___. Viajes de misioneros franciscanos a la conquista del Nuevo México (Seville, 1915).

Manje, Juan Mateo. Luz de tierra incógnita en la América septentrional... (Mexico, 1926).

Mecham, J. Lloyd. "The Second Spanish Expedition to New Mexico," New Mexico Historical Review, I (1926), 265-91.

Ocaranza, Fernando. Establecimientos franciscanos en el misterioso reino de Nuevo México (Mexico City, 1934).

Ortega, José. Historia del Nayarit, Sonora, Sinaloa y ambas Californias (Mexico City, 1887).

Prince, L. Bradford. The Spanish Mission Churches of New Mexico (Cedar Rapids, Iowa, 1915).

Salpointe, J. B. Soldiers of the Cross (Banning, Calif., 1898).

Sauer, Carl O. The Road To Cíbola (Ibero-Americano No. 3, Berkeley, 1932).

Scholes, France V. "Church and State in New Mexico, 1610-50," New Mexico Historical Review, XI (1936), 9-76, 145-78, 283-94, 297-349; XII (1937), 78-106.

___. "The First Decade of the Inquisition in New Mexico," New Mexico Historical Review, X (1935), 195-241.

___. "Problems in the Early Ecclesiastical History of New Mexico," New Mexico Historical Review, VII (1932), 32-74.

___. "The Supply Service of the New Mexico Missions in the Seventeenth Century, "New Mexico Historical Review, V (1930), 93-115 186-210, 386-404.

___. "Troublous Times in New Mexico, 1659-1670," New Mexico Historical Review, XII (1937), 134-74, 380-452; XIII (1938), 63-84.

Smith, T. Buckingham. Relation of Alvar Núñez Cabeza de Vaca (Washington, D.C., 1851, and several later editions).

Vetancurt, Agustín de. Teatro mexicano, 4 vols. (Mexico, 1870-71).

Villagrá, Gaspar de. History of New Mexico, 1610. Translated and edited by Gilberto Espinosa and F. W. Hodge (Los Angeles, 1933)

Wagner, Henry R. The Spanish Southwest, 1542-1794 (Berkeley, 1924; 2d ed., Albuquerque, 1937).

Winship, George P. The Coronado Expedition, 1540-1542 (Washington, D. C., Bureau of Ethnology, 14th Annual Report, 1896).

Wyllys, Rufus Kay. "Padre Luis Velarde's Relación of Pimería Alta, 1716," New Mexico Historical Review, VI (1931), 111-57.

__. "The Spanish Missions of the Southwest," Arizona Historical Review, VI (1935), 27-37.

__. Pioneer Padre, the Life and Times of Eusebio Francisco Kino (Dallas, 1935).

Zárate Salmerón, Gerónimo de. "Relaciones de todas las cosas que en el Nuevo México se han visto y sabido..." Documentos para la historia de México, 3d series (Mexico, 1856).

University of New Mexico
Library
Albuquerque

Manuscripts collection:

The collection consists chiefly of enlargement prints from microfilm and some transcripts of papers from a number of archives, libraries, and other collections in the United States, Mexico, Spain, and Italy. In general, these copies have been collected because of their interest for the history of the Southwest, but they also include a fairly large number of important documents of broader historical interest, or pertaining to related areas such as New Spain in general, northern Mexico, and the Californias.

The collection is divided into several natural groups or sections. (1) The true New Mexico archives or the Spanish archives of New Mexico. These are labeled Documents and have been bound in a chronological series running from 1621 to 1846. There are very few documents for the period prior to the Pueblo Revolt of 1680, and a large number for the eighteenth and the first half of the nineteenth centuries. (2) Papers selected from the Archivo General de la Nación (Mexico) by several scholars, including France V. Scholes, Lansing B. Bloom, and George P. Hammond. These concern a wide variety of subjects and cover the whole colonial period. (3) Similar selections from the Archivo General de Indias (Seville). (4) Similar selections from the Biblioteca Nacional de México. (5) A few items from the Museo Nacional de México. (6) Some items from the Archive of the Sacred Congregation of Propaganda Fide, Rome. (7) Miscellaneous papers from the Museum of New Mexico. These supplement the New Mexico archives. (8) Miscellaneous items from other collections and private papers.

Books:

The Van de Velde collection of Mexican materials, consisting of 8,686 bound volumes, 93 maps, and 50 linear feet of pamphlets, was purchased in 1939 by a special appropriation of the state legislature. It contains much rare and valuable material dealing with the history, archeology, ethnology, geology, folklore, literature, and art of Mexico.

The Catron collection, of 9,574 volumes, is an extensive and valuable library begun by Julia W. and Thomas B. Catron and given to the University of New Mexico Library by C. C. Catron, T. B. Catron, F. A. Catron, and J. W. Catron. Outstanding items are several hundred Spanish and Mexican publications of the sixteenth to nineteenth centuries.

The Otero collection, given by former Governor and Mrs. Miguel A. Otero in 1939, contains 465 volumes on the Southwest and general fields, as well as a valuable manuscript and museum collection.

Art objects:

The Field collection of old Spanish and Mexican art, which includes 96 pieces of silver and 69 other art objects, was given by the estate of Will B. and Mary Lester Field in 1939.

University of New Mexico
Museum of Anthropology
Albuquerque

The nucleus of the collection of the Museum of Anthropology is essentially local. Archeological material is stressed, with the emphasis upon considerable collections of pottery, stone, bone, and shell from the excavations of the sites of Kuaua, Puaray, and Quaray, all of these being Pueblo IV and Pueblo V sites in the vicinity of Albuquerque. The glazeware series of pottery vessels is from these sites, as well as a third of the collection of glazeware from the excavations at Pecos.

Early archeological material of the same nature is represented by a large series of several years' excavations by the university at various sites in Chaco Canyon. Material in this sequence includes a considerable collection from Basketmaker III, and Pueblos I, II, and III. Pottery vessels in this Chaco series number approximately 100 whole pieces, with some 3,000 stone, bone, and shell items.

The museum also possesses collections of approximately

100 to 150 items, respectively, from the Chihuahua and Mimbres areas.

As a supplement to the above items, the museum possesses a considerable quantity of dry-cave material in excess of 5,000 pieces, from the caves in the vicinity of Albuquerque, and large portions from the cave sites in the Mogollón Mountains, New Mexico.

Ethnological material is represented by some 50 specimens of the plains category (for the most part, Sioux), and a collection from various of the pueblos in the Rio Grande Valley, comprising some 200 specimens.

Some somatological material is represented by a fairly complete series of casts of the fossil men of the Old World, both on display and in study collections. Of complete or fairly complete bone material for study or measurement, the museum has a series from Puaray of 206 individuals; Kuaua, 235; Chaco, 40; Quaray, 13; and miscellaneous sites, 50.

University of New Mexico
University of New Mexico Press
Coronado Cuarto Centennial Publications
Albuquerque

The Coronado Cuarto Centennial Publications are being published by the University of New Mexico Press in commemoration of the four hundredth anniversary of the discovery and exploration of a large part of the Southwest by the Coronado expedition, 1540-42. They consist primarily of the most important documents relating to the discovery and exploration of the Southwest down to the end of the colonial period.

Following are the works already published:

Aiton, Arthur S. New Spain after Coronado.
Bolton, Herbert E. Coronado on the Turquoise Trail.
Espinosa, José M. First Expedition of Vargas into New Mexico, 1692.
Hackett, Charles W. The Pueblo Revolt of 1680, 2 vols.
Hammond, George P., and Rey, Agapito. Don Juan de Oñate, First Colonizer of New Mexico, 2 vols.
___. Narratives of the Coronado Expedition, 1540-1542.
Hodge, Frederick W., Hammond, George P., and Rey, Agapito. The Benavides Memorial.

Pfefferkorn's Description of Sonora. Translated from the German
   by Theodore E. Treutlein.
Scholes, France V. New Mexico in the Latter Seventeenth Century.
Thomas, Alfred B. The Plains Indians and New Mexico, 1751-1778.
White, Leslie A. Pioneers in American Anthropology, the letters
   of Adolph F. Bandelier to Lewis H. Morgan, 2 vols.

Museum of New Mexico
Santa Fe

The Museum of New Mexico functions in co-operation with
its affiliates, the Historical Society of New Mexico and the Archaeological Society of New Mexico, and with the research organizations,
the School of American Research and the Laboratory of Anthropology.
It maintains four units: the Palace of the Governors (historical and
archeological displays), the Art Gallery (contemporary Southwestern
art), the Hall of Ethnology, and the Laboratory of Anthropology.

The School of American Research and the Museum of New
Mexico were founded in 1906 and 1907, respectively, by Dr. E. L.
Hewett, their director until his death in 1946. He was succeeded
by Dr. Sylvanus G. Morley (d. 1948), and by the Hon. Boaz Long.

The Historical Society was first founded in 1859. Adjourned
sine die in 1863, it was reorganized in 1880, since when it has func-
tioned continuously. Mr. Paul A. F. Walter has been its president
since 1926.

The Laboratory of Anthropology, accepted in 1949 by action
of the state legislature as a unit of the Museum of New Mexico, was
established as a privately conducted scientific and educational institution in 1927. It is now the research unit of the museum.

Interests of the Museum of New Mexico, the Archaeological
Society of New Mexico, and the Historical Society of New Mexico
are confined almost exclusively to New Mexico, but sometimes in
clude neighboring areas of the Southwest. The School of American
Research has operated in national and international fields—notably
the Southwest in general, Missouri, and California in the United
States; and Mexico, Central America, and Ecuador. The Hispanic
materials of these organizations include archives, study and display
collections, and library holdings.

The most important archival collection is the body of manuscripts known as the Spanish Archives of New Mexico. These have
been catalogued in R. E. Twitchell's work of the same name (Vol.

II; Vol. I lists holdings now in the U. S. Cadastral Office, Albuquerque). Somewhat greater in number are the papers of the Mexican period (1821-46), which are not completely or adequately catalogued. Minor collections include the Historical Society of New Mexico, the Twitchell, and the Read papers, all miscellaneous in content. Translations of the documents listed in R. E. Twitchell's Spanish Archives, Vol. II, have been made. The collection of the Historical Society of New Mexico is constantly growing, since the society is by law custodian of official state documents, but the bulk of such material since 1846 is still in the office of the New Mexico Secretary of State.

The museum and the Historical Society possess important cultural materials of interest to the student of Hispanic culture. Half of the Palace of the Governors' floor space is devoted to display of collections belonging to the Historical Society. Many pieces are stored for study or for safekeeping. These include a large number of Spanish colonial items illustrating the way of life and work of the times, and including notable specimens of furnishings (colchas, sabanillas, and the like) and ecclesiastical art. The Laboratory of Anthropology houses similar materials.

Library holdings of the various organizations affiliated or co-operating with, or under the management of, the Museum of New Mexico are administered by a central library; the Laboratory of Anthropology has separate facilities, as does the new Museum of International Folk Art, both of which are under centralized supervision. The Historical Society has provided most of the works relating to Hispanic phases of history, but the School of American Research and the Laboratory of Anthropology have collected many such titles. The total number of volumes is about 8,500. There is also the most complete file of New Mexico newspapers in the state.

These organizations have published in all a total of more than 250 titles, exclusive of magazine issues and leaflets. The school has been publishing since 1908; the Historical Society, since 1881; the Laboratory of Anthropology, in the period 1931-48—monographs, papers, handbooks, bulletins, memoirs, and reprints under various headings.

Both The New Mexico Historical Review (Historical Society of New Mexico) and El Palacio (School of American Research, Archaeological Society of New Mexico, Museum of New Mexico, and Laboratory of Anthropology) are journals of long standing—the Review since 1925, and El Palacio since 1913. These magazines published much material in the Hispanic field.

Publication is under way of E. N. Ferdon's archeological

survey of Ecuador and of Tonalá, Chiapas, Mexico. A preliminary
report on the Ecuador survey is already published under the title
Studies in Ecuadorian Geography.

A study of the Toltecs is under preparation for publication
by Dr. Bertha P. Dutton.

The Museum of New Mexico has co-operated with the U.S.
National Park Service and the University of New Mexico in an archeological survey of the Chama River region of New Mexico, where
damming of the river will inundate a large number of archeological
sites. Mr. Stanley A. Stubbs has undertaken the preparation of
reports on this work for the museum.

Translation of the Aztec text of the Florentine Codex
(Sahagún's Historia general de las cosas de Nueva España) is in
progress by Dr. Arthur J. O. Anderson, School of American Research, and Dr. Charles E. Dibble, University of Utah, using microfilm secured for the school by the late Lansing B. Bloom. Book
I ("The Gods") has been issued, and the rest will be published as
completed.

Museum of New Mexico
Museum of International Folk Art
Santa Fe

The Museum of International Folk Art was founded and
built by Miss Florence Dibell Bartlett and given to the State of New
Mexico to be operated as a section of the Museum of New Mexico.
It is the first folk art museum in the world of an inherently international character. Its function is twofold: to foster through folk
art an intelligent awareness of other peoples and cultures, and to
assist others engaged in the study of folk art and related subjects.

At the time of opening (September 5, 1953), the museum's
collections included folk art material from over fifty-five countries
or regions, totaling approximately 4,000 items. These holdings
include not only European handicrafts but also the artistic products
of other folk cultures.

Mexico is represented by nineteenth-century lacquered
bateas, chests, and boxes; representative examples of nineteenth-
century majolica; some costumes and textiles from various regions;
toys; and masks.

From Guatemala comes a selection of textiles and costume
items, the majority from Chichicastenango.

There is a fine collection of textiles from Peru, Bolivia, and Ecuador, both pre-Columbian and modern; a sizable group of shawl pins, brooches, and other silverwork from Peru and Bolivia; a selection of featherwork and beadwork from Indian tribes of the Amazon region and British Guiana.

The museum also has a small collection of embroidery and a small group of furniture from Spain.

Brooklyn Museum
Eastern Parkway at Washington Avenue
Brooklyn 17

Hispanic material has always been of particular interest to the Brooklyn Museum, which is especially strong in ethnographical, archeological, and primitive art material from New Mexico, Arizona, Mexico, Costa Rica, and Peru. The archeological material from Colombia, Ecuador, and Venezuela is also of major interest. Collections from colonial Latin America include the important Algara collection from Mexico, consisting of portraits, dinnerware, laces, fans, and documents from the eighteenth, nineteenth, and twentieth centuries; and the Braden collection from Brazil, Peru, and Chile, consisting of furniture, paintings, sculpture, textiles, and some metalwork. Other interesting colonial material includes a rare Jamaican tortoise-shell casket and combs, a large Mexican lacquer tray, and a Peruvian rug.

In addition to the Hispanic material mentioned above, the museum owns the following:

Brazil: large burial urn with modeled decoration and painting, Marajó island; collected during the museum expedition of 1933.
Colombia: examples of Quimbaya, Sinu, and Chibcha goldwork.
Costa Rica: large stone metate in the form of a jaguar; ceremonial stool; large stone figure of a crocodile god holding a human head; large sculptured slab with three kneeling figures; effigy jar with bird modeling on it; tripod jar with modeled figures and negative painting; bowl with tripods of jaguar heads; effigy jar of a jaguar; effigy bowl of animal form in rectangular shape. (All the above objects date ca. 1000 A.D. from Mercedes, Costa Rica; part of the Minor C. Keith collection.) Also, the museum purchased in 1934 gold pendants of birds, humans, gods, spiders, dolphins.
Mexico: large stone statue showing the apotheosis of a chief, Huaxtec culture; large stone statue of a goddess, Huaxtec culture; stone

altar bowl with serpents, Huaxtec culture, fifteenth century;
stone yoke, Totonac culture, ca. 1100 A.D.; stone sculpture
of a king, ca. thirteenth century; stone sculpture of the goddess
of vegetation, Aztec culture, ca. fourteenth century.
Panama: gold consisting of plaques, cuffs, ear rods, nose ring,
sheathing for teeth, and necklace from Coclé.
Peru: large wrap-around shirt, Paracas; mantle with birds on
red squares with black background in checkerboard pattern,
Paracas; mantle with condors on dark blue background in checkerboard pattern, Paracas; mantle with double fish design, Paracas;
textile with simple weave center and borders of three-dimensional
needle-knitted figures, Paracas, 300 B.C.; poncho with over-all
face design, Tiahuanaco culture; feather hat with face design,
Tiahuanaco culture; tapestry mantle, Ica-Tiahuanaco; poncho of
stump-work and plush, Chimu culture, 1000-1500 A.D.

Also from New Mexico: mask of Siatasha and mask of
Nahatasha, from Zuñi Indians; collected in 1903.

Articles on various items in the museum may be found
in its publications, The Brooklyn Museum Quarterly and The Brooklyn
Museum Bulletin. In addition, Mr. Charles Upson Clark has just
completed a study of Hispanic documentary source materials in libraries and collections in Europe under a grant from the Wenner-
Gren Foundation, sponsored by the Brooklyn Museum.

Albright Art Gallery
Buffalo 22

The Albright Art Gallery owns 3 paintings by Picasso, and
1 each by Juan Gris, Joan Miró, Tapies, Rufino Tamayo, and Paul
Uribe. It also has the following sculptures: life-sized kneeling
figures in marble of the Duke and Duchess of Maqueda (Juan de
Cárdenas and Juana de Ludena), by Pompeo Leoni, after 1591;
stone sculptures of the Aztec, Totonac, and Mayan cultures; contemporary sculpture by Picasso and Maria Martins.

Corning Museum of Glass
Corning

The Corning Museum of Glass is a part of the Corning
Glass Center, opened in 1951 on the centennial of the Corning Glass
Works. Examples of glass from pre-Christian times are shown.
The Spanish collection consists largely of eighteenth-century pieces.

Included among the Spanish pieces are the following: 3

cantirs, one of which is of exceptional quality (see "Glass from the
Corning Museum of Glass," 1955, p. 36); 2 Almorratxa (J. Gudiol
Ricart, "Los Vidrios Catalanes," Barcelona, 1941); 2 vases (A.
Wilson-Frothingham, "Hispanic Glass," 1941, Fig. 63); 2 cut pieces,
probably from La Granja de San Ildefonso (A. Wilson-Frothingham,
Fig. 87); 3 enameled eighteenth-century pieces, one of which bears
the Spanish royal coat of arms and the inscription "Viva Carlos III";
and a possibly unique milk-glass candlestick with thread decoration,
from the seventeenth or eighteenth century.

Sunnyside
Irvington

Washington Irving lived in Sunnyside from 1836 until his
death in 1859, except for the period 1842-46, which he spent in
Madrid as United States Minister to Spain. The house, which has
been restored by Hugh Grant Rowell and Alice M. Runyon through
the generosity of John D. Rockefeller, Jr., contains the library of
Washington Irving, the richness of which in old Spanish items is
exemplified by the appended list of titles of books published prior
to 1700. However, little attempt has been made to collect Irving's
manuscripts, since Yale University has assembled a large collection
of Irvingiana, which has formed the basis of the writings of Dr. Stanley
Williams.

Abarca. P. de. Los Reyes de Aragon en anales' historicos, 2 vols.
   (Madrid, 1682-84).
Avicenna et Geber. Artis chemicae principes (Basil: P. Pernam,
   1572).
Beuter, P. A. Coronica general de toda Espana, y especialmente
   del Reyno de Valencia, 2 vols. (Valencia, 1604).
Bleda, Jaime. Coronica de los Moros de Espagna (Valencia, 1618).
Cárdenas y Zuñiga, Jaime de. Historia del rebelion y castigo de
   los Moriscos (Malaga, 1600)
Davila, G. G. Historia de la vida de Don Henrique Tercero de
   Castilla (Madrid, 1638).
Díaz del Castillo, Bernal. Historia verdadera de la conquista de
   la Nueva Espana (Madrid, 1632).
Garibay y Zamalloa, Esteban de. Compendio historial de las
   chronicas y universal historia de todos los reynos de Espana
   (Barcelona, 1628).
Illescas, G. de. Historia pontifical y catholica (Barcelona, 1606).
La Puente, J. M. Epitome de la cronica del rey don Iuan el Segundo
   de Castilla (Madrid, 1678).

Mendoza, R. de. Historia eclesiastica y secular de la ciudad de Guadalaxara (Madrid, 1653).

Morales, Ambrosio de. La Coronica general de Espagna, Vols. I and III (Alcalá, 1574 and Cordoba, 1586).

Ocampo, Florián de. Los Cinco libros primeros de la Coronica general de Espana (Alcalá, 1578).

Quevedo, Francisco G. de. Carta Luis XIII Rey Christianissimo de Francia (Madrid, 1635).

Saavedra Fajardo, Diego de, and Nuñez de Castro, A. Corona gothica castellano y austriaca, 3 vols. (Madrid, 1670-78).

Sandoval, Prudencio de. Historia de los reyes de Castilla (Pamplona, 1634).

Sevilla. Ordenanzas de Sevilla (Seville, 1632).

Zurita, Gerónimo de. Collected works, in Spanish, 8 vols. (Zaragoza, 1604-80).

Cornell University
Library
Ithaca

Colonel Francis Reginald Hull (1872-1948) was an English engineer who lived the major part of his life in Brazil. He joined the São Paulo Railway as a young engineer and worked in different capacities in railroad companies and public utilities both in São Paulo and in Ceará. During the last period of his active professional life, he was general manager of the Ceará Light and Power Company and English vice-consul at Fortaleza. The large library which Colonel Hull collected was acquired by Cornell University Library in 1948. The acquisition was made possible through the generosity of Mr. Herbert F. Johnson, a trustee of Cornell University and a close friend of Colonel Hull.

The Hull Brazilian collection comprises approximately 4,000 volumes and gives a comprehensive description of the political, cultural, and economic development of Brazil. It can be roughly divided into four major parts with the following points of concentration:

1. Political history of Brazil with special emphasis on: the era of discovery, represented by about 300 books (sixteenth- and seventeenth-century travel descriptions); the Dutch colonization; Brazil as a Portuguese colony; the Braganza Empire; the republic; local history, mostly Ceará and Bahia.

2. Cultural development of Brazil, with specific collections on the following points of interest: the Indian aborigines,

language and customs; the Portuguese society, Jesuit missions and
their influence; Negro importations; European immigration in the
nineteenth century (the English influence, the Germans in Rio Grande
do Sul); modern Brazilian sociological investigations describing the
blending of the three races; Brazilian literature and art.

3. Economic development: a number of general works
sketching the six economic cycles best represented by the raw
products which were essential (dye wood in the sixteenth century,
sugar cane in the seventeenth century, gold and diamonds in the
first half of the eighteenth century, cotton in the second half of the
eighteenth century, coffee in the nineteenth and twentieth centuries,
and rubber around 1900). Colonel Hull's special attention was focused
on cocoa, perhaps because of the importance of this plant for the
economy of Bahia.

4. General historical and cultural background for South
America, consisting of a great collection of nineteenth-century
travel books.

The most valuable single item is a collection of 90 unpublished water colors made in Rio in the 1820's. These water
colors are most important documentation for Rio de Janeiro as
capital of the Brazilian Empire.

The collection also contains a manuscript of the diary
made by Francisco Zavier Ribiero de Sampaio during his travels
in Brazil in 1774-75. Colonel Hull was of the opinion that the manuscript is the original diary; it is now considered a copy of the late
eighteenth century. The collection also includes 2 copies of the
first printed edition of the diary, Lisbon, 1825.

The most important printed books are sixteenth-century
imprints of travel and exploration, including the following:

Acuña, Christoval de. Nuevo descubrimiento del gran río de las
Amazonas (Madrid, 1641).
Grynaeus. Novus Orbis (Basel, 1532).
Herrera, Antonio de. Historia general de los hechos de los
Castellanos (Madrid, 1601-15).
Lery, Jean de. Histoire d'un voyage fait en la terre du Brazil,
autrement dite Amerique (Geneva, 1594).
Montalboddo. Itinerarium Portugallense (1508), and Paesi
novamente ritrovati (1517).
Peter Martyr. Decades tres (Basel, 1533), and The Decades of
the New World or West India (London, 1555).
Schmidel, Ulrich. Vera historia admirandae navigationis
(Nuremberg, 1599).
Thevet. The Newe Founde Worlde or Antartike (London, 1568).

American Geographical Society
Broadway at 156th Street
New York 32

The American Geographical Society, founded in 1852, is the oldest geographical society in the United States. It is devoted to geographical research and to the advancement of geography, cartography, and exploration in their scientific, cultural, and educational aspects. The society publishes the Geographical Review, a quarterly magazine, and Focus, a monthly (except July and August) bulletin which views with geographical perspective areas and resources in the news.

It has assembled a library of over 125,000 volumes and a selected map collection of 236,000 examples. The file of scientific periodicals related to geography is without question the most extensive in the country, and since 1923 these have been card-indexed in such a manner that subjects may be located conveniently by regions and topics throughout the world. A list of the monthly additions to this catalogue, Current Geographical Publications, is now available in mimeographed form and provides bibliographical information available under normal circumstances only through the means of a central collecting bureau or library.

Studies in Hispanic American geography have played an important role in the society's research program. In 1920, a department of Hispanic American research was established, one of the immediate aims of which was the gathering of material for and the construction of an entirely new map of all the territory between the southern boundary of the United States and Cape Horn. The need for such a map was quite apparent to students of Latin America in view of the widely scattered nature of cartographic material. The scheme, scale, and standards of the International Map of the World were adopted with certain modifications.

The society has issued the following publications related to Hispanic America, which deal with a widely varied group of subjects ranging from regional and political geography to cartography.

Special publications:

Bowman, Isaiah. The Andes of Southern Peru: Geographical
    Reconnaissance Along the Seventy-third Meridian (1916).
—. Desert Trails of Atacama (1924).
Discovery of the Amazon According to the Account of Friar Gaspar
    de Carvajal and Other Documents (1934).
Johnson, G. R. Peru from the Air (1930).

Pioneer Settlement. Cooperative Studies by Twenty-six Authors (1932).

Rich, John Lyon. The Face of South America (1942).

Research series:

Jefferson, Mark. Peopling the Argentine Pampa (1926).

__. Rainfall of Chile (1921).

__. Recent Colonization in Chile (1921).

McBride, George M. The Agrarian Indian Communities of Highland Bolivia (1921).

__. Chile: Land and Society (1936).

__. The Land Systems of Mexico (1923).

Sullivan, Henry B. A Catalogue of Geological Maps of South America (1922).

Map of Hispanic America publications:

Catalogue of Maps of Hispanic America (1930-33).

Davis, William Morris. The Lesser Antilles (1926).

Ogilvie, Alan G. Geography of the Central Andes: A Handbook to Accompany the La Paz Sheet of the Map of Hispanic America on the Millionth Scale (1922).

Platt, R. R., Wright, J. K., Weaver, J. C., and Fairchild, J. E. The European Possessions in the Caribbean Area: A Compilation of Facts Concerning Their Population, Physical Geography, Resources, Industries, Trade, Government, and Strategic Importance (1941).

Map of the Americas, 1:5, 000, 000 (1942)

    (1) Mexico, Central America, and the West Indies

    (2) South America, Sheet North

    (3) South America, Sheet South

    Index pamphlet

Index to Map of Hispanic America, 1:1, 000, 000 (1945). (See pp. 270-71).

Map of Hispanic America, 1:1, 000, 000 (1922-45); 107 sheets.

American Museum of Natural History
Central Park West at 79th Street
New York 24

For the purposes of this report, the term "Hispanic" applies to the Southwest, Central America including Mexico, South America with the island of Tierra del Fuego, and the West Indies exclusive of Bermuda, that is to say, the Bahamas and the Greater and Lesser Antilles. The island of Trinidad is here treated with the West Indies. The Iberian peninsula is not included because the American Museum has nothing peculiar to it, with the exception of some archeological material.

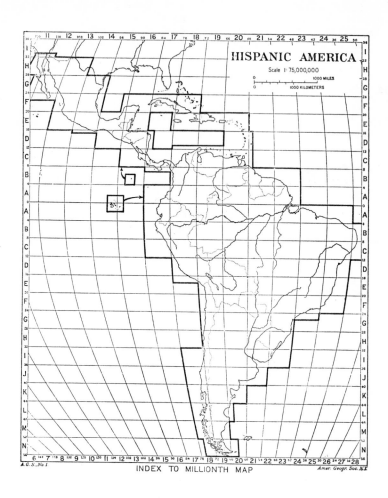

INDEX TO MILLIONTH MAP

MAP OF HISPANIC AMERICA

LIST OF PUBLISHED SHEETS

Map of Hispanic America, 1:1,000,000 [15.78 miles to 1 inch], Provisional Edition
Price: $2.50 per sheet; to Fellows, $1.87

North H-11, Baja California Norte*
North H-12, Sonora
North H-13, Chihuahua
North G-12, Baja California Sur*
North G-13, Culiacán
North G-14, Monterrey
North F-13, Guadalajara
North F-14, San Luis Potosí*
North F-16, Yucatán*
North F-17, Habana
North F-18, Santiago de Cuba
North E-13, Colima
North E-14, Ciudad de México
North E-15, Istmo de Tehuantepec
North E-16, Belize
North E-18, Kingston-Port au Prince
North E-19, Santo Domingo-San Juan
North E-20, Lesser Antilles North†
North D-15, Ciudad Guatemala
North D-16, Tegucigalpa
North D-20, Lesser Antilles South*
North C-16, Lago de Nicaragua
North C-17, Panamá
North C-18, Barranquilla
North C-19, Caracas
North C-20, Boca del Orinoco*
North B-18, Bogotá
North B-19, Río Meta*
North B-20, Roraima
North B-21, Georgetown
North B-22, Cayenne
North A-17, Río Mira-Islas Galápagos
North A-18, Cali
North A-19, Rio Uaupes
North A-20, Rio Branco*
North A-21, Alto Trombetas*
North A-22, Amapá*
South A-17, Quito
South A-18, Iquitos
South A-19, Putumayo-Içá*
South A-20, Manáos
South A-21, Santarém
South A-22, Pará
South A-23, São Luiz
South A-24, Fortaleza
South B-17, Piura
South B-18, Loreto
South B-19, Río Juruá*
South B-20, Rio Purús*
South B-21, Rio Tapajóz*
South B-22, Rio Araguaya
South B-23, Teresina
South B-24, Jaguaribe
South B-25, Paraíba
South C-17, Trujillo*

South C-18, Cerro de Pasco
South C-19, Acre*
South C-20, Rio Madeira
South C-21, Rio Juruena
South C-22, Rio Tocantins*
South C-23, Rio São Francisco
South C-24, Aracajú*
South C-25, Recife
South D-18, Lima
South D-19, Puno-Río Beni*
South D-20, Rio Guaporé
South D-21, Cuyabá
South D-22, Goyaz
South D-23, Carinhanha
South D-24, Bahia*
South E-19, La Paz*
South E-20, Sucre
South E-21, Corumbá*
South E-22, Paranahyba
South E-23, Bello Horizonte*
South E-24, Mucury*
South F-19, Iquique
South F-20, Río Pilcomayo*
South F-21, Rio Apa
South F-22, Paranapanema*
South F-23, Rio de Janeiro
South F-24, Victoria
South G-19, Atacama
South G-20, Tucumán
South G-21, Ascunción
South G-22, Curityba*
South H-19, Coquimbo-San Juan
South H-20, Córdoba-Santa Fé*
South H-21 Uruguayana
South H-22, Porto Alegre*
South I-18, Cauquenes e Islas Esporádicas*
South I-19, Santiago-Mendoza
South I-20, Rosario
South I-21, Buenos Aires-Montevideo
South I-22, Lagôa Mirim*
South J-18, Concepción*
South J-19, Parral-Neuquén*
South J-20, Bahía Blanca
South J-21, Mar del Plata
South K-18, Isla Chiloé*
South K-19, Lago Nahuel-Huapi*
South K-20, Golfo de San Matías*
South L-18, Península de Taitao*
South L-19, Comodoro Rivadavia
South M-18, Isla Wellington-Lago Argentino*
South M-19, Santa Cruz
South N-19, (combined with parts of N-18 and N-20) Tierra del Fuego*

* Out of print
† Without layer tints

Revised sheets listed in italics were published 1949-1952.

American Geographical Society, Broadway at 156th Street, New York 32, N. Y.

The anthropology department of the American Museum has made basic studies in the Southwest, Middle America, and South America, and the fruits of the expeditions to these regions are, of course, in the museum. Peru is particularly well represented, and the Costa Rican collection is one of the finest in the world. The archeological material from Mexico is as good as any outside of Mexico itself. The museum has some original manuscripts, including a fascinating collection of tax records from Mexico made by Indians on native paper, with Spanish notations, and a complete collection of reproductions of old manuscripts. The museum has an excellent working library for all the Hispanic American countries.

The museum is particularly strong in the archeology and ethnology of the Southwest. These collections have been derived from the various expeditions of the Hydes and those sponsored over a period of years by the Committee on Primitive Peoples of the Southwest, and they have been rather thoroughly described and published.

Archeological materials from Mexico and Central America are well represented in the museum, the collections being especially strong for the Valley of Mexico, Oaxaca, the Gulf Coast, and western Mexico. These collections include pottery, tools, ornaments, sculptures, and models of temples. There are also plaster casts of many of the important large monuments of the Maya, Aztec, and Olmec cultures. There are large collections of archeological materials from Costa Rica. The ethnographic collections from Middle America are not extensive except for the Huichol of western Mexico.

The South American anthropological section has extensive ethnographic collections from the tropical forests of eastern Peru, with smaller samplings from other parts of the continent. The archeological material, starting with the Bandelier collections from Bolivia and coastal Peru, has been built up largely through systematic field research by the museum staff. Now represented are southern and northern Chile, Bolivia, Peru, and to a lesser degree Ecuador, Colombia, and Brazil. For some regions the time span covered is far greater than that represented by any other collection.

Although there is no department of the museum which does not have material from some parts of Hispanic America, the most extensive collecting has been done by the departments of ornithology and mammalogy, now two, but in the early years a single department reporting on its combined acquisition of birds

nd mammals. The Maximilian collection forms the nucleus of both
he bird and mammal collections from South America.

The collection of birds in the museum is in general representative of the whole of Hispanic America with the exception of El
Salvador, from which there is practically nothing. This includes the
birds from the Maximilian collection, the Elliot collection of humming-
birds, the Lawrence collection, about 5,000 specimens from the
Dwight collection from tropical America, 40,000 specimens from
Central and South America in the Rothschild collection, and the Brewster-
Sanford collection of oceanic birds, in addition to a great many large
and small collections accumulated almost annually since the founding
of the museum.

The museum's mammal collection from South America is
excellent; there is nothing lacking with the possible exception of a
few subspecies. The museum has in many instances considerable
topotype material when at the time of the original descriptions only
the type specimen was known. Much of the material has not yet been
described, but the staff of the department of mammalogy is working
on it constantly. The collection from Central America is not so good,
but it is adequate.

Other notable collections include fossil material from the
Cope Pampean collection and the Patagonian expeditions. There are
also collections dealing with entomology, herpetology, ichthyology,
and geology.

The history of the acquisition of collections, the names of
donors, and in some instances the number of specimens received
yearly will be found in the various publications of the museum. These
include the Annual Report; the History, Plan and Scope of the American Museum of Natural History (up to the year 1911); Anthropological
Papers; Bulletin; Memoirs; and Novitates, as well as guide leaflets
and handbooks.

Association of the Bar of the City of New York
42 West 44th Street
New York

The Association of the Bar of the City of New York has in
its library an extensive collection of legal works covering Spain,
Portugal, and Latin America. Under each of these countries, the
library has secured reports, digests, statutes, session laws, codes,
constitutional material, legal treatises, and periodicals. It has the
official gazettes for some of the jurisdictions and also the official
papers in many of the boundary disputes.

The eminent Argentine statesman Estanislas Severo Zeballc
was interested in the library's collection, and through his good offic
a large collection of the law of that republic was built up, many worl
being received as the gifts of the respective authors.

In 1909, a complete set of the official Spanish laws and
reports was secured, from the time of Carlos IV to the present, and
also the legal portion of the library of Luis Montt, the national librarian of Chile, which represents years of collecting on the part
of Señor Montt and his father, a former president of Chile.

In 1915, Edwin M. Borchard, then law librarian of the Library of Congress, was sent by that library to South America for
the purpose of buying books on South American law and securing
data for a report on the laws of South America.   The association
was permitted to avail itself of his valuable services in securing
many important additions.

The association is in communication with agents in practically
every capital and is thus able to keep its collections up to date.   It
has also been fortunate in securing the interest of the various consuls in New York City, who have obtained from officials and scholar
in their home capitals expert advice as to purchases.

The library is rigidly a reference library, but accredited
scholars engaged in research are cordially accorded its privileges
when introduced by members of the association.

The collection is fully catalogued on cards, but no printed
catalogue is available, nor have check lists been issued.   However,
attention should be called to the publications of the association's
committee on foreign law, which include such authorities on Latin
American law as Phanor J. Eder, Thomas W. Palmer, Edward
Schuster, and others.

Basque Delegation
30 Fifth Avenue
New York 11

The Basque Delegation has in its files many publications
and manuscripts covering the period since the Basque Autonomous
Government was established in 1936.   They include almost all the
magazines and papers on Basque affairs printed in the Americas
and Europe.   Some of the original documents are still restricted.

The following magazines are perhaps the most useful:

Revista Internacional de Estudios Vascos, up to 1936; Euzko
Jakintza, from 1947; Euzko Deya, edited in Paris; Euzko Deya,
edited in Mexico; Euzko Deya, edited in Buenos Aires; Alderdi,
edited in Bayonne (France) by the Basque Nationalist Party; and the
daily news bulletin edited by the Basque Government-in-Exile, 50
rue Singer, Paris.

Chase National Bank
13 Broad Street
New York 15

The money of Hispanic America is well exemplified in the
Chase National Bank's Museum of Moneys of the World. The collection consists of approximately 75,000 specimens of mediums of
exchange covering all periods and political divisions, and, with a
library, is maintaned for the educational advantage of the public
at the bank's head office. Associated with the main exhibition are
several small collections available for display by the bank's numerous branches, bank correspondents, and commercial customers.

From the time of the first minting of coins in the Western
Hemisphere (Mexico, 1535) to the present day, the political changes—
conquest, revolution, rebellion, and tranquility—of the geographical
divisions of Hispanic America may be read from the coins in the
museum. The paper money, particularly that associated with revolution since the eighteenth century, contributes to the story.

There is more than conventional coinage: coins divided
and perforated for convenience in making change, and those of one
political division countermarked for use in another are notable.
The Portuguese "joes" and the Spanish "doubloons," "pieces of
eight," "bits," and "flips," were money of the realm in the early
development of the United States. From the southern tip of the New
World, there is the gold coinage of Tierra del Fuego ("gramos")
issued by Julio Popper, "Red Rover of Fireland." The numerous
coins of Morelos and others are tokens of Mexico's struggles with
Spain. Those of the seceding state of Oaxaca tell of later political
strife.

Among the pre-Columbian mediums of exchange, cocoa
beans, as well as hand-wrought copper pieces shaped in the form
of chopping knives or chisels, are attributed to the Aztecs, and gold
in fanciful forms to the Incas. Hacienda money tokens, particularly
those of stamped leather, are collectors' items.

Probably nowhere else will be found as great a variety

of the paper money of Hispanic America as that displayed by the
Chase Bank. Uncommon items are the notes of San Dimas (1870),
Nicaragua's revolutionary notes of 1910, and those of Yucatán,
Puerto Rico, Haiti, St. Thomas, and the various states of South
America. The military scrip (1856) of the adventurer and filibustere
William Walker, who made Nicaragua a republic and himself presi-
dent, served a purpose until Walker's execution in 1860.

Stephen Carlton Clark Collection
46 East 70th Street
New York

The private art collection of Stephen Carlton Clark, an
executive of the Singer Sewing Machine Company and a long-time
trustee of the Metropolitan Museum, is distinguished by the quality
of its pieces. Among the noteworthy Hispanic items is "St. Andrew,"
by El Greco. This picture, showing a bearded, cross-bearing
saint, is done in contrasting hues of gray, blue, and green. It was
acquired by Mr. Clark in Munich in 1954, and is one of the most
important Hispanic art objects to enter the United States in recent
years.

Cooper Union for the Advancement of Science and Art
Museum for the Arts of Decoration
Fourth Avenue and Seventh Street
New York 3

In 1902 the recently formed Cooper Union Museum received
from the late J. Pierpont Morgan a gift of three textile collections:
the Baron collection purchased in Paris, and the Vivés and the Mique
y Badía collections formed in Spain. Among these materials were
many Spanish textiles covering roughly the twelfth through the eighteenth centuries. Additions through succeeding years have built up
a collection representative of the weaves and styles of textiles from
this country of great craftsmen. They run from the rare Hispano-
Moresque silks, through the fifteenth-, sixteenth-, and seventeenth-
century velvets, to the patterned silks of the eighteenth and nineteenth
centuries. A group of wool and linen weavings of the sixteenth and
seventeenth centuries is interesting and examples of simpler folk
handicraft are present, as well as typical Spanish embroideries
and some 15 samplers from the sixteenth to the nineteenth centuries.

By far the most important of the Spanish textiles are those
included in the group of Hispano-Moresque materials, those woven
in Spain while still under the artistic domination of her Mohammedan

conquerors and which cover roughly the eleventh to the fifteenth centuries. Of these, as well as a group of sixteenth-century silks exhibiting Mohammedan influence, the museum possesses at present 54 examples. These range from the textiles of marked Persian style, such as the famous "Lion Strangler," a twelfth-century silk from the tomb of St. Bernard Calvo; and the geometric designs of the thirteenth century, such as the fragments from the tomb of Don Felipe (died 1274), son of Ferdinand III; through the silks of the fifteenth century, where a gradual freeing of pattern and elaboration of arabesques merges into the Spanish style of the sixteenth and seventeenth centuries.

For further information of the museum's Hispano-Moresque textiles, the reader is referred to the article by Dorothy Shepherd in the Chronicle, the annual publication of the museum, for December 1943.

Portugal is represented in the collection by a small group of silk brocades of the late seventeenth century, with the designs of huntsmen, flowers, and animals.

The collection of Peruvian textiles, while small (about 100 in all), is comprehensive and provides a useful survey of the techniques and patterns of weaving and embroidery of pre-Columbian Peru, as well as several examples of sixteenth- and seventeenth-century work. One of the most striking is a poncho fragment of wool, in interlocking cloth weave, with curious designs of human heads on a brilliant red ground, catalogued as Paracas, before 500 A.D. Two beautiful mantles of the sixteenth to seventeenth centuries, in tapestry weave, one of wool and metal, are unusually fine examples of Peruvian textiles after the Conquest.

Mexico and Guatemala are represented by a small but useful collection of belts, bags, tunics, and various fragments of Central American textiles.

Foreign Policy Association
22 East 38th Street
New York 16

During the collaboration of the Foreign Policy Association and the World Peace Foundation, both organizations, with the co-operation of the Fletcher School of Law and Diplomacy, sponsored the Committee on Latin American Policy and published in 1933 the Committee's Recommendations as to the Pan-American Conference at Montevideo. Foreign Policy Committee Reports No. 1.

In 1934, in response to an invitation given by President Mendieta of Cuba to Raymond L. Buell, president of the association, the Commission on Cuban Affairs, an unofficial group of experts, was organized. After a period of intensive research in Cuba, the commission brought together the individual members' studies for publication after careful consideration by the entire group. The recommendations appeared as Problems of the New Cuba: Report of the Commission on Cuban Affairs (1934). An edition in Spanish was published simultaneously.

In 1938, Charles A. Thomson of the Foreign Policy Associa tion staff went to South America on a grant from the Rockefeller Foundation. While there, he attended the Eighth International Conference of American States at Lima, and wrote a report on it.

The research department of the association formerly published, at intervals of a fortnight, studies dealing with foreign affairs These studies, first entitled "Information Service Pamphlets," and later "Foreign Policy Reports," are now incorporated in the semimonthly "Foreign Policy Bulletin." The following "Foreign Policy Reports" deal with Hispanic countries:

The Mexican Land and Oil Law Issue (December 22, 1926).
Pan America and the Pan American Conferences (November 25, 1927).
Mexico, the Caribbean and Tacna-Arica (January 20, 1928).
The United States and Latin America (Special Supplement, January 1928).
The Sixth Pan American Conference, Part I (April 27, 1928), Part 2 (July 6, 1928).
The United States and the Nicaraguan Canal (May 25, 1928).
Arbitration on the American Continent (October 28, 1928).
The Monroe Doctrine and Latin America (December 7, 1928).
The Problem of Puerto Rico (January 18, 1929).
The United States and Colombian Oil (April 3, 1929).
Cuba and the Platt Amendment (April 17, 1929).
Spain under a Dictatorship (September 4, 1929).
The Pan American Arbitration Treaty (November 13, 1929).
The American Occupation of Haiti (November 27 and December 12, 1929).
Unsettled Boundary Disputes in Latin America (March 5, 1930).
American Supervision of Elections in Nicaragua (December 24, 1930).
The Revolution in Brazil (March 4, 1931).
Debts, Dictatorship and Revolution in Bolivia and Peru (May 13, 1931).
The United States and Central American Stability (July 8, 1931).

The United States and Central American Revolutions (July 28, 1931).
Argentina's Revolution and Its Aftermath (October 28, 1931).
Panama and the United States (January 20, 1932).
South American Conflicts. The Chaco and Leticia (May 24, 1933).
The Caribbean Situation—Cuba and Haiti (June 21, 1933).
The Caribbean Situation—Nicaragua and Salvador (August 30, 1933).
The Montevideo Conference and the Latin American Policy of the
    United States (November 22, 1933).
Spain under the Republic (December 20, 1933).
Chile Struggles for National Recovery (February 14, 1934).
The Seventh Pan American Conference, Montevideo (June 6, 1934).
Latin American Policy of the Roosevelt Administration (December
    19, 1934).
Brazil's Political and Economic Problems (March 13, 1935).
Church and State in Mexico (July 3, 1935).
The Cuban Revolution: Fall of Machado (December 18, 1935).
The Cuban Revolution: Reform and Reaction (January 1, 1936).
Dictatorship in the Dominican Republic (April 15, 1936).
The League and the Chaco Dispute (July 15, 1936).
Toward a New Pan Americanism (November 1, 1936).
Spain: Issues Behind the Conflict (January 1, 1937).
Spain: Civil War (January 15, 1937).
The Buenos Aires Conference: 1936 (July 1, 1937).
Mexico's Social Revolution (August 1, 1937).
Mexico's Challenge to Foreign Capital (August 15, 1937).
Trade Rivalries in Latin America (September 15, 1937).
U. S. Neutrality in the Spanish Conflict (November 15, 1937).
Fascism and Communism in South America (December 15, 1937).
The War in Spain (May 1, 1938).
The Mexican Oil Dispute (August 15, 1938).
Exchange Controls in Latin America (February 15, 1939).
The Lima Conference (March 15, 1939).
Raw Material Resources of Latin America (August 1, 1939).
War and United States—Latin American Trade (December 1, 1939).
Progress of Pan-American Cooperation (February 15, 1940).
Spain after Civil War (May 15, 1940).
Economic Defense of the Americas (August 1, 1940).
The Havana Conference of 1940 (September 15, 1940).
Export-Import Bank Loans to Latin America (June 15, 1941).
The Resources and Trade of Central America (September 1, 1941).
Toward Free Trade with Latin America (October 1, 1941).
U. S. Trade Ties with Argentina (December 1, 1941).
Portugal: Beleaguered Neutral (December 15, 1941).
Wartime Economic Cooperation in the Americas (February 15, 1942).

Economic Projects for Hemisphere Development (March 1, 1942).
The Rio de Janeiro Conference of 1942 and Some Recent Books on
 Latin America (April 15, 1942).
Hemisphere Solidarity in the War Crisis and An Outline of Pan-
 American Machinery (May 15, 1942).
Impact of War on Mexico's Economy and Mexico's Military Organiza
 tion (June 15, 1943).
Agricultural Cooperation in the Americas and Recent Export-Import
 Bank Loans to Latin America (September 15, 1943).
Some Latin American Views on Post-War Reconstruction and Latin-
 American Organizations for Post-War Planning (March 15, 1944)
Argentina in Crisis and Argentina and the United States (May 1, 1944
Anglo-American Caribbean Commission and Caribbean Dependencies
 of the United States, Great Britain, France and the Netherlands
 (December 15, 1944).
Can Latin America Build a New Economy? and Latin American Trade
 in Pre-War and War Periods (April 1, 1945).
The Mexico City Conference and Regional Security and Act of
 Chapultepec and Economic Charter of the Americas (May 1, 1945)
Brazil: Rising Power in the Americas and Status of Brazilian-U.S.
 War Agreements (October 15, 1945).
Argentina—Focus of Conflict in the Americas and Axis Ties with
 Argentina (February 1, 1946).
Spain in the Post-War World and Spain's Foreign Relations (August
 1, 1947).
Chile: Microcosm of Modern Conflicts and A U.S. Market for
 Chilean Copper (July 15, 1946).
Puerto Rico: An American Responsibility and Progress of Public
 Enterprises in Puerto Rico (March 1, 1947).
Latin America and the United States and Latin America in the Marshall
 Plan (January 15, 1948).
Peron's Greater Argentina and the United States and Background of
 the Anglo-Argentine Railways Transactions (December 1, 1948).
Spain and Portugal—A Dilemma for the West and Portugal: Free
 Nations' Partner (May 1, 1949).
Army Challenge in Latin America and Latin American Dictatorships
 and the U.S. (December 15, 1949).

     The association has also published the following numbers
in its "Headline Series": Challenge to the Americas (1940), The
Good Neighbors, 3d ed. rev. (1941), Mexico: The Making of a Nation
(1942), The Amazon: A New Frontier? (1944), Latin America: Lan
of a Golden Legend (1947), Mexico: Land of Great Experiments (1952),
The Economy of Spain (1952), The United States and Latin America (1953

Frick Art Reference Library
10 East 71st Street
New York 21

The Frick Art Reference Library was founded in 1920 by Miss Helen C. Frick in memory of her father, Henry Clay Frick. It is internationally recognized as the source of authoritative art information for all serious students of art, as well as for museums, art galleries, art critics, and art dealers.

The library has a reference collection of about 330,000 reproductions of works of art and about 108,000 books, catalogues, and periodicals covering European and American painting, drawing, sculpture, and illuminated manuscripts. The reproductions are, for the most part, black and white, 8- by 10-inch photographs, mounted, with the history of each work of art typed on the reverse of its mount. Each work of art is indexed in an alphabetical card catalogue by artist, title, subject, and collection.

There are on file photographs of over 35,000 Spanish and Portuguese paintings, over 8,000 photographs of Spanish sculpture, as well as a very full file of reproductions of Spanish illuminated manuscripts. The book and periodical material on Spanish art is exceptionally complete.

Frick Collection
1 East 70th Street
New York 21

Henry Clay Frick (1849-1919), of Pittsburgh and New York, bequeathed his New York house together with its remarkable contents and an endowment fund, to be maintained after his wife's death for the purpose of "encouraging and developing the study of the fine arts. " Mrs. Frick died in 1931. The house was then remodeled in part and considerably enlarged, and opened as a museum in 1935.

The collection chiefly consists of 161 paintings by fourteenth- to nineteenth-century masters, with the Renaissance Italians, the seventeenth-century Dutch, and the English and French Schools of the eighteenth century being especially well represented. A Summary Catalogue of Paintings was published in 1935, followed in 1937 by a more comprehensive Handbook.

Among the paintings are 7 of the Spanish School:

Goya.   "Doña María Martínez de Puga"; "El Conde de Teba (?)"; and "The Forge."

Greco, El. "Expulsion from the Temple"; "Saint Jerome"; and
"Vincentio Anastagi" (the inscribed tablet at the left and perhaps
the Maltese cross on the subject's breast appear to be by another
hand).
Velázquez. "Philip IV"; the Fraga or Parma portrait.

Hispanic Society of America
Broadway, between 155th and 156th Streets
New York 32

The Hispanic Society of America, a free, public, endowed,
membership institution was founded in 1904, although the founder,
Archer M. Huntington, had begun collecting a Spanish library as
early as 1885 and had taken Spanish letters as his life interest.
A visit to Mexico soon after made it possible to extend this activity,
and during the period 1887-1904 the collecting of books gradually
became extended to works of art, with a view to the foundation of
an institution related to Hispanic culture in as broad a sense as
possible. In a visit to Spain in 1892, the founder traveled for a
year continuously and visited all the important cities and towns of
the Iberian Peninsula, including Portugal. At this time, a rough
draft or outline plan of the future society was made. In 1904, the
society came into existence, and from that time to the present the
collections have been augmented, in each case or type, to the point
where a fair amount of basic information and descriptive material
has been made available for the public and staff.

The plan was to indicate in brief outline the history of
Hispanic culture, either by books, manuscripts, objects of art, or
products of the crafts, and to issue descriptive publications. The
object was not the collecting of endless duplicates or series, but
only of such types as could best be made the basis of a general understanding of the culture of the Hispanic peoples.

Such a plan might be extended indefinitely, and it has been
the chief aim of the founder to limit each field of artistic presentation to the essential basic material which a student could use as a
first step, before going abroad to expand his knowledge and experience
by contact with the greater works of art, which can only be seen
there. Music is not seriously considered, as it is more than amply
presented by other institutions.

No plan of teaching is involved. The staff, which is a
slowly developed group of specialists, devotes itself to research
and the publication of material explanatory of or collateral to the

collections. The society consists of a hundred members, and to this
are added corresponding members, from which group the members
are usually drawn.

Museum collections:

Paintings of the fourteenth- and fifteenth-century Catalan,
Aragonese, Valencian, and Castilian schools are the earliest in the
collection. Representative artists of the sixteenth century are
Morales and El Greco; of the Baroque period, Zurbarán, Carreño
de Miranda, Ribera, and Velázquez; of the eighteenth century, Goya.
Modern artists include Rico, Vierge, Sorolla, and López Mezquita;
two rooms are devoted to the paintings of Zuloaga and Viladrich.
Expressly for the exhibition room in the west wing Sorolla painted
a series of 14 canvases which offer a pictorial document of the fast-
disappearing customs, costumes, and fiestas of the regions of Spain.

The sculpture group comprises engraved ivories in Phoeni-
cian style, pre-Roman and Roman bronzes, a tenth-century carved
Hispano-Moresque ivory box, and jet statuettes and amulets. Among
the polychrome wood carvings is a Mater Dolorosa of the thirteenth
century. Of the work in marble and alabaster, 2 early sixteenth-
century wall tombs from Cuéllar are remarkable for showing the
transition from Gothic to Renaissance style.

Pottery from the prehistoric through the Roman period as
well as Roman glass, excavated from the environs of Carmona and
Seville (Itálica), is on exhibition in the gallery. Of singular importance is the display of Hispano-Moresque and Spanish lustre pottery,
numbering over 150 pieces. Tiles and pottery from Talavera de la
Reina, Cataluña, Valencia, and Seville, early Capodimonte and Buen
Retiro porcelains, and glazed earthenware from Puebla, Mexico,
are also represented in the ceramic collection. Of the Spanish glass
objects, the sixteenth-century enameled glasses from Catalonia are
rarities.

Textile exhibits present varied examples of thirteenth-
and fourteenth-century Hispano-Moresque silks, gold and silver
brocades, and velvets made in the fifteenth and sixteenth centuries.
Also may be seen ecclesiastical vestments, Spanish and Portuguese
embroideries, a group of Spanish peasant laces, and rugs from the
famous rug-weaving centers of Cuenca, Salamanca, and Alcaraz.

Metalwork is exemplified by objects from pre-Roman times
through the eighteenth century. Iron knockers, reja bands, and
locks date from the Gothic to later periods. Works in silver for
ecclesiastical use are represented by Gothic and Renaissance

crucifixes, paxes, censers, and a <u>custodia</u>, dated 1585, by Cristóba
Becerril of Cuenca. Examples of Portuguese silverwork are on
display.

Furniture used during the seventeenth century is typified
by tables, benches, chairs, cabinets, and braziers. Distinctive
of the Spanish cabinetmaker's work are the writing desks (<u>vargueños</u>
sixteenth- and seventeenth-century pieces showing decorative iron
mountings on the exterior, and carving, inlay, or gilding inside.

Library collections:

Books in the fields of history, literature, and the arts of
Spain, Portugal, and colonial Hispanic America are available for
reference use. Those printed before 1650 are restricted, though
microphotographic reproductions will be supplied to readers.

Exhibited manuscripts include: private and papal documents
codices; church service books, commonly called choir books, with
calligraphic and illuminated decorations; holograph letters; early
maps and charts for navigators; and letters patent of nobility with
their heraldic paintings. The library has one of the four known
"black" books, the Book of Hours of Queen María, consort of
Alfonso V of Aragon. This fifteenth-century manuscript is written
partially in silver and gold on black-stained vellum. A Hebrew
Bible written, in part, in gold letters upon vellum is an excellent
example of workmanship and illumination.

Printed books begin with some 250 Hispanic incunabula,
with several by that "master of arts" Lambert Palmart of Valencia,
followed by over 8,000 volumes of first and early editions of important Spanish authors, such as Cervantes, Góngora, and Lope de
Vega. Thirty-six editions of the <u>Celestina</u>, mainly from the famed
collection of the Marquis of Jérez de los Caballeros, cover the perio
from 1499 to 1635. Among the Portuguese volumes are those rare
books of discovery, as well as the first and other sixteenth-century
editions of <u>Os Lusíadas</u> by Camões. Notable among early American
imprints are those from Mexico and Peru. The library collection
includes many unique copies.

Arrangements were made in 1927 for the Library of Congress to assume responsibility for collecting books concerning
modern Hispanic America. The Huntington Fund, established for
this purpose, was the origin at the Library of Congress in 1939
of the Hispanic Foundation.

In the print collection of the Hispanic Society are woodcuts, engravings, etchings, and lithographs from the fifteenth to the twentieth century, including religious and historical subjects, portraits, landscapes, and costumes. Of special note are works by Ribera, Fortuny, and Goya, the latter's etchings and lithographs being most fully represented.

Photographs, available for study, present a comprehensive survey of the fine and decorative arts of Spain and Portugal. An important section is devoted to scenes and costumes in these countries.

Publications on the collections:

Anderson, R. M. Gallegan Provinces of Spain (1939).
—. Spanish Costume: Extremadura (1951).
Burr, G. H. Hispanic Furniture (1941).
Caskel, Werner. Arabic Inscriptions. Translated from the German by Beatrice Gilman Proske (1936).
Frothingham, Alice Wilson. Catalogue of Hispano-Moresque Pottery (1936).
—. Hispanic Glass (1941).
—. Lustreware of Spain (1951).
—. Prehistoric Pottery in the Collection from El Acebuchal (1953).
—. Sigillate Pottery of the Roman Empire (1937).
—. Talavera Pottery (1944).
Gilman, Beatrice I. Catalogue of Sculpture (13th to 15th centuries) (1932).
—. Catalogue of Sculpture (16th to 18th centuries) (1930).
The Hispanic Society of America Handbook: Museum and Library Collections (1938).
A History of the Hispanic Society of America, Museum and Library (1904-1954) with a Survey of the Collections, prepared by members of the staff (1954). Issued for the fiftieth anniversary of the founding of the society.
Irving, Washington. Diary, Spain 1828-1829. Edited from the manuscript in the library, by Clara Louisa Penney (1930).
Johnson, A. M. Hispanic Silverwork (1944).
May, Florence Lewis. Catalogue of Laces and Embroideries (1936).
—. Hispanic Lace and Lace Making (1939).
Miles G. C. The Coinage of the Umayyads of Spain. Published jointly by the American Numismatic Society and the Hispanic Society of America (1950).
—. The Coinage of the Visigoths of Spain, Leovigild to Achila II. Published as above (1952).
Penney, Clara Louisa. The Book Called Celestina in the Library (1954).

—. The Hispanic Society of America. Catalogue of Publications (1943).
—. List of Books Printed before 1601 (1929).   Reprint with additions
    (1955).
—. List of Books Printed 1601-1700 (1938).
Proske, Beatrice G. Castilian Sculpture (Gothic to Renaissance)
    (1951).
Spalding, Frances. Mudejar Ornament in Manuscripts (1953).
Trapier, Elizabeth du Gué. Catalogue of Paintings (14th to 15th
    centuries) (1930).
—. Catalogue of Paintings (19th and 20th centuries) (1932).
—. Daniel Urrabieta Vierge (1936).
—. Eugenio Lucas y Padilla (1940).
—. Luis de Morales and Leonardesque Influences in Spain (1953).
—. Martín Rico y Ortega (1937).
—. Ribera (1952).
Van de Put, Albert. The Valencian Styles of Hispano-Moresque
    Pottery, 1404-1454 (1938).

International Business Machines Corporation
Fine Arts Department
590 Madison Avenue
New York 22

The IBM Fine Arts Department was conceived by Mr.
Thomas J. Watson as a project for bringing artists and businessmen
into a closer relationship for their mutual benefit, and for broadening
the basis of art appreciation. The project began with the acquisition
of two paintings by living artists in each of the seventy-nine countries in which IBM was represented—canvases chosen in every case
by local art juries as characteristic of the art and life of the individual countries. The collections were organized for and first
exhibited in the 1939 World's Fairs at New York and San Francisco.

During a period of fifteen years the collections have been
expanded. The general field of concentration has been the Western
Hemisphere, with the primary core devoted to the development of
the arts from pre-Columbian times to the present. The collections
cover the field of oil painting, water color, sculpture, print making,
American Indian artifacts, models of inventions, and other categories

The Fine Arts Department schedules touring exhibits to
museums, educational institutions, civic groups, and other non-
commercial organizations, upon written request. Exhibits are made
available without charge. Loans are usually for a period of three
or four weeks.

For details on the collections see Contemporary Art of 79
Countries (International Business Machines Corp., 1939) and Art
of the Americas (Art News Annual XVIII, The Art Foundation, Inc.,
1948).

Robert Lehman Collection
625 Park Avenue
New York

The remarkable private art collection of the investment
banker Robert Lehman was started by his father, the late financier
Philip Lehman, in 1911. Among other noteworthy Hispanic objects
are a portrait by Goya and above all a portrait of St. Jerome by El
Greco. This, considered to be the finest of several versions done
by the painter around 1600, was purchased by the Lehmans in 1915.

Metropolitan Museum of Art
New York

Department of Mediaeval Art

Most of the Spanish medieval objects are in the Pierpont
Morgan Wing and are discussed in Joseph Breck and Meyric R.
Rogers, The Pierpont Morgan Wing, a Handbook (New York, 1929)
and also in A Guide to the Collections (New York, 1937), Pt. 2,
"Mediaeval Art, " pp. 1-16. The collections given the museum by
J. Pierpont Morgan and his son, J. P. Morgan, include several
unique Spanish ivories and metalwork objects.

Sculpture:

Most of the museum's collection of medieval Spanish architectural and free-standing sculpture is to be seen at the Cloisters
(see pp. 289-292). Among the important Spanish pieces in the main
building are a monumental, fourteenth-century Catalan wood statue
of St. Peter which is in a remarkable state of preservation, with
its original paint virtually intact[*]; a thirteenth-century Catalan wood
statue of the Virgin and Child; a fifteenth-century alabaster relief
of the Virgin and Child. The museum also has the following:

Two alabaster statues, St. James the Less and another apostle,
originally from the superstructure of the tomb of Juan de Padilla
(d. 1491), which is now in the Museo Arqueológico at Burgos.

[*] See Metropolitan Museum Studies, III (1930), Pt. 1.

The tomb is the work of Gil de Siloé, and these statues are
attributed to his workshop and are dated about 1500. Also from
the Siloé workshop is a griffin said to have come from one of
the royal tombs at the convent of Miraflores, Burgos.
Six alabaster panels, decorated with angels and coats of arms and
nude boys supporting shells, are early sixteenth-century carvings
in the style of Siloé and come from the tomb of Don García Osorio
(d. 1502) and his wife, Doña María de Perea (d. 1499), which was
formerly in the church of San Pedro at Orcaña.

Ivories:

From the eleventh century are a panel with a legendary
scene, probably the "Testing of the True Cross," in the style of the
reliquary shrine of St. Aemilianus at San Millán de la Cogolla, and
the silver-gilt book cover from the cathedral of Jaca with applied
ivory figures representing the crucifixion. The latter was made
for Queen Felicia (d. 1083), wife of Sancho Ramírez, king of Aragon
and Navarre.

A large ivory panel from a diptych in the monumental figure style, with scenes of the journey to Emmaus and the Noli me
tangere; a small crucifix; and an ivory panel with St. Mark and the
lion are significant ivory sculptures of the twelfth century.

Metalwork:

The book cover noted above and a companion piece, and
the silver-gilt processional cross from the church of San Salvador
de Fuentes near Villaviciosa in the province of Oviedo, are most
unusual pieces. The twelfth-century crucifix bears an unusual
Latin inscription which, in translation, reads "In honor of Our Holy
Savior, Sanccia Guidisalvi made me."

A twelfth-century baptismal font, a group of Hispano-
Moresque bracelets and necklaces, and two Spanish or Portuguese
silver-gilt plates decorated with foliage, animals, and figures are
the most outstanding of the other metalwork objects in the collection.
There is also an iron horse bit of the Visigothic period. The miscellaneous pieces of ironwork, fourteenth- and fifteenth-century
crucifixes, and other liturgical objects are less worthy of mention.

Enamels:

Present-day scholarship tends to assign certain enamels
heretofore called Limoges (French) to Spain. Of the many enamels
in the Pierpont Morgan collection, the 6 plaques from a chasse with
representations of Sts. Peter and Paul, Christ between Sts. Mary

Magdalen and Martial, together with the symbols of the evangelists, are among those now considered thirteenth-century Spanish work.

Ceramics:

There is a small collection of enameled earthenware, which includes a Paterna enameled earthenware plate of the fourteenth century, combining interlaced patterns with coats of arms; a large glazed earthenware bowl of Teruel manufacture from the late fifteenth or sixteenth century; and some Hispano-Moresque plates.

Textiles:

Besides 2 fifteenth-century rugs with geometric designs, under Moorish influence, the museum has some vestments and textiles; also 3 fifteenth-century embroidered panels—St. Michael, St. John, and St. Barbara.   The large fifteenth-century Brussels tapestry, representing "The Redemption of Man, " like its companion piece "The Nativity, " at the Cloisters, was probably woven in the workshop of Pieter van Aelst and both taken to Spain by Philip the Handsome.   For generations they were part of the treasures of the cathedral of Burgos.

The Cloisters

The Cloisters is a branch of the Metropolitan Museum of Art devoted particularly to medieval art.* It is situated at the upper end of Manhattan in Fort Tryon Park, New York City.   Although the building housing the collections is not copied from any medieval building, nor is it a composite of various buildings, there are many modern architectural elements which recall medieval Spanish precedents.   As the plan was developed to a large extent around the reconstructed cloister from the Abbey of Saint-Michel-de-Cuxa, some of the features of a tower still standing at Cuxa were employed in the design of the tower.   (Stylistically, the architecture and sculpture from Cuxa are Spanish; geographically, Cuxa is now on the French side of the Pyrenees, but from time to time it belonged to what is now Spain.)

The original elements from Saint-Michel-de-Cuxa, almost all carved in pink marble from Ría and Villefranche, include the following, in addition to miscellaneous capitals, fragments from

---

*See James J. Rorimer, The Cloisters.   The Building and the Collection of Mediaeval Art—in Fort Tryon Park (New York, 1938).

doorways, windows, arches, etc.: 2 white marble capitals of the Corinthian type from the ciborium described by the monk García in 1040; and, from the cloister, 36 late twelfth-century capitals, some vigorously carved with figures consisting of human and animal forms, some suggesting capitals of the traditional Corinthian and composite types, and others ornamented with human heads and figur lions, apes, birds, acanthus leaves, and various conventionalized motifs; 19 abaci, of which 2 are ornamented; 25 bases; 12 shafts; 7 arches; and part of the parapet coping.

Besides the frescoes and tempera paintings which form an important part of the Cloisters collection (noted on pp. 297-301), the Cloisters has the following unusual Spanish objects which are listed according to period:

A twelfth-century crucifix is one of the most distinguished sculpture of its kind. It was found, after years of neglect, in the convent of Santa Clara (near Palencia) in the Spanish province of León. It is in an especially fine state of preservation; both the figure of Christ and the cross (the ends are restored) retain most of their original paint. The figure of Christ is practically identical in style with the ivory figure of Christ on the interior of the famous reliquary in the Cámara Santa of the cathedral of Oviedo, made for Gonzalo Menéndez, who was bishop from 1162 to 1175.

The monumental ecclesiastical sculpture of the late Romanesque period is represented by the 4 sculptures composing the Adoration group. These sculptures come from Cerezo de Riotirón and are dated, on the basis of stylistical comparisons, about 1188. The group consists of the Virgin and Child, Joseph, and two kings. There is no reason for supposing that a third king has disappeared from the group, as photographs of the group taken in situ show the group to be complete as it now is.

Somewhat later are the 80 fragments from the entrance doorway of the church of San Vicente Mártir at Frías, which was presumably made in the early thirteenth century at the order of Alfonso VIII, king of Castile (1158-1214). These stones now make up a reconstructed doorway based upon a study of the individual stones and related monuments in Spain. The various voussoir blocks illustrate, among other subjects, scenes from the life of Christ.

An altar frontal from the parish church of Ginestarre de Cardós is a pendant to one dated 1223 which was formerly in the Barcelona Museum. It is decorated with the Virgin and Child enthroned in a mandorla supported by four angels, and eight apostles in arched niches, the whole composition surrounded by borders with inscriptions. The altar frontal is of raised and painted gesso work simulating enameled metalwork with precious stones.

The fourteenth-century tomb of Armengol VII, Count of Urgel, is a fully developed type of sepulchral monument. In fact, in quality it is one of the finest of the many Spanish tomb groups and the best of those from the Premonstratensian monastery of Santa María de Bellpuig de las Avellanas, which Armengol and his wife, Doña Dulcia, founded in 1146 or 1166. It was in the presbyterium at the epistle side of the main altar of the church. Three lions support the sarcophagus, which is ornamented on the front with carvings in high relief of Christ enthroned in majesty, and the twelve apostles. The sarcophagus lid, cut from a massive block of stone, depicts the effigy of Armengol, behind whom are small figures of lay mourners. On the superimposed panel, part of the funeral rites, the absolution, is shown. Above this there is a representation of the soul of the deceased ascending to heaven escorted by angels. This monument was built at the order of Armengol X, who died in 1314.

In addition to the tomb of Armengol VII, 3 other tombs from the monastery of Santa María de Bellpuig de las Avellanas have been added to complete the group at the Cloisters. They are the tombs of Doña Dulcia, wife of Armengol VII, of Armengol X, who ordered the series of four tombs made, and of Don Alvaro de Cabrera in full armor. Don Alvaro, the brother of Armengol X, was killed fighting in Sicily in 1299.

Two over-life-sized Catalan sculptures of female saints display unusual preservation of their polychromy. One is St. Margaret, the other unknown, and they date from the third decade of the fourteenth century.

A recent acquisition is a seated wooden Madonna and Child from northeast Spain of the late thirteenth century. This work has unusually well-preserved original paint, which shows her to have been garbed in a silver mantle. She is closely related to a large group of similar figures found at the juncture of the provinces of Alava, Logroño, and Navarre. See Richard H. Randall, Jr., "A Spanish Virgin and Child," Metropolitan Museum of Art Bulletin, Dec. 1954, pp. 137-43.

A large Catalan alabaster retable from the workshop of Pedro Juan de Vallfogona (d. 1447) made for the archbishop of Saragossa, Don Dalmacio de Mur (d. 1456), was originally in the archiepiscopal palace at Saragossa. The reredos consists of five panels sculptured in high relief surmounted by canopies. The substructure is decorated with reliefs showing two bearded men holding shields

with the arms of the archbishop.   Between these reliefs is a
modern altar containing three related alabaster shields.   This
is probably the largest medieval sculptured retable in America.
A painted fourteenth-century stone Virgin and Child recalls sculptures from León cathedral.
A fine Gothic ceiling dating from the fifteenth century is the predomi-
nating note in the "Spanish Room" at the Cloisters.   The ceiling
probably came from a palacio at Illescas, the half-way stopping
place between Madrid and Toledo.   It is reported to have been
removed from a bedroom where Francis I stayed in 1526 when
he was held a prisoner by Charles V.   The story is told on good
authority.   It is impossible, however, to substantiate the claim,
for the town of Illescas was completely demolished in the Civil
War of 1936-39.   The ceiling is related to the late fourteenth-
century ceiling covering the cloister walk of the monastery of
Santo Domingo de Silos, though the latter is simpler in construction.   The ceilings are also similar in the arrangement of the
beams and paneling.   At a later date the lower frieze of the
Cloisters ceiling was repainted with animal motifs, which re-
semble closely those of the beams and frieze at Silos.   Both
ceilings are of red pine coated with a thin gesso foundation and
painted.

Armor Department

        Among the noteworthy Spanish objects in the Armor Depart-
ment is a collection of armorial pendants of enamel, dating mainly
from the fourteenth century.   Some were badges of recognition worn
by heralds or messengers, others were used to ornament horse
trappings.

        Of fifteenth-century Spanish armor, there are only isolated
elements, including 2 helmets (a chapel-de-fer and an armet-a-
rondelle) and a series of face defenses which were worn with sallets.
There is also a fine fifteenth-century brigandine, the steel plates
of which are attached with brass rivets to green brocaded velvet
with design in bouclé gold thread.   This enriched defense may be
compared with a purely utilitarian mid-sixteenth-century brigandine,
of which the overlapping iron plates are attached to buckskin with
brass-headed rivets.   Among the early weapons is a breech-loading
cannon dated about 1500; 2 Hispano-Arab daggers of the fourteenth
and fifteenth centuries; "eared" daggers of the fifteenth to the seventeenth centuries; and a sword dated about 1500, with Hispano-Arab
hilt chased with strapwork.

        Among the shields may be mentioned a late fifteenth-century

targe of wood covered with leather and gesso, and painted with the "Spectacle" blazon of the Quiñones family; a Hispano-Moresque bilateral shield (adarga) of iron dated about 1500; and a wooden, leather-covered adarga of the guard of Philip II of Spain.

Equestrian equipment is represented by elements of horse armor (rump defense and 2 peytrel plates) of the early sixteenth century, of leather, covered with gesso and painted light yellow; 6 horse bits of the sixteenth and seventeenth centuries; a sixteenth-century cantle plate etched with classical figure subjects illustrating Spanish proverbs; a series of spurs and stirrups of the sixteenth to the eighteenth centuries, including a pair of spurs dated 1738 and elaborately pierced and chased with animal and scroll forms; bit bosses of bronze-gilt and copper enameled, of the sixteenth and seventeenth centuries; Mexican spurs of the eighteenth century; and stirrups of the so-called "Conquistador" type.

Objects are attributed to twenty-five Spanish historical personages among whom are the Emperor Charles V and Philip II; but most of the arms and armor made for the courts of these rulers are of German workmanship.

A cape of mail of steel and latten rings includes among the inscriptions the motto of the Emperor Charles V: "Plus Oultra" (what lies beyond, i. e., the "New World" discovered by Columbus, and, as they fondly imagined, "The Indies"). One of the museum's outstanding firearms is the double-barreled, double-wheel-lock pistol which appears in the contemporary illustrated inventory of the emperor.

There are 3 harnesses associated with Philip II. One came from the arsenal of Segovia, a provenance which would seem to indicate that it belonged to the king, for the arms and armor of the sovereigns were formerly kept in the treasury at Segovia. Another, a double suit, is similar in decoration to a harness made in 1549 for Philip II, then Príncipe de Asturias. The third is a composed armor with elements which belong to the suite of harnesses made on the occasion of the marriage of Philip II of Spain and Queen Mary of England in 1554.

Belonging to the armor of Philip III in the Royal Armory in Madrid is a pair of child's gauntlets richly damascened. Another pair of gauntlets, of Pamplona workmanship, belongs to the armor of the son of Philip III, the Infante Cardinal Don Fernando de Austria.

Other historical objects are a helmet of Don Carlos; an embossed Milanese half-armor and a brigandine of the Duke of Alba;

a jousting armet, bearing a crowned anagram which may be read—
"Fadrique de Toledo" (son of the Duke of Alba); and an embossed
half-armor of Gonzalo Fernández de Córdoba.

There is a series of cup-hilted rapiers of the second half
of the seventeenth century. Their hilts are pierced and sculptured,
and their hemispherical guards have a recurved edge for entangling
the point of the adversary's sword. The work of such great blade-
smiths as the Elder Sahagún, Sebastián Hernández, Juan Martínez,
and Sebastián Ruiz are represented. Supplementing these rapiers,
and with hilts of similar workmanship, are the left-handed daggers,
a highly specialized weapon used for parrying. Some of the blades
are provided with irregular or serrated backs which were used for
catching or deflecting a sword blade. Among other "white" arms
may be mentioned a series of seventeenth- and eighteenth-century
dirks with handles of disks of bone and brass built up like a string
of beads.

In addition to the Emperor Charles V's pistol is a wheel-
lock pistol (about 1630) bearing the personal badge of Diego Felipe
Guzmán, first Marquis of Leganés; a seventeenth-century pistol
holster of leather, velvet, and gold thread; a pair of pistols dated
1687, made at Ripoll, Catalonia; and a fowling piece dated 1796,
of Charles IV. Also included are a number of firearms with Spanish
miquelet locks, a characteristic of which is that the mainspring is
on the outside.

Other items of unusual interest are a richly damascened
mace used by Henry II of France before his accession to the throne,
signed by Didacus de Çaias, a Spanish damascener; a seventeenth-
century state baldric, embroidered with the insignia of the Grand
Veneur of Spain, with pockets for hunting knives and for instruments
for dissecting game; and a collection of about 20 flags dating from
the seventeenth to the nineteenth centuries, several of them bearing
the heraldic arms of Spain.

There are also 2 noteworthy Portuguese objects: the
armor of Dom Pedro II, King of Portugal, dating from about 1690—
blued, gilded, and elaborately ornamented in punched work; and a
dress sword bearing the arms of Portugal, together with its embroidered belt and hanger, worn at the court of Maria I (1777-1816).

Finally, there are in the Armor Department as collateral
material a few paintings and some sculpture representing arms and
armor. These include a Catalonian painting by Domingo Valls
(active 1366-98) representing a combat of knights; a painting of about

1475, representing a battle scene, attributed to the so-called
Palanquinos Master, an Hispano-Flemish painter active in the province of León; an early sixteenth-century Valencian painting representing St. Michael the Archangel in armor, attributed to the Cabanyes
Master. Other contemporary documents include a kneeling knight
sculptured in sandstone, North Spanish, of the twelfth century, and
a bronze-gilt ornament from bookbinding, dated about 1300, representing a mounted knight in armor.

Department of Renaissance and Modern Art

Spanish sculpture of the sixteenth century is well represented in the museum by 2 alabaster tondos, containing portraits
of St. Jerome and St. Agnes. They are unusual in that they still
have their original vivid polychromy. Also, of the same period
are an interesting alabaster Pietà, originally painted; a Joseph of
Arimathea from an entombment group, carved in wood and painted,
and still showing medieval influence; and a small oval marble relief
of the Madonna and Child, attributed to Diego de Egás. Spanish in
subject and perhaps in provenance is the portrait of Philip II, from
the workshop of Leone Leoni, the Italian sculptor, who, with his
son Pompeo, worked in Spain for the Spanish monarchs. Two interesting pieces of sixteenth-century architectural sculpture with
grotesque decorations are said to be the work of Alonso Berreguete,
who studied in Italy with Michelangelo. Dating from the seventeenth
century is a wooden crucifix, the best example of Spanish sculpture
of this period in the museum. Two representatives of the present-
day renascence of art in Spain are the cock of forged iron by Pablo
Gargallo, and the Javanese panther in diorite by Mateo Hernández.

The museum owns very little Spanish furniture, the best
example being a seventeenth-century walnut armchair upholstered
in tooled leather. Leather, it may be added, was a popular material
in Spain, entire walls sometimes being covered with it. Among
several examples of Spanish seventeenth-century leatherwork, an
attractive and characteristic panel with a floral design, stamped,
painted, and gilded in the baroque style, is outstanding. There
are also a sixteenth-century Gothic bench of wood; a fifteenth-
century leather, iron, and wood chest; a sixteenth-century iron
lectern; and another wrought-iron lectern of the fifteenth or sixteenth century.

Perhaps Spanish art is best represented in this department in the field of ceramics. Altogether there are about 50 pieces
of pottery (plates, jars, jugs, tiles, etc.), many of which are lustreware decorated in the so-called Hispano-Moresque style. The ma-

jority of these, which represent a continuation of medieval Spanish decorative forms, were made in Valencia during the sixteenth and seventeenth centuries. In addition to such handsome and colorful potteries, the ceramic collection contains a few porcelains, including about 10 pieces made in the eighteenth century in the Buen Retiro manufactory in Madrid. The museum's large representation of Spanish glass includes a number of extremely fine and rare examples dating from the sixteenth, seventeenth, and eighteenth centuries.

Four sixteenth-century reliquaries and 6 pendants, elaborately wrought of various precious materials, show that the goldsmith's craft flourished in Spain during the Renaissance. An unusual seventeenth-century reliquary has for its central and principal ornament a beautifully carved Byzantine sapphire. Also to be mentioned are a number of examples of silversmith's work, including 6 chalices dating from the sixteenth and seventeenth centuries. Truly extraordinary, however, is the large silver-gilt dish worked in elaborate repoussé and containing a number of small enameled panels decorated with Moresque ornament. The arms of France, Castile, and León appear on the shield in the center of the dish.

There is also a small collection of steel knives and forks, dating from the sixteenth through the nineteenth century; and a collection of ironwork containing nearly 40 miscellaneous examples dating from the seventeenth century, among which are several andirons and fire screens.

In the field of textiles, mention must be made of 10 Spanish rugs dating from the sixteenth through the eighteenth century. Some are knotted, others embroidered. The best example is a large knotted carpet with a repeating ornament that calls to mind Italian Renaissance classical decoration, but with a combination of colors that suggests Moorish work. The museum owns altogether about 250 examples of woven textiles and needlework, and about 150 pieces of lace and network from the sixteenth to the nineteenth century, many of outstanding importance. Two large embroidered hangings of about 1600, showing the adventures of a twelfth-century hero of the Moorish wars, are pieces of great richness and rarity. The best brocades, velvets, and embroideries are expressive of the finest work in those media produced in Spain during the Renaissance. There are also about 20 printed fabrics, samplers (including a rare seventeenth-century book of embroidery specimens), and costume accessories, among which may be mentioned such items as gloves, collars, and fans. Spanish textiles are also well illustrated in the collection of costumes. The museum has about 30 ecclesiastical garments—chasubles, dalmatics, copes, albs, etc.—a number of them being very excellent pieces. The use of rich velvet and of embroidery in costly metal threads gives some of these costumes a truly sumptuous effect. Even more remarkable from the point of view of rarity are 5 unusual secular costumes: a handsome brocaded courtier's cape of the sixteenth century; a child's dress of the end of the same century, which, embroidered in gold and colored silk, brings to mind formal court portraits of the time; a man's suit of about 1780, said to have belonged to Charles III of Spain; a charming little boy's costume of about 1785, believed to have been worn by Ferdinand VII as an infant; and a mantle of a Knight Grand Cross of the Order of Charles III, dating from the beginning of the nineteenth century.

Art of colonial Spain is represented by a large collection of pottery made in Mexico during the seventeenth, eighteenth, and nineteenth centuries. Altogether there are about 135 pieces of this kind of work, which is based on Spanish models, but which also shows strong local influence. From the Philippines, formerly a Spanish colony, comes an interesting collection of some 30 pieces of white embroidered piña cloth, costumes, or parts of costumes of the nineteenth century.

Paintings

Spanish painting before the sixteenth century is rather meagerly represented in the museum, and most of the examples worthy of note are installed in the Cloisters. Two exceptionally handsome Castilian frescoes date from the first quarter of the thirteenth century. These panels, representing a lion and dragon which surmount friezes of fantastic animals, were taken from the chapter house of the monastery of San Pedro de Arlanza. A Catalan fresco of the late thirteenth or early fourteenth century depicts an episode in the life of St. John. Frescoes of the Virgin and Child, and two side panels of the Archangels Michael and Gabriel with the Three Kings   Melchior, Balthasar, and Gaspar—are by the Master of Pedret, ca. 1130.

Castilian in style is a late fourteenth-century panel representing "Scenes from the Creation and from the Life of St. Andrew," although the altarpiece of which it formed a part is said to have come from a church in Balaguer in Catalonia.

Fifteenth-century paintings in the Cloisters include: "St. Andrew with Scenes from His Life," a Catalonian altarpiece; an

Aragonese altarpiece dated 1473, having as a central panel the Virgin
and Child on the knees of St. Anne; "Six Scenes from the Passion, "
also Aragonese; a Catalonian retable representing "St. John the
Baptist with Scenes from His Life." The latter corresponds closely
in style with the altarpiece by Solibes in the chapel of the Piedad
at San Llorens dels Morunys.

In the armor galleries of the main building are to be seen
a fourteenth-century Catalonian painting of a "Combat of Knights"
and a fifteenth-century "Battle Scene" of the Schools of León or
Castile.

Several Spanish paintings of the fifteenth century are in
the galleries of paintings in the main building. Probably painted
by a follower of the Catalan painter known as the Master of St.
George is the "Christ Among the Doctors." Three panels illustrating scenes from the life of John the Baptist give every indication
of having come from the same workshop as the retable of Saints
Cosmas and Damian in the chapter house of the Barcelona cathedral.
Most authorities agree in dating them close to 1450. Two early
fifteenth-century Valencian panels, one representing "St. Giles, "
the other the "Mission of the Apostles" and "Christ Triumphant
over Satan," formed part of an altarpiece painted for the chapel of
the priory of the Knights of St. John of Jerusalem in Valencia of
which other parts belong to the Hispanic Society Museum, of New
York. A Majorcan or Valencian School "St. Michael and the Dragon"
and a Castilian "Virgin and Child with St. Anne" complete the tale
of the fifteenth-century works.

A portrait of the Infanta Isabel by Sánchez Coello is a
typically meticulous work by this artist.

With the late sixteenth and early seventeenth century the
museum's Spanish collection achieves distinction with 6 magnificent
canvases by El Greco. They were all painted well along in the
artist's career; the earliest must have been made close to 1600.
This is the formidable "Portrait of the Cardinal Don Fernando
Niño de Guevara, " Grand Inquisitor. Rich in color, brilliantly
complex in technique, and somber in its spiritual implications,
this is considered one of El Greco's greatest portraits. The
"Portrait of a Man, " formerly in the Beruete collection, is believed
by some scholars to be a portrait of the artist himself; the face,
which recurs in several of El Greco's works, is appropriate in its
psychological aspects to what is known of the artist's personality.
A group of typically elongated figures compose the "Adoration of
the Shepherds, " painted probably after 1600. The museum also

has another "Adoration of the Shepherds" and a "St. Catherine."
The "View of Toledo" is one of the two landscapes known to have
been painted by El Greco. It is a fantastic view of the old city,
with its Alcázar and cathedral looming up against wildly tossed
clouds, and is famous as one of the master's most powerfully dramatic works.

Velázquez is represented in the museum by 4 paintings.
The magnificent "Portrait of Philip IV, King of Spain," from the
Altman collection, is the earliest extant representation of this king.
It was purchased from Velázquez by Doña Antonia de Ypeñarrieta,
and the museum owns a document dated December 4, 1624, in which
Velázquez acknowledges receiving 800 reales in part payment for
this painting and two others. "Portrait of the Artist" and the "Infanta
María Teresa" were formerly in the Bache collection. The "Portrait
of Cardinal Borja" was in the Kress collection.

The Velázquez School pieces may also be mentioned:
"Christ and the Pilgrims at Emmaus," and bust portraits of "Don
Gaspar de Guzmán, Count of Olivares," of "Prince Baltasar Carlos,"
and of "Mariana of Austria, Queen of Spain." The two latter appear
to be contemporary copies of full-length portraits now in the Vienna
Gallery and the Prado respectively.

Francisco de Zurbarán is represented by 2 strongly con-
trasted aspects of his work. "The Young Virgin" is thought to be
an early work. The figure is delicate in modeling and gentle and
homely in sentiment, but the still life and curtains are energetically
painted. The "Battle with the Moors at Jerez" was painted in the
1630's at the height of the artist's powers. It is a large canvas depicting the Virgin and St. James of Compostela interceding for the
Christians in the battle against the Moors at Jerez in 1340. It is
one of a series of scenes which Zurbarán painted for the Cartuja in
Jerez de la Frontera. Others of the series are in Grenoble and in
the museum of Cádiz.

By Murillo, the museum owns a fine full-length portrait of
a man with a dog, "Don Andrés de Andrade" and a "Virgin and Child";
by Ribera, a beautiful late work, "The Holy Family with St. Catherine,"
signed, and dated 1648; and by Carreño, a "Pietà."

A splendid group of 10 paintings by Goya covers most of
the phases of the work of this many-sided genius. The "Portrait of
Don Sebastián Martínez" displays the delicacy and silvery tonality
characteristic of his eighteenth-century painting. The one of the
"Infanta María Luisa Holding Her Infant Son" is probably a study for
her portrait in the great painting of the family of Charles IV (Prado)

which was completed in 1800. Another portrait of about this period
is that of the artist's young kinswoman, "Doña Narcisa Barañana
de Goicoechea." "Majas on a Balcony" is one of several paintings
of the same composition. This one comes from the collections of
Don Sebastián de Borbón y Braganza, the Duke of Marchena, and
H. O. Havemeyer. Its broad decorative character is reminiscent
of Goya's paintings for San Antonio de la Florida and some of his
tapestry cartoons. The "Bullfight" is similar in composition to
Goya's lithograph of the divided bull ring. The dispersal of incident
which focuses the interest on the whole scene rather than on any
of its parts, forecasts the change in point of view which dominated
the latter half of the nineteenth century. Goya's preoccupation with
the fantastic reveals itself in "City on a Rock," which must have
been painted after 1815. The idea of the rock is seen also in one
of the wall decorations which Goya made for his country house. A
portrait of the artist's friend, the architect "Don Tiburcio Pérez,"
dated 1820, is broadly painted in the sober colors characteristic
of Goya's late work. The museum's more recent Goya acquisitions
include "Don Manuel Osorio de Zuñiga" (Bache), "Don Bernardo
de Iriarte" (Harkness), and "Ferdinand VII, King of Spain" (Fri-
bourg).

Four nineteenth-century Spanish paintings in the museum
are: "Girls at a Window," "Masquerade Ball," and a "Portrait of
Samuel P. Avery," by Madrazo; and an exceptionally handsome work
by Fortuny, the "Portrait of Mme Gaye."

Early in 1955 the museum acquired its first painting by
Dali. "The Crucifixion," a work more than six feet high, was
completed in 1954 and was given to the museum by Mr. Chester
Dale.

Prints and Books

The outstanding Hispanic prints in the museum are to be
found in the work of Goya. Among other Goyas, the museum owns
first editions of the "Caprices," the "Disasters of War," and the
"Tauromachia." It also has the following rarities: "The Blind
Guitarist," Delteil 20; "The Garrotted Man," D. 21; "The Giant,"
proof state, D. 35; "Caprices," proof state, D. 46, 50, 52, 62;
"Disasters," proof state, D. 129-37, 139-44, 146, 149, 160, 163;
"Disparates," proof state, D. 202-3, 206; "The Bordeaux Bulls,"
D. 286-89.

The museum's collections also contain a showing of prints
by the Spaniards Fortuny, José Ribera (called Spagnoletto), and

Vierge, as well as work by modern Mexicans such as Amero, Charlot, Díaz de León, Guerrero, Ledesma, Manila, Mauricio, Méndez, Mérida, Orozco, Posada, Diego Rivera, Romero, Siquieros, Tamayo, Zalce, and others.

The museum owns a number of Spanish writing books, among which are the following:

Anduaga y Garimberti. Arte de escribir (1781).
Casanova. Primera parte del arte de escrivir (1650).
Lucas. Arte de escrevir (1580).
Morante. Nueva arte de escrevir (after 1639).
—. Quinta parte del arte de escrevir (5 woodcuts).
Olod. Arte de escribir (1768).
Ortiz. El Maestro de escrivir (1696).
Palomares. Arte nueva de escribir (1776).
Paluzie y Cantalozella. Paleografía española (1846).
Perez. Arte de escrevir (1599).
Polanco. Arte nuevo de escribir (1719).
Servidori. Reflexiones sobre la verdadera arte de escribir (1789).
Torío. Arte de escribir (1798).
Yciar. Arte subtilissima (1550).
—. Libro subtilissimo (1564).

The museum also owns St. Jerome, Espistolas (Seville: Cromberger, 1537).

Library

Since the Hispanic Society of America has a large library, the museum has to some extent avoided a duplication of material which students can find there. Nevertheless, the museum has a very adequate collection of works on Spanish art and culture from the prehistoric period to the present day, including a good representation of the art of Spain from the Romanesque period through Gothic times.

The important works on all the great Spanish painters and sculptors are to be found, and many general histories of Spanish painting, sculpture, and architecture, as well as books on costume and the industrial arts. There are also many catalogues of Spanish museums and galleries, and of important exhibitions which have been held in Spain or which relate to Spanish art. These are supplemented by histories of Spain, books of travel and description, and guide books.

The museum keeps abreast of current Spanish art activities by subscribing to over 20 Spanish periodicals.

The material on Hispanic art also includes books on Mexico, and on the architecture and arts of other countries of Spanish America. The museum maintains exchange relations with the important museums of South America, and in this way is gradually accumulating bulletins, annual reports, and other publications on the art of this continent, in which the library has been deficient.

Among outstanding works on Spanish architecture is a copy of Monumentos architectónicos de España; pub. . . bajo la dirección de una comisión especial creada por el Ministerio de Fomento; ed. por José Gil Dorregaray (8 vols., fol., Madrid, 1859-81).

Students of Velázquez will be interested to see exhibited in the museum the letter signed "Diego Velazquez Dec. 1624," acknowledging receipt of payment for three portraits, including one of King Philip IV of Spain, in the Altman collection in the museum.

Spanish art in Spain is represented in the reference photograph division of the library by about 17,500 photographs, which are classified under four subject headings—sculpture, painting, architecture, and the minor arts. The largest representation is of architecture, of which there are 9,800 titles, with emphasis placed on the Romanesque and Gothic periods. Sculpture from the fourth to the twentieth centuries, and painting, including anonymous work from the tenth to the seventeenth centuries, together with work of well-known painters such as El Greco, Murillo, Velázquez, Zurbarán, and others, number about 5,000. The remainder is unevenly distributed through the minor arts subjects. Gold and silver objects number about 200; there are 275 textiles, 270 ivories, etc.

The museum has not more than 500 photographs of Spanish art in Mexico and South America.

The extension division of the library has a lending collection of 7,675 slides on Spanish art, of which 5,150 cover the minor arts. A small collection of photographs is available for lending. In addition, there are about 300 slides of Mexico, and a very few photographs.

Museum of the American Indian
Heye Foundation
Broadway at 155th Street
New York 32

The collections in the Museum of the American Indian dealing with the Southwest United States and Hispanic America are described below.

South America
   Argentina:
   The collections of archeology comprise, largely, the material excavated by the Thea Heye—La Plata Expedition in 1925, conducted in conjunction with the Museo de la Plata and under the direction of Samuel K. Lothrop. These numerous specimens, principally of pottery and bone, augmented a more generalized collection made by the director the previous year. The Thea Heye—La Plata Expedition findings have been reported in S. K. Lothrop, "Indians of the Paraná Delta, Argentina, " Annals of the New York Academy of Sciences, XXXIII (1932), 77-232.

   Tierra del Fuego: An almost complete ethnological collection was formed in 1924, when Samuel K. Lothrop conducted an extensive study among the Ona, Haush, Yahagan, and Alacaluf groups in this area and the Tehuelche to the north. The specimens include watercraft, household, hunting, fishing, and other utilitarian implements, clothing, dance masks, and ceremonial paraphernalia. A report of this expedition has been published in Samuel K. Lothrop, "The Indians of Tierra del Fuego, " M. A. I. H. F. Contributions,[*] Vol. X (1928).

   Bolivia:
   The collection of gold ornaments came as a gift in 1927. Many of these pieces are described and illustrated by S. K. Lothrop in "Gold and Silver from Southern Peru and Bolivia, " Journal of the Royal Anthropological Institute of Great Britain and Ireland, LXVII (1937), 305-25. The acquisition of the Blackiston collection in 1930 added considerable material to the archeological collection of the museum.
   Through the years 1924-26, A. Hyatt Verrill conducted an expedition among the Pano and Changa groups of the Bolivia-Peru boundaries from which the basis of the museum's ethnological collections from Bolivia was formed. Later, by purchase and by gift, these earlier materials were augmented by collections from the Aymaras. The collections include textiles, costume material, arms, domestic implements, etc. Other tribes represented in the collections are the Guaranis, the Moxos, and the Pacaguaras.

   Brazil:

   Earlier gifts of collections from among the Tukano Indians of the Brazil-Colombia border made by MacCreagh, and of an extensive collection made among the Carajas, have been augmented

---

   [*] M. A. I. H. F. is the abbreviation for "Museum of the American Indian, Heye Foundation. "

by collections made in 1937 by Sasha Seimel among the Bororos,
Cadioeos, and Parecis groups of Mato Grosso. Material represented
includes articles of household, fishing, and hunting use, examples
of featherwork, ceremonial costumes, and ceramics.

Other tribes represented in the collections are: Conebos,
Campas, Ararras, Yurunas, Apalaiis, Makusis, Mundurucus,
Ararandeuaras, Barbudos, Wapisianas, Nambikuaras, Chicriabas,
Vananas, Tarianas, and Caingangs.

Chile:

Early in its history, the museum acquired the extensive
G. T. Arms collection of archeology, largely from Temuco,
province of Cautin. A gift to the museum in 1920 of a large collection of textiles from the Araucanian-speaking groups stimulated
a subsequent expedition (1925) among these peoples, directed by
A. Hyatt Verrill. Not only was the earlier textile collection augmented,
but a representative collection of silver ornaments, implements,
and costume material was made.

In 1929 and again in 1931, Dr. Lothrop headed expeditions
to the Mapuches of the central coastal areas. They resulted in the
collection of hundreds of specimens representing the material culture of this group. A preliminary report of the textiles collected
has been published in S. K. Lothrop, "Notes on Indian Textiles of
Central Chile, " M. A. I. H. F. Indian Notes, VII, No. 3 (1930), 324- 35.

Other tribes represented in the collections are the Atacamenos
and the Chilotes.

Colombia:

The museum's collection of gold objects, a large portion
of it from the Sinu river district, department of Bolívar, came as
a series of gifts from 1916 to 1923. A representative collection of
archeological material from Santa Marta, made by J. Alden Mason,
came to the museum in exchange with the Chicago Natural History
Museum (formerly the Field Museum of Natural History). It is described in J. Alden Mason, Archaeology of Santa Marta, Colombia,
Field Museum of Natural History, Anthropological Series, XX (1931-
36), Nos. 1 and 2. This was augmented in 1931, when Gregory
Mason visited the same districts under the auspices of the museum,
by many pieces of pottery and stone.

Ethnological material was collected among the Mocoas in
918 and 1920 by Theodoor de Booy. The MacCreagh collection,
nentioned under Brazil, from the Tukanos, was acquired in 1922;
nd in 1931 and 1935, Gregory Mason made extensive ethnological
ollections among the Arhuaco and Goajira groups of the Goajira
eninsula. Other tribes represented in the collections are the
ïuambinos, the Chocós, and the Akawais.

Ecuador:

Expeditions headed by Marshall H. Saville to the provinces
f Manabí and Esmeraldes from 1906-10 built up large collections
rom these areas. Saville published two volumes covering these
xpeditions: "The Antiquities of Manabí, Ecuador, " M. A. I. H. F
Contributions to South American Archeology, Preliminary and
Final Reports (1907-10). In addition to a large number of gold,
ottery, and stone pieces, there is a representative collection of
tone seats and carved slabs.

In 1921, Saville made another trip to Ecuador, at which
ime he was able to acquire for the museum an exceptional collec-
ion of gold objects from Sigsig, discovered in 1889. These he
lescribed in The Gold Treasure of Sigsig, Ecuador, M. A. I. H. F.
ueaflet No. 3 (1924).

Additional important objects have been acquired through
xchange from the collection of Señor Jijón y Caamaño.

The museum maintained an expedition under the direction
f S. A. Barrett among the Cayapa groups in northwestern Ecuador
n 1908-9. A representative collection of specimens of the material
ulture of these Indians was made, and the findings of the expedition
vere published in S. A. Barrett, "The Cayapa Indians of Ecuador, "
M. A. I. H. F. Indian Notes, Misc. XL (1925), 2 vols.

An extended trip among the Jívaro, Canelos, Otavalo, and
Zaraguro peoples of Oriente was made by Wolfgang von Hagen from
1934 to 1936, which brought to the museum additional specimens from
hese areas. During those years, von Hagen also spent some time
mong the Tsatchela (or Colorado) Indians of the western cordillera
n the provinces of Pichincha and Esmeraldes and made a representa-
ive collection among this tribe. His report, "The Tsatchela Indians
f Western Ecuador, " appeared in M. A. I. H. F. Indian Notes, Misc.
LI (1939).

Other tribes represented in the collections are: Caras,
Napos, Zaparos, Mainas, Sarai-Yacus, and Isabellas.

Paraguay:

In 1924, a gift of a numerous collection of specimens from the Matitines was presented to the museum. Other tribes represent« are the Chamacocos, the Tumrahas, and the Macikuis of the Gran Chaco.

Peru:

A comprehensive collection of wooden ceremonial objects, including keros and pacchas, paddles, staffs, etc. was presented to the museum in 1920, together with many specimens of feather ponchos, and a group of exceptionally fine textiles of both the pre- and post-conquest periods. In 1912, the director acquired the so-called Echenique plaque. Markham reported on this golden disk in 1856 and described it more fully in 1910. A later monograph on it was prepared by M. H. Saville, "A Golden Breastplate from Cuzco, Peru, " M. A. I. H. F. Indian Notes, Misc. XXI (1921). Still later Ruth Cutter Nash wrote "Calendrical Interpretation of a Golden Breastplate from Peru, " M. A. I. H. F. Indian Notes, Misc. LII (1939).

The acquisition of the Gayoso collection of gold, silver, copper, and fabrics in 1930 and 1931 and of the Blackiston collection of ceramics added materially to earlier collections from Peru.

From 1924 to 1926, as noted under Bolivia, collections were made under the museum's auspices among the Pano-Changa groups. To these have been added, by acquisition and gift, many articles from the Quichua peoples. In 1937, a comprehensive collection made by William Schaeffler among the Yuhna, Cashibo, Piro, and Champa groups was acquired from him, and thus many objects not before represented were added to the collections from this area.

In 1941, a comprehensive collection of costume and ceremonial pieces as well as domestic implements and musical instruments from the Yagua, Witoto, and Bora Indians of the upper Amazo. drainage areas was presented to the museum by the Viking Fund, now the Wenner-Gren Foundation for Anthropological Research.

The collection was made by the Wenner-Gren Scientific Expedition to Hispanic America when it was among these peoples from December 1940 to August 1941, under the direction of Paul Fejos. Dr. Fejos illustrates much of the material obtained from the Yagua in Ethnography of the Yagua, Viking Fund Publications in Anthropology, No. 1 (1943).

The following year a smaller collection, largely of costume pieces and domestic implements, collected from the Campa
and Karneri Indians by the same expedition, was presented by the
Viking Fund.

Venezuela:

Archeological specimens from Venezuela comprise basically
the large Warfield collection presented to the museum. In 1916,
Theodoor de Booy made collections from the island of Margarita.
For a description, see Theodoor de Booy, "Notes on the Archeology
of Margarita Island, Venezuela, " M. A. I. H. F. Contributions, II
(1916), No. 5. In 1918, de Booy made an ethnological reconnaissance
among the Motilones, which brought to the museum a collection of
specimens representing their material culture.

Middle America

British Honduras:

A goodly portion of the Gann collection made in British
Honduras and in contiguous areas of Guatemala and southern Yucatán
came as a gift to the museum. These pieces have been figured and
described in Thomas W. F. Gann, "The Maya Indians of Southern
Yucatan and Northern British Honduras, " Bureau of American
Ethnology, Bulletin 64 (Washington, D. C., 1918).

In 1928 and 1931, Gregory Mason, under the auspices of
the museum, made investigations among the caves of this area and
in Guatemala. The collections made have been reported upon in
Gregory Mason, "Pottery and Other Artifacts from the Caves of
British Honduras and Guatemala, " M. A. I. H. F. Indian Notes, Misc.
XLVII (1928).

Costa Rica:

In 1916, the Minor C. Keith collection, made through a
quarter-century beginning in 1871, came to the museum. The
principal part of this material has been described and figured in
S. K. Lothrop, "Pottery of Costa Rica and Nicaragua, " M. A. I. H. F.
Contributions, Vol. VIII (1926), 2 vols. The excavations made
under the auspices of the museum, in 1916, by Alanson Skinner in
Mercedes brought a comprehensive collection to augment the vast
Keith material and the Sanger collection, the latter largely Nicoya
pieces. Skinner's notes are published in part in the Lothrop paper.
Numerous objects of gold have been added to the collections of pot-
tery and stone through gift and acquisition.

In 1917, Skinner spent some months among the Bribri groups.

The ethnological specimens collected for the museum have been in great part described in Alanson Skinner, "Notes on the Bribri of Costa Rica," M.A.I.H.F. Indian Notes, Vol. VI (1920), No. 3.

El Salvador:

The archeological collections made by Samuel K. Lothrop augmented many earlier acquisitions by, and gifts to, the museum. These have been reported upon in part in S. K. Lothrop, "Pottery Types and Their Sequence in El Salvador," M.A.I.H.F. Indian Notes, Vol. I (1927), No. 4.

In 1925, Lothrop, under the auspices of the museum, visited the Pipil, Lenca, and Ulva peoples of this country and made a representative collection of their material culture.

Guatemala:

A unique vase presented to the museum in 1917 has been figured and described by Saville in A Sculptured Vase from Guatemala, M.A.I.H.F. Leaflet No. 1 (1919). The collections were augmented by those made by Saville in 1918, by a gift of Rodman Wanamaker of a group of stone carvings, and by a collection made by Samuel K. Lothrop in 1925.

Lothrop also conducted an ethnological reconnaissance for the museum in 1926 and 1927. This he described in "Notes on the Indian Ceremonies in Guatemala," M.A.I.H.F. Indian Notes, IV, No. 1 (1927), 68-81; and VI, No. 1 (1929), 1-25. In 1936, the museum acquired a representative part of the Morse collection of textiles and ceremonial material from groups in this area. The tribes represented in the collections are the Quichés and the Cakchiquels.

Guianas, the:

In 1916 and 1917, A. Hyatt Verrill made extensive collections among the Indians of British Guiana; and collections have been added from the Carib peoples of French Guiana and the Bush Negroes of Surinam.

Other tribes represented in the collections are: Waikas, Arecunas, Akawais, Makusis, Akurias, Atoradis, Wapisianas, and Piros.

Honduras:

Marshall H. Saville made a trip to Honduras in 1916 and collected several of the alabaster jars in the museum's collection. In 1930, a comprehensive archeological collection made by Dorothy

Wilson Popenoe was acquired, and much pottery and stone from the
Bay Islands came to the museum as a gift from F. A. Mitchell-Hedges,
who conducted an expedition there in 1934. In 1937, Wolfgang von
Hagen led an expedition among the Miskito and Xicaque groups and
returned with a collection representative of this people. His report,
"The Jicaque (Torrupan) Indians of Honduras, " appeared in M. A. I. H. F.
Indian Notes, Misc. LIII (1943).

Mexico:

From 1916 to 1921, the Ledwidge collection of Casas
Grandes pottery, the Rice collection of mirrors and carved jades,
and a gift of 18 examples of turquoise mosaics augmented several
lesser acquisitions. The mosaics have been figured and described
in M. H. Saville, "Turquoise Mosaic Art in Ancient Mexico, "
M. A. I. H. F. Contributions, Vol. VI (1922). To these have been
added a large collection of archeological material from Puebla,
Oaxaca, and Vera Cruz, the Avery collection of pottery, and the
Stein collection (made about 1885) of gold, stone, and pottery. A
large collection of carved wooden objects has also been reported on
in M. H. Saville, "The Woodcarver's Art in Ancient Mexico, "
M. A. I. H. F. Contributions, Vol. IX (1925).

From 1922 to 1925, E. H. Davis made ethnological collections among the Seri, Huichol, and Yaqui groups. In 1933-35,
D. W. Amram collected among the Lacandones; and in 1936-37,
Donald Cordry studied ceremonials and collected specimens for the
museum among the Coras, the Aztecs, the Tarascans, the Huichols,
the Tarahumaras, and the Otomis. Augmenting these representative
collections, the Morse collection of material culture from the Tarascans,
the modern Aztecs, and the Mayas was acquired.

Other tribes represented in the collections are: Mayos,
Chinalbos, Chinantecs, and Zapotecs.

Nicaragua:

The archeological collections from Nicaragua are based
on the extensive Barrios collection, largely from Rivas. D. E.
Harrower, in 1924, visited the Ramas of the Bluefields lagoon, the
Mosquitos of the coast and large rivers, and the Sumus of the in-
terior, among which groups extensive collections were made. A
brief report on this expedition has been published in D. E. Harrower,
"Rama, Mosquito and Sumu, of Nicaragua, " M. A. I. H. F. Indian
Notes, Vol. I (1925), No. 1.

Panama:

Alanson Skinner, in 1916, made a collection of gold, pottery, and sculptured stone; and in 1925, A. Hyatt Verrill collected for the museum a group of representative gold objects from Coclé. Many of these have been described and figured by Lothrop in "Coclé, an Archaeological Study of Central Panama, Part 1," Memoirs of the Peabody Museum of Archaeology and Ethnology, Harvard University, Vol. VII (1937).

Verrill, in 1924-26, visited several tribes and made extensive collections of ethnological material among them. In 1929, Lady Richmond Brown and F. A. Mitchell-Hedges, who had spent much time among the Chucunaques, presented the museum with an extensive collection representing the textile and wood-carving arts of these people.

Tribes represented in the collections are: Kunas, San Blas, Chokois, and Tupi-Towalis.

West Indies:

The archeological collections of pottery, stone, and wood from the West Indies, probably the most extensive in the world, were made under the auspices of the museum by M. R. Harrington in 1915 and 1919 in Cuba, and as early as 1907 by Thomas Huckerby, and later by Theodoor de Booy, in Trinidad, Virgin Islands, Martinique, Puerto Rico, Santo Domingo, St. Vincent, Grenada, Tobago, Santa Lucia, Carriacou, and the Grenadines. These expeditions are described by Theodoor de Booy and Thomas Huckerby in various monographs appearing in the American Anthropologist and reprinted in the M. A. I. H. F. Contributions series. See also M. R. Harrington, "Cuba before Columbus," M. A. I. H. F. Indian Notes, Misc. XVII (1921), 2 vols.

In 1916, these collections were augmented by the gift of the large Lady Blake collection from Jamaica. In 1934, Lewis Korn conducted excavations under the auspices of the museum, on the island of St. Croix, which resulted in a comprehensive collection from that area. In 1938, Frank R. Crumbie, Jr. visited the island of La Gonave, Haiti, and made an interesting collection, included among which are several unusual carved wooden objects.

United States

Arizona:

The basis of a comprehensive collection of archeology was the gift of the David W. Lord collection made at the time of the

Hemenway expedition (1887-89). To the large ethnological collection of George H. Pepper, acquired in 1918, have been added many hundreds of specimens from extant groups, largely by gift. These include textiles, jewelry, and ceremonial objects of all descriptions, as well as utilitarian articles of everyday use. To the Pepper collection have been added several collections of Hopi ceremonial material including, by exchange, a part of the Voth collection of Kachina masks and dolls.

Other tribes represented in the collections are: Navajos, Papagos, Pimas, Havasupais, Walapais, Supais, Chemehuevis, Mojaves, Yavapais, Maricopas, and Yumas.

California:

The Davis, Doran, Dreyfus, Glidden, and Sanger collections of mainland and Channel Island archeology were acquired largely by gift from 1916 to 1926. Much of this material has been figured and described, as follows:

Heye, George G. "Certain Aboriginal Pottery from Southern California," M. A. I. H. F. Indian Notes, Vol. VII (1919), No. 1.
__. "Certain Aboriginal Artifacts from San Miguel Island, California," M. A. I. H. F. Indian Notes, Vol. VII (1921), No. 4.
Oetteking, Bruno. "Skeletal Remains from Santa Barbara, California," M. A. I. H. F. Indian Notes, Misc. XXXIX (1925).
__. "Morphological and Metrical Variation in the Skulls from San Miguel Island, California—the Foramen Magnum, " M. A. I. H. F. Indian Notes, Misc. XLV (1928).

A large collection of carved-stone and shell-inlaid specimens from the coast of Los Angeles County, acquired through excavations from 1938 to 1941, are described by Edwin K. Burnett in "Inlaid Stone and Bone Artifacts from Southern California, " M. A. I. H. F. Contributions, Vol. XIII (1944).

Ethnological collections from the tribes of southern California are extensive, the Diegueños, Luiseños, Mission groups, Kawais, and Yaquis being represented.

New Mexico:

From 1917 to 1923, under the museum's auspices, excavations were carried on by Frederick W. Hodge at Hawikuh. A large collection of articles was acquired in the course of this expedition, some phases of which have been reported upon by Hodge, as follows:

"Hawikuh Bonework, "M. A. I. H. F. Indian Notes, Vol. III (1920), No. 3.

Turquoise Work of Hawikuh, New Mexico, M. A. I. H. F. Leaflet No.
2 (1921).
"Circular Kivas near Hawikuh, New Mexico, " M. A. I. H. F. Contri-
butions, Vol. VII (1923), No. 1.
History of Hawikuh, New Mexico, Frederick Webb Hodge Anniversa
Fund, Publication No. 1 (Los Angeles, 1937).

While at Hawikuh, some investigations were made at
Kechipauan by Hodge and Lothrop. A description of some of the
findings occurs in Frederick W. Hodge, "The Age of the Zuñi Puebl
of Kechipauan, " M. A. I. H. F. Indian Notes, Vol. III (1920), No. 2.
The Lord collection, mentioned under Arizona, contained a large
number of archeological pieces from New Mexico; and much Navaje
and Pueblo Indian ethnology was included in the Pepper collection,
already noted.

Texas:

In 1927, M. R. Harrington, and in 1929, E. F. Coffin,
conducted work under the museum's auspices at basket-maker and
bluff-dweller sites in southwestern Texas. A comprehensive collection of this material was thus acquired.

Library

The library of the late Marshall H. Saville, relating to
Mexico, Central and South America, and that of Frederick Webb
Hodge, covering the Southwest, were acquired in 1927. To these
originally large collections, important books are constantly being
added. While it is primarily a working library to which no especia
attempt has been made to add titles solely for their rarity, still
many unusual volumes are upon its shelves. Among some of the
rarer titles in the Hispanic American field are: Kingsborough,
Antiquities of Mexico; Humboldt, Vues des Cordillères; Flores,
Arte de la lengua kakchiquel (1753); Vilagran, Historia de la Nueva
Mexico (1610); Molina, Vocabulario (1555), in which a gloss of the
Matlatzinca language parallels the original throughout; and Cogollu
Historia de Yucatan (1688).

Many volumes on linguistics are represented; and Rudolph
Schuller's extensive vocabulary of the Kekchi tongue is to be found
among the manuscript material.

Publications of all the societies and institutions interested
in Hispanic America are among the serial collections; and thousan
of pamphlets are available for reference.

Museum of Modern Art
11 West 53rd Street
New York 19

Of the Spanish artists represented in the Museum of Modern Art, Picasso is by far the most important. There are in the collection 18 oils, 15 drawings, 3 gouaches, 1 sculpture, 1 water color, 1 collage, and a rug designed by the artist. The oils include: "Les Demoiselles d'Avignon," 1907, which is considered by many critics to be the most important canvas of the first decade of the twentieth century; "Three Musicians," 1921; "Night Fishing at Antibes," 1939; "Girl before a Mirror," possibly the finest canvas of 1932, a gift of Mrs. Simon Guggenheim; "Three Women at the Spring," 1921; "The Studio," an abstract composition of 1928, the gift of Walter P. Chrysler, Jr. In the Bliss collection, bequeathed to the museum in 1931, are "Ma Jolie," 1911-12, "Harlequin," 1915, "Woman in White," and the cubist "Green Still Life." "Guernica" is on view at the museum as a loan from Picasso.

Juan Gris, another of the four great cubist artists (of whom Picasso was the leader) is represented by 8 oils, of which "The Chessboard," 1917, and "Guitar and Flowers," 1912, are generally considered the most important. There is also a 1917 conté crayon drawing, "Fruit Dish and Bottle."

The most important Catalan painter of the avant-garde, Joan Miró, is represented by 9 oils, 1 wood and metal relief, 1 gouache, 1 drawing, and a rug designed by the artist. The oils include the famous "Catalan Landscape," 1923-24, "Person Throwing a Stone at a Bird," 1926, "Dutch Interior," 1928, and the very large "Composition," 1933.

The museum owns 3 oils and 2 drawings by Dali; among these, "The Persistence of Memory" is Dali's most famous painting and one of the monuments of surrealism.

The museum has two wrought-iron sculptures by Julio González: the great "Woman Combing her Hair," 1936; and "Head," also 1936.

Among the minor Spanish artists, Pablo Gargallo is represented by a wrought-iron head, "Picador," 1928; Manuel Manolo, by a small bronze nude; Oscar Domínguez by an oil and a decalcomania (a method which he invented) in ink, 1936; Luis Quintanilla, by 2 ink drawings done during the Spanish civil war. José de Creeft, Spanish born, now an American citizen, is represented by a large lead relief, "Saturnia," 1939.

Among the Mexicans, Rivera and Orozco are each represented by a large original fresco, "Agrarian Leader Zapata" and "Dive Bomber and Tank," respectively. There are also a group of oils, water colors, and drawings by Rivera. Orozco's famous oil painting "Zapatistas," 1931, "Barricade," 1931, and a number of smaller works are in the collection. Siqueiros is also strongly represented by famous works such as "Echo of a Scream," 1937, "Collective Suicide," 1936, "Proletarian Victim," 1933, "Ethnography," 1939, and 2 other oils. The museum owns Tamayo's well-known "Animals," 1941, 2 other oils, and 1 gouache.

The collection also contains work by the following Mexicans: Anguiano, Castellanos, Charlot, Cuevas, Guerrero Galván, Kahlo, Mérida, Meza, Montenegro, O'Gorman, Reyes Ferreira, Rodríguez Lozano, Ruiz, Soriano, Tebo, and Zalce.

Many of the more important Spanish works are on permanent exhibition in the museum building; others can be seen in the study collection by request, providing (as often happens) they are not out on tour. For the further study of the collection, a library of books on modern art, architecture, films, etc. is open to the public. Additional information may be found in Painting and Sculpture in the Museum of Modern Art, 2d ed., 1948; supplementary lists have been published in the Museum of Modern Art Bulletin (Vol. XVII, No. 2-3, 1950; Vol. XVIII, No. 2, Winter 1950-51; Vol. XIX, No. 3, Spring 1952; and Vol. XX, No. 3-4, Summer 1953). A catalogue of the museum's collection of drawings is in progress.

In 1939 the Brazilian government gave the museum the large mural decoration by Portinari, "Festival, St. John's Eve." The museum also owns other works by Portinari, both oils and lithographs. A large jacaranda wood figure of Christ by the Brazilian Maria Martins was presented to the museum by Nelson A. Rockefeller in 1941.

Hispanic directors are represented in the museum's film library. Among these are the Catalan Luis Buñuel's surrealist Un Chien andalou (1929) and the Brazilian Alberto Cavalcanti's Rien que les heures (1926).

In 1942 the Latin American collection in the museum was greatly expanded through the gift of an anonymous donor. Nearly 200 works of art were acquired. Artists from Argentina, Brazil, Chile, Ecuador, Peru, Colombia, Uruguay, Cuba, and Mexico are included in the group. For a description, see Lincoln Kirstein's Latin American Collection of the Museum of Modern Art, 1943.

New York Botanical Garden Herbarium
Bronx Park
New York 58

The herbarium of the New York Botanical Garden, with more than 2, 250, 000 specimens, ranks with the largest herbaria of the world in its collections from Hispanic America.   These are especially rich and unusually complete for the flora of Cuba, Puerto Rico, Venezuela, and Bolivia; secondarily for Colombia, Ecuador, and Amazonian Brazil.   All other Hispanic American countries are also well represented.   Since these specimens are not segregated, an accurate statement of their number cannot be given, but it may be conservatively estimated at 300, 000.

The library, with more than 60, 000 volumes, is fully equipped for research work on the botany of any of the Latin American countries and contains all important literature on the subject, all standard works of botanical reference, and all current botanical indices.

For over fifty years, members of the staff have actively prosecuted research on the flora of these countries.   The results have been presented in Flora of the Bahamas, Flora of Puerto Rico and the Virgin Islands, North American Flora, and in scores of shorter articles in technical journals, amounting in the aggregate to thousands of pages.   Major attention is currently being devoted to Venezuela and the Guiana highlands.

New York Historical Society
170 Central Park West
New York

The New York Historical Society possesses the following Hispanic paintings and manuscripts:

A collection of 14 paintings in oil on canvas, of fourteen Incas of Peru, bearing inscriptions designating the name and succession of each monarch.   They are said to be the original pictures from which the portraits of the Incas were engraved for the work of Antonio de Herrera, Historia general de los hechos de los castellanos, published at the beginning of the seventeenth century (1601-15) and reproduced in the edition by Andrés Barcia (1726-30).   These paintings were presented by Frederic de Peyster in 1873.   The fourteen Incas represented are: Manco Capac, Sinchi Roca, Lloque Yupanqui, Mayta Capac, Capac Yupanqui, Inca Roca, Yahuar Huacac, Viracocha, Urco, Pacha cutec, Tupac Yupanqui, Huayna Capac, Huáscar, and Atahualpa, put to death by order of Pizarro, August 29, 1533.

Collection of Buckingham Smith (1810-71). Twenty-four thin volumes of transcripts from Spanish archives, sixteenth to eighteen
centuries, relating to North America, and more particularly to
Florida. Essential for the history of Florida. Microfilms of
the entire collection are in the Florida State Historical Society.

A logbook in French, March 1713 to August 1715, of a ship that
called at South American ports. At the end is a list of provision
obtained at the several ports.

A fairly extensive collection, including many rarities, of Spanish-
American printed material of the sixteenth through eighteenth
centuries, largely from the Buckingham Smith collection.

A detailed report of the wine and alcoholic liquors made from grape
exported from the jurisdiction of El Paso del Norte, New Mexico
(1762-64, 1766-69), certified by Don Pedro Joseph de la Fuerte,
mayor.

The large collection of the papers of Rufus King (1755-1827), Ameri
can minister to Great Britain. It contains letters and papers to,
from, and about Francisco de Miranda (1798-1805). Some of
these are included in the six printed volumes of the Life and
Correspondence of Rufus King, edited by Charles R. King (1894-
1900).

The papers of Chancellor Robert R. Livingston, including a large
collection in English, French, and Spanish relative to the purchase of Louisiana by the United States.

Papers of Ephraim George Squier (1821-88), relating to Central
America, consisting of: 4 volumes of drafts of his dispatches
(1849-50); 1 volume of copies of dispatches to him from the
Department of State (1849); 1 large scrapbook of letters and news
paper clippings relating principally to the Clayton-Bulwer Treaty
(1856); and 1 volume of letters relating to the Honduras Interoceanic Railway (1857-59).

New York Public Library
Fifth Avenue and 42nd Street
New York 18

This large, general, and public library has important
collections and many great rarities in the Spanish language. While
it prefers originals, it must perforce be satisfied in many instances
with reprints, later editions, or photographic reproductions. In
the selection of materials, content is emphasized. The following
description is indicative, rather than exhaustive, and is in no sense
a catalogue.

The collection of general and literary periodicals is useful and representative. Here the files of such periodicals from Spain are more numerous and complete than those from Latin American countries, though, in exception, Puerto Rico Ilustrado is complete from 1911 to date. The less common titles among Madrid publications include: La América (1857-66); Blanco y Negro (1895-1936); Ilustración Española y Americana and its predecessor El Museo Universal (1858-1921); La Lectura (1901-20); Raza Española (1919-30); Razón y Fe (1901 to date); Revista Contemporánea (1883-1907).

There is an unusually good collection of publications of academies and societies from Spanish-speaking countries. Files are generally complete of such bodies in Spain as the Academia de Ciencias Exactas, Físico-Químicas y Naturales de Madrid, the Academia de Ciencias Morales y Políticas, the Academia Española, the Real Academia de Bellas Artes y Ciencias Históricas de Toledo, and others. The Mexican representation includes the Sociedad Científica Antonio Alzate; the Cuban, the Academia de Ciencias de la Habana, the Academia de Ciencias Médicas, Físicas y Naturales de la Habana, and others. From South American countries come the publications of such organizations as the Academia Nacional de Ciencias (Córdoba), the Instituto Paraguayo, the Museo de la Plata (Universidad Nacional), the Universidad de Chile.

Hispanic newspapers include numerous files of papers in the Spanish language, published during the nineteenth century. The most important are Mexican, such as El Monitor Republicano and others which appeared during the 1840's. For the twentieth century, there is from Madrid La Epoca (1900-1936, with small breaks); and from Barcelona, La Veu de Catalunya (1917-33).

Of Latin American newspapers, those of Mexico and Cuba are the strongest, with only a few from Central America and the West Indies. The South American ones date chiefly from about 1920. The more important Mexican papers include: Excelsior (1917-26), El Universal (1916 to date), and El Universal Gráfico (1924-38). The Cuban papers include: La Lucha (1901-12), El Mundo (1918-20), and El Diario de la Marina (1922 to date).

Finally, there are New York City's Spanish newspapers, the most extensive files of which are Las Novedades (1905-18) and La Prensa (1915 to date).

Spanish literature and philology are well represented in the library. The literature section is particularly strong in printed collections, as "Biblioteca de autores españoles," Semanario Erudito, and the publications of the Sociedad de Bibliófilos Españoles. Of the literary collections listed in Foulché-Delbosc and Barrau-Dihigo, Manuel de l'Hispanisant, the library has a large number, including the important "Parnaso español" (Madrid, 1768-78). The important authors of Spain are represented by their individual works, although there are relatively few first editions. One of interest is Bernardo de Balbuena, El Bernardo (Madrid, 1624). Collected editions have been and are usually acquired if added text or editorial treatment makes them important.

The most important single representation is the Cervantes collection formed by Dr. Wendell Prime. Though it does not contain the first (1605) Madrid edition of Don Quixote, it does have that of Valencia, published the same year, as well as the first Madrid edition of the Segunda Parte (1615). Dr. Prime's gift contains many of the seventeenth-century Spanish editions; the Brussels printing (1607), which popularized this classic throughout northern Europe; and a number of the seventeenth- and eighteenth-century English and other translations. There are likewise early editions of Cervantes' other works. A catalogue, "Cervantes Literature in The New York Public Library," was printed in the library's Bulletin for 1899. Additions have since been made, a first edition of Don Quixote now being in the Berg collection.

The imposing feature of Spanish literature, however, is published plays. The number is roughly estimated at more than 12,000. The collection is particularly rich in works published after 1750.

Of special note is a Spanish literary manuscript of Lope de Vega, El Brasil restitudo. In addition, the work of a twentieth-century novelist and playwright is represented by a collection of original manuscripts, the scripts of 10 plays by Miguel de Zárraga. There are also the scripts of 2 stories by Vicente Blasco Ibañez. The library has the principal collection of the late Isaac Goldberg, the translator of numerous Blasco Ibañez works as well as a writer on Latin American literary taste.

There is a group of Spanish chapbooks of the 1814 period, from Madrid.

The older authors of Central and South America and of the West Indies are represented—some in early editions, others in reprint from the publications of universities and other academic bodies, as the "Biblioteca aldeana de Colombia." Contemporary authors are represented by their important works. Cuban and Mexican literature are both especially good.

Philological materials constitute a good working collection. They include the important periodicals, such as the Revista de Filología Española, and are strong in grammars and dictionaries. The collection contains an interesting representation of older text-books, including American "conversation manuals."

In connection with Hispanic literature and philology, the library has, in its rich collections relating to the American Indian, many early Spanish imprints dealing with the Mexican language. Probably the most notable representation is that of Alonso de Molina's works, including a perfect copy of his Aqui comiença un vocabulario (Mexico, 1555), one of the earliest books published in the New World. Among others, the library has his Vocabulario (Mexico, 1571), Doctrina Christiana (Mexico, 1578), and 2 copies of his Confessionario mayor (Mexico, 1565). Another rarity, of which the library has a perfect copy, is Pedro de Arenas, Vocabolario manual de las lenguas Castellana, y Mexicana (Mexico, 1611). One of considerable scarcity is Pedro Beltrán de Santa Rosa María, Arte de el idioma maya (Mexico, 1746). Other Indian languages are well represented.

History is one of the notable features of the library's collections. Therefore, most of its strongest resources and many of its "treasures" in the realm of Spanish books are historical, in fact or by implication.

Manuscripts are an important feature. The nucleus is the Obadiah Rich collection, 142 volumes relating to Spanish America. The greater part was formed by Don Antonio de Uguina, of Madrid. It comprises almost everything of interest that was collected by his friend Juan Bautista Muñoz for the Historia del Nuevo Mundo, of which only the first volume was published. (The library has 2 copies of this work and, in this collection, a transcript of Volume II.) Uguina, a friend of Martín Fernández de Navarrete also, furnished him with many of the materials for his Colección de los viages. After Uguina's death, his manuscripts were purchased by M. Ternaux Compans, of Paris, who had already collected many manuscripts on Spanish America. The whole collection afterwards came into the possession of Obadiah Rich, who added some manuscripts from the collection of Lord Kingsborough and a few articles he had procured in Spain. It was purchased by James Lenox in 1848. It includes, in addition to original papers, many eighteenth-century transcripts from Simancas and other archives, churchmen's chronicles, historians' writings in manuscript, etc., relating to the role of Spain in the New World. The larger portions concern California, Florida, Mexico and Central America, New Mexico, Peru, and the West Indies.

Another collection of interest is a volume of letters to Joel Roberts Poinsett over the period 1814-40, mainly from Mexican and Chilean officials, during his ministry to Mexico.

The Ford collection and the library's "miscellaneous papers" may yield a small amount on almost any Latin American topic. No scholar undertaking a biography or concerned with any dominant figure in Spanish American history should neglect them.

Manuscript Collections in The New York Public Library (1901) and a supplement (1915) have been published in the Bulletin and issued separately. More comprehensive, up to 1941, is the volume A Guide to the Reference Collections of the New York Public Library. These describe and analyze the principal collections of the library. Annual lists of important accessions of manuscripts appear in the Bulletin currently.

Among printed works on political, social, and religious Spain, the library's resources cover all periods. Of formal histories, few major works, in either the original edition or a satisfactory reprint, are wanting. Important titles covering antiquities include the Memorias of the Junta Superior de Excavaciones y Antigüedades, from 1916 to 1933. For political and religious history, of early dates, the library has, so far as its holdings have been checked, over three-fourths of the works cited in E. D. Richardson, A Union List of Collections on American History in American Libraries.

Another important general feature is historical and political periodicals. Long, though in some cases incomplete, files include: El Año Político, Nuestro Tiempo, Revista de Archivos, Bibliotecas y Museos, the Boletín of the Sociedad Española de Excursiones, and the various publications of the Academia de la Historia.

Historical works on Spain include early editions of many of the early writers. For example, there are a number of works by Marineo Siculo (Lucius Marineus), as De Primis Aragonie Regibus (Saragossa, 1509), and others, primarily important to the library because they contain references to America, as his Opus de Rebus Hispaniae Memorabilibus (Alcalá, 1533), and Obra compuesta (Alcalá, 1539). Other writers' works which are of interest include Gualberto Fabricus de Vagad, Coronica de Aragon (Saragossa, 1499), having passages on the discovery, and Pedro de Medina, Libro de grandezas y cosas memorables de España (Seville, 1548), containing references to America. In the latter is also a contemporary map.

For what was colonial Spain, there is a good representation
f the great collections of voyages and travels and of the original
litions of which they were composed, due to the enthusiastic col-
:cting of James Lenox. His original interest broadened to include
1ything relating to the great "Age of Discovery, " and finally to
verything he could secure on North and South America. Some of
1e prized works are mentioned in subsequent paragraphs.

The library, continuing the interest of Mr. Lenox, has
1ng specialized in collecting Americana and works containing
eferences to the Americas. These include some of its most in-
:resting early Spanish works. The library has most of the works
sted in Henry Harrisse, Bibliotheca Americana Vetustissima...
.492-1551); those which it lacks and which it feels only a remote
ossibility of securing, it is acquiring in some facsimile repro-
uction. However, there are many titles not mentioned in Harrisse,
s Francisco de Ossuna, Norte de los estados (Burgos, 1541).
Iost of the early works cited in this description are, in some way,
mericana, as parenthetical notes usually indicate. In connection
ith bibliography, it is worth noting that the library has a copy
f Antonio de Leon Pinelo, Epitome de la Biblioteca Oriental i
ccidental (Madrid, 1629), said by Joseph Sabin to be probably the
rst work to contain a catalogue of books on America, and of
.. González de Barcia's 1737-38 revision, called by Rich the most
omplete bibliography of geographical works, travels, and mis-
ionary reports, and of particular value for its list of manuscripts.
. manuscript bibliography of great importance is Antonio de Alcedo,
iblioteca Americana (1807), in the Rich collection.

Later resources include many of the printed documentos,
uch as Joaquín Francisco Pacheco, Colección de documentos inéditos
Madrid, 1846-71), and those of Martín Fernández de Navarrete and
thers. Works covering individual countries include Documentos
ara la historia de México (Mexico, 1856), and the printed collec-
ions of Joaquín García Icazbalceta and of Juan E. Hernández y
ávalos. In passing, it may be remarked that the library also
as extensive and valuable collections of contemporary printed
rchives and documents published—generally in serials or as mono-
raphs—by Latin American national libraries, university faculties,
tc. Its strong collections in the field of American history include
1ost of the significant modern publications relating to Latin America.

Among Spanish imprints, the choicest single item is the
olio of Christopher Columbus' letter to Luis de Santangel, dated
'ebruary 1493, printed in Barcelona, 1493, and the only known copy.

Around this exists a strong Columbus collection containing the 5 earliest Latin editions of the letter to Gabriel Sánchez and over 250 pieces of manuscript, including transcripts in the Rich collection, and a list of some 46 documents (then in the family archives); the list was given by the Duke of Veragua after their display at the Chicago Exposition in 1893.

Post-Columbian works include Martín Fernández de Enciso Suma de geographia (Seville, 1519), said to be the first book printed in Spanish relating to America, and, among later editions, that of 1530, unknown to earlier bibliographers. Early accounts include Peter Martyr Anghiera, Opera (Seville, 1511), first and second issues, containing the first of the Decades in which Peter Martyr embodies valuable information gleaned from Columbus and other early navigator friends; and Joseph de Acosta's famous De Natura Novi Orbis (Salamanca, 1588), described by Rich as one of the earliest books to treat of America and its productions philosophicall Geographical works of this period include Valentin, Repertorio del mundo particular (Madrid, 1548).

Early materials relating to the exploration and settlement of the American continents are of interest. Perhaps the most important single primary source is the "Jesuit Relations" (1632-74), of which the library's collection covers every year; there are also variant issues of several years. A description of copies then in the library appears in the "Collation of a Set of the Jesuit Relations," issued by the Lenox Library as No. 11 of its Contributions to a Catalogue, in 1897. Dr. Victor Hugo Paltsits, Chief of the American History Division and Keeper of Manuscripts, has described part of the set and individual copies elsewhere, since that time.

Individual rarities covering or emphasizing particular portions of the continents are numerous. Only a few can be cited here. The Relacion de la gente de mar (Madrid, 1633) gives an account of ships, carrying silver from America, which were wrecked off the Florida coast. For the conquest of Mexico, there is an excellent collection of letters of Cortés, including the second, published in 1522; the third, in 1524; and the rare second edition of the fourth, 1526. The Cortés collection and other rare and important works are included in a reference list on Mexico, published by the library in its Bulletin (1909). A later acquisition is Luis La Marca, Teatro historico (Valencia, 1690), containing a history of Cortés.

For the West Indies and Mexico (and for other parts of the Middle American area), there are more than 60 early imprints of the works of Las Casas. A description of editions in various languages, together with an extensive collection of other works relating to the West Indies, appears in the Bulletin for 1912.

In a previous paragraph on manuscripts in the library, reference is made to several parts of what is now the southwestern United States. There are a number of early Spanish imprints, one of the most important of which is Alvar Núñez Cabeça de Vaca, La Relacion (Zamora, 1542), containing the first account in print of what is now Texas; it is the only perfect copy of three known. Another rarity on Southwestern history is Pedro de Castañeda de Nágera, Relacion de la jornada de Cibola, a unique transcript made at Seville in 1596 of a manuscript dated 1540, which has since disappeared; it is the most important narrative of Coronado's expedition, written by a soldier who accompanied him. These and other rare and interesting works are described in a catalogue of an exhibition, "Texas, 1836-1936," which was printed in the Bulletin in 1937.

Of rare Spanish works relating to South America, only a few may be recorded. For Peru, there is Alonso Venero, Enchiridiö de los tiempos (Salamanca, 1543), mentioning its discovery, and La Conquista del Peru (Seville, 1543), one of two copies known. Of interest to Venezuelan history is the Relacion cierta y verdadera (Seville, 1643), telling of a conflict with the Dutch (1633), who were fortified some leagues from Cumaná.

Additional titles, including histories and other types of Americana, are noticed in final paragraphs devoted to early Latin American imprints.

Of considerable importance to the student of history are the official publications of countries, states, and cities. Only a few of the longer, more important files of the library's quite extensive collection in this field are mentioned here. The disturbed world conditions of recent years has made difficult the task of keeping these files complete. In some cases documents are listed "to date" for cataloguing purposes, but scholars might find incomplete files with some recent numbers or issues of publications during the period of World War II missing in the collection.

The collection of Spanish official publications is strong. For foreign affairs, there are such series as the "Documentos diplomáticos" ("Libros rojos"), 1865-1911 (incomplete), the Colección de los tratados convenios y documentos internacionales and the later Tratados y documentos internacionales, together covering the period 1834-1912. Older collections include Joseph Antonio de Abreu y Bertodano, Colección de los tratados (Madrid, 1740-52). For the study of internal affairs, there is the Gaceta de Madrid, from 1808, an incomplete but very substantial file, and the Diario of the Cortes, from 1811, as well as the publications of all constitutional assemblies and a strong representation of administrative documents. Laws begin with the Colección de los decretos y órdenes (1810-91), and the various "Jurisprudencia" series. The library has many codes, including early compilations, as the Libro (Salamanca, 1503), Las Pragmaticas (Seville, 1520), etc. Resources in law include special materials relating to former Spanish colonies, as the rare Leyes y ordenanças (Alcalá, 1543), of which there are examples of both the paper and the few known vellum copies. In addition to routine administrative series, there are many separate official publications of every reign from Philip II to the present government.

The South American collection of documents includes the Argentine Diario de Sesiones of the Cámara de Diputados, complete from 1885, with some earlier volumes; that of the Senadores is fairly complete from 1862 to 1926; the Registro Nacional runs from 1873 to 1908. The Bolivian parliamentary proceedings are fairly complete from 1900 to date; the Annuario administrativo is complete from 1855 to 1929. The Chile Boletín of the Cámara de Senadores and that of the Cámara de Diputados are both fairly complete from 1860 to date; the earlier Sesiones de los Cuerpos Legislativos, 1811 á 1845 are complete and the Recopilación de decretos-leyes, from the beginning 1898. The Colombia session laws are fairly complete from 1877, and the contemporary Codificación nacional de todas las leyes is complete as far as it has been published. The Ecuador Anuario de legislación ecuatoriana is complete from 1896 to 1925. The Panama Leyes Expedidas and its Gaceta Oficial are complete from 1904 to date. The Paraguay Registro Oficial is complete from 1869 to date. The Peru Leyes y Resoluciones is fairly complete from 1860 to 1905 and is strongly supplemented by compilations of earlier laws. The Uruguay Diario de Sesiones of the Asamblea General is complete from 1830 to 1932, and that of the Representantes, from 1858 to 1928; the Registro Nacional and its predecessor, Colección legislativa constitute an almost complete file from the beginning, 1825. The Venezuela Gaceta Oficial is complete from 1902.

The collection of public documents from Spanish-speaking portions of the West Indies and from Central America is, on the whole, not so strong in administrative reports as are those of South American countries. Cuban documents, however, are relatively numerous, with the Gaceta de la Habana and its successor, Diario, incomplete but very substantial from 1827 to date, and the Colección Legislativa complete from 1902-18. Perhaps one of the most interesting representations in the entire collection is a volume of original "Haytian Papers, 1841-1846, " which includes some transcripts, but contains mainly decrees, official publications, etc., of that period. Of the titles listed in J. B. Childs, The Memorias of the Republics of Central America and of the Antilles, the library has well over two-thirds and is adding these administrative annual reports as rapidly as it can.

Mexican national publications are relatively strong. The Diario Oficial (under its various titles) is fairly complete from 1722. The laws are especially good, including an early imprint, Ordenãças y cõpilacion de leyes (1548), the first law book published in America. The representation of administrative publications of the various Mexican states is not extensive; it consists principally of some of the early reports of the gobernadores and of broken files of official gazettes of the late nineteenth and twentieth centuries.

The historical materials also include important resources for the study of the Philippine Islands during its Spanish colonial period. Elsewhere, something is said of the Rich collection on voyages and exploration. For example, the library has Maximilianus (Transylvanus), De Moluccis Insulis (Cologne, 1523), the first published account of Magellan's voyage (1519-22), and of the discovery of the islands. Manuscripts consist principally of transcripts of early accounts, in the Rich collection. The collection of books includes a number of eighteenth-century histories and works of description, as Joseph Torrubia, Disertacion historico-politica y... geográfica de las Islas Philipinas (Madrid, 1753). Early printed accounts are numerous, including Antonio de Herrera Tordesillas, Historia general de los hechos de los Castellanos (Madrid, 1601-15); Antonio de Morga, Sucesos de las Islas Philipinas (Mexico, 1609); Pedro Ordóñez de Cevallos, Viage del Mundo (Madrid, 1614); Antonio de Remesal, Historia general de las Indias Ocidentales (Madrid, 1620); Balthasar de Medina, Chronica de la Santa Provincia de San Diego de Mexico (Mexico, 1682); Gaspar de San Agustín, Conquistas de las Islas Philipinas (Madrid, 1698); and others. Additional early and later published materials, to the date of publication, appear in a reference list on the Philippines which appeared in the library's Bulletin in 1900.

Several important books on Philippine languages have

been added in recent years: Matheo Sánchez, Vocabulario de la
lengua Bisaya (Manila, 1711); Domingo Ezguerra, Arte de la lengua
Bisaya (1747); Diego Bergaño, Arte de la lengua Pampanga (Manila,
1729); Sebastian de Totanes, Arte de la lengua Tagala (Manila,
1745); Thomas Ortiz, Arte y reglas de la lengua Tagala (Sampaloc,
1740); and Domingo de los Santos, Vocabulario de la lengua Tagala
(Sampaloc, 1794).

Work of more modern character in this field is represented
by the acquisition of a collection of papers of the late Carlos Everett
Conant (1870-1925); these relate to his studies of several of the
dialects of the islands and include some manuscript poetry and a
Visayan drama.

Although other subjects cannot boast as large a number of
early printed Spanish and Hispanic American works as history,
there are some titles of sufficient importance, scarcity, or rarity
to merit attention.

Art and architecture are worth notice principally for im-
portant nineteenth- and twentieth-century works. Included are
Aníbal Alvarez and others, Monumentos arquitectónicos de España
(Madrid, 1859-1905) and José de Madrazo y Agudo, Colección
lithográphica de cuadros del rey de España (Madrid, 1826-32).
Contemporary works include Ivori, Vestidos típicos de España
(Barcelona, 1936); Ribot, Costums de Catalunya (Barcelona, 1935);
Arte y decoración en España (1917-28); and Escultura en Andalucía
(1927—, still incomplete).

In the prints collection, the most notable Spanish representation is that of Goya: "Caprichos" (1793-98), first three
editions; "La Tauromachie" (1815); "Los Desastres de la guerra"
(1863); and "Los Proverbios" (1864). There is a single lithograph
by Zuloaga. Of Fortuny's works, there are some 20 etchings.
Contemporary Spanish print makers are represented mainly in a
gift, received in 1935, from the Museo Nacional del Prado and
from the artists themselves. These include "reproductive etchings"
by F. Esteve Botey, J. Galván, Bartolomé Maura, and J. Núñez;
original etchings by Bertucci, Enrique Brañez de Hoyas, Castro
Gil, Botey, Pedro Gil Moreno de Mora, J. Espinós de Gisbert,
P. Pascual, Rafael Pellicer, Julio Prieto Nespereira, Francisco
Reyes, Ricardo Baroja, T. Campurzano, Juan Espina, and Enrique
Vaquer; and a monotype in color by Leoncio Rivacova.

Among notable illustrated books, there is a representation
of those published from the sixteenth to the eighteenth century,

including Lucius Marineus (Marineo Siculo), De Primis Aragonie Regibus (Saragossa, 1509); Juan de Yciar, Arte subtilissima (Saragossa, 1550); and perhaps two dozen others of this period. Of later imprints, the 1780 edition of Don Quixote, with plates by Antonio Carnicero and others, and Los Españoles, pintados por sí mismos (1843-44), containing engravings on wood after designs by Alenza, Moranda, and others, are outstanding. Modern works include 2 editions of Don Quixote—those published at Barcelona in 1930 and 1933.

Philosophical and religious works are, on the whole, adequate, though there are not so many rarities in these general fields. Among titles which might be named is the Complutensian Biblia Polyglotta Ximenii (Alcalá de Henares, 1514-17), the earliest of the great polyglots. There is an unusual collection of religious works in Indian languages.

Scientific works are principally of interest to the library's collections as Americana. The fullest representation consists of an unusual collection of the astronomical works of Joannes de Sacro Bosco, including at present some 98 editions of De Sphera Mundi; among them is the Spanish edition of 1545; one of earlier date, Opusculum de Sphera Mundi (Alcalá, 1526), is the first edition printed in Spain which mentions the expedition sent by Ferdinand of Spain, in 1491, which, after four months, discovered islands. The technical arts include Pedro de Medina, Arte de navegar (Valladolid, 1545), which mentions America. Of great rarity is Nicolas Monardes, Dos Libros (Seville, 1561-69), a materia medica of Mexico. Among anthropological works is Gregorio García, Origen de los Indios del Nuevo Mundo (Valencia, 1607), which Sabin describes as a "work of vast erudition," but erroneous in theory. A work of interest is Antonio Gómez de Melgarejo y Andrade, Vera Relatione (Milan, 1626), describing a bird-monster. Recent additions to Spanish navigation rarities are Antonio de Najera, Navegacion especulativa y practica (Madrid, 1669) and Lázaro de Flores, Arte de navegar (Madrid, 1673).

There is an outstanding collection of Latin American imprints to 1800, numbering more than 1,200 titles. It includes a fair number of rarities listed in the José Toribio Medina bibliographies. In 1941 a notable collection of nineteenth-century imprints was acquired. It was particularly strong in Mexican pamphlets of the Independence Movement, with a remarkable representation of works by Fernández de Lizardi.

One collection, received from Mr. E. S. Harkness, a

former trustee of the library, included a noteworthy group of documents relating to the earliest printing in South America, beginning with the first year of the first press, in Lima, Peru, and continuing until the death of the second printer, in 1618. There are also important later titles, as Francisco de la Puente, Tratado breve de la antiguedad del linaie de Vera (Lima, 1635), dealing with the history of an old Spanish family, Vera, several members of which held important positions in Spanish America; and J. Antonio Dávila Morales, Practica de la Doctrina Christiana (Lima, 1730), worthy also of notice as a religious work and as representative of a large collection of manuals in Indian languages, to which was recently added Diego González Holguín's Vocabulario dela... lengua Quichua (Lima, 1608).

The representation of Mexican printing includes two varieties of Juan de Zumárraga, Dotrina Breve (1543-44); the Missale Romanum Ordinarium (1561); Francisco Bravo, Opera Medicinalia (1570), the first medical work published in America; and the Mexican Leyes of 1548, previously mentioned as the first law book printed in America. Other "firsts" include Maturino Gilberti, Grammatica (1559), the first Latin grammar published in America; and Mateo Alemán, Ortografia Castellana (1609), the first Spanish grammar printed in America. Of unusual interest is Baltasar de Medina, Chronica de la Santa Provincia de San Diego de Mexico (1682), containing a map (also dated 1682), "the earliest specimen of a copperplate engraving done in Mexico, " according to Sabin. Other outstanding works include Henrico Martínez, Repertorio de los tiempos (1606), on natural history, of considerable rarity; and José Francisco de Cuevas Aguirre y Espinosa, Extracto de los autos de diligencias (1748), of the utmost topographical and historical importance, according to Henry Stevens.

In January 1944, the Arents collection of books relating to tobacco became a part of the reference department of the library as the gift of Mr. George Arents, of New York City. The collection, now well over 6, 000 items, has a substantial number of books, manuscripts, and letters in Spanish and relating to Spanish America. There is a considerable body of records concerning tobacco in the works of Spanish historians and travelers.

The great books of Spanish Americana were already among the holdings of the Lenox collection, but in several fields the Arents books have been notable additions. Among these is the rare Nueva prematica de reformacion (Saragossa, 1635) by Tomás Román, and Bartolomé Ximenez Paton's edition of Talavera's Reforma de Trages (Baeza, 1638). There is in the collection the apparently unique copy of a Spanish printing in broadside form of the first papal bull forbidding the use of tobacco, Seville, 1642.

Quite early in Spain the taxes on tobacco were made into a monopoly and leased for the benefit of the crown. Many of the rare laws and regulations relating to this trade are in the Arents collection, including the important "Renta general del Tabaco" (Madrid, 1740) and "Ordenanzas de la real renta del tabaco" (Mexico, 1768). Legal cases, local edicts, and separate enactments relating to the monopoly are also included.

Among the interesting unpublished manuscripts bearing on the history of tobacco in Spanish America is a series of letters (1742-1823) to and from Lima, Peru, on the subject of the tobacco monopoly in that country. The most important Spanish manuscript, "Instruccion general de el cultivo de tavacos, " was written by Nicolas José Rapun, the general manager of the tobacco administration in Cuba; it was engrossed especially for the Conde de Ricla, governor of the island, and is dated from Havana, October 12, 1764. This work is beautifully illustrated with a map of Cuba and thirty-four other water colors of tobacco plants, fields, leaves, and sheds.

The finest Portuguese item in the Arents collection is a manuscript entitled "Memoria sobre as especias de tabaco que se cultivao no Brazil, " by Joaquim de Amorim Castro, written in 1792 in the city of Cachoeira, Brazil.

Rockefeller Foundation
49 West 49th Street
New York 20

The Annual Reports of the Rockefeller Foundation which record its activities in Latin America are available in most public and university and college libraries in the United States.

Technical articles on the studies carried out in Latin American countries, particularly on yellow fever and malaria, have been published in various medical and entomological journals. Reprints of all technical articles by members of the Foundation's International Health Division staff (including those on work in Latin America) have been bound yearly in volumes as "International Health Division of The Rockefeller Foundation—Collected Papers, " and currently as "Division of Medicine and Public Health of The Rockefeller Foundation—Collected Papers. " An index of these volumes has been prepared through 1943, and a supplement through 1950. These volumes are distributed to various institutes of public health in Latin America and other foreign countries, and to schools of hygiene and public health and departments of preventive medicine and hygiene in medical schools in the United States.

A volume published by McGraw-Hill in 1951, entitled Yellow Fever, is a summary of the foundation's research in that disease. This book is distributed commercially by the publishers.

A booklet issued in 1950, Mexican Agricultural Program, relating to the foundation's agricultural program in Mexico since 1943, was distributed to university and college libraries in the United States.

A brief summary of the foundation's work in Latin America follows:

Public Health

All aid provided by the Rockefeller Foundation in public health was given with the co-operation of the governments concerned central or local governments usually contributed to the work and eventually, if a project was a continuing one, the government agency took it over altogether.

Work in the control of hookworm disease was begun in British Guiana in 1914 and concluded in 1922. A total of $73,958 was expended for this purpose.

Control of intestinal parasites, principally hookworm, was extended to other Latin American countries as follows: Brazil (1916-25), Colombia (1919-32), Dutch Guiana (1915-23), Paraguay (1924-29), Venezuela (1927-28), Costa Rica (1914-26), Guatemala (1914-28), Honduras (1922-24), British Honduras (1916, survey), Nicaragua (1914-24), Panama (1914-29), El Salvador (1916-21), Mexico (1924-27), and the West Indies (1914-29). Total expenditures by the foundation for this work were $2,388,413.

Malaria studies and control were carried out in Argentina (1921, 1925-29), Brazil (1919, 1922-29, 1938-44), British Guiana (1939-46), Colombia (1929, 1932-37, 1947-48), Ecuador (1920), Venezuela (1927-33, 1946-50), Costa Rica (1930-40), Guatemala (1932), Nicaragua (1921-25, 1932-35), Panama (1931-39), El Salvador (1934-42), Mexico (1931-33, 1937-39, 1942, 1944-50), and in the West Indies—including Cuba, Grenada, Haiti, Trinidad and Tobago, Jamaica, and Puerto Rico—within the period 1920-50. Total expenditures for malaria investigation and control through December 31, 1950, were $1,286,464.

The intensive campaign to eradicate the Anopheles gambiae mosquito in Brazil during the period 1939-42 was one of the better-known campaigns against a malaria vector because of the threat of this mosquito to the whole hemisphere. The Malaria Service of the Northeast was organized for the campaign, which was carried out in co-operation with the International Health Division of the Rocke-feller Foundation under the direction of Drs. F. L. Soper and D. Bruce Wilson, foundation staff members who were working with the Brazilian government in the investigation and control of yellow fever. Total expenditures for this purpose amounted to over $2,000,000, of which the foundation supplied roughly one quarter, the Brazilian government providing the remainder. The intensive campaign, which included the application of larvicides and the spraying of houses in all suspected areas, as well as the examination and spraying of such means of transportation as boats, ships, trucks, and airplanes, succeeded in eradicating the Anopheles gambiae mosquito from Brazil.

The largest sum spent by the foundation for the investigation and control of any one disease was that for yellow fever, of which $6,610,265 was expended in Latin America, and $5,090,682 of this amount in Brazil (1917-19, 1921-49). Other Latin American countries in which yellow fever control measures and studies were carried on were: Bolivia (1932-34, 1940-41), British Guiana (1940-46), Colombia and Venezuela (1923-25), Colombia (1934, 1938-48), Ecuador (1918-22, 1933-34, 1946-47), Paraguay (1932-34), Peru (1921-22, 1933-34, 1939-48), Panama (1940-47), Cuba (1935-36), and Mexico and Central America (1921-26).

Respiratory diseases, including tuberculosis, were studied in Argentina (1940-46), Costa Rica (1939-40), Panama (1934), Jamaica (1928-42); and Puerto Rico (1938-39), at a total expenditure of $248,923.

Studies in yaws and syphilis were carried out in Jamaica from 1932 through 1937. Total expenditures were $90,081.

Studies in nutrition were made in Mexico (1942-45), $40,384, and in Puerto Rico (1931-32, 1936-39), $41,259.

Although the principal work of the foundation in public health in Latin America has been the study and control of the three diseases—hookworm, malaria, and yellow fever—aid has also been given, in co-operation with state and local governments, to stimulate improvement in general public health services, such as public health administration, public health laboratory work, sanitary engineering, local public health work, and the training of public health personnel.

Schools and institutes of public health have been aided in São Paulo and Bahia (Brazil), Santiago (Chile), Bogotá (Colombia), and St. Augustine (Trinidad). Schools of nursing have been aided in Buenos Aires (Argentina), São Paulo and Rio de Janeiro (Brazil), Bogotá (Colombia), Quito (Ecuador), Montevideo (Uruguay), Caracas (Venezuela), and Panama. Expenditures for schools of nursing have been $312,506, and for schools and institutes of public health $404,425.

Medical Sciences

In the early years of the foundation, beginning in 1917, aid was given to develop the faculty of medicine and surgery of the University of São Paulo in Brazil. A total of $1,177,822 was provided toward the construction of laboratories (of anatomy, physiology, chemistry, and pathology) and an institute of hygiene; to defray the expenses of a visiting professor of pathology during the years 1921-26; and toward maintenance of the work in hygiene during the years 1917-26.

In Argentina aid was given in 1943 to the University of Buenos Aires for its Institute of Physiology under the direction of Professor B. A. Houssay, and continued to the Institute of Biology and Experimental Medicine which was later set up in Buenos Aires independently by Professor Houssay. Aid has been given for research in universities and institutions in other Latin American countries, often to help former fellows continue work for which they were trained during the period of their fellowships. Among other grants, the sums of $18,000 in 1946 and $35,000 in 1949 were given to the National Institute of Cardiology, Mexico City; and $20,000 in 1946 to the University of San Marcos in Lima, Peru, for equipment and supplies for the department of pathology.

Natural Sciences

The foundation's program to aid agriculture in Latin America was begun in 1941 by a survey of opportunities for assisting agriculture in Mexico. So far, more than $4,000,000 have been appropriated for the Mexican program, and a foundation staff of fourteen agricultural experts is working with Mexican government experts to improve agricultural crops and increase the food supply. The program has demonstrated a pattern for other areas, and has also offered training to personnel from other countries. Agricultural aid was extended to Colombia in 1950. A program to improve the yield and quality of the basic food crops, with emphasis in the beginning on corn and wheat, is being conducted under the direction of ten members of the foundation's agricultural staff with the co-operation of the Colombian government. A number of modest grants have recently been made to schools of agriculture or veterinary medicine in Mexico, Colombia, Chile, Argentina, Uruguay, Brazil, Honduras, Peru, and Costa Rica.

Grants totaling more than $1,000,000 in support of research in the basic natural sciences have been approved during the period since 1941. Among the principal projects in modern experimental biology to which foundation support has been given are those at the Research Institute of Biological Sciences in Montevideo; in various biological departments of the faculty of philosophy, sciences, and letters, as well as the faculty of medicine of the University of São Paulo; at the Institute of Biophysics of the University of Brazil; and at the Institute of Chemistry of the University of Mexico. In addition, more modest assistance has been extended to active investigators in other institutions in, for example, Brazil, Argentina, Chile, and Uruguay.

Social Sciences

Prior to 1939, aid to Latin America for work in the social sciences was given indirectly through grants to institutions in the United States; for example, grants of $45,000 and $27,500 were made to Tulane University for its Department of Middle American Research; $90,000 was appropriated to the American Geographical Society for its Millionth Map of Hispanic America; and $35,000 was given to the Foreign Policy Association for a commission to study Cuban economic and social conditions.

Pending development of the foundation's social science program in Latin America, few grants in the social sciences have been made in this area during recent years. Those grants which have been made have been for comparatively small amounts, chiefly for visits to Latin America by professors interested in Latin American subjects, or for visits by Latin American professors to the United States. Exceptional grants have been $18,650 in 1948 to the University of Puerto Rico for a study of social anthropology in Puerto Rico, conducted by Columbia University in co-operation with the university's Social Science Research Center; and grants totaling $33,000 to the Escola Libre de Sociologia e Política de São Paulo, Brazil.

Humanities

While grants in the field of the humanities were made to universities and institutions in the United States for Latin American

studies beginning in 1934, such as grants to the Universities of
New Mexico and Texas for studies in Hispanic American culture
($5,000 and $7,500, respectively); to Tulane University for a survey of archives and libraries in Central America ($17,000); to the
Pan American Union for Latin American broadcasts ($12,820); and
to the American Council of Learned Societies for production of a
Handbook of Latin American Studies ($15,000), it was not until 1939
that a grant was made directly to an institution in a Latin American
country. In that year $8,000 was given to the University of Chile
for development of its central library.

The foundation's program of aid in the humanities has continued both to institutions in the United States for Latin American
studies, and to institutions in various countries of Latin America.
Among the institutions in Latin America to which most assistance
in the humanities has been given are the National Institute of Anthropology and History, Mexico City, which has received grants totaling
$125,615, and the Colegio de México, to which grants totaling
$215,352 have been appropriated.

Syracuse University
Department of Geography
Collection of Professor Preston E. James
Syracuse

Professor James has been engaged in a study of Latin
America as a whole, and in a more specific study of southeastern
Brazil. In the general field of Latin America he has compiled
several new maps of the continent on a scale of 1:5,000,000, showing
surface features, climate, natural vegetation, distribution of people
(dot map, and with urban centers indicated by circles), density of
population, land use (including mines), and transportation. These
maps, and a considerable amount of the more detailed material
on which they are based, are available in the department of geography.
Many of them are published in his Latin America (New York: Odyssey
Press, 1950). Small-scale black and white maps, generalizing
some of these data, were published in C. C. Colby, Geographic
Aspects of International Relations (Chicago: University of Chicago
Press, 1938). The maps included in this volume refer to surface
features, natural vegetation, distribution of population, and land
use.

Concerning the area of more specific study, southeastern
Brazil, Professor James has a large amount of statistical material
and maps, some compiled from various sources, some resulting

from field observation, and some published by various agencies. This material follows the more general and small-scale maps in his published articles, the most important of which have appeared in the Geographical Review, the Annals of the Association of American Geographers, and the Papers of the Michigan Academy of Science, Arts and Letters.

It should also be noted that the department of geography at Syracuse University has a fine collection of Latin American maps.

University of North Carolina
Library
Chapel Hill

The University of North Carolina library has an unusually complete collection of Spanish and Spanish American bibliography. In Spanish America, for example, practically all the works of José Toribio Medina are there. The Spanish play collection consists of over 20,000 plays, principally from the eighteenth, nineteenth, and twentieth centuries. Many of these are first editions, the most important of which are for the eighteenth century and the Romantic period. The Cervantes collection does not have first editions, but there are many early editions.

In the Latin American field, the University of North Carolina is specializing in Argentina, Chile, Paraguay, Uruguay, and Venezuela, and has very good collections in these fields. Long runs of newspapers from these countries are in the library. Sturgis E. Leavitt has in manuscript an index to 50 Spanish American magazines covering the period 1842-1935. This index was prepared with the collaboration of J. R. Spell of the University of Texas and Madaline W. Nichols of the University of New Mexico.

Duke University
Library
Durham

The Duke University library contains a strong collection for Hispanic American studies in general, and for several countries has collections of considerable distinction.

In 1929, the library acquired the Peruvian collection of 3,000 volumes formed by Francisco Pérez de Velasco. The Peruvian seller, Luis Ferreyros, prepared a printed catalogue of this collection, Catálogo de la Biblioteca Peruana, propriedad de Dn.

Francisco Pérez (Lima, 1918). The bulk of this material relates
to the colonial period, yet the original collector had broad interests
and set no arbitrary restrictions. There are many pamphlets of
the colonial period, most of them bound up in 35 volumes of Miscelá-
neas. Although there is not a great deal that would interest a collector in incunabula, the American imprints go back to mid-seventeenth century. Most of the works of Pedro de Peralta Barnuevo
are here, the rare Mercurio Peruano, 85 volumes of the Guías del
Perú (including 25 issues, 1735-97, of the celebrated Conocimientos
de los tiempos), and the Anales universitarios del Perú (32 volumes)
all of which lend solidity to the collection. Indeed, the chief value
lies not in rare items but in such solid sets as M. Mendiburu,
Diccionario histórico biográfico (both editions), the Ateneo de Lima
(38 volumes, 1889-1907), and both editions of the compilation of
historical and literary documents of Peru by Manuel de Odriozola.
Manuscript material falls into three groups: commerce and industry
literary activity, and religious and social history, ranging from
original manuscript cédulas of the Spanish kings to recent typewritte
mensajes of Peruvian presidents. The manuscripts are described
in Tilley and Goodwin, Guide to the Manuscript Collections in the
Duke University Library (Durham, N.C.: Duke University Press,
1947).

In 1940, the library acquired the collection of Filipiniana
(5,000 items) formed by the late James A. Robertson, pioneer
editor of the Hispanic American Review, with a collection of
Robertson's letters and papers (about 500 items). The library
later acquired an additional collection of Robertson papers (about
1,400 items). Dr. Robertson was one of the editors of the monumental collection of source materials, the Philippine Islands, 1493-
1898 (55 volumes), served for five years as librarian of the Philippine library at Manila, was connected with various governmental
and philanthropic agencies interested in the Philippines, and remained an assiduous collector of Filipiniana until his death in 1939.

Virtually all phases of Philippine affairs are represented
in this collection. The proportion of printed bibliographies, manuscripts, and governmental reports is relatively high. Among the
bibliographic items may be mentioned Pérez and Güemez, Adiciones
y continuación de la imprenta en Manila de José Toribio Medina
(Manila, 1904); Colección general de documentos relativos a las
Islas Filipinas existentes en el Archivo de Indias de Sevilla (1493-
1529); Emma Osterman Elmer, Checklist of Publications of the
Government of the Philippine Islands (Manila, 1918). Philippine
conditions immediately after the Spanish-American war and early

United States administrative policies are illuminated by correspondence of William Howard Taft, first Civil Governor; Dean C.
Worcester, member of the first and second Philippine commissions,
and first Secretary of the Interior of the Philippine Islands (1901-
13); T. H. Pardo de Tavera, bibliophile and Philippine member of
the second Philippine commission; James A. LeRoy, private secretary to Dean Worcester; David Prescott Barrows, director of education, 1903-9; and many Philippine leaders. There are also many
of Dr. Robertson's working notes, drafts, and typescripts of his
published writings.

Dr. Robertson was much interested in the missionary program conducted by the Spanish government and religous orders in
the Philippines, and the collection contains some material of special
interest on this topic. There are, for example, the pastoral letters
(1776-83) of Santa Justa y Rufina, archbishop of Manila; Boletín
eclesiástico del Arzobispado de Manila (1876-91); E. J. Pérez,
Catálogo bío-bibliográfico de los religiosos Agustinos. Furthermore,
there is a basic selection of books and pamphlets by and about José
Rizal y Alonso, celebrated Filipino author, medico, and patriot,
with several editions of his first political novel, Noli me tangere.

About 300 volumes of the Robertson collection are more
recent works by scholars of various nationalities. Among them are
works of Austin Craig, professor of history at the University of the
Philippines; Teodoro M. Kalaw, Filipino nationalist, statesman and
author; Wenceslao Emilio Retana y Gamboa, Spanish bibliographer
and historian; and Fedor Jagor.

In 1940, the division of humanities of the Rockefeller
Foundation made a grant to Duke University, the University of North
Carolina, and Tulane University to support a co-operative project
for the acquisition of Latin American materials. Under the plan of
this grant, Duke University Library assumed responsibility for
materials relating to Bolivia, Brazil, Colombia, Ecuador, and
Peru. During the years 1940-46, Duke University used its grant
of $25,000 for the purchase of books and manuscripts in two cate-
gories: (1) history and related fields and (2) Hispanic American
literature; 7,624 volumes were received. The library had shown
special activity between 1925 and 1940 in collecting the records of
Latin American legislatures, special congresses, and supreme
courts; therefore, special attention was devoted to documentary
sets of source materials for the Latin American countries in the
Duke sphere of interest. Extensive purchases of collections of
government documents were also made in Argentina and Chile. At

the same time, the library supplemented Rockefeller funds with
several thousands of dollars for additional purchases in the Latin
American and related fields. The following are typical of the resources now available for research students as a result of this program and the library's continuing purchases, many of the sets being
complete.

Argentina:

Cámara de Diputados. Diario, 1854 to date.
Cámara de Senadores. Diario, 1854 to date.
Corte Suprema. Fallos, 1863 to date.
Ministerio de Relaciones Exteriores y Culto. Memoria, 1852 to
    date.
Nación, La (Buenos Aires daily newspaper), 1928 to date.

Bolivia:

Anuario de leyes..., 1855-1934.
Cámara de Diputados. Redactor, 1832-1932.
Cámara de Senadores. Redactor, 1832-1932.
Congreso Nacional. Redactor, 1832-1932.
Corte Suprema. Gaceta judicial, 1858-1934.

Brazil:

The library has long had an interest in materials on the
history of Brazil, and its collection is now strongest in modern
government publications and the publications of Brazilian academies
and learned societies. Alan K. Manchester's "Descriptive Bibliography of the Brazilian Section of the Duke University Library,"
in the Hispanic American Historical Review, XIII (1933), 238-66,
495-523, describes the collection at that time. There are good
bibliographical aids and considerable material on the colonial
period, divided largely between the subjects of discovery and exploration, Jesuits, the Inquisition, the captaincies, and the wars
with the Dutch and French; there is also material for primary
documentation on such subjects as foreign affairs in general, and
boundary disputes in particular. Among long sets are the following:

Bibliotheca Nacional. Documentos históricos, 1928 to date.
——. Anais, 1876 to date.
Cámara dos Deputados. Annaes, 1826-1936.
——. Estados de sitio, 1892-1925.
Colecção das leis, 1808 to date.
Decisões do govêrno..., 1808-1917.
Senado. Annaes, 1826-1935.

Chile:

Boletín de las leyes..., 1839 to date.
Mercurio, El (Santiago daily newspaper), 1928-43.

Colombia:

Anales del Consejo de Estado, 1915 to date.
Gaceta Judicial de la Corte Suprema de Justicia, 1887 to date.
Popayán, 1907-47.

Ecuador:

The principal purchase in this field was the collection of about 2,000 volumes brought together during a period of more than twenty-five years by Leonardo J. Muñoz, regarded as the chief bibliographer and collector of the country. The Muñoz collection is unusually strong in printed source materials and has been supplemented by the purchase of pamphlets and other materials about Ecuador and by Ecuadorians.

Diario de debates de las Cámaras Legislativas, 1894-1930.
Diario Oficial, 1889-95.
Mensajes de los diferentes departamentos del gobierno..., 1833-57.
Mensajes de los diferentes presidentes..., 1833-1939.
Mensajes del Presidente de la Corte Suprema..., 1903-42.
Leyes del Ecuador y documentos relacionados, 1830-1942.
Informes of various ministries, 1867-1941 (300 volumes).

Peru:

Anuario de la legislación peruana, 1906-41.
Calancha, Antonio de. Coronica moralizada del Orden de San Augustin en el Peru..., Barcelona, 1638.
Cámara de Diputados. Diario de los debates, 1868 to date.
Cámara de Senadores. Diario de los debates, 1868 to date.
Ministerio de Fomento. Memorias..., 1896-1937.
Peruano, El. 1826 to date.

Newspapers, 1945-49: Nearly 2,000 issues, forming many complete files, of the official organs of Peruvian political parties, such as La Tribuna (Partido Apristo Peruano), Nos. 1-1,100, 1945-48; Labor (Partido Comunista Peruano), Nos. 1-98, 1946-48; Hoguera (Partido Demócrata), Nos. 1-125, 1945-50.

Uruguay:

Alta Corte de Justicia. Jurisprudencia..., 1930 to date.
Cámara de Representantes. Diario, 1830-1931.

The Duke University library maintains a large number of

serial and periodical subscriptions for Latin American material, and receives currently several Latin American newspapers. The Hispanic American Historical Review (q. v.), has since 1926 been subsidized and published by the Duke University Press; John Tate Lanning, professor of history, and Robert S. Smith, professor of economics at Duke, are currently serving on the board of advisory editors and the board of editors, respectively.

Cincinnati Art Museum
Cincinnati

The art of Spain is not strongly represented at the Cincinnati Art Museum. Only in one division of the arts, in painting, are there a few representatives of exceptional importance. A list of the Spanish paintings follows:

Fortuny, Mariano. "The Mazarin Library," water color.

Greco, El. "Crucifixion with View of Toledo," oil on canvas.
Acquired in 1932 for the J. J. Emery collection of the museum.
See Walter H. Siple, "Crucifixion with View of Toledo by El
Greco," Cincinnati Art Museum Bulletin, Vol. III (1932), No. 2.

López y Portana, Vicente (attributed to). "Portrait of the Countess
de Quinto" (?), oil on canvas.

Murillo. "St. Thomas of Villa Nueva Dividing His Clothes Among
the Beggar Boys," oil on canvas. A part of the Mary M. Emery
collection bequeathed to the museum in 1927. It was painted for
the convent of St. Augustine in Seville. Of it, Dr. Mayer has
said, "The most beautiful genre picture he ever painted." See
Catalogue of Paintings from El Greco to Goya (New York: Metropolitan Museum of Art, 1928).

Rico y Ortega, Martín. "Riva della Calcena," oil on canvas.

—. "Canal San Giovano," oil on canvas.

Sánchez-Perrier, Emilio. "Landscape," oil on canvas.

Sorolla y Bastida, Joaquín. "The Little Grandson," oil on canvas.

—. "Rose Bay," oil on canvas.

Velázquez. "Head of Philip IV," oil on canvas. A part of the Mary
M. Emery collection. It dates from the artist's later years,
around 1650-55. See Royal Cortissoz, "Velázquez," International Studio, XC (1928), 39.

—. (attributed to). "Head of a Woman," oil on canvas. This splendid strong canvas, the gift of Frank Duveneck in 1915, has long
been attributed to Velázquez, although before its cleaning no
one of recognized authority had spoken definitely to that effect.
It would date from the early period of that master's work if the
attribution should be established.

Zamacois, Eduardo. "Child and Dog, " oil on canvas.
—. "The Guard, " oil on panel.
Zurbarán. "The Recovery of the Image of the Virgin of El Puig"
(The Legend of the Bell), oil on canvas. A gift in 1917 of Miss
Mary Hanna, Mr. and Mrs. Charles P. Taft, and Mr. Stevenson
Scott, in memory of Charles F. Fowles. See Francis W. Robinson,
"Notes on a Painting by Zurbarán, " Cincinnati Art Museum Bulle-
tin, Vol. VII (1936), No. 1.

Following is a list of other Hispanic objects in the museum
(Spanish unless otherwise noted): missal from the abbey of Roda,
1744; a Charles IV silver coin; medal, Grand Cross of Isabel la
Católica, 1876; 7 nineteenth-century ceramic water jugs; 6 nineteenth-
century Portuguese dolls in peasant costume; nineteenth-century
brooch and pin; lace vest, sixteenth century; seventeenth-century
leather book cover; double harp, 1750; bandarri; Portuguese guitar;
various textile pieces, sixteenth to nineteenth centuries.

Cincinnati Institute of Fine Arts
Taft Museum
Cincinnati

The Taft Museum, under the management of the Cincinnati
Institute of Fine Arts, comprises the art collection and former home
of Mr. and Mrs. Charles Phelps Taft, given by them to the institute
in 1927 and opened to the public in 1932.

Hispanic material is limited to 2 paintings by Goya and 1 by
Mariano Fortuny. They are:

Fortuny, Mariano. "An Arab Guard, " signed, and dated 1863.
Collections: Mrs. Bloomfield Moore.
Goya. "Queen María Luisa. " This is similar to the portrait of
the Queen in the large group of the royal family in the Prado.
It was painted about 1800 and belongs to a group of four portraits
representing the Queen, King Charles IV, the Infante Ferdinand
and the Infanta Isabel, which were formerly in the Palace of
San Telmo, Seville. Collections: Comtesse de Paris.
—. "Joaquín Rodríguez Costillares. " This is one of three similar
portraits of the celebrated bullfighter. Collections: Conde de
Asalto; Enrique Puncet.

Cleveland Museum of Art
Cleveland 6

The Cleveland Museum of Art has a remarkable group of
Spanish textiles, the most important pieces being the group to which

is generally given the name Hispano-Moresque. Among them are
2 fragments from the vestments of San Valero, Lérida, Spain.
These were probably woven in Almería about the year 1200. There
are also 2 fine fragments found in the tomb of the Infante Don Felipe,
who died in 1274, and are, therefore, documented as to their approximate date. Don Felipe was the son of Ferdinand III, King of Castile
(1199-1252).

There is a fascinating roundel within which are seated two
musicians before a hanging lamp, a piece which reveals very clearly
the fact that Spain was all-important as a bridge from the Near East
to Europe. The Mohammedan worker of Spain translated into his
own idiom the Near Eastern motif and in turn influenced the de-
signers of Europe. Textiles from the Iberian Peninsula were sought
everywhere in the marts of trade.

There are also 2 important mantles of silk brocade. These
came from churches where they had been used as mantles for precious
statues of the Virgin. The earlier, of blue silk and gold brocade,
thirteenth or fourteenth century, came from a church near Valencia.
It must have been cut down for its purpose and bears an Arabic
(Nashki) inscription which reads, "Glory to our Lord the Sultan,"
and "The King"—a title referring to minor Moorish sultans in Spain.
The other mantle is of blue and red brocade, of the fifteenth century, and came from Granada. A romantic legend is attached to it,
that at one time it belonged to Boabdil himself.

There are in addition many other pieces of Hispano-Moresque
weaving and a group of Spanish weavings of the Renaissance period.

In the realm of sculpture, the museum owns 2 very fine
figures in wood, Castilian, about the year 1275. They represent
the figures of St. John and the Virgin and come from a Crucifixion
group. They are among the most important figures of an atelier
whose products have been found in Castile or nearby sections of
Catalonia. Very fortunately, their original polychromy has been
preserved in remarkably good condition.

There are a number of other objects of minor importance—
small sculptures and carved wood and stone panels.

In any large collection of arms and armor, works of
Spanish provenance are always to be found, and this is the case in
the Cleveland museum. In the Severance collection, most of these
are works of the seventeenth and eighteenth centuries, with a few
pieces of the fifteenth and sixteenth centuries. The collection was
studied by the late Don José Florid, Keeper of the Real Armería in
Madrid, when he was in America in the twenties.

The Spanish and Mexican paintings owned by the museum are:

Cantú, Federico. "Mujer recostada," water color on paper.

Charlot, Jean. "Two Women Standing," water color on cardboard.

Goya. "Portrait of Don Juan Antonio Cuervo," oil on canvas.

___. "Don Juan María Osorio Alvarez" ("Boy with a Linnet"), oil.

Greco, El. "Holy Family," oil on canvas. The museum's example is of approximately the same size as the one of the same subject in the Van Horne collection, Montreal. Between these two pictures there is a close analogy, while an even closer one exists between the Van Horne painting and one in the Bucharest Gallery. The figures in all three are closely related to the Virgin and angels in the upper part of a picture formerly in the chapel of San José in Toledo, and now in the National Gallery of Art, Washington, D. C. The same model certainly served for St. Anne of the "Holy Family" of the Prado and for the same figure in the Cleveland picture. Mayer dates it between 1592 and 1596. It therefore antedates slightly these other paintings, but it is typical of El Greco's middle period. Collections: Parish church of Torrejón de Velasco near Toledo; Don Juan Gutiérrez, Albarrán; E. O'Rossen, Paris; M. von Nemes, Budapest; Gentile di Guiseppe, Paris.

Jiménez y Aranda, José. "Corridor Around a Spanish Courtyard," oil on wood.

Nicolau-de-Albentosa, Pedro (attributed to). "Coronation of the Virgin," tempera on panel.

Orozco, José Clemente. "Echate la otra," oil on canvas.

Picasso. "Nude" (pink period), water color. Painted about 1905 as a study for the central figure of "Figures," in the collection of Leonard C. Hanna, New York. Collections: Marie Harriman Gallery, New York; Hinman B. Hurlbut.

___. "La Vie" (blue period), oil on canvas.

Tamayo, Rufino. "Women Reaching for the Moon," oil on canvas.

Spanish sculpture in the Cleveland Museum of Art includes:

Wooden St. John, ca. 1275, Castilian; original polychromy.

Wooden Virgin, ca. 1275, Castilian; original polychromy.

Wooden doors, fourteenth or fifteenth century; mudéjar style; covered with a gesso-like material and then gilt; a mixture of Moorish interlacing and Spanish Gothic motifs.

Marble head of mourner, probably fifteenth century; from Poblet. Interesting document of influence of Burgundian sculpture in Spain.

Two fifteenth-century stone bosses; traces of polychrome painting in blue and red; from vaulted ceiling of a monastery in northern Spain.

Marble Pietà (1500-1530), probably by an artist under Flemish influence; bas-relief of white marble, yellowish with age, showing slight traces of red and green.

Carved wood panels, sixteenth century; painted and gilded; figure of Faith in canopied niche, surrounded by groups of Amorini. Not a superexcellent work in any case.

Carved oak plane, seventeenth century.

Wood panel, seventeenth century; formal foliage design and birds arranged around floral urns. Used as model for impressing embossed designs in Spanish leather.

Spanish and Mexican artists represented in the museum's department of prints and drawings include Federico Cantú, Dali, Goya, Orozco, and Rivera.

In addition to the textiles previously mentioned, the museum owns a Spanish rug (ca. 1500), similar, but with different border, to one in the Boston Museum of Fine Arts. See Cornelia Bateman Faraday, European and American Carpets and Rugs (Cedar Rapids, Mich.: Dean Hicks Co., 1929). There are also over 100 other pieces dating from the thirteenth through the nineteenth centuries.

In the department of decorative arts are 2 studio doors of the sixteenth century, in sculptured wood of fourteen panels; a silver crucifix of the sixteenth century; various bowls, plates, and plaques; and a glass bowl made by Steuben Glass Co. with decoration by Salvador Dali. This is signed and dated 1940, and shows figures of a sleeping woman, a sleeping male figure, children, a swan and a shell; the drawing for this is in the museum's department of prints and drawings and entitled "Marsupial Figure."

The John L. Severance collection of arms and armor includes

Two thirteenth-century Spanish spurs.

Fifteenth-century Spanish crossbow and winder; befor (1450-80); 2 spurs; and 2 two-handled swords.

Sixteenth-century Spanish suit of armor; powder flask (1591); muzzle; mace; dagger; morion (1580); rondache; banner; rapier; halberd; cabasset; and 2 stirrups.

Seventeenth-century sword; schiavone; rapier (Spanish or Neapolitan); 3 spurs; stirrup-miniature; estoc; dagger, main gauche; 2 rapiers; cannon; snaphance pistol; and wheel-lock gun (1618).

Eighteenth-century sword hilt; 4 banners; knife; and flintlock (ca. 1750).

Nineteenth-century miguelet lock.

Pair of brass stirrups (Madrid), date unknown.

Cleveland Public Library
Cleveland 14

The John G. White collection of the Cleveland Public
Library specializes in folklore, Orientalia, and chess. It has 116
books on Spanish folklore, 24 on Portuguese, 194 on Latin Ameri-
can. In addition there are 70 books on Spanish ballads, 44 on
Portuguese, 169 books on the native tribes of Latin America, 101
Spanish chapbooks, and 90 Portuguese.

Among the more unusual items are the Revista d'Ethnologia
e de Glottologia, 4 vols. (Lisbon, 1880-81), the only volume published of the Annuario para o Estudo das Tradições Populares
Portuguezas (Oporto, 1883), Tradição, 6 vols. (Lisbon, 1899-1904),
and the possibly unique earliest edition known of Gomes de Santo
Estevam's Libro del infante don Pedro de Portugal [Seville (?),
ca. 1520]. On this last item see More Books, the bulletin of the
Boston Public Library (April 1944), p. 152.

Oberlin College
Oberlin

An interesting exhibit in the Allen Memorial Art Museum
of Oberlin College is a seventeenth-century baldachin, or processional canopy, the gift of Mr. Haig M. Prince, acquired by him
some years ago from the estate of Mrs. Cora Huntington, of Los
Angeles. The canopy of silver, repoussé, is 96 inches high and
52 inches wide. Internal evidence shows that in 1637 it was given
to the convent of Santa Clara in Carmona, province of Seville,
by Doña María de Rueda, a nun of the convent. An inscription
giving these details appears on the dome. Another inscription, on
the base, indicates that it was altered or repaired in 1747. Un-
fortunately, there is no trace of the artist's mark or signature.

The museum owns also a cubist painting, "Glass of
Absinthe," by Picasso, an oil on canvas painted in 1911, acquired
by Oberlin in 1947.

The Spanish drama collection in Oberlin College Library
consists of approximately 7,500 dramatic works dating from the
last quarter of the seventeenth century to the year 1924. It contains a variety of drama as great as Spanish invention could make
it: comedias famosas, comedias nuevas, autos sacramentales,
tragedias, tragi-comedias, dramas, zarzuelas, juguetes, pasillos,
monólogos, bailes, and so forth. Of these, some 2,000 are dated
after 1900, approximately 4,500 belong to the nineteenth century,

while the remaining are principally of the eighteenth century. Only
a few were published in the seventeenth century—the earliest date
is 1678. Several hundred, including many of the musical plays, are
translations or adaptations from the foreign theater. A two-volume
catalogue prepared by Professor Paul P. Rogers and published by
Oberlin College Library offers not only a careful description of
each item, but a title index and a list of composers, printers, and
theaters.

Toledo Museum of Art
Monroe Street at Scottwood Avenue
Toledo 2

The Toledo Museum of Art has felt strong ties with Hispanic
art due to the close friendship between the city and its Spanish name-
sake. The museum is particularly proud of 2 brilliant paintings by
the leading artist of its parent city, El Greco. In 1946, the museum
purchased El Greco's "Christ at Gethsemane" (ca. 1580) from the
collection of Arthur Sachs. The second El Greco painting, "The
Annunciation" (1586), was acquired in 1951 from the collection of
Ralph M. Coe. Preceding the El Greco paintings in date are 2 oil
panels: "Epiphany" (1490) by Fernando Gallego, and the "Adoration
of the Magi" (ca. 1500) by the Játiva Master. The rich collection
of seventeenth-century paintings includes "Man with the Wine Glass"
(ca. 1622) by Velázquez; "Flight into Egypt" (ca. 1630) by Zurbarán;
"Portrait of a Musician" (1638) by José Ribera; and "Young Spanish
Prince Dressed as a Cardinal" by Juan Bautista del Mazo. Goya is
represented by an oil, "Bullfight" (1820), and a good set of the
"Tauromachios" lithographs. Three fine paintings by Picasso, with
2 paintings by Joseph Mompou and the contemporary stage designer
Mariano Andreu bring the collection of Spanish paintings to date.

Most of the paintings mentioned are reproduced and discussed in Spanish Painting, by José Gudiol, published by the Toledo
Museum of Art in connection with an exhibition held from March 16
to April 27, 1941. The exhibition, with its extensive catalogue,
culminated the professorship of José Gudiol y Ricart, the last of a
series of outstanding annual professors.

In 1942, the Toledo Museum of Art sponsored jointly with
the Republic of Chile, the University of Chile, and the Co-ordinator
of Inter-American Affairs, an exhibition of contemporary Chilean
art. Blake-More Godwin, director of the museum, received the
Order of Merit from the President of Chile for the organization of
the exhibition. The works of several Chilean painters—Caballero,

Danitz, Humeres, Lira, Perotti, and Pedraza—were acquired from the exhibition. They are reproduced and discussed in Chilean Contemporary Art, published by the Toledo Museum of Art.

In addition to the paintings, Hispanic material will be found throughout the collection. Polychrome wood sculpture can be seen in a twelfth-century Virgin, a Catalan figure of St. John and a large fourteenth-century Crucifix said to come from San Juan de Loria, Andorra. Six excellent pieces of Hispano-Moresque pottery date from the fifteenth and sixteenth centuries. The museum's extensive collection of ancient and modern glass includes fourteenth-century Arabic cups, of a type which may have originated in Spain, as well as a collection of delicate seventeenth- and eighteenth-century Spanish glassware. An antiphonary leaf of the twelfth century, perhaps from Montserrat, is believed the earliest music from Spain in an American collection. The rare woodcut picture of Columbus landing in the New World is bound in Verardus' Historia Baetica, printed by Bergner in 1494 in Basel. Rare books from Peter Hagembach's press in Toledo, Spain, and from Juan Cronberger's Mexico City press of 1544, the first in the New World, complete the museum's compact but significant collection of Hispanic material.

Portland Art Museum
West Park and Madison
Portland 5

The pre-Columbian collection of the Portland Art Museum consists of 74 objects (clay, stone, wood, and textiles) covering the area of Mexico (archaic, Mayan, and Aztec), Central America, and Peru. This collection has gained accessions in the years 1942, 1949, 1950 and 1952, mostly through gifts, although the Peruvian textiles were purchased from the John Wise collection.

By far the largest number of objects come from Mexico: an early Mayan stone mask from Chiapas; from Nayarit, 12 Tarascan clay objects, one of which is dated as late archaic; 9 clay sculptures from Colima; 4 Mayan clay sculptures from the Isle of Jaina, Yucatán, and 2 from Tabasco; 2 primitive stone masks from Guerrero; a Nahua clay vase, Cholula; 2 Toltec clay pots and a stucco relief; 3 stone palma and a stone frog yoke from Vera Cruz; a Mixtecan stone idol from Oaxaca; 3 Zapotecan funeral clay urns; a wooden mask with mosaic inlay, Yucatán; a late Aztec carved stone altar from Mexico City; an obsidian mask, 5 sculptures of gods, and other pieces from the Valley of Mexico.

Other objects in the collection are: a Mayan polychrome clay vase from Honduras; 9 pottery pieces from Costa Rica; 2 Mayan terracotta animal heads from Nicaragua; 2 ceremonial stone sculptures from Panama; and from the central coast of Peru, Tiahuanaco period, a woven poncho and a woven bag (curled-tail puma design).

In addition to the pre-Columbian collection the museum owns a bronze "Head of a Woman," by Picasso; an oil by Luis Jiménez y Aranda—"Learning to Walk"; and prints by Jean Charlot, Dali, Leopoldo Méndez, Orozco, Miró, and Picasso.

Barnes Foundation
Merion

Among the Hispanic objects owned by the Barnes Foundation are a number of examples of early Spanish wrought-iron work (forks, fireplace spits, candleholders, etc.) and a sixteenth-century Spanish decorated iron jewel box. There are 31 New Mexican santos and 2 New Mexican bultos. Three wood panels, fifteenth-century Spanish primitives, are owned by the foundation. One of these, the "Sanctification of a Woman," is illustrated in Albert C. Barnes and Violette de Mazia, The French Primitives and Their Forms (Merion, Penn.: Barnes Foundation Press, 1931).

Hispanic painters represented in the foundation are as follows:

Goya. Three pictures. One, "Don Galos," is illustrated in Albert
    C. Barnes, The Art in Painting, 3d ed. (New York: Harcourt,
    Brace and Co., 1937), p. 276.
Greco, El. Four paintings. The "Annunciation" and "Vision of
    St. Hyacinth" are illustrated in Albert C. Barnes, op. cit.,
    pp. 24 and 58. The "Mocked Christ" is illustrated in the same
    book (p. 82) under the title of "Christ Bafoué."
Miró. Three paintings—"Women Surrounded by Birds," "Group
    of Women," and "Group of Personages." Also "Composition,"
    a modern French tapestry made from a Miró cartoon under the
    direction of Mme Paul Cuttoli, Paris.
Picasso. Forty-five paintings. "Composition," "Girl with
    Cigarette," "Harlequins," and "Still Life" are listed in Albert
    C. Barnes, op. cit., pp. 59, 475, 23, and 476. In addition to
    the paintings, the foundation owns "Inspiration," a modern French
    tapestry made from a Picasso cartoon under the direction of
    Mme Paul Cuttoli, Paris.
Vieira, Sylvia. A recent acquisition by this Portuguese painter is
    "Symphonie Domestique."

Academy of Natural Sciences of Philadelphia
Nineteenth and the Parkway
Philadelphia

During its history, covering over 140 years, the academy
has accumulated very important Hispanic natural history materials,
using the term Hispanic to cover collections as well as published
volumes or contributions. A very considerable part of the information available on the natural history of Hispanic American countries
first appeared in the publications of the academy, and in numerous
cases as the results of explorations conducted under the institution's
auspices. The correspondence files contain numerous letters from
nineteenth-century Latin American scientists.

The library of the academy is rich in works dealing with
the natural history of Hispanic America, including memoirs such
as Martius' 41 folio volumes of the Flora brasiliensis, the voyages
of Humboldt and Bonpland, d'Orbigny, and many others of the late
eighteenth and early nineteenth centuries. A complete set of the
great Biologia Centrali-Americana is also in the academy library.
Virtually all the publications of important societies and institutions
dealing with natural history in all the Hispanic countries throughout
the world are in the same library.

In the academy will be found the following major reference
series of material, grouped by subjects:

Birds: Important collections, representing the results of numerous, chiefly ornithological expeditions from the academy to parts
of Mexico, Guatemala, Honduras, Nicaragua, Panama, Colombia,
Ecuador, Venezuela, British Guiana, Peru, Brazil, and Bolivia.
Especially comprehensive are the series representing seven years
of field work in Peru and Bolivia in a survey of the birds of the
two countries carried out between 1929 and 1938. These two
series total approximately 16,000 specimens of a grand total of
65,000 from South America alone. In the academy's collection
of South and Central American birds are many old historic types,
mainly Lafresnaye, Cassin, and others, as well as those of
numerous recently described species and subspecies.

Insects: Some hundreds of thousands of insects from Hispanic
America are in the academy series, including the most important
and extensive existing one of the order Orthoptera, as well as
similarly ranked representatives of certain sections of other orders.
The original type specimens of Hispanic American insects forming the basis of such studies of G. H. Horn, Calvert, E. T.
Cresson, Sr., E. T. Cresson, Jr., Hebard, Rehn, Williams, etc.,

represent some thousands of species. Representative sets of
the Coleoptera and of the Odonata reported in the great Biologia
Centrali-Americana are in the academy series, as well as much
of the collections, including types, on which a portion of the
Orthoptera work for the same series was done by Bruner. The
academy series also contains important and representative series
of certain orders of insects from the Iberian Peninsula.

Mammals: Important collections representing the results of academy
expeditions to parts of Guatemala, Honduras, Nicaragua, Panama,
Venezuela, Ecuador, Peru, Brazil, and Bolivia.

Minerals: The academy's series contain extensive collections from
numerous localities in Bolivia and Peru and several in Chile,
largely secured by its own field explorations in past years. While
much of the representation remains to be studied, investigations
already completed and published on these series have made known
five new species of minerals.

Mollusks: Practically all countries of Central and South America
and the West Indies are represented in the exceptionally extensive collections of this group. Many publications have been based
on this material, and large numbers of types of Pilsbry, Tryon,
H. B. Baker, and other authors are included. These collections
have formed the basis of many volumes of the classic Manual
of Conchology by Tryon and Pilsbry.

Plants: The herbarium of the academy contains important series
of higher plants taken by Pringle, Palmer, Wright, Holton,
Fendler, Couthouy, and other well-known collectors in Mexico,
Venezuela, Cuba, Colombia, Ecuador, and Brazil. Dr. Francis
W. Pennell did extensive field and laboratory investigations on
the flora of Mexico, Colombia, Peru, and Chile. There are many
fern collections of Hispanic America, one of the more important
being that of J. N. Rovirosa, which contains many types and iso-
types. Algae: extensive diatom collections from Mexico, Brazil,
Chile, and Peru. Dr. Ruth Patrick is the author of several papers
dealing with Brazilian diatoms, in which many new species are
described. The same author is actively working in fossil diatoms
from Mexico.

Reptiles and fishes: The academy series are rich in historic types
of Hispanic American forms, particularly large numbers of
species described by Cope from Ecuador, Peru, and Brazil,
and the more modern discoveries of Fowler in the fish fauna of
Venezuela, Honduras, Brazil, etc. Classic collections at the
academy in these fields are those made by Orton (Peru), Hauxwell
(Ecuador), H. H. Smith (Brazil), Van Rijgersma (St. Martin,
West Indies), and Hering (Surinam).

Vertebrate and invertebrate fossils: In its invertebrate fossil collections the academy has a large number of type specimens of Tertiary fossils from the Dominican Republic, described by Gabb, Pilsbry, and Johnson; Tertiary forms from Colombia—described by Pilsbry, A. P. Brown, and Olsson—as well as from Cuba and Bolivia; Cretaceous and Tertiary types from Peru; and other species, but not types, from Ecuador and Bolivia.

John G. Johnson Collection
Parkway and 25th Street
Philadelphia 30

The John G. Johnson collection comprises some 1,286 pictures representing the European schools of painting. It was assembled by John G. Johnson, a prominent lawyer, and bequeathed by him to the city of Philadelphia in 1917. The collection, originally housed in Mr. Johnson's old home, is on display in the Philadelphia Museum of Art.

A 3-volume catalogue was published by Mr. Johnson in 1913. This privately printed catalogue was limited to an edition of 300 copies and presented to scholars and libraries throughout the world. A smaller catalogue published in 1941, as well as photographs of all pictures in the collection, and a picture book carrying 288 reproductions may be purchased upon request.

Following is a list of the Hispanic pictures in the collection:

Castilian artist, second half of fifteenth century. "Religious Procession," wood panel.
__. "Mass of St. Gregory," transposed to canvas.
Castro, del (Castilian, late fifteenth century). "Founding of the Franciscan Order," panel. See Valerian von Loga, Die Malerei in Spanien (Berlin, 1923), p. 54.
Espalargucs, Pere (Lérida, late fifteenth century). Six wood panels ("St. Peter," "Mater Dolorosa," "St. John Evangelist," "Sts. Magdalene, Ermengold, and Catherine," "Sts. John Baptist, Bridget, and Michael," "St. Paul") from a retablo, the main portions of which are in the Hispanic Society, New York. The work was ordered from Espalargucs in 1490 by men from the village of Enviny.
Fortuny, Mariano. "Statue of Dionysus," signed and dated lower left—"Roma, 11 Janvier, 1858."
__. "Arab Chief," in lower left—"Fortuny '74."
Gallegos, Fernando. "St. Bernardino of Siena," ca. 1480, formerly attributed to Flemish artist.

Goya. "Portrait of the Actor Máiquez, " canvas. See Frank J.
Mather in Burlington Magazine, IX (1906), 357; J. Kirby Grant
in Connoisseur, XXII (1908), 3-4; and M. Soria, "Portraits of
Isidro Gonzales Velásquez and His Wife, " Art Bulletin (September
1943).

—. "Portrait of the Wife of Máiquez, " canvas. See references above

—. "Mounted Cavalier with Garrocha, " canvas. See Frank J.
Mather, op. cit., 358.

Greco, El. "Pietà, " wood panel. See Frank J. Mather, op. cit.,
p. 357; August L. Mayer, Domenico Theotocopuli (Munich,
1926), p. 17.

—. "Portrait of a Lady, " 1594-1604, wood panel. See Manuel B.
Cossio, El Greco (Madrid, 1908), p. 419; Malcolm Vaughan in
International Studio, LXXXVI (March 1927), 22; J. Kirby Grant,
op. cit., p. 3; E. Bertaux in La Revue de l'Art, I (1911), 406;
L'Art et les Artistes (1905), p. 205.

—. "Crucifixion, " 1604-14, canvas. See August L. Mayer, op.
cit., p. 17.

Iriarte, Ignacio de. "The Vision of St. Anthony of Padua, " canvas.

Jiménez, Juan. "St. Michael, " wood.

Juanes, Juan de (Vicente Juan Mucip). "Madonna Enthroned with
Saints, " wood panel. See J. Kirby Grant, op. cit., p. 3;
Valerian von Loga, op. cit., p. 44.

Lucas, Eugenio, the Elder. "The Love Letter, " canvas, in lower
left signed and dated, 1864.

Martorell, Bernardo. "Virgin Surrounded by Six Virtues, " wood
panel, ca. 1450, formerly attributed to an unknown French
artist.

Marzal de Sas, Andreas. Two companion wood panels, "Nativity"
and "Death of the Virgin, " ca. 1400, formerly attributed to
unknown French artist.

Mazo Martínez, Juan Bautista del. "Portrait of a Young Lady, "
canvas. See Sedelmeyer Gallery, One Hundred Paintings of
Old Masters (Paris, 1892), p. 74; August L. Mayer, Murillo,
in "Klassiker der Kunst" (Stuttgart and Berlin, 1913), p. 231.

Murillo. "Christ in the Desert, " canvas. See August L. Mayer
in Art in America, III (1915), 315.

Olot Master (Catalan, height of activity ca. 1500). "Collection
of Manna, " wood panel, ca. 1470, formerly attributed to a
Castilian artist.

Osono, Rodrigo de, and son (attributed to). Three wood panels—
"Christ in the Garden of Gethsemane, " "Pietà, " and "The
Resurrection"—late fifteenth century, which very likely formed
the predella of a large altarpiece; formerly attributed to an
Aragonese artist. See Valerian von Loga, op. cit., p. 78.

Palanquinos Master (Leon, active end of fifteenth century).   Two "Scenes from the Legend of St. Michael," wood panels, late fifteenth century.   Collections: Davanzati Palace.

Pradilla, Francisco.   "A Lackey," water color; in lower left signed and dated [18]93.

Reixac, Juan.   "Crowning with Thorns," wood panel; this and the following were formerly attributed to an unknown artist:of the sixteenth century.

___. "Death of St. Giles," wood panel. See Valerian von Loga, op. cit., p. 29.

Ribera. "St. James the Apostle," canvas.

Rusinol, Santiago. "Cafe Interior," canvas; in lower right appears "S. Rusinol, Champs Mars, 1892."

Unknown, mid-seventeenth century. "Countess Ruffo Bonneval de la Fard," canvas.

Vargas, Luis de. "Crucifixion," transposed to canvas. See Valerian von Loga, op. cit., p. 101.

Velázquez (old copy after). "Maria Teresa," canvas.

Villamediana Master (Palencia, active second quarter fifteenth century). "Birth of the Virgin," wood panel, fifteenth century. Collections: Edouard Aynard.

___. "Sts. Sebastian and Catherine of Alexandria," wood.

___. "Sts. Margaret and Bartholomew," wood companion panel with above, ca. 1475; formerly attributed to Southeast Piedmontese.

Villegas, José. "Alhambra, Interior," canvas.

Zamacois, Eduardo. "Toreador's Toilet," wood; in lower right, "Ed. Zamacois 1866." Collections: P. L. Everard, Paris.

Philadelphia Museum of Art
Parkway at Fairmount Avenue
Philadelphia 30

The Philadelphia Museum of Art has a very generous collection of Hispanic paintings in its galleries dating from the fifteenth to the twentieth centuries. Hispanic items appear in various of the museum's collections.

In the Bloomfield Moore collection is a seventeenth-century "St. Jerome," of the Spanish School. The Commissioners of Fairmount Park collection has a "St. Jerome" by a follower of Ribera. An excellent "Madonna and Child" by Ribera (signed, and dated 1626) in the William L. Elkins collection is worthy of mention.

The W. P. Wilstach collection includes a comprehensive cross section, with 15 paintings in all. Noteworthy among these are "St. Anthony of Padua, " by El Greco; "Christ on the Cross, " attributed to El Greco; a fine "Annunciation" by Zurbarán dated 1650; and a "Portrait of a Peasant, " attributed to Zurbarán. Another painting of superior quality is the portrait of a "Peasant Woman, " attributed to Antonio Puga, a pupil of Velázquez, whose works are very rare. There are also a number of nineteenth-century examples, followed by a fine large painting by Sorolla, "The Young Amphibians, " dated 1903.

The Lamborn collection contains 72 paintings by Mexican artists of the eighteenth and nineteenth centuries. They were collected in Mexico between 1881 and 1883 by the late Robert H. Lamborn. While none is perhaps comparable to the finest examples of Spanish painting done in Spain, they are nevertheless unique documents of work carried out by Spanish colonial artists in the New World, and as such are of great historical interest. Perhaps the two finest examples are a "Self Portrait of Juana Inez de la Cruz" (1651-9?), who, besides being a painter of distinction, was also the earliest known Mexican poetess; and a portrait by an unknown artist of "St. Rose of Lima. " The other paintings are all religious subjects, and the majority of them formerly hung in convents and churches throughout Mexico.

In 1950 Walter Conrad Arensberg presented his 1, 000-piece collection of pre-Columbian and twentieth-century art to the museum. The paintings, which were placed on permanent display in October 1954, include:

Gris, Juan. Five oils—"The Man in the Cafe, " 1912; "La Place Ravignan, " 1915; "The Lamp, " 1916; "The Open Window, " 1917; "The Chessboard, " 1917.

Mérida, Carlos. "Clay Figurines, " 1931, water color; "Two Figures, " 1932, water color and gouache; "The Window, " 1933, water color, gouache and ink; "Deer Dance, " 1935, oil.

Miró, Joan. "The Hermitage, " 1935, oil and charcoal; "Man and Woman, " 1925, oil; "Nude, " 1926, oil; "Man, Woman and Child, " 1931, oil; "Female Torso, " 1931, gouache and water color; "The Lovers, " 1934, pastel and pencil; "Woman, " 1934, pastel and pencil; "Four Figures, " 1934, ink and pastel; "Person in the Presence of Nature, " 1935, oil and gouache.

Montenegro, Roberto. "The Double, " oil.

Picasso. "Old Woman, " 1901, oil; "Sea Shore, " 1905, pencil; "Female Figure, " ca. 1905-6, ink; "Female Figure and Hand, " ca. 1905-6, pencil; "Head, " 1906, ink; "Woman Seated and Woman Standing, " 1906, charcoal; "Landscape, " 1907-8, gouache; "Men,

1908, gouache; "Seated Nude Woman, " 1908, oil; "Female Nude, "
1910-11, oil; "Man with Violin, " 1911, oil; "Man with Guitar, "
1912, oil; "Violin, " 1912, charcoal; "Violin and Guitar, " 1913,
pasted cloth, oil, etc.; "Three Nudes on Shore, " 1920, pencil;
"Still Life, " 1921, pastel.

The Albert E. Gallatin collection of twentieth-century painting
and sculpture has been in the Philadelphia Museum of Art since
1943. The collection is particularly strong in cubist and abstract
work. There are works by the Spanish sculptor Julio González
and the Uruguayan painter Joaquín Torres-García. The 6 paintings
of Joan Miró include his famous "Dog Barking at the Moon. " Juan
Gris is represented by 12 works, including "The Violin, " "Dish of
Fruit, " "Bottle and Fruit, " and "Harlequin. " Picasso is especially
well represented, 23 of his works appearing in the collection. Among
them are a "Self-Portrait, " 1906; "The Three Musicians, " 1921;
"The Mandolin, " 1923; "Dinard—Design for a Monument, " 1928.

In its general collection the museum owns Zuloaga's
"Portrait of Mrs. William Fahnestock. " There is also an excellent
collection of paintings by Mexican artists, including José María
Velasco, Diego Rivera, David Alfaro Siqueiros, Juan Soriano,
Rufino Tamayo, Jesús Guerrero Galván, Ricardo Martínez, Julio
Castellanos, José Chávez Morado, Agustín Lazo. There are drawings
by Guillermo Meza, Diego Rivera, Rufino Tamayo, Julio Castellanos,
José Clemente Orozco, Jesús Escobedo, Federico Cantú, and
María Izquierdo.

University of Pennsylvania
Hispanic Review
Philadelphia

The unfortunate discontinuance of the Revue Hispanique is
closely linked with the origin of the Hispanic Review. M. Raymond
Foulché-Delbosc, founder and for thirty-five years editor of the
former journal, died on June 3, 1929, and every American Hispanist lamented him as one of the outstanding scholars in the field
of Spanish literary history. Moreover, from almost the inception
of the Revue Hispanique in 1894, articles and long monographs by
American scholars had been published by its editor in ever-increasing
numbers. When it was learned that Mr. Archer M. Huntington's
generous subsidy in behalf of the Revue Hispanique was to come to
an end after the publication of the memorial volume (LXXXI),
every American Hispanist was troubled over the loss of a journal
which had meant so much in the development of Hispanism in this
country.

When the Modern Language Association of America met at Washington, D. C. after Christmas in 1930, the late Charles C. Marden called a meeting to discuss the matter, and a committee under the chairmanship of Professor Marden was appointed to take the steps necessary to the creation of a new journal. As a result of the activities of this committee, J. P. Wickersham Crawford agreed to become the editor provided that the University of Pennsylvania could give a small subsidy for the expenses. This subsidy was granted, and it was planned that the first number should be published in January 1932.

For unavoidable reasons there was a serious delay in the carrying out of these plans, but the creation of the new journal remained uppermost in Professor Marden's mind. He modestly declined to serve on the board of editors, saying that such duties could be performed better by younger men, but his aid and counsel were invaluable. To the regret of all Hispanists in the United States, death came to him without warning on May 11, and his picture serves as a frontispiece for the initial number, which appeared in January 1933.

The title, Hispanic Review, was chosen because it was desired to have as a field the literary history and linguistics of all Romance languages spoken throughout the Hispanic Peninsula and Latin America. It was realized at once that while the Hispanic Review had much the same aims as the Revue Hispanique, it could not aspire to fill its place for lack of sufficient subsidy. In its latter years the Revue Hispanique had printed 3 volumes annually, amounting to approximately 1,200 pages. These included many extended monographs of biography and criticism, long reprints, and lengthy articles and editions. The Hispanic Review is a quarterly journal of approximately 350 pages per volume. Its scope is limited to the publication of scholarly articles and notes, and critical reviews of books embodying research on Hispanic literary history and linguistics.

The normal length of articles varies from ten to twenty-five pages, although longer articles of extraordinary interest are published in parts, in two successive issues. A section of "Varia" is reserved for brief notes and discussions. The reviews are by persons of known capacity for the task; and a further section called "Briefer Mention" contains descriptive notices of books whose importance, while real, does not justify a full-length review.

The present editors are Otis H. Green and Joseph E. Gillet. The managing editor is Arnold G. Reichenberger, assisted by Joseph A. Fernández. Associate editors are Carlos Clavería, Alfred Coester, J. D. M. Ford, Hayward Keniston, Sturgis E. Leavitt, María Rosa Lida de Malkiel, S. Griswold Morley, Charles P. Wagner, Edwin B. Williams, and Raymond S. Willis, Jr. The Hispanic Review is now publishing its twenty-second volume. It is felt that it has contributed through the years to the progress of Hispanic studies in the United States.

University of Pennsylvania
Library
Philadelphia

Rennert Collection

Shortly before the death of Hugo A. Rennert, which occurred on December 31, 1927, the university purchased his library of Spanish books. For over thirty-six years he had served as professor of Romance languages at the University of Pennsylvania. When he was a student of Baist at Freiburg im Breisgau in 1891, he bought rare volumes at the sale of the Salvá library, and these were to form the nucleus of what was to become later the most valuable private Spanish library in the United States.

Dr. Rennert combined the enthusiasm of the bibliophile for rare editions, for typographical curiosities, and for superb bindings with the scholar's desire to have at hand reliable source material for his studies. He is known chiefly as the biographer of Lope de Vega, and while preparing his Life (1904), he made a collection of his nondramatic works which consists almost wholly of first editions, and which is unparalleled in this country. In regard to Lope's plays, he had almost a complete set of the twenty-five partes or volumes which were printed between 1604 and 1647.

Early editions of the Spanish lyric poets from Garcilaso to Góngora and rare volumes of the pastoral novels from Montemayor's Diana and its pallid successors are also notable. However, he was catholic in his tastes in buying Spanish books of the sixteenth and seventeenth centuries, and the collection which he made is valuable alike for the specialist who shares Dr. Rennert's tastes, and for the research scholar who is interested in the manifold literary activities of the Golden Age.

No separate catalogue of the Rennert collection has been printed, but all books and manuscripts are recorded in the library's catalogue. The Rennert collection, and valuable additions made since the acquisition of the collection, is shelved in the rare book collection of the university library.

Samuel Putnam Collection

The library of the late Samuel Putnam, former editor of
the Brazilian section of the Handbook of Latin American Studies
and translator of Portuguese and Spanish literature, was presented
to the University of Pennsylvania in 1950. It consists of approximately 750 titles, largely in the field of Brazilian literature but
including some studies in related fields like Brazilian history and
philosophy. This collection, added to the former holdings of the
university, has increased the research value of the university's
collections in the field of Brazilian studies.

University of Pennsylvania
University of Pennsylvania Library
Henry Charles Lea Library
Philadelphia

The Henry Charles Lea library, containing about 15,000
volumes, forms part of the library of the University of Pennsylvania.
It was left to the university at Lea's death, and additions have
since been made to it with the aid of Lea funds. The collection is
housed in a special room built for the purpose, with a card catalogue
of the collection. No printed catalogue has been published. The
items were collected by Lea as a working library and include only
such material as he felt he needed for his research. Practically
every work cited in the footnotes of his various books is on these
shelves.

The library contains manuscripts, early printed books,
and many of the seventeenth- and eighteenth-century collections
of sources for medieval history, the writings of the theologians,
summists, and commentators, and is especially rich in material
dealing with the religious history of Spain and her dependencies.
It also possesses the chief collections of Spanish laws, statutes,
and treaties. A unique body of material is found in the extensive
transcripts of manuscripts from European archives dealing with
the Inquisition in its various forms. For the medieval Inquisition,
there are transcripts from the Bibliothèque Nationale of Paris,
the Bibliotheca Ambrosiana, the Bibliotheca Vittorio Emmanuele
(Rome), and the Florentine and Venetian archives; for the Roman
Inquisition, transcripts from the archives of Naples and Venice
and from the records that found their way to Trinity College, Dublin;
for the Spanish Inquisition, large bodies of material from its archives at Alcalá, Simancas, and Madrid, from the Biblioteca
Nacional (Madrid), and from the municipal archives of Seville.

A few original manuscripts deal with Inquisitional trials at Toledo
and Valencia. The transcripts are of interest not only as the chief
sources for Lea's History of the Inquisition of Spain, but because of
the kind of evidence elicited from witnesses, which throws much
light on social and economic conditions, especially of the lower
middle class of the population.

The Lea library also contains Mr. Lea's correspondence
about the books he wrote, much of this correspondence being with
scholars in Spain and Spanish America.

University of Pennsylvania
University Museum
Philadelphia

The collections available for Hispanic research in the
University Museum are of an anthropological and bibliographical
nature. Material from the Iberian Peninsula is negligible or nil,
but that from America is extensive. The anthropological objects
are mainly archeological, to a less degree ethnological, with a
little somatological material.

The Mexican archeological collections are large, especially
from the southern highlands. The immense collection of potsherds
and fragmentary ceramic objects made by Dr. Boas for the International School of Mexican Anthropology in 1911-12, which formed
the primary basis for the distinguishing of cultural types and horizons
in the Valley of Mexico, consists of many thousands of objects. Another
large collection (purchased) consists mainly of Zapotecan and Mixtecan
objects, with many excellent funerary urns.

The permanent loans of the anthropological collections of
the Academy of Natural Sciences and the American Philosophical
Society consist largely of Mexican archeological objects and contain such old collections as that of Poinsett, the first United States
ambassador to Mexico, made about 1828. Naturally there are many
outstanding and unique objects in these collections.

The Maya collection is one of the world's best, especially
in ceramics from the eastern foothills of Guatemala, and particularly
from the Chama region. The results of the museum's excavations
at Piedras Negras, Guatemala (1931-38), are extensive, but in the
main the objects are not impressive, consisting largely of potsherds,
except for 2 original large stone monuments, one of them probably
the most artistic original Maya stone sculpture outside of Middle
America. These are held on indefinite loan; the other fine examples,
formerly on exhibition, have been returned to the National Arche-

ological Museum in Guatemala City. Maya large stone sculpture and inscriptions are also represented by 4 stelae and 3 altars recently secured by the expedition to Caracol, British Honduras; these are permanently owned. The collection of originals in this category is more extensive than any other in this hemisphere, except in Mesoamerica itself.

The archeological collections from Panama are unusually large, consisting mainly of the results of the expedition to Coclé in 1940 and of an older group from the Chiriquí region. Both of these are among the largest collections of their kinds, and both consist largely of pottery vessels together with many admirable examples of gold ornaments. From the rest of Central America and the Antilles, the collections are rather small.

In South America, the archeological collections from Marajó Island and Santarém, Brazil, are among the largest known, and the Tairona collection from Colombia is one of the best. The Peruvian and Bolivian material is very extensive and well rounded, including not only large series of pottery and textiles, but much other perishable grave furniture, representative of the coastal cultures from the Chira Valley to the Tacna-Arica area. A large part came from Dr. Max Uhle's famous excavations at Pachacamac, and a later expedition under Dr. W. C. Farabee added a rich collection from the Ica-Nazca-Paracas region. Pottery and stone objects from the Andean highlands around Lake Titicaca represent the Tiahuanaco and Inca cultures.

In ethnology, the Middle American material is slight, with the exception of the famous E. A. Osborne collection of Guatemalan textiles. The major part of the ethnological objects was collected by expeditions in South America, the outstanding and most important groups being from British Guiana, the Upper Xingu in Mato Grosso, the Yaruro and Macoa in Venezuela, and the Goajiro and Arhuaco in Colombia. The collection of modern pottery of the Conibo in eastern Peru is unusually large.

In physical anthropology the museum possesses a fairly large collection of Peruvian and Bolivian crania with a number of trephined skulls, and some skeletal material from other parts of Hispanic America.

The museum has the personal library of the late Dr. D. G. Brinton, which is unusually strong in Hispanic American items. The latter incorporates the famous collection of the late Dr. K. H. Berendt of material on, or in, the native languages of Central

America, especially the Mayan. It consists largely of manuscripts, many of them old original sources, others hand-made copies of very rare and important works.

Monographs and articles referring to many of the museum's anthropological collections and unusual objects may be found in the Bulletin and the Transactions of the Free Museum of Science and Art, the Anthropological Publications, the Museum Journal, and the University Museum Bulletin. All of these, except the last, have now been discontinued and replaced by a single series of Museum Monographs. Several special publications in the Latin American field have been issued, such as Max Uhle's report on Pachacamac, and Maya Pottery, an album of reproductions of Maya ceramics in color, and Piedras Negras Archeology, in which the excavations at Piedras Negras are currently being reported in detail. An annotated catalogue of the Berendt Linguistic Collection was published in the Bulletin of the Free Museum of Science and Art, Vol. II (1907), No. 4.

Brown University
Annmary Brown Memorial
Providence

As in the case of other incunabula at the Annmary Brown Memorial, the Hispanic items in the collection were brought together because of the founder's interest in the typography of the fifteenth century. They comprise a Portuguese imprint (Leiria), and 18 titles representative of the work of thirteen Spanish printing firms and of two unidentified Spanish presses. These titles are described in detail in the Memorial's Catalogue of Books... from the Presses of the First Printers Showing the Progress of Printing with Movable Metal Types Through the Second Half of the Fifteenth Century. Collected by Rush C. Hawkins. Catalogued by Alfred W. Pollard (1910); one of the unidentified items, the Constituciones sinodales del Obispado de Jaén, is further discussed by Dr. Konrad Haebler in his Geschichte der Spanischen Frühdrucker (1923), pp. 238-40, and there given the questioned assignment of Jaén, ca. 1480.

The Annmary Brown Memorial possesses also a few Spanish paintings. They are described in Paintings in Oil and Water Colours by Early and Modern Painters, collected by Rush C. Hawkins, catalogued by C. H. Collins Baker, and deposited in the Annmary Brown Memorial at Providence, Rhode Island, 2d ed. (London: Medici Society, 1913).

Brown University
Brown University Library
Providence

The Brown University Library contains about 6,000 volumes
on Latin America, miscellaneous in character, but emphasizing
chiefly history, geography, and biography. This general collection
is supplemented by microfilms of 2,376 titles of Spanish American
imprints before 1800, or of books printed in Europe before that
date which are of Spanish American interest. These are titles not
represented in the John Carter Brown Library. The majority of
them are from the Medina collection in the Biblioteca Nacional in
Santiago de Chile.

Positive microfilms are available for use at the Brown
University Library and the Library of Congress. The cataloguing
of the titles has been completed, and cards have been printed by
the Library of Congress. A list of about half the titles has been
issued by Brown University Library; a complete list is contemplated.
Orders for microfilms of any of the titles may be placed through
the Brown University Library.

In the Harris collection of American poetry and plays are
about 700 volumes of poetry of Latin America. Additions are made
currently to this section of the Harris collection.

The Church collection on South America was received by
the university in 1912 as a bequest of Colonel George Earl Church.
It consists of some 3,500 volumes dealing mostly with political
and economic history and travel but including some literary reviews
and periodicals. Most of the books are in Spanish and Portuguese and
about 100 of them were printed before 1700. There are about 200
titles on Mexico, over 100 on Central America, about 100 on the
West Indies and Panama, and a good 1,200 on the several South
American republics. Standard histories and works less directly
concerned with Latin America comprise the remainder. There is
one important manuscript of the eighteenth century, Historia de la
villa imperial de Potosí. It is, on the whole, a compact balanced
collection whose full usefulness is contingent on completing broken
sets of printed documents included in it and on filling other gaps by
special works that are now available in later editions. As a step
in this direction, about 200 volumes, chiefly on Mexico, have been
acquired for the general collections from the library of George
Parker Winship.

Brown University
John Carter Brown Library
Providence

The De Ricci and Wilson Census of Medieval and Renaissance Manuscripts in the United States and Canada enters 33 single manuscripts or collections of manuscripts of the twelfth, fifteenth, and sixteenth centuries belonging to the John Carter Brown Library. Of these, 21 are of Hispanic American interest and have chiefly to do with the Church, the government, or with the Indians, either from the standpoint of their languages or of their conversion and treatment by the conquerors. One of these collections of manuscripts entered under a single number is the group of 136 viceregal and other political documents, calendared by Father Damian Van den Eynde in the Hispanic American Historical Review for November 1936. Another is a collection, in 14 folio volumes, of 700 informaciones of the Franciscan novitiates of the province of Pueblo de los Angeles, extending from 1594 to 1841. Without doubt the most important and the most interesting of the manuscripts listed by specific title in the De Ricci and Wilson list is No. 22, that is, the Motul Diccionario, Maya-Spanish and Spanish-Maya, attributed to Antonio de Ciudad Real, and written in the closing years of the sixteenth century.

Of books relating specifically to the history, social and economic life, religion, description, literature, science, and linguistics of Mexico and Spanish South America, there are about 3,600 titles in the library. In other classifications—general history of the New World, discovery and exploration, Spanish conquest, European and American wars of the seventeenth and eighteenth centuries, relations between European nations affecting America, maps and atlases—there are something over 2,000 titles more or less directly affecting Spanish interests in America. The total of printed materials relating to Spanish America in the library, therefore, comprises about 6,000 titles.

Collections of particular interest in this Spanish American classification are, first of all, books printed in Mexico and Peru, especially the volumes issued in the earliest years of the press in those countries. Outstanding among these is the group of 70 titles which came from the presses of Mexico City in the sixteenth century. From the press of Peru, the library has 420 imprints of the period 1584-1800. Among these is the unique copy of the first issue of the Peruvian press, the Pragmatica sobre los Diez Dias del año (Lima, 1584), and, immediately following this, 16 of the 29 titles entered in José Toribio Medina, La Imprenta en Lima, as proceeding from the press of Peru in its first twenty years.

Regarding these categories from the standpoint of subject, we find that there is in the library an especially large group of Spanish American books relating to the native languages—grammars, texts, and vocabularies—printed before the year 1801. These include copies of the celebrated Alonso de Molina, Vocabulario (Mexico, 1555), several works printed in Mexico in the sixteenth century compiled by Maturino Gilberti in the Tarascan language, the Juan de Córdova Vocabulario zapoteca (Mexico, 1578), in addition to several doctrinas, confesionarios, and textual works of that century and that place of issue. In the field of the native linguistics of Peru, the library possesses, among other things, a single volume containing numbers three, four, and five of the titles entered in José Toribio Medina, Bibliografía de las lenguas quechua y aymará. Some idea of the importance of the library's linguistic collection is obtained by a comparison of its resources in the field of Peruvian languages with the full Medina bibliography just mentioned; of the 49 titles recorded by Medina as having been published before 1801, the library has 32. There are also in the linguistic collection 2 books of extraordinary rarity from the Jesuit press of Paraguay, namely, Antonio Ruiz de Montoya, Vocabulario de la lengua guaraní, from the press in Santa María la Mayor (1722); and Arte de la lengua guaraní, written by the same author and issued by the same press in 1724.

A special effort has been made to collect works relating to the additions to scientific knowledge made by early writers in Mexico and South America. One of the most notable titles in this field is the Dos libros of Monardes published in Seville in 1565, which is one of two copies recorded of the true first edition of an important fundamental American scientific contribution; many editions of the treatises of Christoval and Joseph de Acosta; the Physica speculatio of Alphonso Vera Cruz (Mexico, 1557); the Summa y recopilacion de cirugia, of Lopez de Hinojoso (Mexico, 1595); and the Instruccion nauthica of Diego Garcia de Palacio (Mexico, 1587). A notable example of completeness is found in the library's possession of 3 printed editions of the works on plants, animals, and drugs of Francisco Hernández, as well as a manuscript epitome of his papers made toward the end of the sixteenth century. Numerous early works on metallurgy, natural history, astronomy, and geography give diversity of interest to this category of works of practical science.

Among works of belles-lettres are to be mentioned 12 editions (of the whole work or of its parts) of the Araucana of Alonso de Ercilla y Zúñiga, published between 1578 and 1776; Bernardo de Balbuena, Grandeza mexicana (Mexico, 1604); Antonio de Saavedra Guzmán, El Peregrino indiano (Madrid, 1599); Martín del Barco

Centenera, Argentina y conquista del Rio de la Plata (Lisbon, 1602); and Francisco Botello, El Nuevo Mundo (Barcelona, 1701).

In connection with sources of the history of Mexico must be mentioned the large number of monastic chronicles in the collection, including early manuscripts of large portions of the chronicles of Pablo de la Concepción Beaumont and Antonio Tello, and the considerable body of material here brought together relating to the Jesuits in America. There are about 1,000 sermons, catechisms, and devotional works printed in Mexico and other Spanish American countries in the seventeenth and eighteenth centuries.

For further information, see Henry R. Wagner, "Hispanic Americana in the John Carter Brown Library," in Essays Honoring Lawrence C. Wroth (1951).

Rhode Island School of Design
Museum of Art
Providence

The most important Hispanic items in the collection of the Museum of Art, Rhode Island School of Design, are to be found among the paintings, which include: "St. Andrew," attributed to El Greco's workshop; a portrait by Sánchez Coello; a large landscape with figures of Hagar and Ishmael, by Francisco Collantes; a Spanish carnival scene by Eugenio Lucas; a park landscape by Sorolla y Bastida; and a still life by the contemporary Uruguayan artist José Cuneo. To these may be added 3 miniatures by Goya, two being portraits of young girls painted on copper, and an earlier one of two heads painted on ivory.

Distinguished among the prints are Goya's "Disasters of War," in the original folders published by the Royal Academy of Noble Arts of San Fernando (Madrid, 1863), the lithograph "Diversión de España" from the series of the Bordeaux bulls, the complete set of "Proverbios," and several etchings after Velázquez.

Spanish decorative arts are represented by textiles and by a few examples of furniture, metalwork, and pottery. Spanish medieval sculpture is fairly well represented in the permanent collection, supplemented by several important pieces on permanent loan.

The metalwork consists of wrought-iron chest locks and nailheads (chatón), and a seventeenth-century iron sconce. The wood carving is of little consequence, consisting of small panels and minor decorative details. The museum collection includes a fifteenth-century walnut chest with a carved front of flamboyant Gothic tracery.

The jewelry is of the peasant type and dates from the seventeenth and eighteenth centuries. The fans all date from the nineteenth century.

There are 52 pieces of Spanish pottery in the collection, including some Talavera majolica and relatively modern peasant pottery from Andújar, Estremadura, Granada, Níjar, Rambla, Ronda, Toledo, Triana, and Valencia, and 10 pieces of Portuguese peasant pottery. Spanish influence may be traced in many of the 112 pieces of Mexican pottery.

Further information on the collection may be found in the Museum's Bulletin, as well as Art News, Art Digest, Pantheon, Sélection, and Masters in Art.

TEXAS

Spanish Missions

Of the five old Spanish missions in or near San Antonio, the best known is the Alamo, now preserved as the cradle of Texas liberty. As the Misión de San Antonio de Valero, it was founded in 1718 and named for St. Anthony of Padua and the Marquis of Valero, Spanish viceroy. In February 1836, Santa Anna and 1,000 Mexicans beseiged 184 Texans under Col. William Barrett Travis in the Alamo. The Texans all were killed, including Davy Crockett and Col. James Bowie. The church, in ruins, was bought about forty years ago from the Roman Catholic Church by the State of Texas. The building has been restored as a memorial to the defenders of Texas.

The other Spanish missions in the San Antonio area are San José, Concepción, San Juan Capistrano, and San Francisco de la Espada.

Following is a select bibliography on the missions:

Arricivita, Juan Domingo. Cronica seraphica y apostolica del Colegio de Propaganda Fide de la Santa Cruz de Querétaro en la Nueva España, 2 vols. (Mexico, 1792).

Bancroft, Hubert Howe. History of the North Mexican States and Texas, 2 vols. (San Francisco, 1884-89).

Bartlet, John Russell. Personal Narrative of Explorations and Incidents in Texas, New Mexico, California, Sonora, and Chihuahua (New York, 1854).

Bolton, Herbert Eugene. Guide to the Materials for the History of the United States in the Principal Archives of Mexico) Washington, D.C., 1913).

——. Athanase de Mézières and the Louisiana-Texas Frontier, 2 vols. (Cleveland, 1914).

——. Spanish Exploration in the Southwest, 1542-1706 (New York, 1916).

——. Texas in the Middle Eighteenth Century (Berkeley, 1915).

Bravo Ugarte, José. Diócesis y obispos de la Iglesia Mexicana, 1519-1939 (Mexico, 1941).

Brown, Henry. History of Texas from 1695 to 1892 (St. Louis, 1892-93).

Castañeda, Carlos Eduardo. Guide to the Latin American Manuscripts in the University of Texas Library (Cambridge, Mass., 1939).

——. Manuscripts for the History of Texas and the Internal Provinces, 1673-1800. Selected and calendared from the Archivo de San Francisco el Grande (Typewritten copy in the Bancroft Library, dated 1931).

——. A Report on the Spanish Archives in San Antonio (San Antonio, 1937).

Céliz, Francisco. Diary of the Alarcón Expedition into Texas, 1718-19, translated by Fritz Leo Hoffmann (Los Angeles, 1935).

Chabot, Frederick Charles. The Alamo: Mission, Fortress and Shrine (San Antonio, 1935).

——. Mission La Purissima Concepción: Being an Account of Its Founding in East Texas, Its Removal to the Waters of the San Antonio, and Its Present Location near the City (San Antonio, 1935).

——. San Antonio and Its Beginnings (San Antonio, 1936).

Chapman, Charles Edward. Catalogue of Materials in the Archivo General de Indias for the History of the Pacific Coast and the American Southwest (Berkeley, 1919).

Clark, Robert Carlton. The Beginnings of Texas (Austin, 1907).

Domenech, Emmanuel Henri Dieudonné. Journal d'un missionaire au Texas et au Mexique, 1846-52 (Paris, 1857).

——. Souvenirs d'outre-mer. Mes missions au crépuscule de la vie (Paris, 1884).

Espinosa, Isidoro Felice de. Cronica apostolica y seraphica de todos los colegios de esta Nueva España de Misioneros Franciscanos Observantes erigidos con autoridad pontificia y regia para la reformacion de los fieles y conversion de los gentiles (Mexico, 1746).

García, Bartolomé. Manual para administrar los santos sacramentos de penetencia, eucharistia, extrema-uncion, y matrimonio ... en las misiones del Rio de San Antonio y Rio Grande (Mexico, 1760).

Garrison, George Pierce. Texas: A Conquest of Civilizations (Boston, 1903).

Heusinger, Edward Werner. Early Explorations and Mission Establishments in Texas (San Antonio, 1936).

Hughes, Anne Eugenia. The Beginnings of the Spanish Settlement in the El Paso District (Berkeley, 1916).

Ilg, John. San José Mission: Queen of the Missions (San Antonio, 1941).

Jaillet, C. Sketches of Catholicity in Texas, 2 vols. (Philadelphia, 1884-88).

Johnson, F. W. A History of Texas and Texans, edited by E. C. Barker and E. W. Winkler, 5 vols. (Chicago, 1914).

Kirwin, J. M. History of the Diocese of Galveston and St. Mary's Cathedral (Galveston, 1922).

Knights of Columbus, Texas State Council, Historical Commission. Our Catholic Heritage in Texas, 1519-1836, 7 vols. (Austin, 1936—).

Linn, John J. Reminiscences of Fifty Years in Texas (New York, 1883).

Morfi, Juan de. History of Texas, 1673-1779, translated, with biographical introduction and annotations by Carlos Eduardo Castañeda, 2 vols. (Albuquerque, 1935).

Oberste, William H. History of Refugio Mission (Refugio, 1942).

O'Rourke, Thomas Patrick. The Franciscan Missions in Texas, 1690-1793 (Washington, D. C., 1927).

Parisot, P. F. History of the Catholic Church in the Diocese of San Antonio (San Antonio, 1897).

Peña, Juan Antonio de la. Diary of the Aguayo Expedition, translated by Peter P. Forrestal (Austin, 1934).

Pichardo, José Antonio. Treatise on the Limits of Louisiana and Texas, translated by Charles Wilson Hackett, 2 vols. (Austin, 1931-34).

Portillo, Esteban. Apuntes para la historia antigua de Coahuila y Texas (Saltillo, 1880).

Revilla Gigedo, Conde de, Viceroy of Mexico. Informe oficial al rey de España, sobre el estado de las misiones de Texas, en 27 de diciembre del año 1793 (no place, no date).

Schmitt, Edmond J. Catalogue of Franciscan Missionaries in Texas, 1528 to 1859 (Austin, 1901).

Shea, John Gilmary, History of the Catholic Missions among the Indian Tribes of the United States, 1529-1854 (New York, 1855).

Smith, Harvey Partridge. The Charm of Old San Antonio (New York, 1931).

Southwestern Historical Quarterly (Austin, 1897 to date). (From 1897 to April 1912 it was known as the Quarterly of the Texas State Historical Society.)

Texas Catholic Historical Society. Preliminary Studies of the Texas
Catholic Historical Society, 3 vols. (Austin, 1931-40). Supple-
mentary Studies (Austin, 1948——).
Thrall, Homer S. History of Texas from the Earliest Visits of
European Adventurers to A. D. 1879 (St. Louis, 1879).
Torrente, Camilo. Old and New San Fernando (San Antonio, 1927).
Winter, Nevin O. Texas the Marvellous (Boston, 1916).
Yoakum, H. History of Texas from Its First Settlement in 1685 to
Its Annexation to the United States in 1846, 2 vols. (Redfield,
1856).

University of Texas
Library
Austin 12

The Latin American collection in the University of Texas
library is particularly rich in manuscripts and in materials for the
history of Mexico. Its newspaper and pamphlet collections are extensive; the field of literature, especially Mexican, is well covered.
Fifty-five thousand volumes of printed books and pamphlets are included, and in addition, some 560,000 pages of manuscripts, 2,500
volumes of newspapers, 1,750 broadsides, and 2,500 maps and
pictures.

The cornerstone of the collection was laid in 1899 when the
Bexar archives—approximately 205,000 pages of military, civil,
and religious records of the Spanish province and the Mexican state
of Coahuila and Texas from 1699 to 1836—were transferred to the
University of Texas. These were later supplemented by 774 volumes
of transcripts of documents relating to the Spanish Southwest in the
various archives in Mexico City and by 286,000 pages from the
Archive of the Indies in Seville, the archives of France and England,
and the provincial archives of Mexico. Important material on Mexico
and early Florida and Louisiana is also to be found among these
manuscripts.

The collection gained distinction with the acquisition in
1921 of the private library of Genaro García (1867-1920), a distinguished Mexican historian and bibliophile. Including large portions
of other famous libraries and the archives of presidents, statesmen,
and diplomats, it offers excellent facilities for the study of the history
of Mexico in all its phases, including the early history of Texas and
the Spanish Southwest, upon whose subsequent development it also
throws much light.

Among the outstanding acquisitions afforded by the García

library are its splendid bibliographical section on Spain and Mexico, the latter complete from Eguiara to Medina; most of the published Mexican codices; a carefully selected group of works on the languages and customs of native tribes; many well-illustrated volumes from the library of the archeologist, Alfredo Chavero; a full collection of the church chroniclers; many Mexican imprints of the seventeenth and eighteenth centuries; complete files of the earliest newspapers and periodicals; a voluminous literature for the independence period, formed in part from the library of Lucas Alamán, a member of the Spanish Cortes from Mexico and one of her best historians; and, for the period after 1821, newspapers and periodicals in increasing numbers, and the private archives of J. M. L. Mora and Servando de Mier. The remainder of the nineteenth century is well covered by printed books and by the archives of such men as Vicente Guerrero and Valentín Gómez Farías, both presidents of Mexico, and Mariano and Vicente Riva Palacio, statesmen and diplomats. A portion of the Andrade library throws light on the period of French intervention.

The Díaz regime has an extensive literature, while that of the 1910-20 revolutionary period abounds in books, pamphlets, newspapers, and ephemeral sheets characteristic of popular movements. There is also a remarkably complete series of government documents, including congressional journals, departmental reports and bulletins, and the Diario Oficial; an extensive law library ranging from the cedularios of Puga and Encinas to the present day; good coverage of the history, geography, statistics, and laws of the several states; and a strong section on Mexican literature.

The importance of the collection was greatly increased when a part of the magnificent library of Joaquín García Icazbalceta (1825-94), an authority on sixteenth-century Mexican bibliography, was purchased in 1937. Mexican imprints of that century were increased by 45 of the rarest, including the first dictionary (1555) printed in America, and the manuscript section was increased by some 18,000 pages of originals of that century, among them a letter of Cortés and a manuscript of Mendieta's Historia eclesiástica. Also added were over 100 Mexican imprints and 32,000 pages of manuscripts of the next two centuries.

Material on the independence period was further considerabl strengthened by the purchase in 1943 of that portion of the Juan E. Hernández y Dávalos collection of manuscripts and pamphlets not included in the six published volumes (1877-82). These date from 1760 to 1840.

Much material for the history of Texas, New Mexico, Arizona, and California before 1836 was acquired with the purchase of the W. B. Stephens collection, which included 1, 200 printed items and over 20, 000 pages of manuscripts. The papers of Justin H. Smith, author of The War with Mexico, added many volumes of notes and transcripts brought together in the course of the preparation of this work.

More detailed study of the neighboring Mexican states of Tamaulipas and Coahuila was made possible through the purchase in 1941 of the library of Alejandro Prieto, author of the best history of Tamaulipas, and in 1943 of the papers of the Sánchez Navarro family, which at one time owned about half of the state of Coahuila. The first of these included complete or partial files of numerous early newspapers and over 3, 000 pages of manuscripts and transcripts, aside from the printed books; the Sánchez Navarro documents, ranging from the middle of the seventeenth century to 1826, relate largely to the personal affairs of the family, but throw much light on the socioeconomic conditions of the area. Photostat copies from the Matamoros archives (67 volumes), the Saltillo archives (48 volumes) and from the San Francisco el Grande archives in the National Library of Mexico also contribute invaluable material on many aspects of the life of the region.

Central and South America began to be more adequately covered in 1932, when a gift from the Hispanic Society of America of some 7, 000 volumes included many duplicates from its own notable collection, as well as a large block of Latin American public documents and laws. In conjunction with the Muñoz collection of over 1, 000 volumes, which was purchased in 1939, it made possible the completion of the laws of Chile from 1810 to 1890 and the journals of the congress of Chile from 1810 to 1858, and added substantially to the laws of Venezuela, Uruguay, and Costa Rica. A special grant from the General Education Board in 1936 made possible the purchase of many needed works on South America and also on the history and literature of Spain. Through the Muñoz collection, over 200 volumes were added to the already strong collection of the works of José T. Medina, distinguished Chilean bibliographer.

More detailed study of the early history and culture of eastern South America was made possible by the further purchase in 1939 of the private library of Manuel Gondra, twice president of Paraguay. It included 7, 500 books and pamphlets, 270 maps, and over 20, 000 pages of transcripts descriptive of sixteenth-century explorations and settlements, colonial, civil, and ecclesiastical administration, and Spanish-Portuguese relations. Of special interest is the printed material on Paraguay, as it includes files of exceedingly rare periodicals and newspapers. For further details, see Calendar of the Manuel E. Gondra Manuscript Collection of the University of Texas Library, compiled by Carlos E. Castañeda and Jack A. Dabbs (Mexico: Editorial Jus, 1952).

The fine arts section of the collection is strong in Mexican architecture and decoration. The history of painting and sculpture is well illustrated by a fairly extensive picture file and some 1,500 slides. Practically all the histories of music in Latin America in general and in the individual countries are present; and of the first ten music books printed in America, the collection has 5. The history of the theater in Mexico also is well covered.

Since 1948, the source materials relative to Mexico have been further strengthened through a grant from the Carnegie Corporation. Microfilm copies of material from the Juárez archive and of correspondence of and instructions to the ministers from the United States to Spanish American republics and to Spain as well as of the Spanish and Mexican ministers to the United States, and rare music from the cathedral of Mexico, additional newspaper files, and many volumes of literary periodicals from various countries have been secured.

In the 50,000 printed volumes of the Texas collection, the most extensive body of material on Texas in existence, much information relative to border history is to be found, as well as to Mexico itself. Among its archival records are the papers of Anthony Butler, acting minister of the United States in Mexico City from 1829 to 1836.

The Latin American collection is also well supplemented by the newspaper collection in the library, which includes over 2,500 volumes of Latin American newspapers, over half relating to Mexico. In 1941, more than 400 bound volumes of Mexican newspapers collected by Luis García Pimentel were acquired; these include almost every important paper of Mexico City between 1846 and 1890.

For further information, see Carlos E. Castañeda and Jack Autrey Dabbs, Guide to the Latin American Manuscripts in the University of Texas Library (Cambridge, Mass.: Harvard University Press, 1939) and Lota M. Spell, Research Materials for the Study of Latin America at The University of Texas (Austin, Texas: University of Texas Press, 1954).

Dallas Museum of Fine Arts
Fair Park
Dallas 10

The Dallas Museum of Fine Arts is decorated with a large mural (18 feet by 10 feet) by the Mexican artist Rufino Tamayo. Entitled "El Hombre," it was commissioned in 1953 and inaugurated in 1954. It was the hope of the Dallas authorities that this example of Mexican art would help eliminate anti-Mexican prejudice in Texas. The painting depicts symbolically man's struggle to rise above his material surroundings.

Other Mexican works include oils, water colors, drawings, and prints by leading contemporary Mexican artists.

Among the pre-Columbian artifacts are pots, huacos, and featherwork from Peru, and Totonacan heads and figures.

A group of seventeenth-century Spanish paintings includes Pablo Legot and examples of the Schools of Madrid and Seville.

Kimbell Art Foundation
Fort Worth

The Kimbell Art Foundation has 2 Spanish paintings in its collection:

Goya. "Portrait of Rita Luna," oil on canvas. This celebrated portrait of the actress, Rita Luna, comes from the de Oliva family in Madrid, and is recorded or reproduced in all the authoritative works on Goya.

Greco, El. "St. John," oil on canvas; signed with initials D. T. Formerly in the church of Almadrones, Guadalajara, Spain, where it formed a part of an incomplete series of Apostle figures. The paintings were discovered in an abandoned church during the Spanish civil war. Four of the paintings were acquired by the Prado Museum of Madrid in 1946; one was kept by the bishop of the church; and three came to the United States. For further details, see J. Camón Aznar, El Greco, Vol. II, pp. 981-90.

Rosenberg Library
Corner Twenty-Third and Avenue I
Galveston

Spanish papers in the Rosenberg Library consist of letters, documents, and printed decrees of the Mexican government, 1822-36, the colonization period of Texas history, relating to business of

Austin's colonies, addressed mainly to Samuel May Williams, Secretary of Austin's colony, by Mexican government officials. The letters have interesting personal and political comment. The official documents relate chiefly to post-office and customs matters. The 39 printed Mexican government decrees date from 1829 to 1834. There are approximately 450 papers from the Samuel May Williams collection.

There are 5 papers relating to Don Bernardo de Gálvez, prepared by the Royal College of Heralds, Madrid, giving biography and genealogy of Gálvez, description of the Gálvez coat of arms, with supporting documents and papers showing seals of the Gálvez family.

Museum of Fine Arts
Main Street and Montrose Boulevard
Houston 5

The Museum of Fine Arts of Houston has examples of Spanish furniture, ceramics, sculpture, painting, and textiles in its Annette Finnigan collection. There is a Goya, "Portrait of Marquis de Caballero, " in the Robert Lee Blaffer memorial collection, and 4 paintings in the Kress collection: another Goya, "A Maja and Two Toreros"; "Virgin of the Annunciation" and "Don Diego de Esquivel y Aldama" by Murillo; and "Portrait of a Boy Holding a Book" by Alonso Sánchez Coello.

Mexicans represented include the following: a painting, "Kneeling Woman with Sunflowers, " by Diego Rivera, as well as 2 drawings and 2 lithographs; the paintings "Taxco" and "Portrait, " 7 water colors, and 2 drawings by Roberto Montenegro; 7 lithographs by José Clemente Orozco.

There are also a bronze sculpture, "Iacy, " by the Brazilian Maria Martins, and a painting, "Off for the Honeymoon, " by the Uruguayan Pedro Figari.

San Jacinto Museum of History Association
San Jacinto Monument

The San Jacinto Museum of History Association was chartered to instill and encourage historical inquiry, collect and preserve the materials of history and spread historical information, illustrate the chronological story of the region as determined from authoritative history by means of exhibits worthy of a museum of the first rank, extend and diffuse knowledge of our history and promote and perpetuate peace, friendship, and sympathetic understanding between the people of Texas and the people of Spain, France, and the Latin American republics.

In its period of operation, the museum has acquired through unrestricted gifts a large collection of material relating to pre-Columbian America, New Spain, Mexico, the Spanish Southwest, and early Texas. The manuscript collection consists of approximately 400,000 pages, including codices; colonial grants and conveyances; papal bulls; royal cedulas and viceregal decrees; acts of the Council of the Indies; orders of the Inquisition; chronicles and reports of the missionaries; records of haciendas, pueblas, convents, presidios, colleges, and the Spanish galleons and the navy of the Republic of Texas; schedules of taxation; mining regulations; manifestoes of political juntas; documents pertaining to the Republic of Texas, the Texas frontier, and political leaders of Texas; and personal, family, and business documents.

The relic collection consists of approximately 7,000 items including primitive sculpture in stone; castings in bronze; ceramics; wood carving; clay and wooden materials used in pre-Columbian printing; official, royal, church, and private seals; household utensils and equipment; costumes, uniforms, ecclesiastical vestments, arms and armor; coins, medallions, military medals and insignia; gold, silver, copper, and wrought-iron materials; agricultural, domestic, religious, and cultural relics of the Texas frontier; and personal and family memorabilia.

The picture collection consists of 1,400 items, including paintings of historic personages, prints, engravings, photographs, copperplates, and miniatures on ivory and copper.

The library contains 85,000 issues of newspapers and 15,000 publications, including rare books and reference books, pamphlets, imprints, gacetas nacionales, periodicals, early and current Texas newspapers.

The general plan of the museum's permanent exhibits outlines the history of the region in a continuous, chronological line stemming from the Indian civilization which Cortés encountered to Texas, a state in the Union, and embracing the highlights of ten historical periods: the pre-conquest native; conquest and exploration (1518-1685); France and the establishment of Spanish Missions (1685-90); Spanish colonial life (1690-1810); the Mexican Revolution (1810-21); Anglo-American colonies (1821-35); the Texas revolution (1835-36); Sam Houston and Texas (1832-63); the Republic of Texas (1836-46); and Texas' early statehood (1846-61).

Publications:

Texas Newspapers, 1813-1939, a Union List of Newspaper Files
  Available in Offices of Publishers, Libraries, and a Number of
  Private Collections, 1941.
The Battle of San Jacinto and the San Jacinto Campaign, by L. W.
  Kemp and Ed Kilman, 1947.
A Check List of Manuscripts Including an Eyewitness Account of the
  Battle of San Jacinto, 1949.
The First Ten Years of the San Jacinto Museum of History Associa-
  tion, 1950.
A Picture Book Introduction to the San Jacinto Museum of History,
  2d ed., 1950.

University of Vermont
Pringle Herbarium
Burlington

The Pringle Herbarium, an excellent collection of Mexican
plants, is located at the University of Vermont. Cyrus Guernsey
Pringle, who collected and mounted the plants, began his botanical
work as a plant breeder immediately after the Civil War, collecting
plants as a basis for his horticultural work. In 1885, he turned
his attention to Mexico and from that time until 1910 made thirty-
six collecting trips in that country. He usually spent from six to
eight months of each year in the field, shipping his plants home for
classification and distribution. His numerical list of Mexican plants
collected runs from 1 to 15,790. His collection includes fungi,
lichens, and mosses, but the greatest number collected consisted
of ferns and seed plants.

Pringle was collecting in a new field, and his herbarium
contains many plants new to science at that time. He discovered
five new genera, over four hundred new species, and several new
varieties.

The herbarium is arranged according to the Engler-Prantl
classification.

As a result of some unfortunate experiences, the board of
trustees of the university, at Pringle's request, passed a ruling
forbidding the loan of his plants. However, every facility is offered
visiting scientists to examine the collection at the university.

The university published in 1936 a volume prepared by
Helen Burns Davis on the life and work of Cyrus Guernsey Pringle.

This work gives the diaries of his Mexican trips, maps showing the
areas in which collections were made, notes on Mexican travel,
classified and numerical lists of plants collected, and a list of his
plants in the "Type Herbarium" in the National Herbarium.

Joseph Winterbotham Collection
Burlington

Mr. Joseph Winterbotham has in his house at Burlington,
Vermont, a private art gallery rich in the works of modern artists,
contemporary Spanish and Mexican painters being well represented.

The outstanding Hispanic works are:

Greco, El. "Christ at the Supper-Table of Simon Peter."
Pissarro. "The Duck-Pond," pastel.
Utrillo. "Sunday Afternoon in France."

State College of Washington
Library
Pullman

The most significant material of Hispanic interest in the
library of the State College of Washington is a collection of the
Mexican manuscript papers of the condes de Regla, a prominent
family of Mexico, whose titles were established in the late eighteenth
century. The first conde de Regla was one of the wealthiest men
in all the Indies. Mexico's silver mines were the source of his
great wealth and generosity, which included even a fully equipped
battleship as a gift to the king.

The manuscript papers, some 25,000 pages in all, cover
the whole of the family's interests, their lands, titles, wills, liti-
gations, public and private transactions with the viceroys and directly
with the crown, and many other matters. Many of the documents
bear the signatures of the kings of Spain, the viceroys of New Spain,
and many other persons of importance in the early history of Mexico.
There is a large number of sixteenth-century documents, the earliest
bearing the date 1534. The papers cover the entire period from
this date to 1875; they are legible and, with few exceptions, well
preserved. Some of the earlier material was bound in vellum in
1783, making seven volumes of more than 1,000 pages each. There
are a few maps of the properties held by the family.

Seattle Art Museum
Volunteer Park
Seattle 2

The pre-Columbian collection of the Seattle Art Museum
is richest in the field of ceramics. All of the major ancient cultures

of Mexico and Central and South America are well represented in about 100 items, including vessels, figures, whistles, and masks. The Tarascan and Costa Rican groups are especially strong.

The collection includes representative Totonac stone sculpture in the form of palmas and axes, a jaguar yoke with distinct Olmecan affinities, 4 Aztec basalt sculptures carved from volcanic rock, and a few fine Costa Rican stone items. The Peruvian sculpture, aside from the pottery vessels, is represented by a Chimu wooden standing male figure and a few small pieces of silver and gold of the same cultures.

Over 50 examples of Peruvian textiles show excellently most of the techniques and motifs of design.

The museum's Spanish sculpture consists of a pair of late Gothic gesso-covered wooden angels holding candlesticks; a wooden polychrome figure of St. Paul of the sixteenth century; and a small gilt bronze statue of St. John of about 1600.

In incidental art, the museum has 5 Hispano-Moresque lustre plates of the sixteenth-seventeenth century; a Buen Retiro cup and saucer of about 1760; 3 excellent textiles consisting of a section of a fifteenth-century Mudejar silk brocade, an embroidered altar frontal depicting the Flight into Egypt of about 1700, and a large eighteenth-century floral velvet hanging.

In Latin American art, the only colonial item is a large painting of "Scenes from the Life of St. Libania, " which is an excellent example of the work of the early eighteenth-century artist, Nicolás Rodríguez Juárez.

In contemporary art of Mexico, the collection includes water colors by Mérida and Covarrubias, 6 paintings by Emilio Amero, and a number of prints by Rivera and Orozco.

University of Wisconsin
Seminary of Mediaeval Spanish Studies
Madison

The objectives of the Seminary of Mediaeval Spanish Studies are: the edition of the unpublished works of Alfonso X; and the preparation of a vocabulary of all the works of Alfonso X. The seminary, founded in 1931 by the department of Spanish and Portuguese of the University of Wisconsin, was under the direction of the late Professor A. G. Solalinde, its initiator, until the time of his death (July 1937). It is at present directed by Professor Lloyd A. Kasten,

with the collaboration of Professor J. H. Herriott, Mr. Mack
Singleton, and Mr. V. R. B. Oelschläger. Professor Américo
Castro was, during his stay at the university, general adviser to
the seminary.

In 1930, Professor Solalinde published Part I of the General
Estoria. Since that time, the efforts of the seminary have been directed toward the edition of Part II, the most difficult and complicated
of the five parts still to be published, because of the large number
of manuscripts and the lack of a manuscript from the Royal Scriptorium.
Eventually a final volume of linguistic, literary, and ideological
studies will be published. The printing of Part II had already begun
before the outbreak of the Spanish Civil War. Two hundred and
eight pages had been printed in final form, 22 pages were in page
proof, and 70 galley proofs were on hand. These represented the
first 498 pages of the typewritten copy. Since then the remaining
1,697 pages have been completed, but publication has not yet been
resumed.

Part III of the General Estoria is now nearing completion,
and a considerable amount of work has been done on Part IV. Parts
III and V are represented by few manuscripts and are in part fragmentary. Only a small fragment of Part VI remains. It is planned
to publish the General Estoria in five volumes with the text and
variants (Parts V and VI in one volume). The study of sources,
language, and culture of the Alphonsine period will appear in additional
volumes along with the indices.

Other Alphonsine texts prepared for printing are the Primera
Partida, edition of J. H. Herriott; Juicio de las estrellas, edition
of V. R. B. Oelschläger and J. H. Herriott; Canones de Albateni,
edition of M. H. Singleton and D. L. Bolinger; and Lapidario, edition
of J. H. Nunemaker. The Libro de las cruzes, edited by L. A.
Kasten and L. B. Kiddle, had been printed in Madrid up to page 128
at the beginning of the Spanish Civil War. Editions of the Picatrix
by G. S. Darby (a doctoral dissertation at Harvard University), of
the Libro de Ajedrez by A. Steiger (of the University of Zürich),
and of the Septenario by K. Vanderford (a doctoral dissertation at
the University of Chicago), have also been prepared, and the results
will be incorporated into the Alphonsine project. Professor J. H.
Herriott, with the help of skilled workers, has been engaged for a
number of years in the preparation of materials for a definitive
edition of the Siete Partidas of Alfonso X. Mrs. Jesusa Alfau de
Solalinde has prepared A Glossary of Names of Textiles in Spanish
Manuscripts of the XIIIth Century and Costumes as Reflected in
Spanish Illuminated Manuscripts of the XIIIth Century.

At present, all the well-edited works and several unpublishe works of Alfonso X have been included in the vocabulary. With the exception of a few common words of frequent occurrence, every word appears in context in accordance with the method used by Professor C. C. Fries, of the University of Michigan, in his preparation of the Early Modern English Dictionary. The files contain now a total of 616,247 entries. To aid in the preparation of etymologies, an accumulative index of Spanish etymologies is being compiled. All possible etymological references are being included.

Related to the seminary projects, several doctoral dissertations in the Spanish medieval field have been prepared. These include: J. R. Ashton, Ovid's 'Heroides' as translated by Alphonso the Wise, 1944; E. C. Munro, An Etymological Vocabulary of Military Terms in the Works of Alfonso X, 1949; J. Y. Causey, A Cultural Study of the Agricultural Terms in the Works of Alfonso el Sabio, 1940; T. H. Shoemaker, Alfonso X as Historian, 1941; H. A. Van Scoy, Spanish Words Defined in the Works of Alfonso X, 1939. Mr. V. R. B. Oelschläger has revised, with Professor Américo Castro, his Preliminary Spanish Word List of First Appearances up to Berceo. Consult also J. Ortega, "Datos sobre la obra de A. G. Solalinde (1892-1937)" in Hispanic Review, VI (1938), 4-9.

The seminary has its own quarters and is provided with special photographic equipment (cameras, dark room, etc.) for the reproduction of rare books and manuscripts; a large bibliographical card catalogue of Spanish literature and general linguistics; a fairly complete library of books on medieval and philological subjects, including the collection of Professor Solalinde which was purchased by the university on his death; and several thousand photostats and numerous sets of films. Most of the manuscripts of the Alphonsine texts and other rare manuscripts and printed books are reproduced in this material.

Organizations Without Specific Location
American Association of Teachers
of Spanish and Portuguese

The American Association of Teachers of Spanish and Portuguese, founded in 1917, has as its aim the fostering of the study and teaching of Spanish and Portuguese in the United States. The association is governed by a president, three vice-presidents, a secretary-treasurer, the editor of Hispania, and an executive council of nine members. The association holds an annual meeting at which members read and discuss papers on literary, linguistic, and pedagogical subjects. There are, in addition, regional meetings arranged by the forty-five chapters of the association. Membership, at present 3,500, is open to any teacher of Spanish or Portuguese or to any person interested in the Hispanic cultures. There are members in every state and in many foreign countries, as well as subscribing libraries. Dues, now three dollars a year, include subscription to Hispania, the quarterly journal of the association.

Hispania is published in February, May, August, and November. Each issue, from 96 to 128 pages in length, contains articles on the Hispanic literatures and on the Spanish and Portuguese languages, as well as pedagogical articles. The papers read at the annual meetings of the association appear usually in the February and May issues. There are special departments: Official Announcements, The Hispanic World (notes on new books and events of importance to the culture of the Spanish- and Portuguese-speaking countries), Chapter News, Questions and Answers, Notes and News, Spanish in the Elementary Schools, and Reviews. In each May issue is published a list of the doctoral theses completed or in preparation in American universities on the Hispanic languages and literatures. The list is prepared by Professor L. L. Barrett, of Washington and Lee University.

The editor of Hispania from 1917 to 1926 was Professor Aurelio M. Espinosa, of Stanford University; from 1927 to 1941, Professor Alfred Coester, of Stanford University; from 1942 to 1948, Dean Henry Grattan Doyle, of Columbian College, The George Washington University. The present editor is Donald Devenish Walsh. Editorial offices are at The Choate School, Wallingford, Connecticut.

Bibliographical Society of America

The Bibliographical Society of America has three functions: the holding of two meetings a year at which papers are read and round-table discussions held; the publishing of these papers and other essays and bibliographies in its Papers; and the publishing of a quarterly News Sheet, which contains bibliographical news from both North and Spanish America, a record of projected or recently published bibliographies, etc. It does not maintain a library but does act as a clearing house for bibliographical information and, through its officers, council, and permanent secretary, does all it can to encourage the compiling and publishing of scholarly bibliographies on all subjects. The present secretary is Herbert W. Liebert, of Yale University Library.

The News Sheet of the society has frequently announced or

reviewed current Hispanic American bibliographies; its officers have corresponded with Hispanic American bilbiographers, including the late José Toribio Medina, who was an honorary member of the society; and the Papers, now in its fiftieth volume, have included many contributions of Hispanic American interest.

Handbook of Latin American Studies*

The Handbook of Latin American Studies had its origin in the need of scholars in the field for an annual selected and critical bibliography. The first volume, containing publications of the year 1935, appeared in 1936, under the sponsorship of the Committee on Latin American Studies of the American Council of Learned Societies and with the financial support of the council. The succeedin volumes through No. 8 continued to be issued with private sponsorship and financial support. The latter came, on occasion, from the Rockefeller Foundation, as well as from the council.

Beginning with No. 9, the Library of Congress assumed responsibility for maintenance and operation of the editorial office of the Handbook, as an integral part of the Hispanic Foundation. With No. 11, an advisory board began to function, consisting of four scholars in the Latin American field and a representative of the Library of Congress. Members were Clarence H. Haring, Harvard University, chairman; Henry G. Doyle, The George Washington University; Leslie W. Dunlap, the Library of Congress; George Foster, Smithsonian Institution; and Cornelius Krusé, American Council of Learned Societies. For Handbook No. 12, Burton W. Adkinson succeeded Leslie W. Dunlap as the Library of Congress representative, and Miron Burgin, of the School of Advanced International Studies, became a sixth member of the board.

The editors of the Handbook, like its sponsors, have changed from time to time. The first five volumes were edited by Lewis Hanke. Raul d'Eça served as associate editor of No. 4, and Miron Burgin was joint editor of No. 5. Beginning with Handbook No. 6, Miron Burgin assumed the editorship and was responsible in this capacity for the succeeding five issues. No. 12 was edited by Francisco Aguilera, with Charmion Shelby as assistant editor. Succeeding numbers have the same editorial staff.

Throughout its career the Handbook has been fortunate in obtaining the collaboration of specialists representing most of the

---

*From article of Charmion Shelby appearing in Review of Inter-American Bibliography, I (1951), No. 2.

important centers of Latin American studies in this country and
several in Latin America. Through No. 14, 113 individuals have
served as contributing editors. An important degree of continuity
has resulted from the fact that some of these contributors have served
without interruption over a period of years.

The purpose of the Handbook has remained the same from
its beginning. That is, each volume aims to record, with critical
and informative notes, the year's important publications in the
fields of humanistic and social science studies. The volume is
selective and not comprehensive and is designed to be a permanent
work of reference. The number of titles included has varied from
2, 343, for the year 1935, to 5, 731, for 1941. Each item consists
of a bibliographical entry giving the most complete information
available, and a brief descriptive or critical comment by the contributing editor. Most of the editors preface their sections with
an introductory statement concerning the material included or with
other matters of interest to scholars in the respective fields.

Organization varies from section to section with the nature
of the material, and no attempt is made to follow one arbitrary
system throughout. Thus, subdivisions of a section may be upon
a geographical or a topical basis. The special interest of each
contributing editor governs to some extent the content of his section. In the earlier volumes, each contributing editor was largely
responsible for titles appearing in his section. More recently,
the editorial staff has prepared bibliographical cards for titles
noted in the Handbook offices, examining for this purpose thousands
of books, pamphlets, and periodicals from current acquisitions of
the Library of Congress. The cards are distributed to the various
editors, who may use or reject them. The editors continue to make
contributions of their own as well. The editor-in-chief and assistant editor make final selections of all material, and edit all material for bibliographical form.

The fields covered in the Handbook, and their subdivisions,
have varied somewhat from volume to volume. At one time or another,
the following main sections have been included: Bibliographies,
General Works, Anthropology, Archives, Art, Economics, Education,
Folklore, Cartography, Geography, Government, History, International Relations, Labor and Social Welfare, Language and Literature, Law, Libraries, Music, and Philosophy. The larger disciplines,
such as anthropology, history, and literature, have topical, regional, or chronological subdivisions, or a combination of these, and
are distributed among several contributing editors.

The Carnegie Institution for International Peace made possible free distribution of earlier volumes of the Handbook, to appropriate libraries and other institutions in Latin America and Europe. More recently, the Library of Congress, through its international exchange program, has continued to distribute the Handbook outside the United States. The volumes through No. 13 may be purchased from the Harvard University Press, and, beginning with No. 14, from the University of Florida Press.

Hispanic American Historical Review

The erudite Spanish historian, Professor Rafael Altamira, first suggested the founding of a review to deal with Hispanic American history, at the special meeting of the American Historical Association held in California in 1915. In 1916, Professors Charles E. Chapman, of the University of California, and William S. Robertson, of the University of Illinois, while delegates to the American Congress of Bibliography and History held in Buenos Aires, discussed the founding of such a review with leaders of the congress. The hearty response elicited led them to send a communication to the American Historical Review which appeared in that organ in October 1916. Later, discussion of the matter by Professor Chapman and Dr. J. Franklin Jameson led to the special group dinner on December 29, 1916, at the meeting of the American Historical Association in Cincinnati. As one result of the meeting, a committee on organization, of nine members, and a nominating committee, of three members, were appointed. A financing campaign, conducted during 1917, realized the small sum of $3,675, but it was decided after considerable discussion to begin publishing. The first editorial board consisted of Charles E. Chapman, Isaac J. Cox, Julius Klein, William R. Manning, James A. Robertson, and William S. Robertson; and an advisory board of editors, of Herbert E. Bolton and William R. Shepherd. James A. Robertson was elected managing editor and occupied that position until his death in 1939. Subsequent managing editors have been John Tate Lanning, 1939-44, James F. King, 1945-49, Charles C. Griffin, 1950-53, and Lewis Hanke, 1954--.

The first number of the Review was published (through the Waverly Press, of Baltimore) in February 1918. The general policy of the Review, as expressed in the communication published in the American Historical Review for October 1916, has been followed, namely: "The said review should be devoted to the history (political, economic, social, and diplomatic, as well as narrative) and institutions of Spain, Portugal, and the Latin-American

states; that bibliographical material be published, and that articles
n Spanish and Portuguese be printed as well as those in English. "
Documents are also printed in the language of origin.

With varying fortunes, the Review was able to keep afloat
until the completion of its fifth volume in 1922, when, because of
financial losses following World War I, it had to be suspended.
In August 1926, publication was resumed through the interest of
the Duke University Press, and the Review has been published continuously since that time.

In addition to the managing editor Lewis Hanke, John P.
Harrison is associate editor for archives and John Finan, associate
editor for bibliography. The present board of editors consists of
John F. Bannon, S. J. (St. Louis University), Robert S. Chamberlain
Washington, D.C.), William J. Griffith (Tulane University), Rayford
W. Logan (Howard University), Charles E. Nowell (University of
Illinois), Walter V. Scholes (University of Missouri), Engel Sluiter
University of California, Berkeley). The advisory editors are
Isaac Joslin Cox (Northwestern University), Clarence H. Haring
Harvard University), John Tate Lanning (Duke University), Irving
A. Leonard (University of Michigan), Dana G. Munro (Princeton
University), J. Fred Rippy (University of Chicago), William S.
Robertson (University of Illinois), Arthur P. Whitaker (University
of Pennsylvania). Associate editors outside the United States are
Enrique M. Barba (Argentina), Jorge Basadre (Peru), Dantès
Bellegarde (Haiti), Alice Canabrava (Brazil), Daniel Cosío Villegas
(Mexico), Edmundo Favaro (Uruguary), Héctor García Chuecos
(Venezuela), Robin A. Humphreys (Great Britain), Richard Konetzke
(Germany), Enrique Ortega Ricaurte (Colombia), Eugenio Pereira
Salas (Chile), José Manuel Pérez Cabrera (Cuba), Virginia Rau
(Portugal), Rafael Heliodoro Valle (Honduras).

Instituto Internacional de Literatura Iberoamericana

The Instituto Internacional de Literatura Iberoamericana
was organized in Mexico in the summer of 1938, and reorganized
in Los Angeles, California, in 1940. Its main purpose is to broaden
and intensify cultural relations among the Americas, and to promote the study of Iberoamerican literatures—Spanish American
and Brazilian.

To this end, the institute has provided for the publication
of the Revista Iberoamericana, which is printed in Mexico City
three times a year, in volumes of.some 250 pages each; and for
the publication of the memorias of the various congresses or con-

ventions of its members. These congresses take place every two years, more or less. They have been held successively at Mexico City, Los Angeles, New Orleans, Albuquerque, Mexico City, and Berkeley.

The present managing editors are Julio Jiménez Rueda (Mexico), Fernando de Alegría (University of California), and Francisco Monterde (Mexico).

Stanford University
Art Gallery and Museum
Stanford, California

The Stanford University Museum has recently acquired an outstanding group of pre-Columbian objects from the Stendahl collection. These include representative examples from many different Mexican sites and civilizations.

Among the more important pieces are:

Dog of hollow clay with vent in tail; Tarascan civilization, from Colima.

Emaciated man with many ornaments; painted clay; Tarascan civilization from Nayarit.

Fluted vase with parrot effigy legs; Tarascan from state of Colima.

Incense burner in two parts; figure of god or priest made up of clay ornaments to form headdress; from Santiago Ahuizotla.

Incense burner with two-faced monster and entwined snakes handle; clay; Tarascan civilization from Colima.

Seated priestess wearing mantle and skirt; hollow clay with traces of paint; whistle; Mayan from island of Jaina.

Seated warrior wearing quilted cotton armor, woven helmet, and holding lance; Tarascan civilization from Nayarit.

Seated woman; hollow clay with applied decorations and asphaltum paint; pre-Totonac civilization from Elotepec, Veracruz.

Seated woman; hollow painted clay; Tarascan civilization, Colimese style, from Jalisco.

Standing woman holding bowl, dressed in painted cotton shirt and cape; nose and ear ornaments; Tarascan civilization from Nayarit.

Stanford University
Farquhar Papers
Stanford, California

Papers of Percival Farquhar (1864-1953), the Pennsylvania Quaker who was the most important American in the economic development of Brazil, are partly in the custody of Dean Charles F. Park, Jr., School of Mineral Sciences, Stanford University (5 cubic feet of Farquhar's records of his efforts in the 1920's and 1930's to develop his Itabira iron ore project), and partly in the hands of Charles A. Gauld, Hispanic American Studies, Stanford. Gauld, who was in Rio de Janeiro during 1947-54, obtained from Farquhar and his surviving Brazilian and American associates 8 cubic feet of records of Farquhar's Itabira iron project and his vast Brazil Railway Company and its 36 subsidiaries, including correspondence, memorials to the Brazilian government, photographs of Rio's reconstruction during 1904-7, and publications in Portuguese and English on the Brazil Railway and Itabira iron. Gauld accumulated much material for a biography of Farquhar in interviews with Farquhar and his friends and from survivors of Farquhar's $33,000,000 Madeira-Mamoré Railway (1907-13) in which some 875 Americans participated. Additional data on that epic of the selva exists in the archives of the Madeira-Mamoré Association of which Lt. Col. Robert P. Waters is secretary at 5922 Wooten Drive, Falls Church, Virginia, including negatives of several hundred official photographs taken by Dana Merrill at the order of Farquhar. The costly (3,500 lives) rubber-boom railroad was one of the best documented, photographically and in print, of any American enterprise in Latin America. Carbon copies of thousands of pages of Brazil Railway Receivership Papers under Governor W. Cameron Forbes in 1915-19 are in the Baker Business School Library at Harvard, the originals being (unless destroyed) in the Brazil Railway archives in Paris and London.

University of California
The Library
Los Angeles, California

The library of the University of California at Los Angeles has grown, in thirty years, from 50,000 items to much over 1,000,000. The intention has been to supplement rather than to duplicate expensive and highly specialized materials in the Clark Library, and in the nearby Huntington, Los Angeles Public, and County Law libraries. These libraries are rich in Latin American materials, such as the eighteenth- and nineteenth-century Mexican pamphlets of the Huntington and the Public Library, and the massive holdings of legal texts for all of Latin America in the County Law Library.

The university library has relatively little material from Portugal, Brazil, and the Platine countries, but it has substantial collections from Mexico and the Caribbean countries in general, and from Peru and its neighbors in the national era. Its collection of eighteenth- and nineteenth-century travel accounts is outstanding. The eighteenth century in Spain and Spanish America has been emphasized, as has economic life and international relations in general. There are many uncommon contemporary imprints of Mexico.

Some collections have been created by purposeful buying for years, in addition to those given or bought en bloc. None are

necessarily kept as collections. The Clark J. Milliron gift, added
to materials already owned, contains valuable material concerning
the Spanish regime in the Philippines. Among the extensive holdings
for the period of the Napoleonic wars and wars of independence in
Spain and America are the "Papeles varios, " two volumes of pamphlets and flyers printed mostly in Valencia, 1808-1810. The
Spanish literature collections are unusually strong in materials
from Valencia. The Spanish history and literature collections for
the era 1868-1876 includes books, broadsides, long newspaper runs,
and several literary magazines, many of them not in the Union List
of Serials. A notable group of the printed cabildo records of Spanish
America includes the large sets for Buenos Aires, Lima, Mexico
City, Quito, and Santiago, Chile. The 7,000-volume John Fiske
Library contains many of the nineteenth- and early twentieth-
century treatises on the discovery of America, and early cosmog-
raphies and chronicles of the Conquest era. The Robert Ernest
Cowan collection of over 3,000 volumes, pamphlets, maps, manuscripts, and newspapers pertaining to California and the West contains many of the key items relating to Spanish and Mexican activity
in those areas. Among the several hundred Mexican broadsides,
ballad sheets and similar items from the second half of the nineteenth century are works by the anti-Díaz propagandist and "popular" artist, José Guadalupe Posada, 1851-1913. The "Colección
de folletos relacionados con cuestiones del derecho internacional
americano" has several hundred pamphlets and government publications, 1835-1926 (mostly before 1914), bound in 58 volumes.
It was gathered in Colombia, and is strong on the foreign relations
of that country and its neighbors.

There are many lesser groups, such as hundreds of pamphlets on the French West Indies during the Revolution and until
1829, a few dozen contemporary reports by and attacks on the Anglo-
Mexican, United Mexican, and Colombian Mining Associations in
the 1820's and the 100 titles of works by José Toribio Medina.
This group is being added to, but already includes nearly all the
bibliographies (some extremely rare) and histories of the Inquisition.

Although acquisition of rare books has never been emphasized,
many are found in the general collections and the Department of
Special Collections. The following list mentions some outstanding
samples of strong fields, but includes no imprints of the last century or from the very large holdings of Mexicana.

Balbi, Adrien. Essai statistique sur le royaume de Portugal et
d'Algarve, 2 vols. Paris, 1822.

Caro de Torres, Francisco. Historia de las ordenes militares...
Madrid, 1629.

Céspedes y Meneses, Gonzalo. Historia de Don Felipe IIII, Rey de
las Españas. Barcelona, 1634. One of two copies in the United
States.

Colón, Fernando. Historie... della vita... dell Almiraglio.
Venice, 1571.

Conciliador, El, 5 vols. Lima, 1830-34.

Conspiration et trahison admirable des Espagnols... contre... Venise,
7 pp. N. p., 1618.

Cuadro estadístico de la... isla de Cuba... 1846. Havana, 1847.
Some tables lacking.

Dalence, José María. Bosquejo estadístico de Bolivia. Chuquisaca,
1851.

Diario de los literatos de España, vols. 2-7. Madrid, 1737-42.

Dictamen de los comisiones... sobre el restablecimiento y reforma
de las casas religiosas, 79 pp. Cadiz, 1813.

Discusión del proyecto de decreto sobre... la Inquisición.
Cadiz, 1813.

Encyclopedia metódica dispuesta por orden de materias, 10 vols.
Madrid, 1788-94. Complete text, but a volume of plates is
missing.

Expediente instruido por el Consulado de la Habana sobre...
agricultura y comercio. Havana, 1808.

Fernández de Medrano, Sebastián. El Perfecto arquitecto... militar.
Brussels, 1700.

González de Mendoza, Juan. Dell historia della China. Venice,
1586.

González Vigil, Francisco de Paula. Compendio de la defensa de
la autoridad de los gobiernos contra... la Curia Romana, 2 vols.
Lima, 1852.

Hevia Bolaños, Juan de. Curia philipica. Madrid, 1657.

Horozco, Sebastian de. Tesoro de la lengua castellana, 2 vols.
Madrid, 1673-4.

Llaguno y Amirola, E. Noticias de los arquitectos y arquitectura
de España, 4 vols. Madrid, 1829.

Mapa puntual que manifiesta las armadas de mar y tierra...
Seville, 1762.

Mejía, Pedro. Historia imperial y cesarea. Basel, 1547.

—. Silva de varia lección. Lyon, 1556.

Morale pratique des Jésuites, La, 8 vols. N. p., 1682-96.

Noticia de las Ordenes de Caballería de España, cruces y medallas
de distinción, 2 vols. Madrid, 1815. With colored plates.

Olañeta, José Antonio de. Juicio de residencia del excelentísimo señor Don Miguel Tacón... Capitán General que fué de... Cuba. Philadelphia, 1839.

Ordenanzas de S. M. para el régimen...de sus ejércitos. Cadiz, 1810.

Pacheco de Narváez, Luis. Nueva ciencia...de las armas. Madrid, 1672.

Piso, Willem. De Indiae utriusque re naturali et medica. Amsterdam, 1658.

Ramusio, Giovanni Batista. Della navigationi et viaggi, 3 vols. Venice, 1606-13.

Regla del coro y cabildo de la Santa Iglesia Patriarcal de Sevilla y memoria de las processiones, y manuales... Seville, 1760.

Reglamento para el gobierno del Consejo de Estado [Havana, 1812].

Reseña histórica de los principales acontecimientos políticos de... Cali desde...1848 hasta 1855. Bogotá, 1856.

Saavedra Fajardo, Diego de. Idea principis christiano-politici. Amsterdam, 1660.

Sala y Abarca, Francisco Ventura de la. Después de Dios la primera obligación y glosa de órdenes militares... Naples, 1681.

Sánchez Valverde, Antonio. Sermones, panegíricos y de misterios, 2 vols. Madrid, 1783-4.

Soto y Marne, Francisco. Copia de la relación y diario crítico-naútico de el viage desde... Cádiz a la Cartagena de Indias. Madrid, 1753.

Touron, Antoine. Histoire générale de l'Amérique depuis sa découverte, 14 vols. Paris, 1768-70. Complete; such sets are rare.

Veitia Linaje, José de. Norte de la contratación de las Indias. Seville, 1672.

Wytfliet, Cornelius. Histoire universelle des Indes. Douay, 1611.

Zapata y Sandoval, Juan. De justitia distributiva et acceptione... Pro Novi Indianarum... Valladolid, 1609. Only copy in the United States.

Zayas y Sotomayor, María de. Primera y segunda parte de las Novelas Amorosas. Madrid, 1659.

Zurita y Castro, Jerónimo. Cinco libros postreros de la historia del Rey Don Hernando el Católico. Saragossa, 1580.

Northwestern University
University Library
Evanston, Illinois

Northwestern University Library has two notable Spanish American research collections.

The Bolivian manuscripts, part of the Lanza collection, come from the library of the Bolivian scholar and author Nicolás Acosta (1844-93). His library passed into the hands of his nephew Donato Lanza y Lanza, who sold it in 1914 to Walter Lichtenstein, then librarian of Northwestern University. Dr. Lichtenstein was on a book-buying tour through South America on behalf of five co-operating institutions: the American Antiquarian Society, John Carter Brown, Crerar, Harvard, and Northwestern. When the material was divided according to the fields of interest of the participating institutions, Northwestern obtained the manuscripts. The collection includes not only holographs and typescripts, but also printed matter—documents, broadsides, leaflets. There are about 40,000 pieces, the majority in Spanish, a few in Latin and French, covering the period from the late sixteenth to the late nineteenth century. They fill two portfolios and sixty-six bound volumes, to which are added one unnumbered volume of rare broadsides and one volume containing the Bibolotti manuscript on the language of the Moseteno Indians. This last item was published by Northwestern in book form in 1917 under the title Moseteno Vocabulary and Treatises. While the papers are concerned primarily with Bolivia, there is scattered through them much valuable information on the early history of Peru, Colombia, Venezuela, Chile, Paraguay, the Chaco territory, and Argentina. Although the emphasis is on history, the collection has research value in the fields of anthropology, art, economics, law, and religion. For a detailed description of the collection, see Jac Nachbin's "Descriptive Calendar of South American Manuscripts in the Northwestern University Library," Hispanic American Historical Review, Vols. XII (pp. 242-59, 376-86, 503-21) and XIII (pp. 124-42, 267-80, 403-19, 524-42).

The private library of Manuel Segundo Sánchez, director of the national library of Venezuela was acquired by Dr. Lichtenstein in 1913, and divided among the Northwestern, John Crerar, and Harvard libraries. Northwestern's three hundred volumes relate to South America in general and to Venezuela in particular.

See Felix Pollak, "The Spanish American Collections at Northwestern University Library," Hispanic American Historical Review, XXXV (November 1955), No. 4, 499-501.

Indiana University
Bloomington, Indiana

On January 7, 1956 it was announced that Josiah K. Lilly, Jr. had given his library of rare books, first editions, and manuscripts

to Indiana University.   The library, assembled over a period of
thirty years, is concerned chiefly with literature, history, and
science.   Among the Hispanic items may be mentioned two copies of
Columbus' letter printed in Rome in 1493, and a practically complete set of the Jesuit relations.   There are also books by Cortés,
Martyr, Vespucci, and other historians of the New World.

It is estimated that the collection contains over 20, 000 first
editions with a value of about $5, 000, 000.   Indiana University is
planning a new building to house the library.

INDEX

(<u>See also</u> Table of Contents)